WARS AND SOLDIERS IN THE EARLY REIGN OF LOUIS XIV

Volume 7 – Armies of the German States 1655–1690 Part 1

Text and Illustrations by Bruno Mugnai

'This is the Century of the Soldier', Fulvio Testi, Poet, 1641

Helion & Company

Helion & Company Limited
Unit 8 Amherst Business Centre
Budbrooke Road
Warwick
CV34 5WE
England
Tel. 01926 499 619
Email: info@helion.co.uk
Website: www.helion.co.uk
Twitter: @helionbooks
Visit our blog http://blog.helion.co.uk/

Published by Helion & Company 2024
Designed and typeset by Mary Woolley, Battlefield Design (www.battlefield-design.co.uk)
Cover designed by Paul Hewitt, Battlefield Design (www.battlefield-design.co.uk)

Text © Bruno Mugnai 2024
Photographs and illustrations © as individually credited
Maps by George Anderson © Helion and Company 2024
Colour artwork by Bruno Mugnai © Helion & Company 2024

Every reasonable effort has been made to trace copyright holders and to obtain their
permission for the use of copyright material. The author and publisher apologize for
any errors or omissions in this work and would be grateful if notified of any corrections
that should be incorporated in future reprints or editions of this book.

ISBN 978-1-804510-04-9

British Library Cataloguing-in-Publication Data.
A catalogue record for this book is available from the British Library.

All rights reserved. No part of this publication may be reproduced, stored in a retrieval
system, or transmitted, in any form, or by any means, electronic, mechanical, photocopying,
recording or otherwise, without the express written consent of Helion & Company Limited.

For details of other military history titles published by Helion & Company Limited
contact the above address or visit our website: http://www.helion.co.uk.

We always welcome receiving book proposals from prospective authors.

Contents

Acknowledgements		v
Foreword		vi
1	The 'German Universal Soldier'	7
2	Germany after Westphalia	14
3	The Electorate of Brandenburg	28
4	The Electorate of Bavaria	120
5	The Electorate of Saxony	184
6	The Prince-Bishopric of Münster	226
	Colour Plate Commentaries	280
	Currency in Seventeenth-Century Germany	293
Appendices:		
I	Regiments, Battalions, Squadrons and Companies, 1657–1690	294
II	Army Lists and Orders of Battle	337
	Brandenburg	337
	Bavaria	353
	Saxony	359
	Münster	362

Please note that a bibliography for this work will appear in Volume 7 Part 2.

Acknowledgements

The easiest debts to acknowledge are time and means. I would like to thank Helion & Company who gave me the opportunity to write several earlier books whose ideas emerge in these pages, as well as finish this one. My intellectual debts are much more difficult to acknowledge adequately. I cannot begin to thank all of the people with whom over the years I have discussed ideas and topics that emerge in this book, for this would include hundreds of friends, teachers, and colleagues spread out in many countries around the world. I am especially grateful to fellow early-modernists, some of whom I have known writing this series, such as Andreas R. Hofmann from Bochum, and Alexander Querengässer from Leipzig, as well as Paolo Coturri from Florence, whom I have known for more than half my life.

I also owe particular debts to people who helped me with especially tricky issues, or read over chapters and sections, among them Lorenzo Ressel, Niccolò Capponi, Stephen Ede-Borrett, and Serena Jones.

Finally, I would like to remember my good teacher and friend Paolo Fanfani (1957–2023), who would certainly have read this book.

Florence, 7 November 2023
BM

Foreword

The German military experience in the seventeenth century has for long appeared crucial but the focus overwhelmingly has been on the Thirty Years' War of 1618–1648. As a consequence, this interesting study is of particular importance because it enables us to consider its period both in terms of the consequences of the earlier conflict and with reference to the particular challenges of the second half of the century notably that from the France of Louis XIV. Earlier, French forces had advanced east of the Rhine but in large part that capability owed much to alliance with a highly effective Sweden. Again, this was to be an issue in 1741 when benefiting from Prussian action. However, under Louis XIV the emphasis was far more firmly on action by France. This posed major challenges to the fighting effectiveness of German forces and notably in the 1670s. This is the book to read when approaching these issues.

Jeremy Black

1

The 'German Universal Soldier'

Every German soldier who serves in our army is worth twice as much: first, because he fights for us; second, because doing so we deprive our enemies of using him against France (Louis XIV)

The fact that the volume dealing with the states of Germany follows the one dedicated to Italy in this series is no coincidence. Until recent years, the historical trajectory of Germany during the *Ancien Régime* was used as an element of comparison with Italy. Effectively, in the second half of the seventeenth century, Germany and Italy offered very similar scenarios. Both countries were politically divided into many states, often with a history of recent conflicts, and forced to move between the interests of Austria and Spain or with those of Sweden and Louis XIV's France. This assumption then highlighted how, following a similar path, only two states were able to emancipate themselves from foreign influence: Brandenburg-Prussia in Germany and Savoy-Piedmont in Italy. The key of this success was found in the common military policy that would allow both states to rise from regional powers to builders of national unity. The army had been the main instrument for achieving such a considerable result that Bismarck's propaganda would even attribute to it the role of the glue of the Prussian state.

Some historians point out how, both in Italy and Germany, these aspects were elaborated precisely to please the military class, to the point that military history was for the exclusive benefit of the academies where the officers of the new army studied.[1] Having said this, there are authors who state that in Italy the hegemony of Savoy-Piedmont had monopolised the study of military history, relegating the traditions of Italian armies to miserable simulacra. In

---

1   As for Germany, in this regard, Peter H. Wilson, *Iron and Blood. A Military History of the German-speaking Peoples since 1500* (London: Penguin Books, 2022), p.xlv, adds: 'The broad geographical approach will also address a major deficiency present in the few general military histories of Germany, all of which write German history teleologically as the rise and fall of the Prussians ... Most [of these works] truncate German history by starting only in the 1640s, which are commonly, if not accurately, identified as the decade of the 'birth' of the Prussian army. The entire German military past is read through the lens of Prussia's experience, while much of that experience is poorly understood because it is not set in its wider German and European context.'

WARS AND SOLDIERS IN THE EARLY REIGN OF LOUIS XIV – VOLUME 7 PART 1

German soldiers of the late seventeenth century; illustration by Herbert Knötel for Martin Lezius' *Die Entwicklung des Deutschen Heeres von Seinen Frühesten Anfängen bis unsere Tage in Uniformtafeln* (Berlin, 1936). From left: Saxon artilleryman, about 1680; Brandenburg pikeman, 1630; Hessen-Kassel, musketeer of the Life Guard company of 1664; Brandenburg *Leibdragoner*, 1674; Brandenburg musketeer, regiment *Döhnoff zu Fuss*, about 1680; Bavarian cuirassier, regiment Arco, 1685; Württemberg cuirassier, 1683.

Germany, on the contrary, the armies of each state had maintained uniforms and insignia even after the birth of the Empire, as well as the recruitment on the basis of the ancient German states and the tradition of the single regiments.'[2]

In addition to these aspects, in more recent times several accurate studies highlighted – sometimes even drastically altering the hitherto predominant opinion – how in the years preceding the Peace of Westphalia, Italy had gone through a scenario marked by regional conflicts and large-scale wars to an extent not very different from Germany. The influence of war and standing armies on early modern state-building is still intensively discussed by the historians. According to the original military revolution theory, the Swedish (and Dutch) war effort in the late sixteenth and especially the early seventeenth centuries, and the requirements of a strong military machine, forced the state to build up a more effective administrative system. In the case of the early standing army of the German states no such causal relationship can be detected. The armies were often raised by the wishes of the princes with the consent of the estates, which restricted the size to 8,000–10,000 soldiers with few exceptions. This seems rather small, not only compared with the other major armies of Europe, but also to the approximately 26,000 professional troops of Savoy-Piedmont in 1672, and 30,000 soldiers and seamen of Venice in the opening phase of the War of the Holy League.

However, the gradual disinterest of Italian elites in military careers is an argument that is still far from over, while it was well established that the Thirty Years' War had been an event destined to decisively influence the history of the German states, much more so than in Italy. The prolonged state of belligerence was the spring that led to an unprecedented development of the German 'Military', which led to its deep rooting in society. This aspect has recently been underlined by analysis on the functions of modern wars, which are veritable *Staatsbildungskriege* (wars leading to state formation).[3] In Germany, the 'Military' consolidated the preponderance of the sovereigns, because they were able to control the political forces. Finally, the material needs of the standing troops and their growth had a decisive influence on the economic and fiscal development of the German states. The military society

---

2   Raimondo Luraghi, Introduction to Piero Del Negro (ed.), *Guida Alla Storia Militare Italiana* (Naples: Edizioni Scientifiche Italiane, 1997), p.3.

3   As occurred in Italy, in Germany also military history by academics and the fear of talking about it among those who had lived through the Second World War further reinforced the isolation of this branch of the historical discipline. As a result, it was only former and new military personnel who wrote this history, often apologetically, in order to establish a purified memory. The innumerable volumes, rich in illustrations and detail, published by veterans to mark commemorations, could only reinforce the prejudice of academic historians that military history was nothing more than the staging of the army. The creation of military history research institutes under the direction of the army in West and East Germany seems both to have resulted from this isolation and to have perpetuated it. As a result of this development in German historiography, the military factor was neglected until the 1980s, so much so that even in the great works of general history, there is no mention of the 'military revolution' or of the armed forces. It is only in recent years that in Germany historical research has begun to recognise the importance of the military in understanding the modern era. Fortunately, since the 1980s German historiography has undertaken research in this field with very valuable contributions.

was an immense machine for redistributing money. On the one hand, the constant financial demands of the state required the development of other resources, especially in the form of new taxes. The Chambers became responsible for administering these taxes, of which the contribution and excise were the most important, and also for collecting money by force in the event of opposition. On the other hand, these resources were used primarily for military purposes, such as uniforms, equipment, the construction of strongholds, and arsenals. The local economy benefited indirectly. At the same time, by granting privileges and subsidies and setting up specialised factories, the corporate economy underwent forced changes. Infrastructure measures such as the construction of warehouses, grain shops, arms factories, military orphanages, barracks, major roads and waterways further illustrate the interdependence of military development and a mercantilist policy.[4]

Thousands of German soldiers served in the armies of both Germany and the other powers involved in the Thirty Years' War. After 1648 they constituted a pressing priority because they represented an intolerable burden on an exhausted population, and above all they hindered the territorial exchanges that had been agreed. It has been calculated that this mass of unemployed soldiers numbered 180,000 men in 1648.[5] The process of demobilisation required the meeting of a special congress convened in Nuremberg in 1649–50, which arranged a schedule for the demobilisation and coordinated the collection of funds for managing this remarkable labour force. This process was achieved astonishingly quickly. Around two-thirds of these troops had already gone by autumn 1649 to the still warring states, including a significant number who left Germany for the Mediterranean in the war against the Ottomans. Between 1648 and 1700, with the exception of England alone, German mercenaries served in virtually all European armies.[6] Among the states which employed the largest number, Spain paid 16,021 German mercenaries in 1662, increasing to 22,483 the next year just in the army of Estremadura for the war against Portugal.[7] In 1661, France had about 3,500 German infantry, increasing to 4,400 in 1672 and a further 400 cavalrymen.[8]

Thousands of German soldiers served in the armies of Sweden, Denmark, in the Polish Commonwealth, and even in Russia and Transylvania.[9]

---

4   On these issues see Johannes Burkhardt, 'Der Dreißigjährige Krieg als frühmoderner Staatsbildungskrieg' in *Geschichte in Wissenschaft und Unterricht 45* (1994), pp.487–499 ; and by the same author, 'Die Friedlosigkeit der Frühen Neuzeit. Grundlegung einer Theorie der Bellizität Europas', in *Zeitschrift für Historische Forschung 24* (1997), pp.509–574.

5   Wilson, *Iron and Blood*, p.132.

6   Perhaps a few ethnic Germans served for England alongside native soldiers, but it is difficult to determine an approximate number.

7   Antonio José Rodríguez Hernández, 'Financial and Military Cooperation between the Spanish Crown and the Emperor in the Seventeenth Century', in Peter Rauscher (ed.), *Die Habsburgermonarchie und das Heilige Römische Reich vom Dreissigjährigen Krieg bis zum Ende des Habsburgischen Kaisertums* (Vienna: Aschendorff Verlag, 2010), p.284.

8   Belhomme, *Histoire de l'Infanterie en France*, vol. II (Paris, 1893–1902), pp.108, 172; Louis Susane, *Histoire de la Cavalerie Française*, vol. II, p.101.

9   Among the studies dealing with the German mercenaries in the European armies of the seventeenth century, see Georg Tessin, *Die Deutschen Regimenter der Krone Schweden*

THE 'GERMAN UNIVERSAL SOLDIER'

Germany's mercenary market was so dynamic that it was possible to form units by enlisting German mercenaries of the enemy, both deserters and prisoners, as the Portuguese did between 1650 and 1668.[10] Even the United Provinces of the Netherlands, despite the policy of military reduction after the Peace of Westphalia, continued to make use of mercenaries hired in Germany until the next century, whenever the political scenario became bleak again.[11] From the middle of the seventeenth century, the German soldier became the archetype of the mercenary, a true 'universal soldier', much more useful than other professional soldiers of ancient and prestigious tradition, such as the Swiss or the Corsicans, mainly because unlike them, in Germany it was possible to find not only excellent infantry, but also a good heavy cavalry and veteran officers. Not only did France and Spain continue to make use of German soldiers, but also Venice in the war on Crete, and for other states on the Peninsula Germany continued to be the natural recruitment pool for soldiers. The availability was so high and convenient that every Italian prince could easily plan his military policy by resorting to the omnipresent *Alemanni* in case of need, perpetuating the tradition of the Landsknechts. Even when German mercenary units were dismissed for budgetary reasons, many Italian princes kept a German life guard in their service, whose officers had the dual task of serving in the corps and maintaining relations at home in case professional soldiers were recruited.[12]

Contemporaries divided Germany culturally and linguistically into High (south) and Low (north). In the seventeenth century, the two German 'nations' were still regarded as different only by language, and only in Spain were the two categories still considered in the matter of recruitment, but after 1648 this had no implications since the Spanish Monarchy enlisted both *alto* and *bajo* German soldiers. Spain, like other European states, had Catholic and Reformed German mercenaries in its ranks without exception. There is continuity between the 'warlords' of sixteenth century Germany and the

---

1645–1718, vols I–II (Cologne–Graz: Böhlau, 1965–67); Rodríguez Hernández, Antonio José, 'La presencia militar alemana en los ejércitos peninsulares espanoles durante la guerra de restauracion portuguesa (1659–1668)', in L. Ruiz Molina, J. J. Ruiz Ibanez and B. Vincent (eds), *Yakka. Revista De Histudios Yeclanos*, vol. 10 (2015), pp.269–288; Peter H. Wilson, 'The German Soldier Trade of the Seventeenth and Eighteenth Centuries. A Reassessment', in *The International History Review*, vol. 18, n. 4 (IX, 1996), pp.757–792; and the discussed but remarkable work of Fritz Redlich, *The German military enterpriser and his workforce: a study in European Economic and Social history*, vols I–II (Wiesbaden: Steiner Verlag, 1964–5).

10 Bruno Mugnai, *Wars and Soldiers in the Early Reign of Louis XIV, Volume 5 – The Portuguese Army 1659–1690* (Warwick: Helion & Company, 2021), p.99: 'After the infantry regiment recruited in Hamburg … in 1650, some free companies of German mercenaries are registered in the Army of Alentejo in 1652. Then, in 1663 … the Portuguese raised one *terço dos alemães* enlisting prisoners and deserters from the German regiments of the Spanish army. The 300 strong unit was commanded by the Frenchman, Colonel Clairon … Two years later, the *terço* had lost half of its strength, but it was still with the field army that fought at Montes Claros.'

11 The Dutch Republic did not differentiate between Dutch and German recruits, see Bruno Mugnai, *Wars and Soldiers in the Early Reign of Louis XIV. Volume. 1 – The Army of the United Provinces of the Netherlands 1660–1687* (Warwick: Helion & Company, 2019), p.54.

12 German life guards served Genoa, Tuscany and Parma and Piacenza. See Bruno Mugnai, *Wars and Soldiers in the Early Reign of Louis XIV. Volume 6, Part 2 – Armies of the Italian States 1660–1690* (Warwick: Helion & Company, 2023).

Thirty Years' War with the mercenary entrepreneurs of the second half of the seventeenth century. They perpetuated the tradition of Landsknechts, dealing with the recruitment of soldiers, managing equipment, clothing and any other concerns. Experienced contractors were retained on a semi-permanent basis in many larger territories from the early sixteenth century, either to ensure their services in the advent of a major war or to drill the militias. Some families served as mercenaries in several countries at the same time. Among these, the Degenfelds entered the service of Saxony, Bavaria, Venice, Osnabrück, Waldeck-Pyrmont, Denmark, Trier and the Dutch Republic, either as commanding officers or as mercenary contractors as the case may be.

Between 1648 and 1690, other great dynasties of mercenaries served throughout Europe: Trautmannsdorff (Bavaria, Saxony and Venice), Styrum (Sweden, Münster and Venice), Dönhoff (Sweden, Poland, Dutch Republic and Brandenburg), Sparr (Brandenburg, Dutch Republic and Brunswick-Lüneburg), Bielke (Bavaria and Denmark), Flemming (Sweden, Brandenburg, Saxony and Brunswick-Lüneburg), Fürstenberg (Baden, Cologne, France), Francke (Brunswick-Lüneburg, Brandenburg and Dutch Republic) Königsmarck (Sweden, Brunswick-Lüneburg and Venice), Haxthausen (Brunswick-Lüneburg and Denmark), Brockdorff (Brandenburg and Denmark), Wartensleben (Hessen-Cassel and Brandenburg), Bülow (Sweden, Brunswick-Lüneburg and Holstein-Gottorp), Solms (Dutch Republic and Sweden), Truchsess (Sweden, Brandenburg and Würzburg), Ende (Brunswick-Lüneburg and Denmark) Wittgenstein (Palatinate and Dutch Republic), Wolframsdorff (Sweden and Münster), Sydow (Sweden and Brandenburg) just to mention families with prominent exponents as senior commanders or colonel-proprietors. To this crowd should be added several princes of the Empire, often lords of small states, who embarked on careers as military entrepreneurs.

Engraving of Christoph Martin von Degenfeld, 1599–1653. He was one of the major exponents of this Swabian family of mercenaries and military entrepreneurs who occupied a leading position in the 'trade of soldiers' in seventeenth century Germany. (Author's Collection)

Among them, the Margraves of Ansbach-Bayreuth and Brandenburg-Bayreuth-Culmbach, Duke Ernst Ludwig of Saxse-Meiningen, or the *Rheingraf* Johann Ludwig von Salm, and Count Heinrich IV of Reuss, who did not always achieve brilliant results, while others such as Prince Georg Friedrich zu Waldeck-Pyrmont, who instead was considered among the most skiled commanders, politicians and military theorists in the Germany of his time, and Margrave Hermann of Baden, president of the Aulic War Council of Vienna and at the same time military entrepreneur on behalf of Spain.

Most of the recruits enlisted by these military entrepreneurs were of the lower and lowest social classes. Regulations issued in Saxony in 1676, for instance, stipulated that certain social classes, especially the citizens of towns, being craft masters, students and educated men should be exempted from enlistment. Additionally, the ordinance of 1677 encouraged the recruitment of non-settled, unemployed, unmarried and idle folk. Simply said, the ranks of the army should be filled up with people who were not integrated into society. This protected the economy, and gave cash to those who otherwise filled the cities as beggars or criminals.[13] This scenario offers a new insight on the German military scenario of the second half of the seventeenth century. Possibly, historians have to correct the biased and negative view of the German armies of the modern age. Soldiers' living and service conditions were not always like those of Simplicius Simplicissimus, suffering from hunger, punishment and injustice. Military service offered an opportunity to survive temporary crises of subsistence, and guaranteed a surprising number of material and moral rewards.[14]

Gerhard Dohnoff 1632–85

---

13 Alexander Querengässer, *The Saxon Mars and His Force. The Saxon Army During the Reign of John George III 1680–1691* (Warwick: Helion & Company, 2019), p.60.
14 Ralf Pröve, 'La Nouvelle Histoire Militaire de l'Époque Moderne en Allemagne', in *Revue Historique des Armées* 257–2009, p.7: 'The relationship between civilians and the military was also reinterpreted: mutual antipathy, physical violence and forced recruitment are now just one aspect of it. Social relations between peasants or city-dwellers and soldiers, economic cooperation and shared leisure activities seem more characteristic of everyday life at the time. It was the housing system that was largely responsible for reintegrating soldiers into urban life, as it enabled them to prepare for civilian life as soon as they had finished their military service.'

2

Germany after Westphalia

The [German] *Empire is the main limb, Germany is the centre of Europe …, Germany is the ball which (the powers) toss to one another …, Germany is the battlefield on which the struggle for mastery in Europe is fought* (Gottfried Wilhelm Leibnitz, 1670).

The Holy German-Roman Empire was a complex political entity formed by states which enjoyed a unique form of territorial authority that granted them many attributes of sovereignty, although they were never fully sovereign states in the sense that term is understood today, being formally subject to the Emperor. After 1648, the scenario registered a significant change, because the Treaty of Westphalia granted the princes the right to make alliances with each other and with foreign powers, but forbade them to conclude alliances against the Emperor or the *Reich*. This settlement was not always complied with, but in its essential features it lasted until the dissolution of the Empire in 1806.

The German Empire after the Treaty of Westphalia. The territory encompassed 701,085.3km^2 with about 18,000,000 inhabitants at the end of the Thirty Years' War. Parts of it were in a state of 'special union' such as the Duchy of Lorraine and the Low Countries, the latter under Spanish rule, and consequently their connection to the Empire had become very tenuous. These territories were also called 'Lower Germany', in contrast to the *Reich*, and were often not considered part of it at all. Most Germans lived in small communities governed by the heads of the richer well established families, who normally controlled the election or appointment of the village council and law court, except in eastern Germany, where the nobility had greater influence over these affairs.

It is not surprising that the political writers of the time found it difficult to define what the *Reich* really was. Hippolythus a Lapide denied that the Emperor was a sovereign and held that the Empire was an aristocracy of the princes; while Samuel Pufendorf, in *De Statu Imperii Germanici* (1667), aimed at a reconciliation of the different factors wielding influence in the Empire and declared that it was an *irregulare aliquod corpus et monstro simile* (an irregular body like a monster). It was certainly irregular, although perhaps not a monster but a marvel.

GERMANY AFTER WESTPHALIA

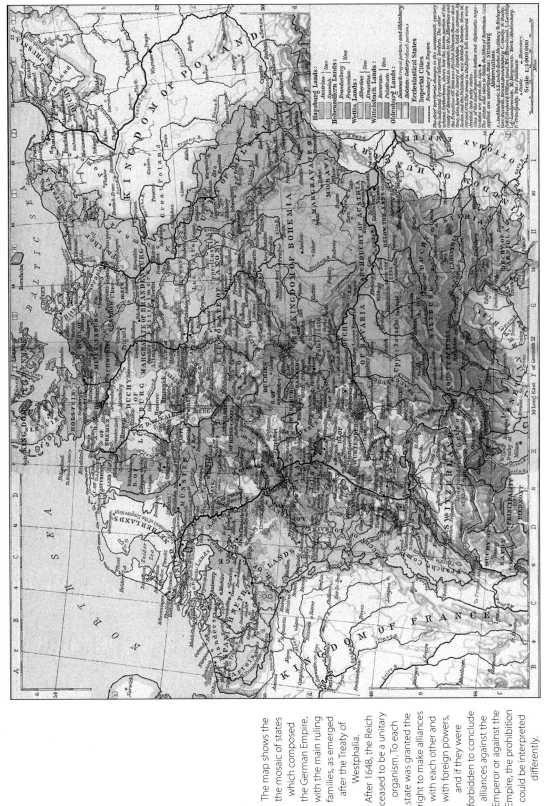

The map shows the the mosaic of states which composed the German Empire, with the main ruling families, as emerged after the Treaty of Westphalia.

After 1648, the Reich ceased to be a unitary organism. To each state was granted the right to make alliances with each other and with foreign powers, and if they were forbidden to conclude alliances against the Emperor or against the Empire, the prohibition could be interpreted differently.

Anna Sophia of Hesse-Darmstadt (1638–1683), Princess-Abbess of Quedlinburg from 1681 until her death. The small state of Quedlinburg was one of the many principalities of the Holy German-Roman Empire, and had its seat in the Circle of Upper Saxony. The Princess-Abbess was the only woman ruling as immediate prince of the *Reich*. (Bavarian State Painting Collections, Münich)

The material to implement this policy was huge. In the late seventeenth century, Germany consisted of approximately 1,800 such territories with 362 among principalities, lordships, bishoprics, knighthoods and Free Imperial cities and villages. The difficulties of government action and the complexity of the political mechanisms of the *Reich* that regulated the internal balance of Germany aroused criticism from contemporary commentators. Historians of the nineteenth century have agreed that the lack of a strong hereditary monarchy was a fundamental weakness, condemning Germany to a largely passive international role until Prussia and Austria acquired sufficient power to act independently and emerge as rivals for political leadership.[1] Imperial politics have often been misleadingly portrayed as a dualism of Princes and Emperor with the former seeking to escape the latter's control and establish their own independent states. Though familiar, this picture no longer stands modern scrutiny, not least thanks to a fuller understanding of French, English and Dutch development as well as revisions to German history.

Recently, historians point out that despite such a critical situation, the institutions of the Empire continued to exist, and in spite of all tensions and rivalries, the internal frontiers fixed by the Peace of Westphalia remained substantially the same for more than half a century.[2] Rule over the secular principalities and lordships was decided by hereditary succession and the prevailing laws of inheritance, which permitted their accumulation and partition subject to formal Imperial approval. Consequently, it was possible for a ruler to exercise different forms of power depending on the combination of land he had inherited. Princes, especially secular electors like those of Brandenburg, Bavaria and Saxony, often held several pieces of land qualifying for full votes along with shares in collective ones derived from possession of relevant counties, and they could also inherit or purchase property belonging to the Imperial knights or within the jurisdiction

---

1 *New Cambridge Modern History*, 'The Ascendancy of France, 1648–1688' (Cambridge University Press, 1968), vol. V, p.432.
2 *New Cambridge Modern History*, p.433: 'Even more stable proved the frontiers drawn between the warring creeds. Protestantism was eliminated from the Habsburg lands, Bohemia, and the Upper Palatinate, but the secularised abbeys and bishoprics were not restored. After 1648 very few German princes exercised their right of driving out those of their subjects who adhered to a religion different from that of the ruler … Many princes were not strong enough, or not fanatical enough, to enforce their religion upon their territories. Thus the Calvinist Electors of Brandenburg and the landgraves of Hesse-Cassel ruled over Lutheran principalities and did not attempt to make Calvinism the state religion. When later in the century the Electors Palatine and the Electors of Saxony became Roman Catholics, Protestantism remained the dominant religion of their principalities.'

of other rulers. Feudal ties were an imperfect match for this complex web of rights and privileges so that while most territories constituted separate Imperial fiefs, held by their rulers as vassals of the Emperor, others were dependencies of secular or ecclesiastical princes.

If the Empire had almost lost the character of a state, the weight of political life had shifted into the principalities. The major princes, adopting the principles of absolute government, tried to gain more power at the cost of weaker neighbours and of their own subjects. Their policy of consolidation and of becoming 'more considerable' was bound to lead to conflicts with the institutions which acted as a brake on such endeavours.[3]

While dealing with matters of foreign policy on the European stage, German rulers seem to be representing a single state, but when dealing with internal matters they had to be careful to respect the constitutional organisations, traditions, and system of their domains. The main actors of this territorial policy were the *Stände* (estates). The organisation by estates was a characteristic feature of medieval and early modern Germany until the eighteenth century. It was mostly a complex hierarchy of personal statuses that marked civil society and had various consequences in legal and political matters. The estates acted as separate bodies, which deliberated separately. In matters of war, tribute and land division, the estates mostly saw their competence recognised by the princes. Jurisdiction also acquired a typical conformation, when the specific competences of feudal, city, ecclesiastical and rural courts were established. As in other European states – notably England – the estates could control the military, because they enjoyed the right to grant a budget for troops and raise extraordinary taxes. Yet the 'absolutism' that historians have frequently applied to this state of affairs often implied a degree of control that no early modern ruler in fact enjoyed. In Germany specifically, all princes had to negotiate with their estates. Indeed, the ambition of some to dispense with this necessity was thwarted by the Emperor when he vetoed a proposal to remove all constraints on the princes' monopoly on taxation. Once again, the princes were tied into a legal structure which entitled estates to appeal to the Imperial courts if their rights were infringed, and which entitled the Emperor to intervene in the domestic politics of a territory to enforce the rights of subjects.

Local struggles between rulers and estates over access to territorial resources were thus linked to national politics by the princes' efforts to legitimise their own militarisation within wider revisions to collective security. There can be no doubt that wide areas of Germany not only suffered severely from the war and its aftermath, but also lost a large part of their population. Armies entailed considerable expense, which is why the estates were often seen as antagonistic to the princes, as professional troops took resources away from the economy of the territories the estates represented. Furthermore, while some states could protect themselves more easily against hostile forces, they suffered all the more severely from outbreaks of plague, which afflicted some areas of Germany until 1679. In this struggle, the princes

---

3   *New Cambridge Modern History*, p.434.

scored a partial success at the 1653–4 Diet in Regensburg despite the general failure to agree a definitive reform. The concluding document was known as the Latest Imperial Recess – *Jüngster Reichsabschied* – because the next meeting of the diet, which opened in 1663, remained permanently in session. The recess strengthened the princes' arguments by establishing a formal obligation of all territorial subjects to contribute taxes towards the upkeep of 'necessary fortresses, fortified places and (their) garrisons.'[4] The estates could no longer refuse all requests for military funding, but the deliberately vague wording permitted them to play a role in fixing the precise levels of funding and allowed the Emperor to intervene when they could not agree. Moreover, by specifying only defensive installations and forces required to fulfil Imperial obligations, the recess denied the princes a firm basis for larger forces capable of independent action.

Several rulers had maintained small numbers of troops even before 1618, but it was not until after the Peace of Westphalia that the first true territorial armies emerged alongside the larger forces that had long existed in the Austrian Habsburg lands. The appearance of these armies had significant consequences for all levels of Imperial politics as well as changing German relations with neighbouring states and their subsequent developments.[5] Habsburg dynastic weakness contributed to these developments by undermining their already vulnerable position within Germany. Moreover, some princes also looked to the Emperor and Imperial constitution to legitimise their accumulation of military power, arguing their forces were

Print after Gerard ter Borch depicting the ratification of the Peace of Münster in Westphalia, 15 May 1648. The settlement prohibited the transfer of soldiers to the ongoing Franco-Spanish War and covert Austrian efforts to support Spain were largely thwarted. The Westphalian settlement brought peace to the European state system, but not for long. The question of the common defence arrangement was deliberately postponed by the Congress to stop discussions on the reform delaying the peace – it was nonetheless clear that there were conflicting options on the matter. As a consequence, the Holy Roman-German Empire, the *Reich*, continued to be the most important area of internal contestation. Confessional differences remained important, in Germany as in Europe more generally, and they repeatedly caused attrition between the states. (Author's Collection)

---

4   Peter H. Wilson, *German Armies. War and German Politics, 1648-1806* (London: UCL Press, 1998), p.31.
5   Karl Staudinger, *Geschichte des Kurbayerischen Heeres Insbesondere unter Kurfürst Ferdinand Maria, 1651-1679*, vol.II (Münich, 1901), p.184: 'On 2 August 1655, the Imperial vice-chancellor Count Ferdinand Siegmund Kurz reported to Ferdinand Maria of Bavaria that the Emperor would send his own troops to the Prince-Elector in case the Swedes prolonged their occupation of the Elector's states, and that the Emperor had increased the army to 27,000–30,000 men for the defence of both his hereditary lands and those of the Empire.'

necessary to fulfil their obligations to uphold the public peace and contribute to collective security.[6]

That the treaties facilitated the interference of foreign powers was shown even more clearly in the Rhineland and Lower Saxony, since renewed international tension increased the uncertainty in some areas. The Swedes attacked the city of Bremen in 1654 in an unsuccessful attempt to deprive it of its autonomy and incorporate it into their own Lower Saxon territory. This was followed by the outbreak of the wide-ranging Second Northern War in 1655 at a time when the French and Spanish were still fighting in Flanders, Franche-Comté and Northern Italy. The princes responded by forming alliances, either through the existing framework of the *Kreise* (Imperial circles) or by direct bilateral agreements. These were intended to enhance mutual security against external dangers and possible Imperial absolutism, as well as providing a vehicle to carry demands for further constitutional revisions in their favour. The Habsburgs' financial crisis strengthened their position and the electors were able to insert further restrictions on the estates' rights of assembly into Leopold's capitulation in 1658. His election also saw the formation of the French-sponsored Rhenish Alliance – *Rheinbund* – led by the influential Prince-Bishop Elector of Mainz, Johann Philipp von Schönborn, who was a natural focal point for princely interests.[7] The collapse of the Rhenish Alliance by 1668 encouraged the emergence of a new group known as the Extensionists – *Extendisten* – because they wished to widen the Imperial legislation to remove all restraints on the princely monopoly of taxation. Joined by Bavaria, Cologne, Brandenburg, Pfalz-Neuberg and Mecklenburg-Schwerin, the group carried the Reichstag, which endorsed their proposals. After this was vetoed by Emperor Leopold I in 1671, the members agreed to establish a common force of 20,000 men to crush potential opposition within their territories and reinforce their lobbying of the Emperor.

These developments were accompanied by act of actual arbitrariness within the domains, as the Princes deployed troops to collect taxes and subdue recalcitrant towns and provinces.[8] The revival of the Austrian

---

6 Staudinger, *Geschichte des Kurbayerischen Heeres*, vol.II, p.30. Soldiers were often designated as *Kreistruppen* while performing police actions within the *Kreis* structure or forming part of a regional contingent to the *Reichsarmee*, even though they were in fact *Haustruppen*, or the Household troops of the prince, who often referred to them as his private property.

7 The aims of the Alliance were the maintenance of the peace treaty, of the liberties of the estates of the Empire, and of a balance between France and the Habsburgs. But the German members were much too weak to pursue an independent policy or to form a third force, and in reality the Alliance became an instrument of French foreign policy. It was renewed several times and joined by other German princes, among them the Prince-Elector of Brandenburg; but it was dissolved in 1668. See also Chapter 1 of the forthcoming Part II of this work.

8 Christoph Bernhard von Galen, the warlike Prince-Bishop of Münster, besieged his capital city three times between 1655 and 1661 with the help of the Rhenish Alliance. Schönborn also called on Alliance support to deprive the enclave of Erfurt of its autonomy from Mainz control in 1664. The Guelph Dukes assembled no less than 20,000 men and 100 cannon in June 1671 to bombard their town of Brunswick, which had refused to submit to their direct authority. These operations, along with the better known use of force by the Prince-Elector Friedrich Wilhelm of Brandenburg against the East Prussian estates in 1661–3 and the city of Magdeburg in 1666, all ended in princely victories.

Habsburgs after 1670 enhanced the ability of the Emperor to intervene in local affairs and helped secure the survival of those estates that chose to oppose their prince. The long-term consequence, however, was to strengthen the German territorial state by forcing it to rely on nonviolent means to extend its authority. Despite the proliferation of military forces, armed conflicts between princes were rare and most preferred arbitration through the Imperial courts to resolve their disputes. However, tensions remained a constant in 1650s Germany. Suspicion of the Austrian Habsburgs remained strong in the Protestant states. At the same time, the desire for security led many into regional alliances that were also anti-Imperial in their basic tendency. In Lower Saxony, Westphalia, the Upper Rhine, and Franconia there was an early revival of the existing circle organisations with a particular anti-Imperial impetus in the Rhineland and Lower Saxony at least. Other states formed new leagues and unions. In the spring of 1651, the Electors of Mainz, Trier, and Cologne formed the League of Frankfurt with members of the Upper Rhine Circle. In February 1652, the Welf family league formed the 'Hildesheim Union' with Hessen-Kassel, the Swedish territory of Bremen-Verden, and other minor north-western territories. Cologne and Paderborn also soon joined. The following year, Prince Georg Friedrich of Waldeck floated a proposal for a grand anti-Habsburg coalition, to be led by the Prince-Elector of Brandenburg and to include the princes of the Hildesheim Union as well as a range of Catholic princes, notably the Elector of Cologne. However, while various schemes for unions of Protestant territories seemed to be viable, it proved impossible to accommodate the interests of the Catholics in them.

From this scenario a few states led by skilled rulers, emerged above the others. Historians traditionally focus on the 'rise' of Brandenburg-Prussia and underestimate the significance of other major territories, such as Saxony, the Welf principalities of Brunswick-Lüneburg (electors of Hanover from 1692, though only finally confirmed in 1708), and Brunswick-Wolfenbüttel, or Bavaria and the Palatinate (the latter now restored as electors and an ally of the Emperor). The Brandenburg Electors certainly now firmly stepped out of the shadow of Electoral Saxony, whose lead they had consistently followed during the last century and a half. However, they stepped into a competition rather than a vacuum. They competed directly with the Welf, Saxon, and Bavarian princes, and Leopold's exploitation and manipulation of that competition in the 1680s and 1690s was one of the key factors in the re-establishment of his authority.

Brandenburg-Prussia was by no means the only territory that aspired to enhance its status. With the exception of Brunswick-Wolfenbüttel and the Palatinate, all the principalities mentioned above did so, and even the Prince-Bishopric of Münster emerged as a major actor under the rule of Christoph Bernhard von Galen. All the major players in Imperial politics pursued their own interests both within the legal and institutional framework of the *Reich* and according to the rules imposed by their feudal hierarchical relationship with the Emperor. As mere princes, however, even the Prince-Electors found it almost impossible to gain recognition at international peace conferences:

in itself a powerful motive for seeking royal status.[9] Indeed, ultimately, even the most powerful of the territories found it difficult to achieve anything without the sanction of the Emperor or against the law and convention of the *Reich*.

The competition between leading princes and the successful manipulation of that competition by the crown was more significant before the eighteenth century than the 'emergence' of Brandenburg-Prussia and Brunswick-Lüneburg Hannover. This competition in turn reflected other major developments. The tension between electors and princes continued. By the 1680s at the latest the electors had lost their struggle to maintain their pre-eminent position, to establish themselves as a governing oligarchy, with royal or quasi-royal status, in the Reich. As a result, their solidarity as a group was undermined. The competition for royal status was as much a reflection of that as it was a reaction against the Emperor's creation of a ninth Electorate for the Brunswick-Lüneburg princes in return for their support, but also to create a balance against Brandenburg. At the same time, Brunswick-Lüneburg Hannover was not the only non-Electoral principality that sought to enhance its status.

Armed and Unarmed States

A crucial distinction that emerged for the first time after 1648 in Germany was between the armed – *Armierten* – and the unarmed – *Nicht Armierten* – territories. Within a decade of the end of the war, there were a dozen armed territories with forces numbering between 1,000 and 10,000 men. They belonged to the first category: the 'armed states'. They had already begun to maintain permanent forces of their own and favoured combining these as a collective army sustained by payments from their weaker unarmed neighbours.[10] This scenario was sanctioned by Imperial law, for after 1654 all subjects were obliged to contribute to the cost of maintaining fortresses and garrisons, which were interpreted by princes to include troops generally for the defence of their territories. But it had implications for the political development of both *Reich* and territories. On the one hand, the existence of territorial armies shaped the development of the *Kreise* and of regional power structures.[11] The owners of such troops were often able to insist on them being regarded as Empire's forces and hence to oblige unarmed neighbours to contribute to the cost of raising and maintaining them; they also obliged their neighbours to provide billets. On the other hand, the maintenance

---

9 Joachim Whaley, *Germany and the Holy Roman Empire. Vol. II: The Peace of Westphalia to the Dissolution of the Reich 1648–1806* (Oxford–New York, NY: Oxford University Press, 2012), p.7.

10 Wilson, *German Armies*, p.23: 'The Emperor's monarchical solution equated with Imperial absolutism while the arguments of the armed princes were in line with the federalist political option. Both solutions were variants of security through deterrence since they relied on the construction of an effective monopoly of violence, either at national or territorial level, complete with an infrastructure of permanent armed forces.'

11 See also Bruno Mugnai, *Wars and Soldiers in the Early Reign of Louis XIV. Volume 2 – The Imperial Army 1657–1687* (Warwick: Helion & Company, 2019), pp.108–121.

of troops also created domestic imperatives. Maintaining an army was but one of the ways in which princes competed for status and prestige. Cultural competition, most notably the construction of palaces and expenditure on a court and residential capital, was equally remarkable. However, no prince could live exclusively either off his own domains or off foreign benefactors. The main burden invariably fell on their subjects and encountering the opposition of the estates. Like these latter in most territories, the unarmed territories argued that permanent forces encouraged war by arousing the fear and jealousy of neighbouring states. In their opinion, it was far better to avoid involvement in other people's quarrels and attend to the immediate task of post-war recovery.

The outbreak of the Franco-Dutch War in 1672 precipitated a political crisis, as the existing mechanism of mobilising collective defence proved incapable of meeting the French challenge, pushing the Emperor into a number of dangerous expedients at the expense of the weaker, unarmed territories. Not only did French troops infringe *Reich* neutrality by using the bishopric of Liège as an invasion route, but both Cologne and Münster actively assisted operations in return for subsidies and political support. While Bavaria, the Welf duchies, Osnabrück and Pfalz-Neuburg continued to remain unengaged, some of them, notably Bavaria, also increased their forces with French help and began pressing for collective diplomatic intervention on behalf of Louis's claims. Brandenburg, followed by Trier, Brunswick-Lüneburg, Celle, Brunswick-Wolfenbüttel and others, began providing auxiliaries for the Dutch army, once it became involved in 1673. In a misguided attempt to deter such interference, Louis XIV deliberately spread the war to western Germany, beginning systematic devastation in the Rhineland early in 1674.[12] Increasingly, Brandenburg, Celle, Saxony and even Hannover, which was still neutral, began demanding billets and contributions from neighbouring German territories on the grounds that these were not pulling their weight for the common cause. Faced with the need to assert his influence and obtain urgently needed additional forces, Emperor Leopold made a virtue of necessity by capitalising on his prerogative to assign billets and arbitrate in territorial disputes. To be successful, this tactic depended on balancing concessions to the armed princes with the need to maintain the loyalty of their unarmed victims, something that became very difficult

---

12   Peter. H. Wilson, *German Armies. War and German Politics, 1648–1806* (London: UCL Press, 1998), p.45: 'Leopold's lacklustre handling of Imperial defence during these years has drawn censure in the past from nationalist historians who have contrasted it with the more energetic involvement of the Great Elector. Even today the German dimension of this Dutch War is fundamentally misunderstood, extending beyond the almost universal mistaken belief that it involved a formal *Reichskrieg* to overlook the profound consequences of Leopold's war management. His decision to avoid a formal declaration of war compelled him to fight a defensive war with the assistance of the larger, militarising territories at the expense of the weaker, unarmed ones. This expedient permitted the growth of the armed princes, who, with the onset of new French encroachments in the *Réunions* policy after 1679, looked set to implement their version of collective security after the war. Abandoned by an Emperor, who was apparently unable to protect them against domestic and external opponents, the weaker territories revolted in the *Reichstag*, paving the way for the reforms that finally stabilised the Imperial constitution after 1681 and provided the political and military framework that lasted until 1806.'

after January 1675. Although Vienna sponsored a conference to regulate matters, he could not prevent the participants rearranging agreements to suit their political objectives. As a consequence, the unarmed Westphalian territories of Essen, Werden and Dortmund were assigned to Münster in 1675 but the Bishop traded them in March 1676 for Brandenburg's billets in the former bishopric of Bremen, which was earmarked for annexation from Sweden. Meanwhile, Brandenburg used its billeting rights in Westphalia to consolidate its hold on the area around Cleves and Mark. The situation in the north was worse, as Leopold was unable to stem the influence of Hannover, Celle, Wolfenbüttel, Münster and Brandenburg, all of which enjoyed diplomatic backing from Spain and the Dutch Republic in return for their renewed contribution to the allied effort in Flanders. On 21 September 1675, Münster, Brandenburg and Denmark agreed to Hanoverian billeting in large parts of Lower Saxony as the price of the Duke's non-intervention in their operations against Sweden.[13]

All these developments severely strained collective defence, and the lesson for the medium territories appeared to be clear: only through possession of their own independent forces would they preserve their political position and escape domination by their neighbours. This scenario naturally angered their neighbours, who were still participating in the *Kreis* contingents, while their exemption from billeting reduced the areas available for the Emperor and armed princes. Matters reached crisis by October 1676, as a shortage of assigned quarters and contributions began to undermine the Great Elector's war effort. Though Brandenburg received about two million thalers in Dutch and Austrian subsidies in 1672–1678, irregularities in payment caused acute cash flow problems, while Swedish intervention disrupted tax collection at a time when the army was expanding in line with political objectives.

Pressure mounted after the close of formal hostilities in 1679. French *Reunions* provided a convenient excuse to continue the wartime exploitation of unarmed neighbours, now all the more vital to the military finance of the armed states given the end of Dutch, Spanish and Austrian subsidies in 1678 after the Peace of Nijmegen. Some, however, clearly wanted more, intending like France to convert temporary occupation into permanent possession as compensation for the disappointing peace. Friedrich Wilhelm of Brandenburg pressed the Imperial Diet in 1679 to confirm his claims to East Frisia and permit the annexation of the Imperial cities of Dortmund, Nordhausen and Mühlhausen as recompense for the efforts on behalf of the common cause.

Having already greatly suffered during the war from enemy and allied depredations, the unarmed states now found themselves the primary targets of their neighbours' reunion-style policies. The structure of the *Kreise* was being eroded in favour of a looser federation of the larger territories, undermining both Habsburg authority and the autonomy of the lesser princes. This process was stemmed by a series of political compromises in 1679–84, defusing the external threat and revising collective security in a manner

---

13 *Ibid.* p.51.

Allegory of the Peace of Nijmegen, by Romeyn de Hooge (Rijksprentenkabinet, Amsterdam). The Peace of Nijmegen was a series of treaties signed in the Dutch city between August 1678 and October 1679. With this Peace the Franco-Dutch War ended. France annexed Franche-Comté and also added further territories of the Spanish Low Countries to those it had gained with the 1659 Treaty of the Pyrenees and 1668 Treaty of Aix-la-Chapelle. In turn, the French King, Louis XIV, ceded the occupied town of Maastricht and the Principality of Orange to the Dutch Stadtholder, William III. The French forces withdrew from several occupied territories in northern Flanders and Hainaut. Emperor Leopold I retained the captured fortress of Philippsburg but had to accept the French occupation of the towns of Freiburg and Kehl on the right bank of the Rhine. The treaties did not result in a lasting peace.

that consolidated the existing hierarchy and extended its life. Crucially, this occurred prior to the Ottoman onslaught on Vienna in 1683, enabling the Empire to survive the prolonged warfare that followed despite the coincidence of renewed dangers from France in the 1680s.

Decisive support to the Habsburgs came from the initiative of Georg Friedrich of Waldeck and Peter Philipp von Dernbach, Prince-Bishop of Würzburg, who since 1679 had planned the creation of a stable army formed by the lesser German states, which evolved in the 'Laxenburg Alliance'.[14] This initiative gave Leopold a decisive advantage over the armed princes, particularly since the alliance utilised the existing framework of the *Kreis*. This provoked the reaction of the armed princes who emphasised their hegemonic ambitions. Ferdinand von Fürstenberg, the new Prince-Bishop of Münster, pledged 25,000 men if Leopold assigned him the entire Westphalian Circle as permanent billets. Friedrich Wilhelm of Brandenburg boasted he would send twice as many troops as Bavaria and Saxony together, if he was made commander of the Imperial army.[15] Fearing it would mean the end of his exploitation of Lower Saxony, Ernst August of Hanover declined Waldeck's offers to head the Laxenburg Alliance proposing a secret plan instead to Leopold in November 1681. This called for a set of alliances to provide 60,000 men from the

---

14 See Mugnai, *Wars and Soldiers*, vol. 2, pp.121–123.
15 Wilson, *German Armies*, p.123.

existing armies of the larger territories for an immediate assault on the *Réunions*. The force was to be divided into three fully independent corps under Hanoverian, Brandenburg and Saxon command and be paid for by the unarmed territories. Such proposals indicate the growing self-confidence of the larger princes, now abandoning their earlier endorsement of reforms based on the *Kreis* structure to advocate solutions resting entirely on their own fully autonomous standing armies. However, they also indicate just how these princes were out of step with the prevailing mood in the Reichstag, which saw Leopold's proposals as the ideal answer to both French aggression and German encroachment. Brandenburg's association with France, which was opposed to any reform, also removed it as an active force at a crucial moment in the discussions.

Though the Empire preserved its territorial integrity, tension grew amongst the Franconians and Swabians, who had fielded their *Kreistruppen* since the 1660s[16] and were angry at the additional burdens placed on them. The Franconians were particularly incensed, since they had negotiated renewed promises of exemption in return for providing extra troops. Resentment was most pronounced in northern Germany, where the outcome of the *Kreis* diets of 1681–1682 had been less than satisfactory. The meeting of the Westphalian Circle in March–April 1682 proved particularly alarming, as the Brandenburg representative proposed that political influence should be commensurate to military contribution. The small territories whose matricular obligations amounted to only a few men should lose their full individual voting rights and be compelled to share a third of a vote each. Although this was rejected, Brandenburg collaborated with the other two executive princes to block a decision to actually form the Kreistruppen, compelling the unarmed members to pay them to provide substitutes in the meantime. Despite numerous disagreements over their share of these contributions, the three executives sustained their domination throughout the 1680s. Brandenburg also collaborated with the Guelphs to divide Lower Saxony on a similar basis, while Electoral Saxony continued to draw cash contributions from the weaker Upper Saxons, except for a few like Anhalt, which managed to gain exemption by sending their own contingents to Hungary. Conscious of the need to retain the support of the lesser states, Leopold I had objected to this continued extortion, but the Ottoman offensive against Vienna required immediate support. Further assistance had to be bought with concessions that consolidated the privileged position of the armed princes within collective security. Leopold I permitted Prince-Elector Johann Georg III of Saxony to take over the financial contributions of the lesser Upper Saxon territories on 7 June 1683, initiating a virtual monopoly of the *Kreis*.

Here, the Prince-Elector managed the matter in an unscrupulous manner, to say the least. Already by 1682, the Prince of Schwarzburg had agreed to pay a three-year contribution to the Prince-Elector of Saxony in return for exemption from billeting. In the event of the money not being paid, the

---

16   See Mugnai, *Wars and Soldiers*, vol. 2, pp.108–121.

Prince-Elector kindly offered to send his army to help collect it.[17] The contract was extended for another two years in 1686, but since the Saxon troops could not avoid crossing the territory of Schwarzburg on their march to the Rhine, the cost for quartering the soldiers was deducted from the payment. Once more the agreement was extended in 1688. Electoral Saxony was particularly active in this kind of contribution. The Abbey of Quedlinburg offered 4,000 thalers per annum in 1684, but paid only occasionally. In April 1685, the Saxon treasury informed Johann Georg III that the war chest was empty, in 1684 Quedlinburg had not sent money, and the first contribution for 1685 was also missing. At the beginning of 1686, after Saxony's request, 3,000 thalers were paid. In April, abbess Anna Dorothea of Saxe-Weimar informed the cousin of Dresden, Johann Georg III, that she could only raise 'with the greatest difficulties' a further 1,300 thalers and therefore wanted to cancel the agreement of 1683. In response, the Prince-Elector sent troops to Quedlinburg. In 1687, no money has been paid, probably because the cost of quartering covered the contribution. In 1688, the abbey paid three of its four contributions which in the 1689 were raised to an annual total of 7,680 thalers, and the year after another of 10,533 thalers.[18]

Although subsidies were scarcely lucrative, since they paid for initial mobilisation and rarely covered the cost of long-term involvement, in the 1680s the 'trade' of contributions continued without pause, but also caused dispute. In 1683 the Count of Stollberg was requested to pay his contribution to Saxony. The Emperor had supported this request having granted the Prince-Elector permission to raise funds in the Upper Saxony Circle, and the local diet, surprisingly, increased the contribution. However, by December 1684 only half of the contribution had actually been collected, and by 1685, the Count was 10,000 thalers in arrears. The Prince-Elector reduced his requirement but also demanded the quarter for a company of infantry, Despite this, in 1687 the estates of the county retained a part of the payment, arguing that the city of Wernigerode, in *condominium* between Stollerg and electoral Brandenburg, was a fief of Berlin, and paid its duties to another Prince-Elector. As the city housed a Brandenburger garrison, it even ignored the repeated orders of the Emperor to pay the contribution to Saxony. Instead of attempting to bring Berlin to heel, in 1689 Leopold simply supported Saxony and placed a further demand.[19] The conflict demonstrated how the two Protestant Prince-Electors struggled for influence over the small principalities of Germany.

Though the difficulties of collecting money were accompanied by not always justified complaints, which were typical in that age, this scenario troubled the major powers, because the contribution of the small states of the *Reich* were considerable, and even vital for the maintenance of the German standing armies.

---

17 Querengässer, *The Saxon Mars and His Force*, p.33.
18 Querengässer, *The Saxon Mars and His Force*, p.34
19 Walter Thenius, *Die Anfange des Stehenden Heerwesen in Kursachsen unter Johann Georg III. und Johann Georg IV*. (Leipzig, 1912), pp.15–16.

A similar arrangement was struck with Hanover on 14 January 1683. In return for holding 10,000 men in readiness, Duke Ernst August was authorised to collect 16,000 thalers a month from the Lower Saxon unarmed territories in addition to a down payment of 50,000 thalers from Austria to mobilise his troops. Saxony sent the largest single German contingent following a further agreement with Leopold on 30 July 1683, but Hanover, along with Celle and Wolfenbüttel, was unable to assist for fear of Brandenburg, which was still allied to France and Denmark.[20]

In 1682, the Laxenburg Alliance had been created the basis for a new *Reichsarmee*. Mobilisation would inevitably be slow, since many territories still lacked sufficient troops to fulfil even their minimum obligations, though the desire to escape continued exploitation by the armed princes was to encourage even small counties to establish permanent forces after 1681. With this act, the *Reich* had opted for a reform of its existing mobilisation system and not, as is often stated, raised a standing army.[21] The revised structure was undoubtedly flawed and became the subject of considerable criticism both at the time and subsequently. Nonetheless, it was the product of a political compromise that sacrificed military efficiency to prolong the life of the traditional Imperial constitution.

---

20 Wilson, *German Armies*, p.182. Leopold I even fined the Great Elector for demanding money from the abbess of Essen despite the end of the war in 1679, but in practice he was powerless to enforce such decisions because he depended on the armed princes' auxiliaries for the Turkish War after 1683, and so left them largely in control of those areas they had established as zones of contribution during the Dutch War.

21 Wilson, *German Armies*, p.66.

3

The Electorate of Brandenburg

As historians have long recognised, the rise of the Prussian state was as unlikely as it was meteoric. There was probably no other state in seventeenth century Europe where the elites were so divided and the monarchy so weak. After 1648, the territories that formed the core of the Electoral state were bizarrely scattered along five parallel river courses in northern Germany. Between Ravensberg, Cleves-Mark, Brandenburg and Ducal Prussia there was no natural connection, and in the confused and fluctuating political conditions of that century there was no reason to suppose that the tenuous ties that bound those territories could have been maintained for long. Despite this, what appeared to be a 'strategic mistake' became a major power in northern Germany within 40 years.

The seventeenth century Electorate consisted of seven distinct territories – the Baltic provinces of East Prussia and eastern Pomerania, the Margravate of Brandenburg, the Rhineland provinces of Cleves and Mark, the county of Ravensberg-Minden, and the former bishoprics of Magdeburg and Halberstadt – each with its own constitutional arrangements and territorial estates. And in three of these territories the sovereignty of the Hohenzollern was either contested (by the Palatinate in Cleves and Mark) or shared (with the Poles in Prussia and the Swedes in Pomerania).[1] To this, deep confessional divisions split the Electorate, particularly between the court, which was predominantly Calvinist, and the subjects, who were overwhelmingly Lutheran. A further difference, of a legal nature, contributed to the poor homogeneity of the Electoral domains. All western territories, including Brandenburg, fell within the borders of the *Reich*, while Prussia belonged to Poland, and therefore was not subject to Imperial jurisdiction. The

---

1   Wilson, *Iron and Blood*, p.131: 'With the Treaty of Westphalia, Brandenburg gained the most territory, receiving the eastern half of Pomerania, plus former church lands as compensation for Sweden acquisition of the western half. Although these gains boosted the revenue by a third, the Prince-Elector remained aggrieved and the desire to acquire the missing half of Pomerania was a major factor dictating subsequent Prussian involvement in European wars. The Prince Lector had not secured these gains through military victories, as his army had performed uniformly badly during the brief involvement in the Thirty Years' War. Instead, he owed his new lands to the Habsburgs' desire to expand Brandenburg as a buffer to contain Swedish influence in Northern Germany.'

THE ELECTORATE OF BRANDENBURG

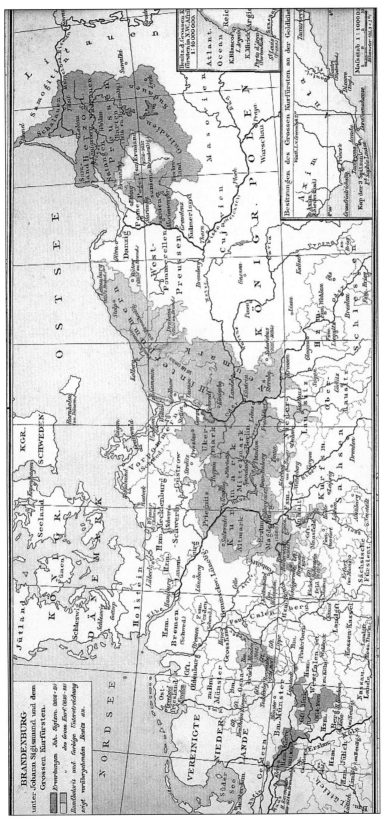

The Territories of the Electorate of Brandenburg in 1648

Hohenzollern were one of the four secular Prince-Electors of the *Reich*, and as a Margrave of Brandenburg, the Elector was a member of the Imperial Circle of Upper Saxony, and as lord of other German territories, he was also represented in the circles of Westphalia and Lower Saxony. Relations between the Elector and the subjects in these territories were therefore regulated according to Imperial laws, and for any disputes, the parties appealed to the *Reichstag*, and after 1648 to the King of Sweden too. In Prussia, on the other hand, the subjects had Poland as protector, since the Hohenzollern were vassals of the *Rzeczpospolita*.

Even from a purely geographical point of view, the differences appeared significant. The Duchy of Prussia was less extensive than Brandenburg, but had a larger population, and due to its geographical location and better soil quality was more developed and prosperous than the Electoral mark. It is estimated that 400,000 inhabitants lived in Prussia at the end of the seventeenth century, while Brandenburg had a population of slightly more than half that figure.[2] Furthermore, Prussia possessed an excellent harbour: the city of Königsberg (today Kaliningrad, Russian Federation), which economically eclipsed every city in the Electorate, including Berlin. In practice, Königsberg's trade volume alone was worth that of the whole of Brandenburg and in the south-eastern Baltic area, its importance was second only to Danzig, with which it had been competing since the sixteenth century. With its 30,000 inhabitants, Königsberg was the largest city in the Hohenzollern states, and for this reason, it was divided into three urban agglomerations each with its own Burgomaster. In the same period, the capital, Berlin, housed only 10,000–12,000 inhabitants.

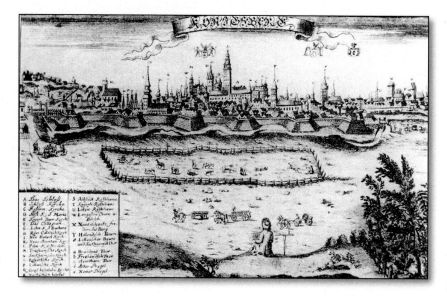

Königsberg in a print dated to 1684. (Author's Collection)

---

2   Francis L. Carsten, *The Origin of Prussia* (Oxford: Oxford University Press, 1979; Italian Edition, Bologna: Il Mulino, 1982), p.243.

THE ELECTORATE OF BRANDENBURG

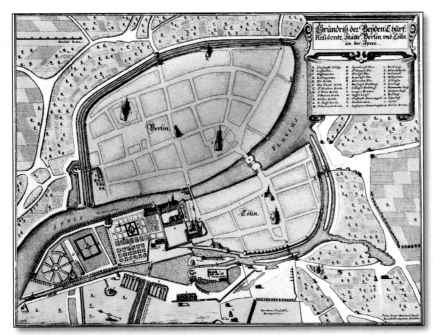

Map of 1652 by Johann Gregor Memhardt, showing the layout of Berlin and the suburb of Cölln. (Author's Collection)

The nobility occupied the dominant constitutional position and controlled the central and provincial administration; however, privileges were not uniform. The nobility of Brandenburg occupied a more prominent position, especially in comparison to the nobility of Prussia, which unlike the former was not exempt from paying taxes, albeit to a much lesser extent compared to the common people. Regardless of where they came from, the nobility of the countryside constituted a very different social body from the aristocracy living in the cities, and for this reason the former were identified with the not always positive term *Junker*.[3] All male nobles from every Electoral domain were still required to serve in the army and procure a horseman for military campaigns.[4] Just as there were differences in the rank of the aristocracy, so too were there differences between one territory and another, especially when it came to taxation. Brandenburg, in fact, paid higher taxes, although it was economically less prosperous, and in turn, the other dominions enjoyed a special legislative and tax regime.

Through a successful marriage policy, the Margraves of Brandenburg had obtained sovereignty over territories in Germany that were far more developed than their original domains. The most important of these was the Duchy of Cleves, which extended beyond the Rhine on the border with the United Provinces, to which it was closely linked economically. Further south-west, in the Ruhr valley, was the county of Mark, which benefited from the flourishing trade resulting from coal mining and iron production.

---

3   In Brandenburg and Prussia, the *Junker* was a member of the landed nobility who owned great estates that were maintained and worked by peasants with few rights. The *Junker* often lay in the countryside outside of major cities or towns. They became an important factor in Prussia, and after 1871, in German military, political and diplomatic leadership.

4   *Lehmpferde*, namely 'feudal horse', which according to its origin was a military public benefit, later converted into private obligations by the nobility.

Christoph von Kannenberg (1615–1673), Major General, Councillor of the Prince-Elector's Secret Council, and Colonel Proprietor of a Brandenburg cavalry regiment in a contemporary print by Lambert Visscher (Rijksmuseum, Amsterdam). Like other prominent families of the Electorate, the Kannenbergs belonged to the 'Junker' aristocracy. The term *Junker* is derived from Middle High German *Juncherre*, meaning 'young nobleman' or otherwise 'young lord' (derivation of *jung* and *Herr*), and was originally the title of members of the higher *edelfrei* (immediate) nobility of Germany. While in Austria and in other parts of Germany the rise of a strong bourgeoisie and the gradual decline of the power of the nobility began, in Brandenburg-Prussia there was a rise of the aristocracy with the worsening of serfdom. The despotism of the Hohenzollerns and the rise of the Junkers sealed the defeat of the bourgeoisie. The predominance of the sovereign's power was the characteristic theme of a state that was not founded on a balance of classes, but on a compromise between monarchy and nobility. Historical sociologists and social historians have long viewed early modern Prussia as one of the purest expressions of 'absolutist' rule. This assertion is not without good reason, for there was perhaps no other state in eighteenth century Europe where the fusion of the elites- nobility, the bureaucracy and the officer corps – and the centralisation of power, social, political and military – were more complete. Even if one regards the term 'absolutism' with suspicion, as many now do, there can be no question that the eighteenth century Prussian state was relatively, if not absolutely, stronger and more autonomous than most, and perhaps all, of its neighbours.

The social structure of the two territories was completely different from that of the Electoral domains in the north-east. Neither in Cleves nor in Mark was there a preponderance of Junkers nor a subjugated citizenry and peasants subservient to the power of the gold masters. Here as in all his domains, the Elector appointed the *Statthalter*, who acted as military governors and lieutenants of the prince, as this rank was the equivalent of the Dutch Stadtholder. In the Rhineland territories, there was a nobility that naturally formed the first estate, in the local diets, but they did not dominate the assemblies as the Brandenburg Junkers did, nor did they possess tax privileges. Furthermore, the power of the nobility was balanced by that of the cities, especially in Cleves, which, unlike other areas of the Rhineland, had been less affected by the economic decline caused by the Thirty Years' War.

THE ELECTORATE OF BRANDENBURG

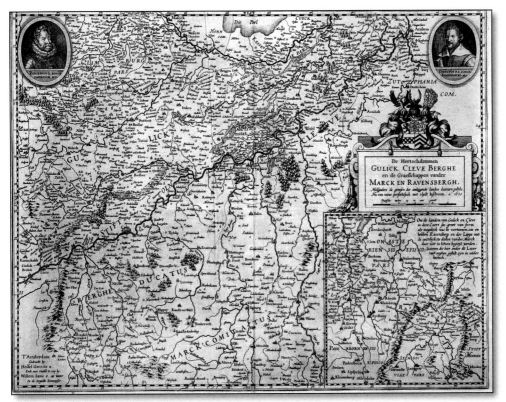

The Duchy of Jülich-Cleve in a German print dating to the 1630s (Author's Collection). The Duchy, approximately 2,100 square kilometres, had a considerable strategic value. Extending to both banks of the Rhine, every crossing point was defended by strong fortifications. By controlling this territory, the Spaniards would have been able to bypass the Dutch defensive line. When the last member of the dynasty reigning over Jülich-Cleve and Berg died out in 1621, Cleve was assigned by succession to the Hohenzollerns of Brandenburg, but was garrisoned by Dutch troops in Emmerich, Rees and Jülich, while the Spaniards held Wesel, Orsoy and Rheinberg, the latter belonging to the Prince-Bishop Elector of Cologne. The Brandenburg troops joined the Dutch garrisons while remaining neutral, but in fact prevented the passage of the Rhine for the duration of the Thirty Years' War.

In the countryside of Cleves and Mark, the peasants were in the majority free, and formed a politically cohesive class. In the Rhineland, the Prince-Electors also ruled the county of Ravensberg-Minden, where a few thousand inhabitants lived.

In addition to these direct domains, there were others not yet fully acquired. With the Treaties of Westphalia, the town of Magdeburg was ceded to the Elector as a 'benefit of war'. The town, which belonged to a prince-archbishop, would only be absorbed by the Electorate after the death of the sovereign, which happened in 1680.[5] By contrast, the other bishopric assigned to Brandenburg in 1648, Halberstadt, was secularised and immediately

---

5   The last prince-archbishop was August of Saxe-Weissenfels (1614–1680). However, as early as 1666 the Great Elector sent 10,000 soldiers to the city as a garrison. During the course of the seventeenth century Magdeburg, which had 30,000 inhabitants before the Thirty Years' War, slowly recovered from the devastation suffered in 1631 and was provided with a modern fortress. The defences were further strengthened, and under Frederick II the fortress reached a

annexed to the state. These territories totalled 38,650 square kilometres altogether with a population of about 800,000 persons. The territories ruled by the Hohenzollern Electoral branch were included in three Imperial *Kreise*: Upper Saxony, Lower Saxony and Westphalia, and this, if properly exploited, would have allowed Berlin wide influence in the affairs of the *Reich*.

Magdeburg in 1640, from Merian's *Theatrum Europeum*. (Public Domain) The city became a Brandenburg possession in 1680, but in 1668 the local authorities were already obliged to swear an oath to the Great Elector.

A German print showing the African fort of Dorothea. (Author's Collection)

---

size of 200 hectares, while the city expanded to only 120. Magdeburg was then considered the most important fortress in all of Prussia.

THE ELECTORATE OF BRANDENBURG

Unique in the history of seventeenth century Germany, Brandenburg had colonial possessions in Africa: the fort-harbours of Grossfriedrichsburg, Sophie Louise, Dorotheenschanze, and Taccarary on the Gold Coast, and that of Arguin in Senegal.

The Birth of a Military-Fiscal State

Friedrich Wilhelm I, who entered history as 'the Great Elector', is rightly regarded as the founder of what was to become the mighty Prussian state. The most important political achievement ascribed to him was the transformation of a small peripheral margravate with obsolete medieval features into a modern state governed according to the principles of absolutism. In this, Friedrich Wilhelm was of course influenced by the example of Louis XIV. The Elector focused his politics in the foundation of new institutions, to the extent that the basis on which he founded the Hohenzollern state remained virtually unchanged throughout the eighteenth century. This result appears even more extraordinary if we consider that during the Thirty Years' War, the Hohenzollerns' rule over their territories appeared little more than formal. Historians who have dealt with the modern Brandenburg-Prussia have concentrated their interest on this transformation, but have rarely investigated the genesis of this politic, which started from very special circumstances, and as is often the case, took shape despite the fact that the original intentions were quite different.

Prince-Elector Friedrich Wilhelm of Brandenburg (1620–1688), Jacques Vaillant. (Public Domain) When the young Friedrich Wilhelm ascended the throne in 1640, there was no electoral state worthy of the name: he simply possessed a number of territories scattered throughout Germany, each with its own government and institutions. But when he died in 1688, there was a fully centralised state governed from Berlin and held together by the army. Writing towards the end of the eighteenth century, the military historian Georg Heinrich von Behrenhorst declared that the Prussian monarchy was not a country that had an army, but an army that had a country which it used as a billeting area, and Mirabeau once made a somewhat similar remark.

From 1637 onwards, the armies of the major powers involved in the Thirty Years' War occupied the Electorate. Consequently, the court had moved to peripheral Prussia, which was less burdened by the war and less exposed to foreign occupation, but this caused a serious loss of prestige for the ruling house. At the same time, the war weakened the power of the estates and shook their political and economic strength. The estates of the Electorate were not very different from those of the other German states. The first of these consisted of the provincial officials – *Landräte* – appointed for life by the prince at the suggestion of his council. They came from the nobility, which in turn formed the second estate; thus the nobility had two estates as opposed to only one formed by the representatives of the towns, the majority of whom were bourgeois. There was also a fourth estate, formed by the non-noble landowners and village chiefs who, however, did not enjoy uniform political representation throughout the state, and in fact in Brandenburg were

35

excluded from all prerogatives reserved for the other Estates. Collectively, the estates were the highest civil authorities in each Hohenzollern domain, exercising local administration, judiciary and tax collection.

Unfortunately, the Imperialists and the Swedes, who took turns occupying Brandenburg, did not seek the consent of the estates when imposing a tax, and resorted to intimidation and forced collection through soldiery.[6] During the years of foreign occupations, the weakness of the estates and the climate of emergency were exploited by the energetic and skilful minister of Elector Georg Wilhelm, Count Adam von Schwartzenberg. He was not a native of Brandenburg, but came from the Rhineland and had been in the service of the Emperor and the last Duke of Cleves before coming to Berlin. The Count succeeded in marginalising the Prince-Elector's Privy Council (*Geheimer Rat*) which he joined in 1625, dominated by the Brandenburg nobility, and in having councillors he proposed appointed, also from the bourgeoisie. The following year, he had the powerful councillor Samuel von Winterfeld arrested on charges of high treason, while two other private councillors accused of complicity were discredited and forced to resign. After these events, the Privy Council ceased to play an important role in state affairs. Gradually, Schwartzenberg concentrated power on himself and his circle, and did not hesitate to use troops to collect contributions without the consent of the estates. In 1630, the Count established a special War Council (*Kriegsrat*), which he also used outside the military sphere, until it became the main instrument of government for all state affairs. According to Schwartzenberg's plan, all government officials were to report the most important and sensitive affairs to the War Council, to establish thorough control over all matters of state. After 1635, all members of the council were foreigners, both nobles and commoners, with just one exception, in order to guarantee greater autonomy from the interests of the estates. When Elector Georg Wilhelm died in 1640, the council comprised 16 members, of whom 10 were bourgeois, as were all lower officials. On that date, the Privy Council ceased to exist. Even in the military, the Count used the same method, forcing officers to obey his orders without question and to refrain from criticism on pain of immediate dismissal.

Despite the great power accumulated by the Count, the estates strenuously opposed his policies. At the diet of 1636, they violently attacked the War Council and refused to vote for any form of taxation whose expediency was not known to them in advance. Nevertheless, Schwartzenberg, using a pretext, disbanded the diet, ordered the imposition of contributions and finally

Count Adam von Schwartzenberg (1583–1641), portrait by Michiel Jansz, shown wearing the white cross of the Order of St John of Malta (Weiss Gallery, Maastricht). A native of Cleve-Mark, the Count inspired the policy of Friedrich Wilhelm to counter the Estates' power in the Electorate.

---

6 When the estates of Brandenburg tried to negotiate a reduction of the war tax with the Swedish commanders, they were advised to bargain with their Prince-Elector, because Sweden only knew about the right of arms and did not care at all about the privileges of the Prince's subjects. Carsten, *The Origin of Prussia*, p.218.

imposed a new tax by decree. In the following years, the estates were forced to adopt a conciliatory attitude, decreeing the final success of the Count, who was able to prevail even over the influence of the Junkers in the government, thus becoming 'the soul of the Elector', as Crown Prince Friedrich Wilhelm bitterly declared.[7] When he succeeded his father on the Electoral throne, many expected a radical change, given the huge difference in temperament between the young prince and his father, and especially because of Friedrich Wilhelm's attitude to taking care of state affairs in person. The hopes of the estates regained strength and implored the sovereign to restore their rights and remove them 'from the subjugation they were in by entrusting the reins of government to them, their loyal and faithful subjects': an insult to the person of the powerful Count Schwartzenberg.[8] It is unlikely that the estates would have made such a direct request had they not known on which side the new Elector's sympathies lay. Friedrich Wilhelm, as a matter of course, had many friendly ties with the Brandenburg nobility, including many of those hostile to Schwartzenberg, and this had been one of the causes of the conflict with his father. However, the issue was already perfectly clear to the young Elector. In fact, he too was convinced of the need to limit the influence of the aristocrats and keep the estates in check, but to succeed in this it was necessary, for the time being, to obtain the support of both of them in order to use them against Schwartzenberg. Although in March 1641 the Count's sudden death made the task less difficult than expected, Friedrich Wilhelm had to remove the entire government structure built by Schwartzenberg. The Elector acted swiftly and a few weeks after Schwartzenberg's death the War Council was removed and the Privy Council immediately reinstated, which also became responsible for military matters. Some of the most prominent officials, compromised by Schwartzenberg's system of government, were forced to resign. However, with the revival of the Privy Council, the power of the estates also resumed. They resumed the management and administration of taxes and even the distribution of funding for expenditure chapters, including those for the army. Alongside the estates, the Junkers once again occupied a leading role in the government. Most of them belonged to the aristocracy of Brandenburg and Pomerania, including such great lineages as Horn, Platen, Kleist, Kannenberg, Schwerin, Dohna, Putlitz, Bergsdorf, Knesebeck, and Treffenfeld; in the absence of the Prince-Elector, some nobles could deliberate on matters of state together with private councillors.[9]

A change in the political climate could hardly have been more radical. The Peace of Westphalia opened a new phase in the history of the Electorate, but Friedrich Wilhelm was aware that this was not a long-term guarantee. The dispute between the countryside and the cities, the bourgeoisie and the

---

7   Carsten, *The Origin of Prussia*, p.219.

8   Carsten, *The Origin of Prussia*, p.219.

9   Even in less important matters, Friedrich Wilhelm took care to respect the wishes of the estates even before they expressed an opinion. In 1648 he went so far as to declare that he could not give his consent for the Jews to reside in Brandenburg because this would have been cause for complaint by the representatives of the estates. See Karin Friedrich, *Brandenburg-Prussia, 1466–1806: the Rise of a Composite State* (Houndmills: Palgrave Macmillan, 2012), pp.106–107.

Marble bust of Joachim Hennigs von Treffenfeld (1615–1688) in the burial ground of Könnigde, Sachsen-Anhalt. Unlike most of the Brandenburg senior commander, Treffenfeld did not serve in the Swedish army and nor he was of noble origin. He entered the electoral cavalry in the 1640s climbing the ranks and becoming a Captain in a short time. A veteran of the campaigns in Poland and Pomerania, he became Colonel Proprietor of a cavalry regiment in 1675. For his brilliant behaviour during the winter campaign against the Swedes, he was ennobled by the Great Elector. In the following campaigns he was promoted Major General.

nobles, had not subsided.[10] With his domains stretching from the Meuse to the Niemen, the Elector guessed that other power conflicts would arise in both east and west, and although Brandenburg remained geographically and politically the centre of his domains, he was convinced of the need to defend each territory from foreign interference. However, any attempt by Friedrich Wilhelm to remedy the existing situation undermined the understanding with the estates, and in the long run it would have been impossible to reconcile his policy with that envisaged by these latter. In any case, he was determined not to take a part like his father, namely the victim among the belligerents. To avoid this, he was convinced of the necessity of possessing a well-trained military force, without which any significant political achievement would have been impossible. He moved with rapidity and tried to exploit the scenario that emerged after the Peace of Westphalia to strengthen the position of his states and possibly gain other territories in the north-east, especially Stettin (today Szczecin in Poland) and the mouth of the Oder, which had eluded him in 1648 and were considered as the key to the geostrategy of the Electorate. In the west, Friedrich Wilhelm's interest focused instead on the Duchy of Jülich, which in 1609 had gone to the rival Dukes of Pfalz-Neuburg in the inheritance of Cleves.

However, the estates of Brandenburg had little interest in the geopolitics of the Lower Rhine or the Baltic. They demanded peace and tranquillity to recover from the economic crisis caused by the war and did not care about the rights of persecuted Protestants in Jülich – which in 1651 Friedrich Wilhelm tried to support through military intervention – nor about the demarcation of the border with Sweden in Pomerania and along the Oder. The estates as a

---

10   Carsten, *The Origin of Prussia*, p.220: 'The biggest problem and source of strife between town and country was that of taxes, which had risen considerably due to foreign military occupations. After lengthy negotiations, a compromise was reached in 1643: from that date, the cities would pay 59 percent of all taxes for the army, both ordinary and extraordinary, while the remaining 41 percent was paid by the countryside. The nobility of Brandenburg, despite the numerous rents they enjoyed, naturally remained exempt from all taxes. This taxation was therefore a major obstacle to the economic recovery of the provinces that had suffered severely from the military occupations.'

THE ELECTORATE OF BRANDENBURG

whole were also convinced that, with the cessation of hostilities, the army would be reduced as it had been every time in the past, and furthermore they would not contribute in any way to financing a military enterprise for the territorial increase of the Electorate. This was the first significant divergence that arose between Friedrich Wilhelm and the estates. In those months, the Elector had repeatedly emphasised to his councillors that he considered his estates, scattered all over Germany, to be parts of a whole. In September 1649, when relations with the estates were still amicable, Friedrich Wilhelm urged the Privy Council not to focus only on the Brandenburg mark, but on all lands and subjects, and the estates should also do the same.[11] The following year, the differences of opinion increased, especially when the estates opposed the spending of money on rearmament of the army to support the Elector in his border dispute in Pomerania. The representatives of the estates addressed their reply to the Privy Council stating that it seemed unlikely to them 'that Pomerania, Prussia or Cleves would help Brandenburg in case of danger', and therefore 'Brandenburg would not interfere in disputes with foreign states', and this had to be applied later on.[12] The greatest disagreements arose in tax matters, as happened in 1651 when the Elector, forced by the need for money for his plans, tried to introduce a tax in the form of a levy without the estates' approval. In the end, Friedrich Wilhelm became convinced that he could never prevail with a conciliatory policy and it became increasingly clear that mere exhortations would bring him no advantage. In March 1652 the Elector convened a general diet, calling together the nobility, city burgomasters and guild representatives. Such a meeting had not been held for 37 years, but it was also to be the last. It is unlikely that at that time Friedrich Wilhelm still believed in cooperation with the estates, and hoped to obtain more with this large assembly than he had hitherto achieved with separate negotiations. The act on which the diet focused was the Elector's proposal to introduce a taxation system modelled on the one existing in the United Provinces of the Netherlands. It was a system based on income and land rent that, among other things, required the nobility to contribute. In practical terms, the reform would have given the Elector an economic disposition not subject to the interference of the estates. The project immediately met with favour in the cities, but was bitterly disapproved of by the aristocracy.[13] Moreover, the estates countered the prince's proposal with a long list of grievances, and reaffirmed respect for their privileges in matters of taxation and justice. The dispute continued throughout the year and the diet was convened seven more times until May 1653. In the end, Friedrich Wilhelm did not insist on conducting the negotiation with the general assembly formula, but requested the presence of restricted delegations trying to negotiate with the most malleable deputies. The result of these deferred negotiations was the

---

11 Oskar Meinardus (ed.), *Protokolle und Relationen der Brandenburgische Geheimen Rathes aus der Zeit der Kurfürsten Friedrich Wilhelm* (Lipsia, 1889–1919), vol. IV, p.274.

12 Carsten, *The Origin of Prussia*, p.222.

13 Carsten, *The Origin of Prussia*, p.223. According to the nobles, this modus, once introduced, would hardly be abolished, and would cause a rift in the institutions and impose equality between the aristocrats and the other princes' subjects.

famous *Rezess* issued in the summer of 1653. In order to obtain it, Friedrich Wilhelm was forced to grant considerable concessions of power to the large landowners who had hitherto been his greatest antagonists. The Junkers' properties were to be transformed from fiefs held in exchange for military services, into land in absolute ownership. By removing the restrictions that had existed in this matter, the Elector recognised the Junkers as the only class authorised to acquire property and confirmed, making them permanent, the privileges they had obtained from his predecessors, such as the right of absolute jurisdiction over their peasants. Finally, the Elector specifically recognised their authority in local affairs and their right to be considered as the ruling class in all matters concerning the state as a whole.[14]

Friedrich Wilhelm of Brandenburg, in a print dating to the early 1660s, wearing the attributes of Prince-Elector. (Author's archive) In the background are musketeers wearing *Leibröcke*. Like two sides of the same coin, the Great Elector's achievements had both positive and negative aspects. The harsh taxation hit the population hard and was one of the least glorious pages of his reign. The architects of this financial policy were the new government bodies, which revolutionised the old administrative system of the state. In the creation of these offices, the Elector showed his positive intentions. Partly due to circumstances, partly due to the impact of foreign policy, and partly due to his personal ambitions, he adopted a policy directed against the Estates and their privileges, and towards the centralisation of power.

The Elector also renounced to introduce the tax reform, but finally achieved his aims: the financing of 530,000 thalers payable in six years with which he could raise a standing army.[15] It was a compromise solution, and

---

14 Gordon A. Craig, *The Politics of the Prussian Army, 1640–1945* (Oxford: Oxford University Press, 1964; Italian Edition, Bologna: Il Mulino, 1984), p.19.
15 Leopold von Orlich, *Geschichte des Preußischen Staats im 17. Jahrhundert* (Berlin: 1838–39), vol. III, p.55. It was, however, a significant fact that the tax reform proposed by the Elector, called

THE ELECTORATE OF BRANDENBURG

formally the estates prevailed, but Friedrich Wilhelm had finally obtained the desired funding. Consequently, an important change occurred in the military administration with the appointment of the *Churfürstliche Kriegstaffe*.[16] Brandenburg's increased military strength gave the prince a prominent position in the North German scenario, and participation in the Swedish-Polish war of 1655–60 marked a turning point in relations between the prince and the estates throughout the state. Indeed, he saw his full sovereignty recognised by both sides with the Labiau and Wehlau Treaties, respectively, which were reconfirmed at the conclusion of the conflict in 1660 with the Peace of Oliva. Henceforth, it would no longer be possible for the estates to obtain the help of Poland or Sweden if their privileges were threatened.

In the early years of the war, Friedrich Wilhelm continued his policy of cooperation with the estates, and in 1656 warned the Privy Council to treat them as leniently as possible, but later considered it the obvious duty of the estates not only of Prussia, which was directly involved in the war, but equally of Brandenburg and Cleves, to finance his military effort, renouncing reliance on neighbouring countries in defence matters.[17] When they refused to do so, the Elector collected the contributions without their consent. Brandenburg repression in Cleves and Mark only proved successful after its alliance with the House of Orange in 1655 removed Dutch backing for the estates, and within eight months its troops had collected 300,000 thalers from the local population.[18] The scenario did not change even when the Electorate changed alliance and sided with Poland and the Emperor. Between 1655 and 1657, in addition to the 530,000 thalers granted by the diet, a further 517,766 thalers were collected in Brandenburg, making a total of 717,766 thalers in just over two years.[19]

---

modi generalis, was implemented in the city of Frankfurt, and that a similar attempt was also made in Berlin in 1658, where, however, it met with strong opposition from the estates and the nobility, who prevented its implementation.

16 Curt Jany, *Geschichte der Königlich Preußischen Armee bis zum Jahre 1807*, vol. I (Berlin, 1928), p.110: 'Whereas the troops had hitherto received their share of the tribute granted by the Estates for their maintenance, and a divided tribute from the district commissions and the municipal magistrates, to whom they were referred, without a state control office supervising both parts, on 6 September 1653, the Elector transferred the supreme direction of the tribute granted by the most recent Diet, to the Privy Chamberlain Christian Sigismund Hendekampf, and the revenue collection to Johan Adam Prunel. This is how the *Churfürstliche Kriegstaffe* came into being.'

17 At the end of 1656, Elector Friedrich Wilhelm made it clear to the governor of Cleves-Mark, Johann Moritz of Nassau-Siegen, that any contact by the provincial estates with a foreign power to demand protection affected his authority over the country and that he 'could not allow them to take precedence in this matters'. See Michael Kaiser, 'Temps de l'occupation – temps de la liberté: les territoires du duché de Clèves et du comté de La Marck sous l'occupation des Provinces-Unies', in J. F. Chanet and C. Windler (eds), *Les Ressources des Faibles: Neutralités, Sauvegardes, Accommodements en Temps de Guerre (XVIe–XVIIIe siècle)* (Rennes: Presses universitaires de Rennes, 2010), p.256.

18 Wilson, *German Armies*, p.32.

19 Carsten, *The Origin of Prussia*, p.227. This figure does not include goods in kind, which reached about the same value. In 1656, 40,000–50,000 thalers were collected monthly in Brandenburg, and the burden increased again until it reached 110,000 thalers per month in early 1659. Complaints were numerous, and as early as 1657, even the councillors of the Elector declared that the towns would be depopulated if contributions did not decrease. The burgomasters

The main factor behind this achievement was the new administrative offices appointed by the Elector in 1656: the *Generalkriegskommissariat*, which was responsible for the control of the financing of the army. The office remained active until 1660, extending its competence to the management of war contributions and, above all, the collection of money. The terrain had been prepared since the early 1650s, with the formation of the *Amtkammer*. With these 'chambers' the Elector attempted to balance the governments of the estates to administer and coordinate the Elector's domains, taxation and privileges. The *Amtkammer* was first introduced in Brandenburg in 1652, then in Cleves and Mark in 1653, in Pomerania in 1654, in Prussia in 1661 and finally in Magdeburg in 1680.

By the end of the war, Friedrich Wilhelm had gained a position of international prestige, and above all had an army that was able to break any internal resistance. After 1660 the estates were no longer able to regain lost ground: as in so many paradoxes of history, the political scene had returned to the one dominated 20 years earlier by Count Adam von Schwartzenberg.

The Peace of Oliva in 1660 led to a significant decrease in the tax burden, but not to a return of the understanding between the Elector and the estates, nor was the army disbanded. However, the Great Elector did not abolish the estates in his various provinces, but merely modified their constitutions, and even temporarily reduced taxes. Bargains, such as that struck with the estates of Brandenburg in 1653, along with the cooption of their members and their integration into princely patronage networks, proved a more effective means of securing funding and advancing absolute rule.[20] After all, the standing army was not an end in itself.

In 1664, the Prince-Elector mobilised 2,000 of his soldiers to join the troops sent by the other German princes in the war against the Porte in Hungary. One year later, the garrison was alarmed at Cleves for the war between the Dutch Republic and England, and by the threatening demeanour of the Prince-Bishop of Münster, an ally of Charles II Stuart. Consequently, the cost of maintaining the troops even in peacetime made the continuation of extraordinary taxation necessary. This was the least glorious chapter of the Great Elector's reign. Protests and harassment continued throughout the 1660s. Year after year, the provinces begged the Prince for a moratorium on taxes because of the progressive impoverishment of the economy and the dramatic depopulation that resulted.[21] The exasperation of the subjects reached a climax, and by the admission of the Privy Council, the tax collection

---

testified that troops were used on a large scale to extort money, and the poor were forced to sell everything, even their beds; moreover, it had become impossible to sell the requisitioned goods, as the cost of such operations was higher than the proceeds. In 1660, in the town of Neumark, half of the houses were uninhabited. In the countryside, peasants were equally affected, and many fled to neighbouring states. Some communities tried to oppose the troops sent to collect the taxes, threatening to 'wring the necks' of anyone who tried to force payment, and in 1656, in the Brandenburg district of Prignitz, a full-blown revolt broke out that prevented the collection of taxes.

20 Wilson, *German Armies*, p.32.

21 Meinardus, *Protokolle und Relationen*, vol. V, p.643. In 1662 the town of Spandau asked for a moratorium, explaining that before the war, 400 families lived in the town and now only 70–80 remained. A year later, a three-year moratorium was granted to Prittwalk because the

THE ELECTORATE OF BRANDENBURG

entrusted to the army was even more detrimental to the population: 'because instead of one non-commissioned officer and two soldiers, officers are sent with many troops, and the communities must also bear the maintenance of all these people.'[22] In 1659, Königsberg refused to pay war contributions and host the Electoral troops from the Rhineland, but under the threat of arms had to give in.[23] The hostile climate against the Elector alarmed the councillors, who warned the Prince against the excesses of his soldiers. They reported that both the nobility and the common people who did not pay taxes had their roof tiles requisitioned, a fact described as 'unprecedented'.[24] The lukewarm summers contributed to this. The years between 1660 and 1662 were of great distress throughout Prussia: the harvest was poor and the price of grain reached record prices. Opposition against Brandenburg rule grew throughout the Duchy, and Friedrich Wilhelm was blamed by his subjects as 'the greatest tyrant and enemy of the people'.[25]

Despite this, the amount of taxation steadily increased and effects on the economy and trade were dramatic.[26] After 1662, Brandenburg alone paid an annual tax of 264,000 thalers, rising to 324,000 in 1666, and falling to 288,000 in 1673. Later, in the course of the war against France and Sweden in 1674–79, taxation increased vertically to 448,000 thalers in 1678 and 549,000 in 1679. After the Peace of Nijmegen the volume of revenue decreased, but never below 340,000 thalers and in the last years of Friedrich Wilhelm's reign it returned to above 400,000 thalers, namely to what it had amounted to during the war of 1655–60.[27] A considerable amount when compared to a population of only 270,000. Altogether, between 1655 and 1661, taxation in the entire Electorate amounted to seven million thalers, averaging around one million each year.[28]

It was evident that the Elector would not be able to maintain an expanding army with the antiquated and unequal method of taxation in use in his states. As far back as 1661, Friedrich Wilhelm submitted a new taxation proposal to the estates, but one that imitated the 'Dutch system' of 1653. The Prince

---

population had decreased to one-sixth, and trade, based mainly on cloth production, was virtually ruined.

22 Meinardus, *Protokolle und Relationen*, p.645.

23 Orlich, *Geschichte des Preußischen Staats*, vol. III, p.61. The Elector was even more annoyed when he heard that the city intended to send a delegation to participate in the peace talks: 'If Königsberg had insisted on this absurd intention, it would have bitterly regretted it.'

24 Meinardus, *Protokolle und Relationen*, vol. VI, p.112.

25 Carsten, *The Origin of Prussia*, p.248.

26 *New Cambridge Modern History*, p.441: 'The trade down the Elbe was so burdened with tolls that even corn – the soul of commerce – was shipped along different routes and transport over land became cheaper. The Elbe tolls at Lenzen were farmed out for some years, with very bad results for trade; but matters did not improve when they were again managed by state officials. The Great Elector considered these heavy tolls entirely justified; three conferences summoned to discuss the Elbe tolls produced no result because, against the advice of his privy councillors, he refused to make any concessions. The governors of Frankfurt-on-Oder and Spandau levied their own duties on passing carriages and ships, and others did the same with travellers, in spite of official prohibitions.'

27 Ferdinand Hirsch, 'Die Armee des Grossen Kurfürsten und Ihre Unterhaltung während der Jahre 1660–86', in *Historischer Zeitschrift*, LIII (1885), p.273.

28 Carsten, *The Origin of Prussia*, p.248.

warned the Privy Council to convene as few representatives as possible, to negotiate in a stronger position. Despite this expedient, the Brandenburg deputies rejected the plan, arguing among other things that with this reform, the nobles would pay taxes 'like the lowly plebeians'.[29] This was a crucial moment in the politics of the Great Elector, who seriously risked losing the support of the Brandenburg nobility. It is highly probable that he realised the danger and in fact from that date onwards moved more cautiously towards the Brandenburg aristocracy. Opposition also remained strong in the Duchy of Prussia, especially in Königsberg, which complained about the imposition of duties affecting trade. In May 1661, the estates of Prussia convened a diet that essentially demanded the abolition of customs and duties, and an end to contributions for troops stationed in the Duchy. The diet lasted two years and ended with a compromise between the parties, but only after bitter negotiations and the arrival of the Elector at the head of his army. The delegates of Königsberg did not adhere to the agreement and the city was surrounded, while the authorities gathered the civic guard to defend it against a siege.[30] In the other domains, tensions never reached a fever pitch, but even then the estates rejected the Elector's proposals.

Friedrich Wilhelm took the blow, but in 1666 returned to the subject. A representative of the diet was summoned to which it was proposed, in view of the misery in which the state found itself, a general tax for all subjects, nobles excluded. This time, the Elector was adept at exploiting the incandescent political climate. He took advantage of popular discontent, especially in the province of Altmark, where the population demanded measures and openly threatened the estates who defended the privileges of the nobility. Both in the cities and in the countryside, people began to see the general tax as the only hope for relief from the old taxation and collection by the soldiers. There were new tensions with the estates and protests throughout the state, but in Königsberg the Elector met with the representatives of the city, to whom he allowed a 'friendly ear'.[31]

The situation remained unresolved until 1667, however, growing popular pressure led to a compromise, which in practice left the cities free to apply the general tax, skilfully circumventing the opposition of the estates and the city nobility. The reform brought mixed results and ultimately fell short of expectations in economic terms, as capital quickly moved to the countryside, where the old taxation system remained in force. Only Berlin, and from 1671 Frankfurt, made the general tax permanent.

In the 1670s, the Electorate was again involved in a war, this time on the Rhine against France. The Elector exploited every funding channel, including foreign ones, when he agreed with the Dutch States General to provide troops to help the Republic. The war once again fuelled the struggle

---

29 Carsten, *The Origin of Prussia*, p.229.
30 Carsten, *The Origin of Prussia*, p.252. The situation deteriorated dramatically and was only resolved by the arrest of one of the opposition leaders, Hieronymus Roth, who was taken from his home in a surprise action by the Elector's troops. Roth became a kind of Prussian 'man in the iron mask': arrested without ever having been convicted, he spent the rest of his life in prison in Brandenburg.
31 Meinardus, *Protokolle und Relationen*, vol. VI, pp.35–36.

between the Prince and the estates of Brandenburg and Prussia, although the latter was later involved when the conflict spread to Sweden, which invaded the Duchy in 1675. Both estates showed no interest in Rhenish affairs, but the Elector tried to use the French invasion of the United Provinces to convince them to vote for more funding. He also evoked the risk of involvement of the Tatars and the Porte, as had happened in 1656. This time, too, the estates proved recalcitrant and declared that they did not believe in the threat posed by Louis XIV, nor by the Ottomans. The Prussian delegates remarked that the French threat on Cleves and Mark did not affect them, and they did not feel the need to participate in all the wars of Europe.[32]

Western cavalry engaging Tatar horsemen in an illustration from Daniel Defoe's novel, *The Life and Strange Surprising Adventures of Robinson Crusoe of York, Mariner. Related by Himself. With upwards of One Hundred Illustrations* (London: Cassell, Petter & Galpin, 1863) (Public Domain). In the war of 1655–1660, Prussia was heavily devastated by the transit of undisciplined troops looting and burning, especially by the Crimean Tatars, who were allied to the Poles. According to a perhaps somewhat exaggerated estimate presented to the Privy Council by the Estates of the Duchy of Prussia, the Tatar incursion in the winter of 1656–57 burnt down 13 towns and hundreds of villages, 23,000 civilians perished and another 34,000 were stolen by the *Han's* horsemen. After the invasion, a plague epidemic killed another 80,000 inhabitants. Even wealthy Königsberg, which was not attacked, suffered from the devastation wrought by the Tatars as they caused a sharp decline in domestic trade.

All provinces justified their refusal by stating that the economy was still fragile and that many towns did not even have the money to send their representatives to Berlin. The deputies pointed out that maintaining the troops was another serious problem, citing the case of Memel, which had to maintain a garrison of 500 men, not counting the wives and children of the soldiers, and that some citizens housed three or four soldiers; while

---

32   Carsten, *The Origin of Prussia*, p.256.

other villages housed garrisons that instead of 25 soldiers had grown to 90 or more.³³

The Elector did not change course, and continued to show great concern for the war, which he considered such a serious emergency that he could cancel all privileges. The Prussian nobility protested against the forced exaction by the army and declared through their representatives that it made no sense to bleed themselves dry for the sake of the Empire, which they had nothing to do with.³⁴ At the beginning of 1674 the nobility of the Duchy gathered in Königsberg, and the governor feared a revolt, but the union between the aristocrats and the people did not materialise. However, the city representatives resolutely rejected any request for contributions for which they had not been consulted. Major-General Joachim Ernst von Görtzke, commander of the Königsberg garrison, recommended the use of force, but the Elector did not make a decision until May, when his soldiers entered the city, removed the gate hinges and occupied squares and streets. The citizens were taken by surprise and the authorities, in tears, assured their devotion to the Prince and offered an immediate payment of 12,000 thalers.³⁵ In the following years, the Duchy of Prussia and Königsberg granted the Elector a war tax of 20,000 thalers per month, rising to 35,000 in 1678. From October 1677 to December 1679, the estates of Prussia agreed to pay more than four million thalers as war tax.³⁶ After the Peace of Nijmegen, Friedrich Wilhelm demanded further contributions, justifying these with the need to defend the state against foreign threats. The amount collected in the Duchy after 1680 was more than 300,000 thalers per year, but still less than that paid by Brandenburg.

In 1680, feeling strong enough to act without any further convocation of the estates or the diet, Friedrich Wilhelm decided to put an end to the ambiguous situation by imposing the general taxation everywhere except for the noble fiefs, and after 1682 in all Brandenburg cities. In the end, the new taxation fully achieved its purpose, namely a solid economic basis for the maintenance of an ever-growing standing army, avoiding the long and complicated negotiations with the representatives of the provinces. Although this

Joachim Ernst von Görtzke (1611–1682). (Public Domain) A native of Brandenburg, he served in the Swedish army from 1631 to 1654. As with many other prominent senior officers, he was Colonel Proprietor of both an infantry and a cavalry regiment of the electoral army.

---

33 Carsten, *The Origin of Prussia*, p.256. The military governor of Prussia, Duke Ernst of Croy, confirmed 'that poverty was widespread and growing in need every day'. In the spring of 1674 the Duke sent to Berlin a bread of the type eaten by peasants, consisting of wheat husks and wood bark, as proof of his assertions.
34 Meinardus, *Protokolle und Relationen*, vol. VI, p.178.
35 Orlich, *Geschichte des preußischen Staats*, vol. III, p.133.
36 Carsten, *The Origin of Prussia*, p.255.

THE ELECTORATE OF BRANDENBURG

was achieved by granting extensive privileges to the nobility, whose social position, and ultimately their opinions, were the same as those of the Prince, Friedrich Wilhelm's absolute rule had its limits in the face of the seigneurial estates, which remained strong enough to exert pressure, remaining master of the peasants and villagers within the noble fiefs. Aristocrats had to serve in the army, but this appeared less functional from a military point of view, as the professional growth of officers and the specialisation of troops required qualities that were not always possessed by the nobles entering the army.[37]

From Brandenburg, the reform was gradually extended to the other territories of the Electorate: in Pomerania, Magdeburg, Halberstadt, Minden, and under its successor in the remaining provinces, but only in the cities. After the regulation introduced in 1684, no more changes were made and the double taxation, town and country, remained in force in Prussia until the beginning of the nineteenth century.[38] The financial burdens were immense. The incomes contributed significantly to military expense, which amounted to roughly a third of central government revenue.[39]

Whatever residual power the estates of Brandenburg had left, was further reduced by the *Kriegskammer*, as the *Generalkriegskommissariat* was generally known, reconstituted in 1680 to manage the army's expansion plans. The officials of the commissariat proved to be particularly active and intransigent, far more determined to execute the will of the Prince against opponents than the Privy Council or the governors. Gradually, the Commissariat replaced the estates, until then in charge of tax administration, directly ordering the collection and distribution of both ordinary and extraordinary taxes. According to some historians, the General War Commissariat became the main instrument of the Elector's state, as it effectively replaced the estates in many matters beyond the specifically military ones. Officials of the Commissariat gave orders, allocated contributions to the districts in quotas, examined petitions, and of course issued provisions on the housing of troops. The office interfered in the administration of all taxes, whereas previously the estates had always negotiated these matters with the Privy Council. For this purpose, all state territories were divided into *Kreise* (circles), so that the collection of contributions could be managed more easily. There could hardly have been clearer evidence of the political decline of the estates before the creation of the *Generalkriegskommissariat* and the definitive establishment in Brandenburg-Prussia of the principles of the modern fiscal-military state.[40]

---

37 In this regard, between 1663 and 1665 the Elector granted a cash payment in return for the nobles' participation in military life. See Hirsch, 'Die Armee des Großen Kurfürsten', in *Historischer Zeitschrift*, LIII, p.269.

38 Carsten, *The Origin of Prussia*, p.233: 'If they had wanted to, the Hohenzollerns would certainly have introduced general taxation throughout the state, as was the case in the United Provinces, but probably they preferred to maintain the separation between towns and countryside, and with it the privileges of the nobility.'

39 Wilson, *German Armies*, p.30.

40 Craig, *The Politics of the Prussian Army*, p.8.

The Electoral Army

Even in more recent times, the raising of the standing army of Brandenburg-Prussia had been considered by historians as an actual turning point for modern Germany.[41] This not because the army created by the Great Elector was the first or the most numerous, records that belonged to other German states, but because it became a fundamental institution in political life and the 'iron ring' that held the Hohenzollern domains together.[42] There is more than a little truth in these observations; the history of Brandenburg-Prussia is essentially the history of its army. From the earliest actions of the Elector's government, the military problem was closely linked to the general question of state administration and local particularism: all aspects that Friedrich Wilhelm bent to his vision of the modern state.

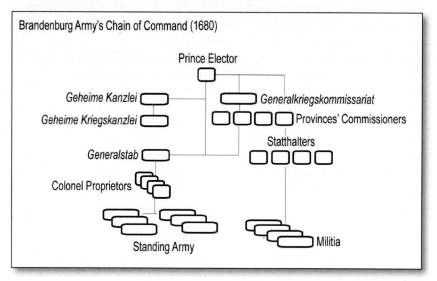

Brandenburg Chain of Command

In 1640, the professional army consisted of approximately 5,000 men,[43] mostly refugees from other armies, 'Landsknechts' of the worst kind, who

---

41 In *Deutsche Geschichte im Neunzehnten Jahrhundert* (München: Deutscher Taschenbuch Verlag, 1987), Franz Schnabel wrote that, 'the foundation of the Prussian state constitutes the greatest political event in German history, since the Hohenzollern domains completely lacked the favourable geographical conditions that facilitated the formation of other great nation states. But it did, and if from the disparate territorial fragments was forged not only a solid political unity, but even a state recognised as one of the great European powers, it was thanks to the concomitance of two decisive factors: the political will of the Hohenzollern rulers after 1640 and the effectiveness of the army they raised.'
42 Walter Goerlitz, *History of the German General Staff, 1657–1945* (New York, NY: Barnes & Noble, 1995), p.7.
43 According to Gerhard Pelet-Narbonne, in his *Geschichte der Brandenburg-Preußischen Reiterei, Teil I. Die alte Armee* (Berlin, 1905), p.6, at the death of Elector Georg Wilhelm, the Electoral army consisted of 4,650 men, 800 of whom were horsemen, divided into two companies of dragoons and four companies of *Reiter*, the latter amounting to 500 men. Ludwig Friedrich von Ciriacy, in the *Chronologische Übersicht der Geschichte der preußischen Heers dessen Stärke, Verfassung und Kriege seit den letzten Kurfürsten von Brandenburg bis auf die jetzigen Zeiten* (Berlin, 1820), p.12, gives a different figure. He proposes 4,000 infantry and 2,000 horse. Finally,

THE ELECTORATE OF BRANDENBURG

were unable to operate effectively against trained troops and terrorised the very provinces to whose defence they had been assigned. The Elector's first move was made to gain the favour of the Estates of Brandenburg and consisted in eliminating all the worst and treacherous elements in the army. In the first years of his reign, the undesirables and inept were dismissed; the unruly colonels who had harassed the provinces and were suspected of peculate were arrested or exiled. At the end of this purge, a small force of 2,202 men remained in arms.[44] The estates, grateful for the reformation of the army, granted the necessary funds to maintain this modest force. The Elector took advantage of this favourable situation and was able to increase the number of troops during the last years of the Thirty Years' War, even between some ups and downs.[45] In 1648, Friedrich Wilhelm had about 8,000 men in his service, including 3,000 horse and dragoons. The existence of these troops was not an insignificant factor among others that secured the concessions made to the Elector in the Treaties of Westphalia. In 1649, all the cavalry was dismissed except for the *Leibcompagnie zu Ross* (brc-i), numbering 152 horsemen, NCOs and officers. However, the Elector was able to continue the policy of increasing military expenditure despite the interference of the estates. Further companies and regiments were raised in 1651, for the inconclusive (and bloodless) 'Cow's War' against Pfalz-Neuburg.[46]

As introduced before, the *Rezess* of 1653 was an extraordinary success for Friedrich Wilhelm's military policy, because after this year the standing army increased at an unprecedented rate.[47] The social and political consequences of this act were historic for the Hohenzollern state. The immediate result of the *Rezess* was the creation of a new Electoral army. Though the funds granted were sufficient to recruit a force of only 5,000 men, an absolutely insufficient number to support the military policy of the Great Elector,[48] two years later, in the climate of emergency caused by the war between Sweden and Poland, Friedrich Wilhelm managed to recruit more soldiers throughout Brandenburg and the Rhineland domains. He ignored the grievances of the estates, and through extraordinary impositions increased

---

Claus von Bredow, author of the *Historische Rang-und Stammliste des Deutschen Heeres* (Berlin, 1905), p.20, offers another total: 4,150 infantry and 500 cavalry in 1640.

44   Jany, *Geschichte der Königlich Preußischen Armee*, pp.99–100. This force comprised 2,050 foot and 152 horse.

45   In the summer 1643, all the cavalry was ceded to the Imperial army of Gallas, and only 125 horsemen remained in Brandenburg, forming the company of the *Leibgarde zu Pferde*. Pelet-Narbonne, *Geschichte der Brandenburg-Preußischen Reiterei*, p.7.

46   In 1651, the Elector gathered seven infantry regiments, while a further seven cavalry regiments and one squadron were raised in a few weeks to make war against the Duchy of Pfalz-Neuburg. These troops did not take part in military actions, and in November they were all disbanded at the Duisburg camp. Jany, *Geschichte der Königlich Preußischen Armee*, p.20.

47   Pelet-Narbonne, *Geschichte der Brandenburg-Preußischen Reiterei*, p.7. In 1653, the cavalry increased to 1,200 *Reiter*, excluding officers, quartered in Brandenburg. In the Rhineland there were 20 companies with a total of 441 horsemen.

48   Pelet-Narbonne, *Geschichte der Brandenburg-Preußischen Reiterei*, p.6, The author quotes Count Schwartzenberg, who in the 1630s stated that at least 25,000 men would be needed 'to keep the provinces under control and discourage the warring powers from invading the Electorate and extorting contributions'.

the army from 8,000 men in September 1655, to 22,000 in June 1656.[49] The numerical strength grew again in the following years, reaching 27,000 men when the Peace of Oliva ended the war in 1660. The 'Peacetime Strength' was established at 5,100 foot, the mounted life guards to 300 horsemen, and four companies of dragoons, approximately 240 men.

Despite the reduction of the standing army, the Elector invested many resources in the technical corps, especially in the formation of an artillery corps, which included drivers and cannon casting personnel in the arsenals. In 1661, all personnel amounted to 1,800 artillerymen, drivers, craftsmen and technicians.[50] The rapid growth of the army necessitated the creation of a new structure for the direction of military affairs. Until 1652, all matters concerning the army were entrusted to the Privy Council, which managed them through a special secretariat headed by an official appointed by the Elector, and chaired in that year by the *Kriegsecretär* Philipp Schreiner. In 1655 the whole organisation was reformed, and a new office called *Geheime Kriegskanzlei* was created and entrusted to the loyal Franz Meinders after Schreiner's death in September 1656. The office still depended on the Privy Council, which in turn assumed the new title of *Geheime Kanzlei* (Privy Chancellery) and later became the *Staatskanzlei* (State Chancellery) under Elector Frederick III. Military affairs were discussed by the *Kommission*s met for each particular topic related to the army and militia, in which the *Statthalter*s participated when the affairs concerned their province.

The expansion in the numerical strength of the army would not have been possible without the work of the *Generalkriegskommissariat*, established in 1655, and entrusted to the talented Count Claus Ernst von Platen. Historians describe him as a clever and indefatigable official, who served the Elector in various assignments until 1669, the year he died. The War Commissariat became the most important military offices of the Great Elector's army: the actual engine of the military financing and administration. The figure of commissioner was a completely new kind of official. While under Prince-Elector Georg Wilhelm commissioners had to organise marches and occasional billeting, in the age of the standing army most of their time was spent creating a system of permanent billeting. This and the increasing number of troop movements during the war against Poland and Sweden caused the increase in personnel. Since its raising, the War Commissariat was responsible for all matters of replacement, clothing, armament, food and shelter. The office was disbanded in 1660, but eight years later, its officials were called back into service to conduct an investigation into the taxable income and financial administration of the Duchy of Prussia. One of the most able and trusted officials, Colonel Barfuss, was appointed to direct the office. The majority of the members of the Commissariat, called *Preussische Kommissariat*, were natives of Brandenburg and received orders exclusively from the Elector.[51] Not as vehemently as in Brandenburg, but

---

49 Craig, *The Politics of the Prussian Army*, p.20.

50 Jany, *Geschichte der Königlich Preußischen Armee*, p.110.

51 Philip Gorsky, 'The Making of Prussian Absolutism: Confessional Conflict and State Autonomy under the Great Elector, 1640–1688', in *The Protestant Ethic Revisited* (Philadelphia: Temple

nonetheless decisively, the estates of Ducal Prussia demanded the removal of the commissioner, who had been appointed in 1660. They only wanted to maintain the garrisons in Pillau and Memel as usual, but demanded the re-establishment of the traditional national defence, 'under a Prussian national commander with war experience and native officers.'[52] In addition, the estates submitted a plan for 'a general stable council' that was to meet every year on one day in the city residence, and every three years on one day in the province. The Elector completely opposed the proposal.

The 'star' fortress of Pillau (today Baltijsk in the Russian Federation) with the external defences on the east side of the Peninsula, as shown in a print dated 1656. (Public Domain) In 1617, the Swedes occupied the town, belonging to the Polish-Lithuanian Confederation. King Gustav II Adolph landed there a second time in May 1626. During their occupation, the Swedes expanded the fortifications and built the five bastioned fort. After charging a ransom of 10,000 thalers, Sweden handed Pillau over to Brandenburg.

In Pomerania, a local war council was established in April 1659 in Colberg, to which the Elector gave all deliberative powers for the 'military and militia' of the province. The council included the military Governors, and from 1668 also the War Commissioner of the province. A 'supplementary instruction,' signed by the Elector in November 1668, entrusted the commissioner with the representation of military interests against both the local estates and the provincial government, especially with regard to quartering and marching. In the same year, in the Rhineland territories of Cleves-Mark and Minden-Ravensberg, the traditional common governorate was not re-established.[53] In Cleves-Mark, by 1661, the *Direktion in Militaribus* was held by *Generalwachtmeister* Alexander von Spaen, as commander-in-chief. In Minden, military power was exercised by *Generallieutenant* Kannenberg;

University Press, 2013), p.155.
52 Jany, *Geschichte der Königlich Preußischen Armee*, p.197.
53 Jany, *Geschichte der Königlich Preußischen Armee*, p.196. The last governor was Prince Georg Friedrich zu Waldeck.

in Ravensberg by *Generalwachtmeister* Eller, in Memel by Friedrich von Dönhoff. Commissioner-in-Chief – *Oberkommissar* – Ludwig was responsible for the economic affairs of the provinces and the administration 'of our military forces in the lands of Cleves-Mark, Minden and Ravensberg' until his death in 1665.[54] A War Commissariat also continued to operate in Halberstadt. War Commissioner Peine, appointed in 1658, held the office until his death in 1678.

Count Friedrich von Dönhoff (1639–1696), Governor of Memel, Major General and Colonel Proprietor of an infantry regiment. (Public Domain)

Gradually, since its definitive reinstatement in 1680, the *Generalkriegskommissariat* extended its influence throughout the state to the detriment of the other authorities, especially in tax matters, unilaterally setting taxes for all subjects. The office extended its authority dealing with the general supervision of the army's recruitment, remounting, provisioning and housing, wages, stores and depots, and the collection of contributions for the army at home and abroad. The office also decided on enforced collections if payments were not paid, and issued orders to local officials to execute rulings. To speed up the deliberations local tax collectors were created, appointed, obviously, by the Commissariat. The *Generalkriegskommissariat* also instructed trials in the event of conflicts between soldiers and rural inhabitants, and was responsible for the return of peasants enlisted in the army to their masters, if the latter requested their discharge.[55]

As before, the Elector retained command of all troops as *Generalissimo*, but with the order of 2 September 1655, he instituted the rank of *General-Feldzeugmester* with which he delegated the direction of the field army to Baron Otto Christoph von Sparr. Previously, Sparr had been commander of all garrisons outside Brandenburg and Prussia since 1651. He was one of the truly great generals of Friedrich Wilhelm. Under Sparr's direction, a generation of young officers was formed who gave practical meaning in terms of command to the unification process. The nucleus of what became an *ante-litteram* major staff was formed, also including 'foreign' officers such as the talented Prince Georg Friedrich zu Waldeck, the counts of Limburg-Stirum, and the Frenchman Pierre de la Cave. They formed the first rank of commanders after Sparr as members of the *General Stab*.

---

54 Jany, *Geschichte der Königlich Preußischen Armee*, p.197: 'Prince Johann Moritz von Nassau-Siegen, who had been Governor of Cleves-Mark (since 1647) and Minden-Ravensberg (since 1658), at the same time lieutenant general of the Dutch army, Field Marshal and governor of Wesel since 1668, increasingly took a back seat in military matters. The Elector's instruction of April 1660 emphasised that all responsibility for the Military lies with Spaen.'

55 Carsten, *The Origin of Prussia*, pp.248–249.

THE ELECTORATE OF BRANDENBURG

Nineteenth century German historians emphasised the birth of the modern concept of the major-state in the Great Elector's army. In effect, the period round the 1650s saw the beginnings of what was later to be referred to by the comprehensive term *Generalstabsdienst*, or 'General Staff Service'. The Swedish army stood at this time in high repute in Northern Europe, and it was on that model that the Great Elector may be presumed to have based himself in creating a quartermaster general's staff. The latter's function comprised all engineering services, the supervision of routes of march and the choice of camping sites and fortified positions, and normally established marching directions together with the field commander. The first mention in the records of a quartermaster general in Brandenburg, the *Obrist Lieutenant* and engineer Gerhard von Belkum (or Bellicum), appears in 1657. He seems to have been assisted by Lieutenant Colonel and engineer Jacob Holsten, who bore the title of Second Quartermaster General.[56] The pay sheets show that they belonged at this time to the Elector's military staff. Among Belkum's successors there was in the years 1670–73 the Huguenot exiled Philippe de Chiese, less well known as a soldier than as the architect of the main building of Potsdam Castle and Berlin Mint, and also famous as the constructor of a post-chaise hung in slings, known as the *Berline*.[57] For all the matters concerning encampments, routes and fortifications, the *Generalquartiermeister* and his lieutenant coordinated the activities of the regiment quartermasters. Further, the army on campaign had two *Adjutants-General*, one *Provendermaster-General*, a *Generalauditeur*, who dealt with matters of military law, a *Wagenmaster-General* and an 'Enforcer-General' – *Generalgewaltiger* – who with his constables was responsible for policing matters in the army.

In fact, neither the quartermaster general nor the commissary-general ranked as senior officer of the General Staff, but this honour fell to the 'master of ordnance' – *Feldzeugmeister* – Otto Christoph von Sparr. All generals belonged to the General Staff, a term that sometimes virtually denotes the generality. Since all generals with the exception of the *General-Feldzeugmeister* belonged to the infantry or cavalry, in the Electoral army the general staff of infantry was usually kept separate from the general staff of cavalry.[58] Together with this corps of senior officers, in the summer of 1656 the rank of *Generalwachtmeister* (general major) was created in the army

Otto Christoph von Sparr (1599 or 1605–1668). (public Domain) A native of Brandenburg, and former Imperial General, in 1655 he became the highest ranking field commander of the Electoral army.

---

56   Goerlitz, *History of the German General Staff*, p.8.
57   Goerlitz, *History of the German General Staff*, p.8.
58   Jany, *Geschichte der Königlich Preußischen Armee*, p.152.

Georg von Derfflinger (1606–1695). Coming from a Protestant family of farmers from Neuhol, Austria, who emigrated in Bohemia, Derfflinger began the military career in the army of Friedrich V of the Palatinate, and then served Electoral Saxony and Sweden. In 1655, he entered the Brandenburg army as cavalry commander.

gathered in Ducal Prussia: two for infantry and one for cavalry.[59] Before the end of the year, a second general major was appointed for the cavalry, and then in June 1657, the rank of cavalry *Generallieutenant* was also created. In the same year Georg Friedrich of Waldeck was appointed *General über die Kavallerie*.[60]

In the 1670s, the rank of *Generalfeldmarschall* was also introduced for senior commanders who managed the direction of larger corps. The first Field Marshal of the Brandenburg army was the skilled Georg von Derfflinger. At the same time, other ranks and functions were established for the army on campaign. Some of them performed operational functions whose characteristics had long been established and belonged to the tradition of the German military world. The *Generalwagenmeister* supervised the army train and directed the work of the regimental *Wagenmeister*, while the *Capitaine des Guides*, chosen from among people who knew the territory, acted as an adviser of the field commanders on campaign. Among the innovations introduced, the most important function was that of the *Oberst-Kommissar*, in charge of the administration of the army, and above all the economic management of supplies on campaign, the medical care staff, which included the *Feldmedicus* (army physician) and the *Feldapotheker* (army pharmacist), and the care of the soul, with the *Feldprediger* (army pastor).

Nineteenth century German historians state that the Brandenburg-Prussian standing army was actually born during the war of 1655–60.[61] The field army gathered in 1656 comprised 51 companies of infantry, 79 companies of cavalry, 14 companies of dragoons, artillery and train;[62] and a further 3,758 infantrymen, 1,530 horsemen, and 730 dragoons were quartered in the garrisons in Prussia, Ravensberg and Cleves-Mark.[63] For

---

59 Jany, *Geschichte der Königlich Preußischen Armee* p.151. The Polish German Joachim Rüdiger von der Golz, and the younger brother of the Prince of Waldeck, Count Wolrad, were appointed for the infantry; for the cavalry Christoph von Kannenberg, already in Swedish service, was appointed.

60 Jany, *Geschichte der Königlich Preußischen Armee*, p.151. Rank attributed to Georg von Derfflinger.

61 Jany, *Geschichte der Königlich Preußischen Armee*, p.115.

62 Jany, *Geschichte der Königlich Preußischen Armee*, pp.139–140.

63 Jany, *Geschichte der Königlich Preußischen Armee*, p.143.

THE ELECTORATE OF BRANDENBURG

Colonels Alexander von Spaen (1619–1692), and Christian Albrecht zu Dohna (1621–1677). In 1653, the Prince-Elector recalled the Brandenburg officers who were serving abroad. From The United Provinces came Colonels Dohna, Eller, Jakob and Alexander von Spaen; from Sweden came Derfflinger, Kannenberg, Pfuhl, Quast; then the Count of Limburg-Styrum and General Otto Christoph von Sparr, formerly in the service of the Emperor; and General Joachim von der Golz and Colonel Pierre de la Cave who were serving in the French army.

the campaign in Schleswig-Holstein in 1658, the Elector called to arms the unprecedented number of 30,000 soldiers and militiamen, of which 14,400 professional soldiers formed the field army.[64] After the Peace of Oliva in 1660, a reduction of the troops took place, but never as large as in the past. In the 1660s, several infantry regiments and almost all cavalry were disbanded, but a core of selected troops continued to man the garrisons of the state. In Brandenburg there were 2,950 foot and 150 horse quartered between Berlin–Cölln, Kustrin, Driesen, Oderberg, Landsberg, Spandau, and Frankfurt. In Pomerania there were 1,600 infantrymen divided between Kolberg, Draheim and other minor garrisons, a further 1,000 in Minden and Ravensberg alongside 300 dragoons, and finally 1,000 infantrymen guarded the strategic posts in Cleves-Mark. The 'peace strength' numbered 7,450 professional soldiers, not including officers and the corps of the artillery.[65]

---

64 Georg Adalbert von Mülverstedt, *Die Brandenburgische Kriegsmacht unter dem Großen Kurfürsten* (Magdeburg, 1888), p.27.
65 Jany, *Geschichte der Königlich Preußischen Armee*, p.195.

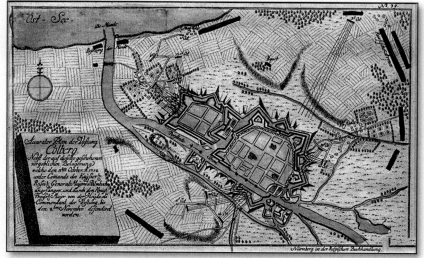

The fortress of Kolberg (today Kołobrzeg, in Poland) was the major Brandenburg stronghold in West Pomerania, and had had a permanent garrison since the 1650s.

From 1661 to 1671, Friedrich Wilhelm was able to maintain a standing army which oscillated between 7,000 and 12,000 professionals. To consolidate this force, he adopted the policy of assigning positions to senior officers who had left the service after 1660, and of giving discharged soldiers land to settle on as free farmers.[66] After all, these years did not see the army inactive. In the autumn of 1663 the Elector raised a *Hilfskorps* for the Habsburg Emperor, who was facing the Ottomans in Hungary. After Montecuccoli's unsuccessful campaign in Transylvania in 1661–62, the Ottoman crisis now lent the matter urgency. The diet agreed to provide financial support to the Emperor for the duration of the war. It was also agreed to raise an army of 30,000 men, but Brandenburg, like Bavaria, Saxony and other German states, refused to contribute troops to raise this force through the *Kreise* system, preferring instead to conclude separate agreements with Vienna. As a result, Friedrich Wilhelm provided troops under agreements against additional payment. In February 1663, Duke August of Holstein-Plön was appointed as commander of the Brandenburg corps for Hungary. The force under his command comprised 1,000 infantrymen divided in eight companies from the regiment *Holstein* (BrI–14); four cavalry troops of 100 horse each from the regiment *Radziwill* (BrC–5) were added to one *Freicompagnie* of horse, alongside five dragoon companies comprising 600 men in all; a further three other companies of dragoons under the *Obristlieutenant* von Block, and three companies of the *Derfflingersche* dragoon squadron under the *Obristwachtmeister* Narwitz completed the contingent.[67] The infantry was officered by the *Obristlieutenant* Anselm Casimir Ferdinand von Sparr, the son of the *General-Feldzeugmeister* Otto Heinrich. The Brandenburg troops took winter quarters in Silesia and then joined the Imperialists in Hungary in March 1664. In April, the infantry was under the Imperial general Jean-Louis Raduit de Souches on the border with Transylvania. Here the Brandenburgers

---

66 Craig, *The Politics of the Prussian Army*, p.20; in the Elector's plans, these settlers formed a trained reserve to recall in the event of a new conflict.
67 Jany, *Geschichte der Königlich Preußischen Armee*, p.201.

fought alongside the Allies at the siege of Niytra, which surrendered on 7 May, and nine days later in the encounter of Szent-Benedek against the Ottoman relief army. On 9 July the Allies repulsed the enemy offensive at Léva, and achieved a great success.[68] On their return to the homeland, the whole cavalry with the exception of a company of dragoons was disbanded; the Duke of Holstein-Plön received the prince's commendation for the successful outcome of the expedition.

New international crises offered pretexts to strengthen the army. In the spring of 1665, the Anglo-Dutch war also involved the bishopric of Münster, whose borders lapped those of the Rhine provinces of the Electorate. In order to secure the domains, 2,500 infantrymen, including 500 from the *Garde zu Fuss* (BrI-9), and the *Trabanten* (brc-i) headed to Cleves-Mark, and before the end of the year, two new infantry regiments were raised. For the raising of one of these, the Prince-Elector obtained permission to recruit volunteers in the Imperial cities of Frankfurt am Main, Nuremberg and Regensburg, while the other regiment was formed with recruits from Cleves-Mark. A third regiment of infantry was raised in March 1666.[69] In the same months, the Elector raised a dragoon regiment of six companies of 670 men overall, which was later joined with two *Frei-Kompagnien* quartered in Cleves, increasing the strength to 800 dragoons.[70] These veterans formed the skeleton of that army which, in protracted disputes between the Elector

Brandenburg infantry, about 1665, by Richard Knötel, from Ewald Fiebig, *Unsterbliche Treue. Das Heldenlied der Fahnen und Standarten des Deutschen Heeres* (Berlin, 1936). Note the pikemen with breastplate and morion helmet, which is also worn by the musketeers.

---

68 See also Mugnai, *Wars and Soldiers*, vol. 2, pp.156–157.
69 Jany, *Geschichte der Preussischen Armee*, p.203. The regiments were *Fargell zu Fuss* (BrI-39), *Siberg zu Fuss* (BrI-40), and *Schmidt zu Fuss* (BrI-41).
70 Jany, *Geschichte der Preussischen Armee*, p.203. Regiment *Kanitz Dragoner* (BrD-9).

and the estates, had maintained its position as standing forces since 1656. While the first decades of Brandenburg army policy were determined by inflating the army in times of war in order to drastically reduce it in the pauses between wars, in the 1660s the tendency arose to constantly maintain a field force ready to be used.

The policy of military strengthening also involved the cavalry. The Elector requested the recruitment of 1,000 *Reiter* and 1,000 horses in Brandenburg, divided into five companies of 200 men each. Pomerania was requested to provide three cavalry companies of 100 men complete with horse and equipment, while Halberstadt was taxed with two companies of the same strength. Finally Minden-Ravensberg and Cleves-Mark were required to raise 110, 120 and 600 *Reiter* respectively. In Prussia, half of the cavalrymen were mounted with horses provided by the province.[71]

A decisive impulse for increasing the army strength was the agreement signed on 16 February 1666 between the Prince-Elector and the Dutch Republic's representatives for hiring 12,000 Brandenburg soldiers. In detail, the *Subsidienvertrag* provided for the delivery of 7,000 foot, 3,500 horse and 1,500 dragoons. The agreement included 32 cannons and two mortars.[72] This contingent was to be employed in the campaign against Münster, but the Peace of Breda, signed on 31 July 1667, made the use of the contingent unnecessary.[73] For the Elector it was a considerable economic loss, but the agreement stipulated that the troops would remain at the disposal of the Dutch Republic in case of further need until 1670, albeit at a lower cost. This contingent, already gathered in the Rhine domains, became useful in April 1668 when it was transferred to Magdeburg, to force the city to swear the oath of homage to the Elector and to host a strong garrison.

The worsening of relations between the Dutch Republic and France reopened negotiations for a new *Subsidienvertrag* with the States General. In the autumn 1671, Friedrich Wilhelm signed a preliminary agreement to keep at the disposal of the Dutch Republic a corps of 20,000 men, consisting of 12,000 foot, 8,000 horse and 50 cannons.[74] The States General bore half the payment of the sum needed to maintain the corps. In January 1673, these troops were distributed between Ravensberg, Minden and Cleves, overall they numbered 7,000 infantry, 6,000 cavalry and 1,000 dragoons.[75]

A few months after the agreement with the Dutch Republic, the Elector was faced with Poland's demand for its rights under the *Bomberger Beitrage* (the Bydgoszcz's contribution). The treaty obliged Friedrich Wilhelm, as Duke of Prussia, to send troops to the war between Poland and the Porte, which began in the summer of 1672. As early as 1671, Poland requested

---

71 Pelet-Narbonne, *Geschichte der Brandenburg-Preußischen Reiterei*, p.38.

72 Jany, *Geschichte der Preussischen Armee*, p.206.

73 Olaf van Nimwegen, *The Dutch Army and the Military Revolutions, 1588–1688* (English edition, Woodbridge, Suffolk: Boydell, 2010), p.429. In 1666 the Great Elector acted in the first person to accommodate for a truce between Galen and the States General.

74 Jany, *Geschichte der Preussischen Armee*, p.211. The agreement lasted for one year, but could be renewed for another 12 months. The Republic paid the Elector 220,000 thalers in monthly tranches of 83,448 thalers.

75 Pelet-Narbonne, *Geschichte der Brandenburg-Preußischen Reiterei*, p.41.

THE ELECTORATE OF BRANDENBURG

the contractual assistance of 1,500 men for the forthcoming war. At first, the Elector wanted half of these corps to come from the regular army and half from the Prussian militia, but the proposal met with resistance from the Duchal authorities.[76] The matter remained unresolved until the following spring, and became an internal affair because it called into question the reputation of the Prince-Elector and his army. On 28 August 1671, putting aside all issues of reputation or prestige, a corps of 1,000 infantrymen from different regiments was formed under the orders of Colonel Hans Adam von Schöning. A further 400 dragoons joined the infantrymen alongside 100 horsemen.[77] The corps headed to Cracow to join the Poles on campaign. In early 1672, while the army was increasing its size to raise the troops for the Dutch Republic, the contingent for Poland was modified, and now comprised 1,000 infantrymen and 500 dragoons. These troops were quartered in Lublin from July to December, without taking part in military activity. A new request from Poland was addressed to Berlin in July 1673. The *Rzeczpospolita* now demanded a contingent of only cavalry and dragoons. Pressed by military commitments on the Rhine, the Elector delayed the formation of the contingent until March 1674, when he ordered the mobilisation of two regiments of dragoons.[78] In August, 1,200 men headed to Lvov and then joined the army of Sobieski in Podolia. In February 1675, the Swedish invasion caused the immediate return to Prussia of the whole corps, which crossed the border in April.

However, since 1672 Germany had also caused concern. After joining the Imperialists in September, in April 1673 under threat of the devastation of his possessions in Westphalia, the Prince-Elector had been forced to sign the treaty of Vossen, interrupting his participation in the war against France. In July 1674, the Great Elector signed a new convention with Emperor Leopold I, with which Brandenburg had to send 16,000 troops to the Rhine.[79] Notwithstanding the Swedish invasion of Pomerania, Friedrich Wilhelm maintained 2,500–3,000 men of infantry and cavalry to support the Dutch and Spanish army of the Low Countries. These troops participated in the major actions against the French, such as the siege of Grave in 1674, Maastricht in 1676 and the Battle of Saint-Denis in 1678. Problems concerning payment and quarters occurred, but what was missing was taken by force. In October 1676, regiments were sent into Franconia to demand billets and contributions, followed by other troops to Hessen-Kassel, Fulda, Anhalt and the Thuringian states the next month, while two regiments occupied Cologne's Westphalian

---

76 Jany, *Geschichte der Preussischen Armee*, p.221: the Prussian authorities declared that 'in so many years the chosen militia has indeed been maintained, and those who could be selected have been provided with the necessary armament, but the officers in the companies have not been appointed'.

77 Jany, *Geschichte der Preussischen Armee*, p.221. The infantrymen came from regiments *Kurprinz* (BrI-11), *Dönhoff* (BrI-43) and the *Preussische Garde* (bri-ii); the dragoons comprised a squadron of the regiment *Derfflinger* (BrD-1) and the *Blockschen* free company; the cavalry was represented by the *Ragozky* company, or Preussische Gard zu Ross (Brc-ii).

78 Pelet-Narbonne, *Geschichte der Brandenburg-Preußischen Reiterei*, p.42; these were the regiments *Schlieben* (BrD-12) and *Hohendorff* (BrD-13).

79 Pelet-Narbonne, *Geschichte der Brandenburg-Preußischen Reiterei*, p.42.

territories.[80] Exploiting all available resources, both internal and external, in the course of the Franco-Dutch War the Electoral army grew to 45,000 men in early 1679. The reduction begun after the Peace of Saint-Germain en Laye brought the available force to 27,000 men, of whom 20,200 were infantry, 5,200 cavalry and 1,600 dragoons at the end of the year. In January 1680, a further reduction of cavalry and dragoons reduced their numbers to 4,900 men in all.[81]

The French army under the Prince de Condé seized the Brandenburg fort of Rees, in the Duchy of Cleve, in June 1672, in a contemporary print. (Author's Collection) The Peace of Vossem was a controversial episode of the Franco-Dutch War. Prussian historians stated that, since he no longer received support from the Dutch Republic, and seeing his Westphalian possessions in French hands, the Great Elector was forced to negotiate a truce with France. With the exception of the fortress of Wesel and the Forts of Lippstadt and Rees, France returned to Brandenburg all occupied places in the Duchy of Cleves, the Principality of Minden and the counties of Mark and Ravensberg. France also promised Brandenburg 800,000 *livres* – which was never paid.

In the summer of 1682, news of another war between the Habsburg Emperor and the Porte brought the Ottoman danger back to the fore

---

80 Wilson, *German Armies*, p.54: 'Poised to drive the Swedes from Pomerania, the Great Elector feared his operations would collapse unless he secured adequate resources, and, complaining bitterly that his demise was imminent, he took the law into his own hands.'

81 Jany, *Geschichte der Preussischen Armee*, p.274; Mülverstedt, *Die Brandenburgische Kriegsmacht unter dem Großen Kurfürsten*, pp.29–30.

THE ELECTORATE OF BRANDENBURG

throughout Germany. In July 1683, the Elector mobilised 1,000 infantrymen and 200 dragoons as a contingent from the Duchy of Prussia to join the forces that Jan Sobieski was finishing to gather in Poland. The small contingent was entrusted to Colonel Wolfgang Christoph Truchsess zu Waldburg.[82] The Brandenburgers joined the Poles at Reidenburg in Bavaria, where the Polish commissioners mustered them on 27 August 1683. Alongside the Royal Polish army, the Electoral troops fought at Kahlenberg and Párkány. In early 1684, the Polish King called for another contingent of 2,000 men. The *Vertrag*, signed on 16 March, provided for two infantry regiments of eight companies, one company of cavalry and one of dragoons.[83] The contingent in Polish service faced several problems due to Hungary's unhealthy climate, and in autumn 1685 returned home, but in 1686 Brandenburg raised another corps, this time paid for by Emperor Leopold I. On 4 January 1686, the sides agreed on a contingent of 7,000 men, to which the Elector voluntarily added in February an infantry battalion of 804 men.[84] The corps was formed with great care and on 6 January orders had been prepared for gathering the troops, which comprised:

General Stab: 50 men
Infantry: 5,916 men
Cavalry: 1,390 men
Dragoons: 779
Artillery: 223 men with eight guns, 2 mortars and 2 howitzers.[85]

The command was entrusted to the skiled *Generallieutenant* Hans Adam von Schöning, with *Generalmajor*s Johann Albrecht von Barfus and Kurt Hildebrand von der Marwitz as seconds. The 1686 campaign, culminating in the conquest of Buda on 2 September, was the last military engagement performed by Brandenburg troops during the reign of the Great Elector. Upon his death in 1688, the army mustered 24,364 infantry,

Hans Adam von Schöning (1641–1696). (Public Domain) After the campaign of 1686 in Hungary, in 1688-1689 Schöning held the command of the Brandenburg troops against the French on the Lower Rhine as *Feldmarschall-Lieutenant*. On 12 March 1689, he won the Battle of Uerdingen, but in September he was dismissed from the command following a dispute with General Barfus and in 1690 he was dismissed from the military service. He then entered the service of the Electorate of Saxony. In 1691, Prince-Elector Johann Georg III appointed him as Field Marshal and war councillor. In 1692, during a stay in Teplitz, he was arrested by order of the Emperor and taken to Spielberg, accused of treasonable negotiations with the French. He was only released in 1694. His health was so weakened by imprisonment that he was only able to serve for a short time as commander of the corps of cadets in Dresden, where he died at the age of 55.

82　Jany, *Geschichte der Preussischen Armee*, p.285. The infantry consisted of four companies from the regiment *Dönhoff* (BrI-43) and four other free companies.
83　Jany, *Geschichte der Preussischen Armee*, p.286. The infantry regiments were assembled with companies from the existing units; the first was assigned to Colonel Karl Emilius zu Dohna (BrI-66), the second to Colonel Alexander von Kettler, Prince of Courland (BrI-67).
84　Jany, *Geschichte der Preussischen Armee*, p.288.
85　Jany, *Geschichte der Preussischen Armee*, p.288; Pelet-Narbonne, *Geschichte der Brandenburg-Preußischen Reiterei*, p.65, states a slightly different force, namely 6,360 infantry and artillery, 1,200 cavalry and 640 dragoons. Sources are also discordant regarding the composition of the expedition corps. Jany, *Geschichte der Preussischen Armee*, p.289, does not include the regiments *Kurfürstin zu Fuss* (BrI-57) and *Straus Cavalerie* (BrC-44), which instead appear in the cartoon preserved in the Hessian archive in Marburg, WHK 6/19: *Plan vom Feldlager der Armee des Kurfürsten von Brandenburg* (1686).

3,883 cavalry, 1,449 dragoons, and 227 artillerymen: an 'establishment of peace' five times more numerous than the one 'of war' of 48 years earlier.[86]

In June 1688, a month after the death of the Great Elector, his son Friedrich III (later Friedrich I as King in Prussia), signed a three-year *Subsidienvertrag* with the Dutch Republic for hiring an auxiliary corps of 6,000 men.[87] The Republic asked for this corps to secure the border between the Waas and Sambre Rivers, after the news of a strong French corps quartered in this area. On 11 October 1688, 5,324 infantry and 612 cavalry were quartered in the Wooser area near Nijmegen, a few days later the French invasion of the Palatinate. The agreement was renewed three years later and thereafter until 1697.[88]

The siege of Buda in 1686, engraving by François Collignon. (Author's Collection) Despite the cordial relationship established between the Great Elector and Emperor Leopold I, disagreements arose at the beginning of the Hungarian campaign. *Generallieutenant* Schöning informed the Prince-Elector of the harsh treatment received by his troops, to such an extent that he could not rule out the possibility of a mutiny.

While the auxiliary corps was marching to the Netherlands, Friedrich III signed an alliance with Saxony, Brunswick-Lüneburg Hanover and Hessen-Kassel, known as 'the Magdeburg Concert', formed on 22 October 1688 for raising an army to face the French in the Middle Rhine area.[89] Brandenburg contributed with 1,500 men, followed by further 8,000 on the Wesel River in 1689.[90]

---

86 Mülverstedt, *Die Brandenburgische Kriegsmacht unter dem Großen Kurfürsten*, p.312.
87 Jany, *Geschichte der Preussischen Armee*, p.361. The negotiation was facilitated by Prince Georg Friedrich zu Waldeck, as representative of William III.
88 Jany, *Geschichte der Preussischen Armee*, p.361.
89 Wilson, *German Armies*, p.183. Saxony contributed with 10,000 men; Hanover with 8,000 (or 7,400); Hessen-Kassel with 6,000; Münster with 6,000; the Ernestine Dukes with 1,000.
90 Jany, *Geschichte der Preussischen Armee*, p.364.

THE ELECTORATE OF BRANDENBURG

Army Organisation

A sign of the supremacy of the Junker military class in the army lies in the ownership of more than one regiment by a single family. Between 1660 and 1680, three members of the important family Sparr were colonel-proprietors of infantry and cavalry regiments, while Dohna, Schwerin and Görtzke held this position with two members each. In some cases, the same officer was Colonel Proprietor of several regiments simultaneously, as happened with Georg von Derfflinger, who in the early 1670s was colonel of infantry, cavalry and dragoon regiments. The army of Brandenburg also registered the case of a female Colonel Proprietor, the rank entrusted to the wife of Prince-Elector Friedrich Wilhelm, Dorothea von Schleswig-Holstein, who obviously held the office *ad honorem*.

Family ties were important for climbing the rank system, and belonging to an influential Junker family was a good precondition for a military career, but officers who did not possess this requisite and held important positions in the army were not an exception. Among the many, Ulrich von Promnitz (1636–1695) represents an exemplary case. Cadet son of a Prussian noble with modest means, in his youth he served in the Imperial army under Montecuccoli in Hungary, and was later appointed as *Obrist-Kommandant*. However, because he was a Protestant with limited resources, he was not able to rise above this rank; in 1671 he entered the service of Brandenburg, and in 1672 became Colonel Proprietor of a cavalry regiment (BrC-40). He served on the Rhine against France and later against the Swedes in northern Germany, where he took part in the Battle of Fehrbellin, which became a very special merit in Brandenburg. In 1675, Promnitz became colonel of the *Leibregiment* (BrC-35), and two years later he was promoted to *Generalwacthmeister*. He was highly regarded as a soldier and his talent enabled him in 1680 to transfer to the Saxon army with the same rank but with a higher salary. In his new post, the veteran commander became

Musketeer of the infantry regiment *Kurfürstin* Dorothea von Schleswig-Holstein, 1683; drawing by Herbert Knötel (*Das Kasket. Handdrucke zur Geschichte der Militärischen Tracht*, Berlin, 1924–25). The regiment wore a red coat with white cuffs and lacing until 1685. Note the cloak in red and white, the ammunition pouch decorated with the Princess's monogram, and the hat edged in red and white. The decorated ammunition pouch was a distinctive mark of the Brandenburg infantry regiments. In the 1680s, regiment Anhalt-Dessau (BrI-39) had the colonel proprietor's coat of arms painted above a blue cover.

63

Portrait of Margrave Philipp of Brandenburg-Schwedt (1669–1711). Oldest son from the Great Elector's second marriage; in 1685, aged 16, he was appointed Colonel Proprietor of an infantry regiment. The Margravate of Brandenburg-Schwedt was created by Friedrich Wilhelm for his secondgeniture, but the title granted no succession.

one of the Prince-Elector's favourite officers and his experience was useful in selecting young cadets for the officer corps.[91]

Apart from the Electress Dorothea, all major officers in Brandenburg had received a military apprenticeship following the classic seventeenth century scheme. Many of them were full-time soldiers, and had risen through the military hierarchy within regiments, into which they had entered at a very young age as cadets or adjutants, in Brandenburg or elsewhere. Alongside them, since 1652 Friedrich Wilhelm established schools for training cavalry officers, which became known as *Ritterakademie*. In 1660 there were three, in Berlin, Kustrin and Colberg. Every year, 60–70 young men were selected to receive instruction to become cavalry officers.[92]

At the unit level, the internal organisation was the traditional one of German armies, and in substance there was little difference between a Brandenburg infantry or cavalry regiment and that of another German state. The company was the basic administrative unit assigned to a captain, *Hauptmann* in the infantry and dragoons, and *Rittmeister* in the cavalry. The first company belonged to the Colonel Proprietor as usual, and the second to his lieutenant colonel, who normally assumed the command of the whole regiment on campaign. Another key figure, the *Obrist-Wachtmeister*, or *Major*,

Portrait of Margrave Carl Philipp of Brandenburg-Schwedt (1673–1695). He was the third son of the Great Elector and Princess Dorothea of Schleswig-Holstein. In 1688, he was appointed an infantry captain and in 1693 fought at Neerwinden, where he was promoted to *Feldmarschall-Lieutenant*. One year later, he joined the Brandenburg corps in Piedmont during the war of the Augsburg League. Here Carl Philipp was involved in a passionate love affair with Countess Caterina de Salmour, who he tried to marry notwithstanding the opposition of his half-brother Friedrich III and the Duke of Savoy. In 1695, the couple's attempt to secretly marry met with the faltering of a Piedmontese priest forcibly summoned by the bride and groom's witnesses. The affair involved the Roman curia, which confirmed the marriage, in the hope that the Margrave would convert to Catholicism. To avoid further complications, Duke Vittorio Amedeo imprisoned Caterina in a convent. While the issue was still being debated, Carl Philip died of a fever or, it was said, of a broken heart in Casale Monferrato. His body was buried in the Hohenzollern family crypt in Berlin Cathedral.

---

91 Anton Balthasar König, *Biographisches Lexikon aller Heiden und Militairpersonen* (Berlin, 1791), vol. III, pp.237–239.
92 Pelet-Narbonne, *Geschichte der Brandenburg-Preußischen Reiterei*, p.8.

was the third in command in the infantry, cavalry and dragoon regiments, especially in tactical matters, since he had the special task of distributing the companies on the field, assigning them in the order of battle, and directing the guard and sentry service in the garrisons and on campaign. He also was the captain of his own company in the regiment. Further ranks dealt with administration, discipline, and other matters, such as the *Quartiermeister*, *Profoss*, *Wagenmeister* and *Secretarius*.

Each company of infantry, cavalry and dragoons had its staff with three or four officers: *Hauptmann* (infantry and dragoons) or *Rittermeister* (cavalry), one or two lieutenants, and an ensign. The rank of NCO was held by the *Feldwebel* in the infantry and dragoons, and the *Wachtmeister* in the cavalry. The infantry company was completed by *Fourier*, accountant, surgeon, and a variable number of drummers and fifes, corporals, lance-corporals and privates. The cavalry had no *Fourier* – he being replaced by a quartermaster – a trumpeter instead of drummer and fifer, and some craftsmen such as a saddler and blacksmith. A dragoon company had the same staff as the cavalry, but the hautboy usually replaced the trumpet, alongside a drummer.

Possibly, the only image known today of a seventeenth century military surgeon is this portrait of Georg Händel (1622–1697), father of the composer George Frederick Handel. (Author's Collection) He was a surgeon in the Brandenburg army in the 1670s, and later became teacher and *Hof-Chirurgus* at the court of Prince-Elector Friedrich III of Hohenzollern.

While the internal organisation of regiments and companies became more or less standard, differences in strength remained a constant in the Electoral army, since the colonel-proprietors could negotiate for the number of men of their units. Differences could be remarkable: In 1656, infantry regiment *Wittgenstein* numbered four companies, increased to five in 1660.[93] Unlike this latter, in 1657 the *Sparr zu Fuss* (BrI-3) had 12 companies of 102 men, while *Belcum* (BrI-6) fielded eight companies with 83 or 84 men; in contrast, the two free companies under *Obristlieutenant* Dobeneck consisted of 100 men each.[94] The 1659 ordinance reported that the field strength of an infantry company comprised 108 *gemeine* pikemen and musketeers.[95]

The reduction of 1661 decreased the number of infantry companies, but the strength increased considerably: the regiment *Dohna zu Fuss* (BrI-2) now deployed six companies of 166 men, while the *Leibgarde* (BrI-9) had the same number of companies but of 200 men; the free companies numbered between 100 and 250 men.[96] Except for the *Leibgarde*, and *Dohna*, all the surviving regiments retained four or two companies.

The differences in strength between one regiment and another also posed no problem for the field army. In the Polish campaign in June 1656, the cavalry fielded regiments ranging in strength from 1,212 to 303 men; in total

---

93 Mülverstedt, *Die Brandenburgische Kriegsmacht unter dem Großen Kurfürsten*, pp.692–693.
94 Jany, *Geschichte der Preussischen Armee*, pp 138, 147.
95 Jany, *Geschichte der Preussischen Armee*, p.183.
96 Jany, *Geschichte der Preussischen Armee*, p.195.

Landgrave Friedrich II von Hessen-Homburg (1633–1708) in a portrait by Pieter Nason (Collection of the Middachten Castle, Gelderland, The Netherlands). Note in the background the cavalry wearing black hats and wearing pale yellow buff coats. Celebrated by Heinrich von Kleist in his drama *Prinz Friedrich von Homburg*, written in 1809–1810, Friedrich II became the archetypal Romantic hero. Keist's emblematic text represents the dichotomy between obeying orders and doing what is right.

there were 6,900 *Einspännige* with 73 officers; the dragoons numbered 3,255 privates with 31 officers, belonging to regiments with a strength between 808 and 303 dragoons. The infantry entered the campaign with regiments of 1,285 and 404 men.[97] As for the number of men in each company, in 1666 this increased to 130 men for the newly formed units.[98]

In the 1660s, the first steps were taken towards a modern system of centralised army administration. The Prince-Elector succeeded in limiting the old recruitment system whereby the colonel-proprietors negotiated the strength of regiments with the Prince, but did not allow interference from him in the administration and command of their troops. At the same time, the activities of the *Generalkriegskommissar* Platen, appointed in 1655, promoted uniformity in the Electoral army just as quickly. With these measures, it was inevitable that gradually the authority of the colonels would diminish. Starting in 1656, the Great Elector sought to decrease the issuing of individual contracts to colonels – the *Kapitulationen* – and limited the right of commanders to appoint officers to their regiments. In this way, he laid the foundations for a system in which all officers without distinction owed absolute loyalty to the sovereign and commander-in-chief of the army. Finally, he attempted – although with much less success than one might imagine from reading Kleist's *Prinz Friedrich von Homburg* – to change the mentality of his officers and persuade them to see themselves less as professionals and businessmen than servants of the state.

Needless to say, the officers enjoyed the privileges typical of their rank and social class. This could easily be seen from the number of horses and carts for their baggage. While each company and regimental staff had one wagon with four horses, a cavalry colonel received 14 horses as 'particular baggage animals'; his colleague of infantry and dragoons received 10 horses, a captain of cavalry six, dragoons five, and of infantry four: lieutenants and ensigns of all the specialties had a couple of

---

97 Jany, *Geschichte der Preussischen Armee*, p.122.
98 Jany, *Geschichte der Preussischen Armee*, p.207; regiment *Schmied zu Fuss* (BrI-41), raised in 1666, had eight companies of 130 men.

horses each.[99] Until the 1670s, the officers continued to use supplementary baggage horses to carry their luggage, so the number of rations that the ordnance issued for them was very high.

German authors of the nineteenth century emphasise the fact that the superiority of the Brandenburg-Prussian army was the result of an extremely strict discipline. In Brandenburg, the basic document in matters of discipline was issued in 1556;[100] this derived from the Landsknecht's Code, issued by Emperor Maximilian I, which was the basis of similar regulations in use in the rest of Germany and also in the Imperial army. This was probably the most brutal and severe military regulation in Europe. In 1659, the Prince-Elector issued a revised version of the code, eliminating some of the outdated articles, but reconfirming many of the heavy corporal punishments. The slightest infraction was punished by 'running through the rows' and 'donkey riding'. However, senior commanders recommended moderation in the application of punishments, advising against maiming the soldier in such a way that he could not be used in service.[101]

Infantry

In 1668, the first orders for a standard composition of companies and *Regiments-Stab* were issued. Alongside the three field officers who held the direction of the regiments – *Obrist, Obristlieutenant* and *Obristwachtmeister* – each regiment of infantry, cavalry and dragoons included:

1 *Regimentsquartiermeister*
1 *Regimentsauditor*
1 *Regimentsprediger* (priest)
1 *Regiments Secretarius*, in charge of the administration of the regiment
1 *Regimentsfeldscherer* (physician)
1 *Regimentswagenmeister*
1 *Regimentstambour* for infantry and dragoons, *Pauker* for cavalry
1 *Regimentsprofoss*
1 *Scharfsrichter* (executioner) with his assistants

In wartime, each infantry regiment was to deploy eight or 12 companies. Each infantry company was to be formed with the following ranks and files:

1 *Kapitan*
1 *Lieutenant*
1 *Fähnrich*
3 *Sergeanten*
1 *Gefreiter-Korporal*

---

99 Jany, *Geschichte der Preussischen Armee*, p.160. The number of horses was established by the *Ordonnanz* dated 12 November 1657.

100 Pelet-Narbonne, *Geschichte der Brandenburg-Preußischen Reiterei*, p.10.

101 Jany, *Geschichte der Preussischen Armee*, pp.170–171.

1 *Fourier*
1 *Capitaine des Armes*
1 *Musterschreiber*
1 *Chirurg*
3 *Korporale*
3 *Tambours*
1 *Pfeifer*
180–200 privates, including 10–12 *Gefreite*

On campaign, the regiments formed a couple of *Eskadrone* (battalions) each with half regiment staff.[102] The scheme followed the traditional 'German pattern' but there were some terms which allude to the French terminology, such as *Kapitan* and *Sergeant*. Furthermore, while the *Capitaine des armes* was apparently another inspiration from the French, in fact this rank derived from that existing in the Swedish infantry companies.[103] In Brandenburg, this rank was held by a junior officer in charge of weapons and ammunition, as well as caring for the sick. According to the *Ordonnanz* of 1668, on the field, the *Capitaine des armes* walked behind the last corporal musketeer 'to keep him determined and to drive them on.'[104]

In the spring of 1672, all infantry regiments were ordered to form companies of 125 privates with a *Primaplana* of 18 officers, non-commissioned officers and musicians, in total 1,144 men; tactically, each regiment continued to field two battalions of four companies. However, only eight regiments could deploy this strength, and the units assigned to garrisons formed only four companies; the newly formed regiment *Syberg* (BrI-46) also fielded four companies. There were notable exceptions, such as the *Chieze zu Fuss* (BrI-50), which assembled four companies of 165 privates.[105] Two years later, the contingent for the campaign in Alsace deployed six infantry regiments of eight companies, two with five companies and two with four.[106]

One-third of the infantry company consisted of pikemen, but this was not an absolute rule, since in 1655 some regiments consisted only of musketeers. Implicit evidence that pikes were not present in all infantry regiments is confirmed by the correspondence between Colonel Wolrad von Waldeck and General Sparr. On 23 July, Waldeck informed the commander-in-chief that his 1,200-strong regiment had received 400 pikes from the arsenal of Lippstadt. However, he reported that, 'since the soldiers are not instructed in the use of the pike, a great confusion is taking place among them, and

---

102 Jany, *Geschichte der Preussischen Armee*, pp.160–161.
103 The *Capitaine des Armes* was the highest non-commissioned officer in the infantry company of the Swedish army until the rank was abolished in 1747 and replaced by a sergeant-major. The rank probably derived from the one existing in the French navy in the seventeenth century. He was the person in charge of the company's weaponry, dealing with care, maintenance and storage, and also training in its use together with the other non-commissioned officers.
104 Jany, *Geschichte der Königlich Preußischen Armee*, p.163.
105 Jany, *Geschichte der Preussischen Armee*, p.214; Mülverstedt, *Die Brandenburgische Kriegsmacht unter dem Großen Kurfürsten*, pp.788–789.
106 Jany, *Geschichte der Königlich Preußischen Armee*, pp.225–226.

therefore I have had all the pikes withdrawn, and furthermore I would like to wait a week for the men to be trained with this kind of weapon.'[107]

The proportion of one pikeman for every two musketeers remained unchanged until the 1690s, and in 1686 the infantry of the auxiliary corps in Hungary retained their pikes. The only exception consisted of a pistol to be carried with a bandolier distributed to each pikeman.[108]

In July 1677, the first order relating to grenadiers was issued shortly before the siege of Stettin. Infantry regiments *Garde zu Fuss* (BrI-9), *Kursfürstin* (BrI-57) and *Kurprinz* (BrI-11) had to 'command' 24 soldiers as grenadiers joining them in a company under a captain, the Scotsman Henry Montgomery.[109] In 1681, it was then established that each infantry regiment

Grenadier *Hauptmann* and private grenadier of the *Garde zu Fuss* regiment (BrI-9), from a series of prints by Peter Schenk dating to 1698. (Zeughaus - Deutsches Historisches Museum, Berlin) The year of printing does not always coincide with the age of the subjects and these uniforms can probably be dated to the mid–1690s. This gives us a fairly detailed picture of the clothing issued to the Brandenburg grenadiers a few years after their introduction. In particular, *Mütze* (mitre cap), similar to the Dutch models, may already have received such shape and decorations in the previous decade. *Hauptmann*: carmine red mitre cap with golden monogram, grenades and edgings, electoral cap embroidered of red, silver and black, silver grenades' flames; white cravat with black ribbon; carmine red coat laced and embroidered of gold, medium blue lining; carmine red breeches and stockings; golden buttons; carmine red bandolier with golden laces; black grenade bag with golden fittings and monogram.
Grenadier private: mitre cap with white plate edged red and golden monograms, silver grenades with red flames, silver Electoral cap, dark blue bag with white tassel; red cravat, dark blue cat with white cuffs and lining and golden buttons; dark blue waistcoat with silver buttons; white stockings; white grenade bag with golden monogram, black grandees, red flames and silver Electoral cap.

---

107 Jany, *Geschichte der Preussischen Armee*, p.179; the regiments formed in Prussia with companies from the militia probably already had pikemen, but the *Culenburg* militia regiment, which remained active even after the Peace of Oliva, still consisted only of musketeers in January 1667.
108 Jany, *Geschichte der Preussischen Armee*, p.329.
109 Jany, *Geschichte der Preussischen Armee*, p.255.

would form a company of grenadiers. Administratively, the grenadiers belonged to the regiment, but tactically they were joined into battalions from four to six companies.[110]

By 1687 the Great Elector established a new organisation of the infantry. In wartime, each regiment had to deploy 1,000 *Gemeine* and 167 *Gefreite* and corporals divided into eight companies. The *Garde zu Fuss* had 12 companies.[111] However, in the peace establishment differences in strength continued and only the foot guards maintained this pattern.

In 1675, Friedrich Wilhelm raised a *Blessirten-Compagnie* (invalids) quartered in Spandau. The company was entrusted to the veteran *Major* Schönebeck who held the command with two lieutenants. In 1688, a second sedentary company formed by unable soldiers was raised in Johannisburg (today Pisz in Poland). In the same year the company of Spandau numbered 150 *Gemeiner*, while the one of Johannisburg had 50 men in all.[112]

As early as the 1680s, the Brandenburg army was among the first to draw up regimental registers containing information on soldiers. For the seventeenth century, this information is as rare as it is valuable, because it gives insight into the origin and social background of the recruits. An analysis of the regiment *Kurfürsten* (BrI-55) in 1681 relates that of 1,105 soldiers, 227 came from Prussia, 175 from the Mark of Brandenburg, 100 from Pomerania, 55 from Saxony, 62 from Westphalia, 71 from Silesia and 30 from Lüneburg. Among the non-Germans, the regiment recorded 25 Danes, 85 Swedes, 47 Poles, 15 Bohemians and eight Hungarians.[113] Only 45 percent of this regiment was composed of recruits from the countryside. The previous professions of the other soldiers were varied: there were carpenters and tailors, shoemakers, woollen workers, butchers and porters, students and even nobles, 'in other words, everything but the rabble or the dishonest.'[114] Most of them had served for a long time: 11 had been under the flag for 30–40 years; 44 for 20–30 years, 156 for 10–20 years, 475 for up to 10 years and 311 for up to five years. A notable feature was the low rate of desertion, since with such a composition, it was not a risk for the Prince-Elector to scatter them throughout the Brandenburg territories.

As far as tactical ordering was concerned, until the 1670s the infantry was arranged in six rows with the pikemen in the centre. However, all commanders of this age, including that of Brandenburg, were in complete agreement that there was no single tactical model to be used in every battle, so the positioning of troops and the battle plan had to take into account their opponents and the lie of the land. During the war against Poland, the deep formation with six rows proved very effective against enemies fighting in open order supported by large numbers of cavalry. When Friedrich Wilhelm reversed the alliance with Sweden in 1657, the infantry continued to deploy

---

110 Jany, *Geschichte der Preussischen Armee*, p.276.
111 Jany, *Geschichte der Preussischen Armee*, p.326.
112 Mülverstedt, *Die Brandenburgische Kriegsmacht unter dem Großen Kurfürsten*, pp.495–496.
113 Olaf Groehler, *Das Heerwesen in Brandenburg-Preußen von 1640 bis 1896. Das Heerwesen* (Berlin: Brandenburgisches Verlagshaus, 2001), p.8.
114 Groehler, *Das Heerwesen in Brandenburg-Preußen*, p.8.

THE ELECTORATE OF BRANDENBURG

Brandenburg infantry, 1675–80, after Richard Knötel (Author's Collection). German historians generally praise the discipline of Brandenburger troops, however, especially when they were deprived of resources, the Great Elector's valiant soldiers also behaved violently towards the civilians. In 1697, when the Brandenburg corps in northern Italy left their quarters in the Duchy of Parma and Piacenza, a local chronicler remarked on the size of the sum paid, concluding with the wish to 'never again [see] such beastly and cruel people.'

in six rows, since the Swedes also had a cavalry that was numerically remarkable. However, with the exception of the landing at Funen and the Battle of Nyborg in 1659, the campaigns were mainly marked by sieges.

In the Alsace campaign of 1674–75, the infantry reduced the number of rows to five,[115] but this was not enough to avoid the defeat at Türkheim. In the following campaigns, the infantry fought on six, five and sometimes four rows in order to achieve a greater extension of troops on the battlefield. Contemporary authors praised the quality of the Brandenburg infantry,

---

115 Heinrich Rocholl, *Der Große Kurfürst von Brandenburg im Elsass 1674-1675* (Strasbourg, 1877), p.47.

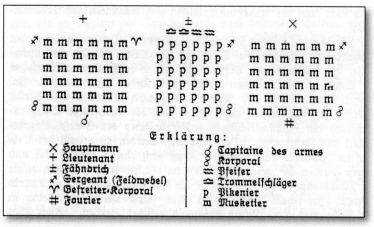

Infantry company deployment after Curt Jany, *Geschichte der Königlich Preußischen Armee bis zum Jahre 1807*, vol. I (Berlin, 1928).

describing them as always in good order and solid. In fact, the Great Elector and his commanders always placed special emphasis on combat discipline, taking the Swedish and Dutch models as a model, and later also some tactical features of the French army. These doctrines governed how the soldiers and their officers were to conduct themselves during the engagement, as the opposing forces came into contact, and dictated whether the attacking infantry was to advance carefully and methodically, or to move spiritedly and quickly. Brandenburg infantry followed both principles and exploited the advantages offered by the former or the latter approach with the usual tactical manoeuvres, which included the doubling of the rows in the assaults, extending the wings of the battalions through the halving of ranks against enemy infantry approaching, or forming the square against cavalry.[116] Fire by platoons or sections, on the Dutch model, was usually employed against the enemy infantry, while the single volley of the whole front at short range offered greater success against the cavalry.

The lesson learned at Brandenburg's expense in Alsace in 1675 against Turenne, favoured the introduction of a tactic less dependent to manoeuvres and more oriented to the solidity of the deployment. Infantrymen were now required to advance at a slow, deliberate step so that an *en muraille* (literally a curtain) formation could be constantly maintained. This tactic required that soldiers advance in close order, in five or six rows, and at a slow pace. Officers were not to order their men to fire, until the enemy did so first, and then only when the battalion had advanced to within 30 or 40 paces. As soon as they received the enemy's fire, they were to stoically reciprocate. The common wisdom was that if the defenders could be induced to fire first, they were likely to be defeated. No one would stand stoically, realising they had been deprived of fire, while the advancing enemy was still able to unleash a single, deadly volley at point-blank range. In this regard, the Brandenburg infantry developed special devices useful in both attack and defence that were as simple as they were effective. Among the most notable was the adoption of multiple fire, achieved by loading muskets with double ammunition. Some colonels trained their infantrymen to load up to five balls to achieve a

---

116 Jany, *Geschichte der Königlich Preußischen Armee*, pp.183–184.

THE ELECTORATE OF BRANDENBURG

devastating short range effect.[117] When 100 paces from the enemy, the ranks were close to within point of the sword, and the ranks were to be half open, at two paces, six feet, from each other. Then, as they further approached, the distance between ranks was reduced to one small pace. Although this method of attacking enemy infantry remained official practice in the following years, there was notable variation among commanders, many of whom advocated and used much more aggressive methods. To what extent this result was achieved through brutal discipline is debatable. Some authors argue that motivations such as honour, sense of belonging and patriotism were of greater importance in the Brandenburg army than the classical view of the soldier who fought valiantly because he was under constant threat from the officers.[118]

Cavalry and Dragoons

The organisation of the cavalry faced a much more complicated situation, and maintained a precarious organisation for a long time due to its higher cost compared to the infantry. Consequently, the cavalry remained more susceptible to reductions in strength, with the disbanding of regiments, and retaining only autonomous companies. In 1656, each regiment deployed six to 10 companies on average, but there were also a couple of regiments formed by a single squadron of three companies. For the 1659 campaign in Denmark, the cavalry regiments fielded four to eight companies, with the exception of the newly formed *Leibregiment* (BrC-12), which had 10 companies. Overall, 10 regiments formed a mounted force of 62 companies, and a further four companies entered the campaign as autonomous units. The size of the company comprised 80 to 100 horsemen.[119] In December 1659, the cavalry recovering in winter quarters numbered 2,680 horsemen divided into 30 companies. Just four units retained the status of regiment with 24 companies of 80–86 men, while six companies of 100 men formed autonomous units. One

Brandenburg cavalrymen, plate XIII.48 from Richard Knötel's *Die Grosse Uniformenkunde* (Rathenow, 1903).

---

117 K.u.K. Kriegsarchiv, *Feldzüge des Prinzen Eugen von Savoyen* (Vienna, 1875), vol. I, p.486.
118 Groehler, *Das Heerwesen in Brandenburg-Preußen*, p.7.
119 Jany, *Geschichte der Königlich Preußischen Armee*, p.121.

regiment had been formed into a temporary corps, with six companies of disbanded units under the *Statthalter* of Prussia.[120]

Although he had dismissed the entire cavalry in 1660, the Elector exploited all options at his disposal to raise a numerically adequate mounted force. Along these lines, Friedrich Wilhelm intended to reintroduce the feudal obligation of the *Lehnpferde*.[121] Envisioning the imminent danger of war against the Porte, on 6 May 1661 he ordered the nobility of Brandenburg, Pomerania, Halberstadt, Minden and Ravensberg to stand ready in case of need. Furthermore, on 14 June 1661, 'in eventum belli', Friedrich Wilhelm appointed a number of officers to 'restore the order in the feudal services.'[122] These officers were to be divided into companies, and for the composition all dismissed persons residing in Brandenburg were taken into account.[123] The candidates responded by complaining of their poverty and also demanded, as they had done in 1656, 'that they be paid a fair wage'. The military budget could not take on any more salaries, as the Elector had reintroduced the feudal obligation precisely to save money. Thus the planned reorganisation did not take place, and it was replaced by the payment of compensation. However, in September 1663 the Elector turned to the feudal obligation, in the form of the hire of a horse, into a tax, allowing the payment of 40 thalers, corresponding to the sum needed to enlist a horseman. The Elector issued the same order in 1665, in 1672, and again in 1683. In 1670, 1677 and 1678 decrees were issued for the supply of feudal horses from Brandenburg, but these were not actually paid.[124]

In 1666, there were seven cavalry regiments, each with six companies of 83 men.[125] Two years later, the cavalry troop was organised with the following war-establishment:

1 *Rittermeister*
1 *Lieutenant*
1 *Kornet*
1 *Wachtmeister*
1 *Quartiermeister*
3 *Korporals*
2 *Trompeter*
1 *Musterschreiber*
1 *Feldscherer*
1 *Schmied*
1 *Sattler*
80 *Einspännige*

---

120 Jany, *Geschichte der Königlich Preußischen Armee*, p.147.

121 *Lehnpferde*, the warhorse which the owner of a fief has to provide to the prince; see also footnote 4.

122 Jany, *Geschichte der Königlich Preußischen Armee*, p.220.

123 Pelet-Narbonne, *Geschichte der Brandenburg-Preußischen Reiterei*, p.43. The Elector ordered the formation of two companies in the Altmark, one in the district of Prigniz, three in Mittelmark, and three in Neumark.

124 Jany, *Geschichte der Königlich Preußischen Armee*, p.220.

125 Pelet-Narbonne, *Geschichte der Brandenburg-Preußischen Reiterei*, p.8; Mülverstedt, *Die Brandenburgische Kriegsmacht unter dem Großen Kurfürsten*, p.22.

THE ELECTORATE OF BRANDENBURG

The regiments fielded six to eight companies.

However, this organisation remained on paper, as until the end of 1671 the whole cavalry consisted of only seven squadrons of two companies with 14 officers and NCOs and 86 horsemen. The following year, seven regiments of six companies with a total of 600 horses were reconstituted from this force. These were joined by another five new regiments, also consisting of six companies. For the Alsace campaign of 1674, the cavalry comprised eight regiments of six companies each, equal to three tactical squadrons. Each company still comprised 14 officers and NCOs and 86 horsemen.[126] Throughout the Great Elector's reign, cavalry regiments were often assembled by joining free companies and squadrons only for the duration of the war or even for a single campaign. This happened in the autumn of 1677, when the Elector sent three squadrons from the field army cavalry to support the Danish invasion of Rügen, and assembled them into the temporary corps entrusted to *Obrist* Johann von Hülsen. As usual in Germany and elsewhere, not only could the establishment strength of units vary, these also generally suffered from considerable attrition. After the Peace of Nijmegen almost all the regiments retained six companies, reduced, however, to 50 horsemen and 14 officers and NCOs.[127]

The dragoons also experienced the same circumstances as the cavalry in the matter of fluctuating strength. In 1656, on the eve of the war against Poland, 3,281 dragoons were assigned to the field army in Poland, grouped into six regiments and two autonomous formations. The number included the 200 dragoons of the *Churfürstliche Leibgarde*, which formed a single large company, while the other companies fielded between 80 and 100 dragoons.[128] The regiments comprised a variable number of companies ranging from three to eight. After the Peace of Oliva, the size of the company decreased to 40–50 privates. This was a cost-saving measure widespread throughout Europe, and the companies would provide NCOs and corporals when the regiments were reconstituted. However, the strength did not increase significantly in subsequent years. In 1666, there were only two regiments, each with five companies of 60 dragoons.[129]

In 1668, the company of dragoons was established as follows:

1 *Kapitan*
1 *Lieutenant*
1 *Fähnrich*
1 *Wachtmeister*
1 *Gefreiter-Korporal*
1 *Fourier*
1 *Capitaine des armes*
1 *Musterschreiber*
3 *Korporale*

---

126 Jany, *Geschichte der Königlich Preußischen Armee*, p.213.
127 Pelet-Narbonne, *Geschichte der Brandenburg-Preußischen Reiterei*, p.47.
128 Jany, *Geschichte der Königlich Preußischen Armee*, p.122.
129 Pelet-Narbonne, *Geschichte der Brandenburg-Preußischen Reiterei*, p.8.

Brandenburg cavalry in action at Rathenow on 14 June 1675, in a drawing of Richard Knötel. Notwithstanding the fact Knötel extensively researched before carrying out his work, two inaccuracies can be found in this illustration. The first is that it was not the cavalry that performed the surprise assault on Rathenow, but the dragoons, and the second is that the village was not manned by Swedish infantry, but by cavalry.

1 *Feldscherer*
2 *Tambours*
1 *Schmied*
80 *Gemeine*

In 1670, the company strength increased to 16 officers and NCOs and 96 privates. The following year, the *Derfflinger Dragoner* (BrD-1), the only unit with the size of a regiment, comprised six companies, each of 16 officers and NCOs (*Primaplana*) and 100 *Gemeine Dragoner*.[130] In the summer of 1672, however, the dragoons, now consisting of two regiments, totalled 776 men in all.[131] By 1674, both regiments had reached a 'regular' strength of 616 men.[132] In the 1680s, the dragoon regiments added two new companies, but with just 64 men.

Finally, in 1687, the 'establishment of peace' fixed the cavalry regiment's 360 rank and file and the dragoons to 608.[133]

Artillery

As in every European army of the seventeenth century, the artillery occupied a special position in Brandenburg. It was less a troop than a guild which retained its own regulations. In peacetime, only a small number of professional artillerymen were employed as NCOs and privates in the fortresses and arsenals, and enlisted as *Zeugmeister*, *Zeugwarter*, *Feuerwerker*, *Petardier* and *Büchsenmeister* (constables). A certain period of apprenticeship was necessary to acquire the technical knowledge that entitled them to be employed as artillerymen and to practise the 'art of shooting and throwing'.[134] Governors of the fortresses and commanders of the garrisons were responsible for the supervision of equipment and personnel. Otto Christoph von Sparr had held this position since 1651; with him, the *Oberzeugmeister* Elias Franke was entrusted with the supervision of the artillery materiel in Brandenburg and held this position until his death in 1660. There were no other artillery

---

130 Pelet-Narbonne, *Geschichte der Brandenburg-Preußischen Reiterei*, p.17.
131 Mülverstedt, *Die Brandenburgische Kriegsmacht unter dem Großen Kurfürsten*, p.789.
132 Jany, *Geschichte der Königlich Preußischen Armee*, p.226.
133 Jany, *Geschichte der Königlich Preußischen Armee*, p.326.
134 Jany, *Geschichte der Königlich Preußischen Armee*, p.174.

senior officers in Brandenburg before the outbreak of the Northern War.[135] The artillery equipment and personnel for the field army were taken from the fortresses. On 12 February 1657, the command of field army's artillery was assigned to *Oberlieutenant* Christian Hochkirch, who also held the direction of the artillery at the Battle of Warsaw. Like Sparr, he came from the Imperial army, where he had been *Zeuglieutenant*, and had found employment in Brandenburg in 1654 as captain of the Halberstadt militia. On campaign, the artillery also had a senior captain – *Oberhauptmann* – with the rank of major, with a variable number of *Stückhauptleute*, *Stücklieutenant* und *Stückjunker* as his seconds.

*Büchsenmeister*s and assistants formed the actual artillery crew. In June 1656, the field artillery numbered 50 *Büchsenmeisters* and 30 private artillerymen under a *Büchsenmeisterkorporal*. If necessary, other personnel were taken from the infantry companies to make up the necessary number of artillerymen. In addition, a large number of technical personnel were needed for explosives and equipment administration, as well as a number of craftsmen, in particular carpenters – who were enlisted in large numbers in the Netherlands – blacksmiths, leather craftsmen and saddle-makers.[136]

After 1660, a special commissioner of the artillery – the *Kommissarius* – was established, assisted by a *Secretarius*. On campaign, *Auditor*, *Quartiermeister*, *Proviantmeister*, *Proviantschreiber*, *Fourier*, *Profoss* and surgeon were also appointed. On 1 January 1672, the first artillery regulation was issued. Though the *Articulusbrief* looked more like a guild's job description than a military regulation, within it were prescribed precise training hours and the maintenance of pieces. Service hours were not to be less than nine hours per day, and penalties included being tied

Brandenburg Gunner, c. 1690. Plate X.46 from Richard Knötel's *Die Grosse Uniformenkunde* (Rathenow, 1900). Black hat with yellow edge; red cravat; dark blue cuffs; leather breeches; medium blue stockings; brass buttons; natural leather belt and bandolier. All gun carriages were painted red, with the metal parts painted black.

---

135 Jany, *Geschichte der Königlich Preußischen Armee*, p.174.
136 Jany, *Geschichte der Königlich Preußischen Armee*, p.174.

to the cannon as well as fines.[137] At the tactical-organisational level, from 1675 onwards a *Feldbattaillons Artillerie* with 12 officers and 200 artillerymen was established.[138]

For the Brandenburg princes, the most important way to turn artillery into a branch of the army was to standardise the training of artillerymen and concentrate them in Berlin. In November 1687, the Prince ordered the training of all artillerymen in the capital.[139] Interest in artillery was further stimulated by the development of several towns into modern arsenals. From 1679 onwards, this was especially true for Berlin, but also for cities such as Kustrin, Frankfurt, Löchnitz, Magdeburg, Pillau, Memel, Königsberg, Minden, Kolberg, Oderberg and Wesel.

Brandenburg 4lb field gun, late seventeenth century (Collection of the Brandenburg-Preußen Museum, Wustrau. Author's Photograph). At the time of the Northern War and in the years that followed, major attempts were made in the Brandenburg to develop the armaments industry, which had already started to produce guns and projectiles for the fortresses of Brandenburg in the first half of the sixteenth century. On 1 May 1658, the Elector Friedrich Wilhelm decreed 'that a high furnace, in which barrels, shells and other things of iron are cast, be built in our fortress of Peitz'. Workers were sent from the Harz region. The blast furnace opened in October 1658 and in 1668 produced 7,336 pieces of bullets of all calibres. Meanwhile, gun barrels also began to be cast in Peitz. On 15 December 1663, Landgrave Friedrich of Hesse-Homburg, who owned the fiefdom of Neustadt an der Dosse, was granted a patent for the production of iron artefacts, sharing profits (and losses) with the Elector. A blast furnace was also built here, used for the production of iron objects of all kinds and clay balls. The old Zehdenik ironworks, which had ceased operation, was reopened in 1653 and the first blast furnace was built between 1664 and 1668. It supplied ammunition for the artillery. Cannon production, however, was also entrusted to private local and foreign foundries. The supply of raw materials also continued to be supplemented by suppliers across the border, especially iron, which was purchased from Sweden until 1672.

---

137 Groehler, *Das Heerwesen in Brandenburg-Preußen*, p.91. The following regulation, issued in 1697, continued along these lines and led to the final formation of an artillery corps, entrusted to a unified general staff that replaced fortress commanders in the directing of the artillery, with modern requirements and in tune with what was happening in the rest of Western Europe.
138 Jany, *Geschichte der Königlich Preußischen Armee*, p.353.
139 Groehler, *Das Heerwesen in Brandenburg-Preußen*, p.91. A company of artillerymen and *Feurwerker*, denominated *Feurwerker und Bombardier-Kompagnie* was quartered in Berlin, comprising 20 *Feurwerker*, three *Korporale*, 39 *Bombardier*, five hautbois, a fife, and two drums.

THE ELECTORATE OF BRANDENBURG

Horses were partly provided by towns and feudal lords on the basis of the aforementioned *Lehnpferde*, and even by private benefactors. If the number remained insufficient, additional horses had to be bought or hired, but the government often resorted to requisitioning horses, and of course this was the practice in enemy territory. The drivers came from the countryside and were only hired for the duration of the campaign. These were not soldiers, received little care and attention from the officers, and according to the coeval sources formed a difficult group to control.[140]

For the 1656 campaign, a certain Johann Muschnau was hired as *Stallmeister* (stable master) of the artillery. He received a monthly salary from the commissioner and had to take responsibility for the care and maintenance of 900 horses, which were delivered to him, together with all harnesses, wagons and carts, with the exception of cannons and equipment. He was provided with quarter and fodder, and losses or damage due to fighting were compensated. The artillery remained in this condition throughout the war, although the individual composition fluctuated according to need. Regiment *Wolrad Waldeck zu Fuss* (BrI-6) already had two regimental pieces when it entered the Elector's service in 1655. In April 1656 he ordered 'that in future four light cannon and four wagons belonging to each regiment shall be used and conducted on campaign, and that therefore the servants and horses necessary for this purpose, which are in total eight servants and 16 horses for each regiment, shall be taken from the quarters in which each regiment is quartered.'[141] In a clear derogation to this order, six conductors and 12 horses were added to each regiment. In the 1656 campaign, six 3-pdr and eighteen 4-pdr cannons were used as regimental artillery. In the campaign of 1658 in Holstein, twenty 3-pdr light guns were used for the same purpose. Each cannon was entrusted to a *Büchsenmeister* with his assistants. The cannons were positioned in front of and between the brigades and served to support the effect of musket fire, which was limited to 100 paces, especially when the enemy was still some distance away. After 1656, there is no evidence of a permanent distribution of cannon to individual regiments.

In addition to the regimental pieces, the field army of 1655–56 had a small number of heavy cannons. In the spring of 1656, the field artillery consisted of four 6-pdrs, four 8-pdrs, two 12-pdrs, as well as four 16-pdr howitzers, making a total of 14 guns. How much the artillery at the Battle of Warsaw helped to repel the enemy's repeated and furious cavalry attacks is stated by War Commissioner Platen, who witnessed the battle and wrote: 'today the artillery did its best'.[142] For the campaign in Schleswig-Holstein in 1658, four 6-pdrs, six 8-pdrs, two 12-pdrs and four howitzers were brought

---

140 Jany, *Geschichte der Königlich Preußischen Armee*. For the march to Prussia in August 1655, as the servants supplied were running away in large numbers, four regiments of infantry had to command 25 men each, capable of handling horses, in order to serve as conductors of the field artillery. Once at the Vistula, the infantrymen returned to their regiments, as they were replaced by conductors hired in the Duchy of Prussia.

141 Ferdinand Hirsch, *Urkunden und Achtenstücke zur Geschichte des Kurfürsten Friedrich Wilhelm von Brandenburg* (Berlin, 1902), vol. XVII, p.314.

142 Jany, *Geschichte der Königlich Preußischen Armee*, p.118.

79

in. The 6-pdrs needed six horses, the 8-pdrs eight, the 12-pdrs 10 to 12, the howitzers four.

The reduction of the military force after 1660 also affected the artillery, which remained represented by one *Reducierte Compagnie* with a staff of three officers.[143] However, in 1672 the field artillery could deploy 28 light 3-pdrs, eight 4-pdrs, four 6-pdrs, four 12-pdrs, two 24-pdrs, four 16-pound howitzers and one 75-pdr firing stone projectiles. The train consisted of 696 horses of which 128 were for the ammunition wagons. The personnel comprised one *Oberstlieutenant*, two *Oberhauptleuten* (one of whom was an explosives expert), two *Stückhauptleuten*, two *Stücklieutenanten*, four *Stückjunker*, 14 *Feuerwerkern*, one *Quartiermeister*, two *Fourieren*, four *Fourierschützen*, three *Büchsenmeisterkorporalen*, 60 *Büchsenmeistern*, 60 *Handlangern* (assistants), two *Tambours* and one *Pauker* with his chart. The command of the artillery corps was entrusted to Colonel Wangelin, a German of Sweden, who held the office 'in very good order and condition'.[144] In the winter 1673–74, for the incoming campaign in Alsace, the field artillery assembled 42 cannons and howitzers. This figure comprised 36 light 3-pdr and 4-pdr guns, two 12-pdrs, two 8-pdrs, and two mortars.[145] Ammunition was transported in wagons and included bullets and canisters for the cannons, grenades and incendiary shells for the howitzers. The whole train required 1,000 draught animals.

Two years later, the artillery corps still numbered 16 officers and 200 men under one *Oberst*.[146] In 1678, at the siege of Stettin, there were 206 guns, mortars and howitzers, served by 300 *Constabler*, alongside 40 *Feuerwerker* and 24 miners.[147] In 168, the artillery corps had a permanent staff with five field officers, six captains, six lieutenants, 16 NCOs, 25 corporals, specialists, administrative personal and artillerymen, 511 men in all.[148]

In addition to its own ammunition, the artillery train also carried the necessary supply of ammunition for infantry and cavalry. In 1656, there were a further 32 wagons with gunpowder, match cords and musket balls. Finally, the artillery managed the necessary equipment for crossing rivers and marshes, which was indispensable due to the condition of roads and bridges in the seventeenth century. On 26 September 1659, the field army used a dismountable pontoon of boats to cross the River Trebel on the Pomeranian border.[149]

143　Mülverstedt, *Die Brandenburgische Kriegsmacht unter dem Großen Kurfürsten*, p.681; June 1550, *Hauptmann* Friedrich von Lesgewang, *Lieutenant* Joachim von Kappen, *Stückjunker* Dietrich von Oppen.

144　Jany, *Geschichte der Königlich Preußischen Armee*, p.214.

145　Rocholl, *Der Große Kurfürst von Brandenburg im Elsass*, p.23.

146　Louis von Malinowsky and Robert von Bonin, *Geschichte der Brandenburgisch-Preussischen Artillerie* (Berlin, 1842), vol. I, p.27.

147　Malinowsky and Bonin, *Geschichte der Brandenburgisch-Preussischen Artillerie*, p.27.

148　Malinowsky and Bonin, *Geschichte der Brandenburgisch-Preussischen Artillerie*, p.27. See the Appendix I for more detail.

149　Jany, *Geschichte der Königlich Preußischen Armee*, p.215.

THE ELECTORATE OF BRANDENBURG

Household Troops

Along with the *Leibregiment* of infantry, cavalry and dragoons, there were in Brandenburg companies of life guards which the Great Elector inherited from his predecessors. For many years, these companies were the first actual standing troops of the Electorate and held the rank of seniority within the army. The oldest unit was the *Märkische Garde*, established in 1615 as a permanent garrison for the Prince-Elector's residences. In 1653 the company numbered 33 officers and NCOs, 20 *Adelburschen* (noble cadets), and 247 lance-corporals and private guards.[150]

The *Markische Leibgarde* in a drawing of Karl Röchling (military post card, Darmstadt 1909).

In 1640, a second foot guard was also raised and denominated *Preussische Garde*. In 1658 there were four companies with 500 private guards, which served in Rastenburg alongside the *Leibgarde* company of the *Statthalter* of Prussia.[151] In 1672, the *Preussische Garde* was disbanded and joined to the regiment *Kurprinz zu Fuss* (BrI-11). The same fate fell on the *Märkische Garde*, which was disbanded and became the sixth battalion of the regiment *Garde zu Fuss* (BrI-9) in 1691. However, the most prestigious was the company of *Trabanten*, raised in 1632 in Berlin and entrusted with the horse escort service for the Prince-Elector and his family. By virtue of their proximity to the person of the sovereign, the *Trabanten* occupied the first rank of the cavalry,

---

150 Jany, *Geschichte der Königlich Preußischen Armee*, p.109.
151 Jany, *Geschichte der Königlich Preußischen Armee*, pp.143 and 147.

Trabanten-Garde in parade uniform, 1690; plate XIII.16 from Richard Knötel's *Die Grosse Uniformenkunde* (Rathenow, 1903). Black hat with gold edge and red ribbon; red cravat, medium blue tunic laced of gold with embroidered Prince-Elector's cross; buff leather coat with medium blue cuffs laced of silver; medium blue breeches; golden buttons; medium blue saddle cover with golden trim.

and in 1638 they became the *Leibcompagnie* of the cavalry regiment formed by joining the autonomous cavalry companies on campaign into a single unit, according to the usual pattern of this age. By 1652, the Prince-Elector raised a company of *Leibgarde zu Pferde* in the Duchy of Cleves with 54 guards.[152] Before the end of the year, the *Trabanten* company was increased to a squadron strength joining the *Leibgarde* of Cleves and the Statthalter' Life Guard. The *Trabanten* accompanied the Prince-Elector on campaign and participated in all the major encounters until 1679. After the Peace of Nijmegen, the squadron numbered 340 horsemen.[153] In 1688 there were two companies each with 150 horsemen, assigned to the Prince-Elector's residence in Berlin, Potsdam, Bernau, and Nauen the first company, and in Oranienburg, Wriezen Müncheberg, Treuenbriezen, Trebbin and Starussberg the second company.[154]

By 1687 the Great Elector raised two more mounted life guards, taking inspiration from the French *Maison du Roi*. The first were the two companies of the *Grands Mousquetaires*, which were composed of French émigré officers. The first company was quartered in Prenzlau under *Obrist Lieutenant* Christian zu Dohna, the second served in Fürstenwalde under *Obrist Lieutenant* du Saint Bonnet.[155] In 1688 the squadron numbered 326 horsemen in all. By November 1687, a company of 65 *Grenadiers à cheval* was also raised and like the *Grands Mousquetaires* included French émigrés ranking as NCOs. While the mounted musketeers became the regiment of *Gens d'Armes* in 1710, the grenadier company was disbanded in 1698.

---

152 Pelet-Narbonne, *Geschichte der Brandenburg-Preußischen Reiterei*, p.7.
153 Mülverstedt, *Die Brandenburgische Kriegsmacht unter dem Großen Kurfürsten*, p.29.
154 Mülverstedt, *Die Brandenburgische Kriegsmacht unter dem Großen Kurfürsten*, p.611.
155 Crouzas, *Die Organisationen des Brandenburgischen und Preußischen Heeres*, p.26.

Militia

By the middle of the seventeenth century, the Brandenburg militia had a long tradition, and unlike similar territorial defence formations was fully integrated into the Electorate and also provided volunteers for the regular troops. Its structure derived from the one existing in Poland, and it was based on the system of the *Wibranzen*, a term that derived from the Polish *Wybrancy*, meaning 'selected'. This word identified the foot militia organised by town and country, and in several respects it prefigured the more modern and familiar Prussian *Landwehr* of the following century. The performance of the *Wibranzen* was excellent, and like the *Landwehr* they formed entire regiments with senior officer and company staff like the professional troops. Although six *Wibranzen* regiments were transformed into regular infantry between 1656 and 1660,[156] the militia had a clear defensive role, since usually the 'selected' troops could be employed only in the defence of the Electoral domains. In 1655, when the regular army joined the Swedes in the war against Poland, the militia replaced the professional infantry as garrisons in the major fortresses. The question of service abroad, especially for noble chivalric horse, remained a matter of contention. In the 1650s the estates of Brandenburg declared that their *Lehnpferde*[157] would not serve outside the margravate. The declaration did not concern the other provinces of the Electorate, since by 1655 a cavalry regiment consisting of only *Lehnpferde* from Pomerania joined the field army.[158] Alongside the *Lehnpferde*, another source for mounted militia was the *Dienstpflichtigen*, namely the recruit of the compulsory service provided by cities and towns. However, according to the foreword for the reform of the militia introduced in 1703 under King Friedrich I, in the last decade of the seventeenth century the mounted militia had been much neglected and basically existed only on paper.[159]

The war of 1655–60 served as a catalyst for the formation of a stable defence system, which was elaborated in the *Defensionwerk* of 1644 by the *Landoberst* of Prussia Sigmund von Wallenrodt, and modified in 1649 and 1650 by the new *Landoberst* Christoph Albrecht von Schönheich. The document mainly served to establish a militia with rules of service, discipline and training updated to the new requirements, and organised into infantry, cavalry and dragoon companies to be entrusted to *Landoffizierer* appointed by the Prince-Elector. By 1655, 13 infantry, 16 cavalry and four dragoon companies had been formed in Prussia among the three districts of the Duchy, 5,570 men in all.[160] In August, the militia of Ducal Prussia

---

156 Georg Tessin, *Die Regimenter der Europäischen Staaten im Ancien Régime des XVI bis XVIII Jahrhunderts – Teil 1* (Biblio Verlag: Osnabrück, 1986), pp.105–106.

157 'Feudal Horse', as already discussed in Chapter 1.

158 Cavalry regiment *Manteuffel*, in Tessin, *Die Regimenter der Europäischen Staaten im Ancien Régime*, p.105.

159 Hermann von Gansauge, *Das Brandenburgisch-Preußische Kriegswesen um die Jahre 1440, 1640 und 1740* (Berlin, 1839), 'Verhandlungen aus den Jahren 1701–1705 wegen Stiftung von Miliz-Truppen in der gesamten Preußischen Monarchie', pp.205–206.

160 Jany, *Geschichte der Königlich Preußischen Armee*, p.112. According to Pelet-Narbonne, *Geschichte der Brandenburg-Preußischen Reiterei*, p.7, there were 18 cavalry troops.

was mustered and established in five infantry regiments of *Wibranzen*, a further four of *Dienstpflichtigen* and two of *Landsdragoner*.[161] This force did not fight during the years of the conflict against Poland and then Sweden. The mounted militia guarded the roads leading to the cities, and controlled the coastline.[162] The difference from the previous mounted militia was that these horsemen performed regular tasks, but their service was considered 'not very practical anywhere' and the funds were used to recruit professional cavalrymen for the field army.[163] Although their employment was limited to territorial control, Friedrich Wilhelm declared himself very satisfied with the ducal militia, to the extent that in 1667 he wrote to his successor: 'The Prussian state militia is fit for war, as I have experienced myself.'[164]

Alongside these militiamen, in the larger towns there were companies of civic guards, called interchangeably *Stadtwache* or *Stadgarde*, under officers who not only directed the activity but also had the task of training their men. The latter served voluntarily and received money for each day's service, usually at the city gates or during fairs and markets. In 1675 in the capital there was a city guard of 1,291 men divided into eight companies, assigned to seven posts in the suburb of Cölln and another 11 in Berlin.[165] After the city guards, each province had its own *Ausschuss* and *Landvolk* companies whose service was very limited, consisting of guarding bridges and border roads. Each province organised the militia according to its traditions, so in Pomerania there were companies of *Landjäger* and *Heidereitern*. The Swedish invasion of 1675 represented a further moment of transformation of the Electoral militia. In spring, Friedrich Wilhelm ordered the mobilisation of all militia companies in Brandenburg, Pomerania and Prussia. In November 1675, the cavalry of the Prussian militia numbered 1,732 *Dienstpflichtige* divided in three Kreisregiments: *Samländischer*, *Ratangischer* and *Oberländisher*. Each company had its own staff with one *Rittmeister*, one *Lieutenant*, one *Kornett*, one *Wachtmeister*, and three *Corporale*.[166] The *Wibranze* deployed a further three regiments from the same Kreis with 1,841 men. Each company had one *Hauptmann*, one *Lieutenant*, one *Fähnrich*, three *Sergeanten*, one *Gefreiter-Corporal*, one

Prince Johann Georg II of Anhalt-Dessau (1627–1693) presumably wearing the officer's uniform of his infantry regiment, dark blue coat laced and embroidered of gold lace and with gold buttons. In his right hand he holds a baton of command. The portrait was probably painted after the work of Jacques Vaillant (Saxe-Anhalt Museum, Quedlinburg).

---

161 Jany, *Geschichte der Königlich Preußischen Armee*, p.117.
162 Pelet-Narbonne, *Geschichte der Brandenburg-Preußischen Reiterei*, p.7.
163 Pelet-Narbonne, *Geschichte der Brandenburg-Preußischen Reiterei*, p.8.
164 Friedrich Förster, *Friedrich Wilhelm, der Grosse Kurfürst, und seine Zeit* (Berlin, 1885), p.103.
165 Jany, *Geschichte der Königlich Preußischen Armee*, pp.236–237.
166 Jany, *Geschichte der Königlich Preußischen Armee*, p.263.

Fourier, one *Capitaine d'Armes*, three *Corporale*, two *Tambours*. As for the dragoons, they comprised four companies with 414 men in all with the same staff of the cavalry, but the *Hauptmann* replaced the *Rittmeister*.[167] According to nineteenth century German historians, the Prince-Elector had at his service in the arsenals personnel trained in the use of rifled muskets 'who was well accustomed to military discipline.'[168] These, in addition to a thorough knowledge of the country, formed the basis of a light troop that was assembled in small detachments of *Jäger* during the war against the Swedes, and used both for the defence of the country and as support for the regular troops. Some of them were mounted, but only used their horses for transport and fought on foot with their firearms.

From Alsace to Pomerania: Brandenburg's War Campaigns 1673–1679

After 1660, the Brandenburg army did not execute campaigns as an autonomous force, but joined with the troops of the other German states, such as in Hungary and Transylvania in 1663–64. In late September 1672, 12,000 Brandenburg troops under general Johann Georg II of Anhalt-Dessau joined the Imperial army near Hildesheim, in the first campaign on the Lower Rhine in support of the Dutch Republic. However, neither Leopold I nor the Great Elector was prepared to face open hostilities with France, and above all the Emperor wanted to prevent Brandenburg taking advantage of the involvement of Cologne and Münster on the enemy side. The impasse was exploited by Friedrich Wilhelm to negotiate a truce with France, signed on 6 June 1673 in the village of Vossen.

In 1674, after entering the alliance against Louis XIV for the second time, the Great Elector gathered a corps of 16,000 men which represented an intermediate step between the small contingent of 1663–64 and an actual field army, because these troops operated alongside the Imperial army and the *Reich*'s contingents in Alsace under *Feldmarschall* Alexandre de Bournonville. On 1 August 1674, 10 regiments of infantry, 13 of cavalry, two of dragoons, and 42 cannons, totalling 15,400 men, of which 5,950 were Reiter and 1,150 dragoons, left the Electorate for the Upper Rhine. Two dragoon regiments joined the allied army on 2 October at Strasbourg, anticipating the rest of the contingents in their march, which arrived in Alsace in early January. On 29 December the Brandenburg dragoons were involved in the Battle of Mulhouse. Notwithstanding the defeat suffered by the Allies, both regiments seem to have performed well, since days later when then Prince-Elector met the Imperial General Dünnewald, he asked: 'How did my dragoons behave?'

---

167 Jany, *Geschichte der Königlich Preußischen Armee*, p.263.
168 Fedor von Köppen, *Preussens Heer in Bild und Wort, 1619–1889* (Glogau, 1900), p.7; Crouzas, *Die Organisationen des Brandenburgischen und Preußischen Heeres*, p.12.

Prince Carl Emil von Hohenzollern (1655–1674), second son of Friedrich Wilhelm and first to survive infancy. He joined his father on the Rhine campaign as *Obrist* of infantry regiment *Kurprinz* (Bri-11). The autumn of 1674 was cold and wet, leading to supply and sanitary problems, and disease in the army. Charles became ill in late November and at the start of December was sent to Strasbourg to recover. After seven days of a rising fever, he died of dysentery.

Dünnewald replied, 'Your Grace, with these boys I could drive the devil out!'[169]

Days later, the Great Elector and Bournonville shared the unfortunate outcome of the campaign against Turenne.[170] During the battle on 5 January, the Brandenburger troops occupied the left wing, which attempted to seize the village of Türkheim, but it was defeated by heavy fire from the French artillery. Losses were considerable: 300 dead and wounded, as claimed Friedrich Wilhelm in his letter.[171] The campaign had been particularly bitter for the Prince-Elector, since his cadet son Carl Emil died of illness on 7 December 1674 while serving with him as an infantry officer. On 10 January the Brandenburgers marched to the quarters assigned in Franconia, and on the same day the Prince-Elector learned the news of the Swedish invasion of Pomerania.

When Field Marshal Carl Gustav Wrangel invaded the Electorate on 25 December 1674, it was because of pressure from France and the need to secure supplies. Though the Swedish military objectives in Pomerania were unlimited, Stockholm was grateful to France for allowing her to retain possession of Stettin and other key locations in Pomerania in the Peace of Oliva. Another decisive factor was the concern of the Swedish court that a French defeat in the Netherlands would result in political isolation. Ultimately the goal of Sweden's entry into the war copied the French plan, and was to occupy undefended territories in the Electorate in order to force Friedrich Wilhelm to withdraw his troops from war zones in the Upper Rhine and the Alsace. Since September 1673, reports of troops movements were received in Berlin. In particular, the *Statthalter* of Brandenburg, Prince Johann Georg II of Anhalt-Dessau, informed the Prince-Elector about a talk with the Swedish envoy, in which he had announced that about 20,000 Swedish troops would be available in Pomerania before the end of the year.[172] The news of an impending attack by the Swedish army grew stronger when, in the second half of October, the

---

169 Pelet-Narbonne, *Geschichte der Brandenburg-Preußischen Reiterei*, p.42.
170 Regarding the Brandenburg participation on the campaign in Alsace, see Mugnai, *Wars and Soldiers*, vol. 2, pp.170–180.
171 Gustav Kortzfleisch, 'Der Oberelsässische Winterfeldzug 1674–75 und das Treffen bei Türckheim nach Archivalischen Quellen Bearbeitet', in *Beitrage Landes und Volkeskunde Elsass-Lothringen*, XXIX Heft (Strasbourg, 1904), p.142.
172 *Theatrum Europaeum*, Vol. XI (Frankfurt am Main, 1682), p.523.

THE ELECTORATE OF BRANDENBURG

Friedrich Wilhelm leads his army against the Swedes in a nineteenth century print (Author's Collection). In the early spring of 1674, when it became clear that the Great Elector would not withdraw from the war against France, the Swedish court issued the order for a stricter regime of occupation to be enforced in order to raise pressure on Berlin to pull out of the war. This change in Swedish policy followed swiftly, with the result that repression of the state and the civilian population increased sharply. Several contemporary chroniclers described these excesses as worse, both in extent and brutality, than during the Thirty Years' War. There was no significant fighting, however, until spring 1675. The *Statthalter* of Brandenburg, Johann Georg II of Anhalt-Dessau, described this state of limbo in a letter to the Elector in April 1675 as 'neither peace nor war'.

Swedish commander-in-chief arrived in Wolgast.[173] In spite of the disturbing news coming from Berlin, Friedrich Wilhelm did not believe that there was an imminent Swedish invasion in Pomerania. He expressed this in a letter to Anhalt-Dessau on 31 October 1674, which stated: 'I consider the Swedes better than that, and do not think they will do such a dastardly thing.'[174] This was a major mistake.

---

173 To support Wrangel, who was over 60 years old, often bedridden and suffering from gout, generals Simon Grundel-Helmfelt and Otto Wilhelm von Königsmarck were appointed alongside him. However, Helmfelt, a veteran of the Thirty Years' War, also suffered from illness and declined his post and was replaced by Conrad Mardefelt.
174 Förster, *Friedrich Wilhelm, der Grosse Kurfürst*, p.128.

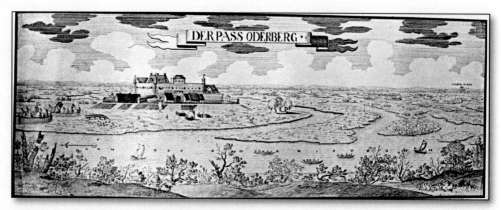

Although the Electorate did not have many modern fortresses, a good defence was ensured by the network of small forts guarding strategic locations. The fortress of Oderberg, in Pomerania, controlled the Oder river crossing and housed a garrison. Before the massive improvement of 1702, the fortifications had already been strengthened in 1688.

In the days after the invasion, Wrangel established his headquarters at Prenzlau, and advanced cautiously in the Uckermark awaiting for the news from the Swedish representative in Berlin. On 30 December 1674, Hagen informed Anhalt-Dessau that the Swedish army would leave the Electorate as soon as Brandenburg ended the war with France. A complete break in relations between Sweden and Brandenburg was not intended however.[175]

Wrangel and Friedrich Wilhelm had known each other personally since 1656, and both considered logistics the most important matter. In this regard, the Swedish general had warned King Carl XI that Pomerania was too poor to support a strong army. Pomerania, like Brandenburg, mostly consisted of sandy plains interspersed with rivers and canals, which made military operations difficult. Although rivers were not large and easily crossable, swamps and marshes represented considerable obstacles, and then each bridge and village became strategically important. The early phase of the invasion was very far from the occupations of the Thirty Years' War. Wrangel ordered the troops not to abuse the population and to pay for their supplies. However, the mild attitude of the Swedish commander did not avoid the flight of the inhabitants, so most provisions had to be taken without pay.[176] The undefined assignment prevented clear orders being issued, so that the advance of the Swedish army continued very slowly. This allowed Berlin to face the threat, at least with the small forces at its disposal. The regular force available in Brandenburg after the departure of the main army for Alsace was very low. The garrisons were under the established strength and many soldiers were old or disabled.[177] The overall strength of the garrison troops that Anhalt-Dessau had at his disposal in early 1674 was around 3,000 men.

---

175 Michael Rohrschneider, *Johann Georg II. von Anhalt-Dessau (1627–1693). Eine Politische Biographie* (Berlin: Duncker & Humblot, 1998), p.239.
176 Michael Fredholm von Essen, *Charles XI's War. The Scanian War between Sweden and Denmark, 1675–1679* (Warwick: Helion & Company, 2019), p.57.
177 Jany, *Geschichte der Königlich Preußischen Armee*, p.230.

THE ELECTORATE OF BRANDENBURG

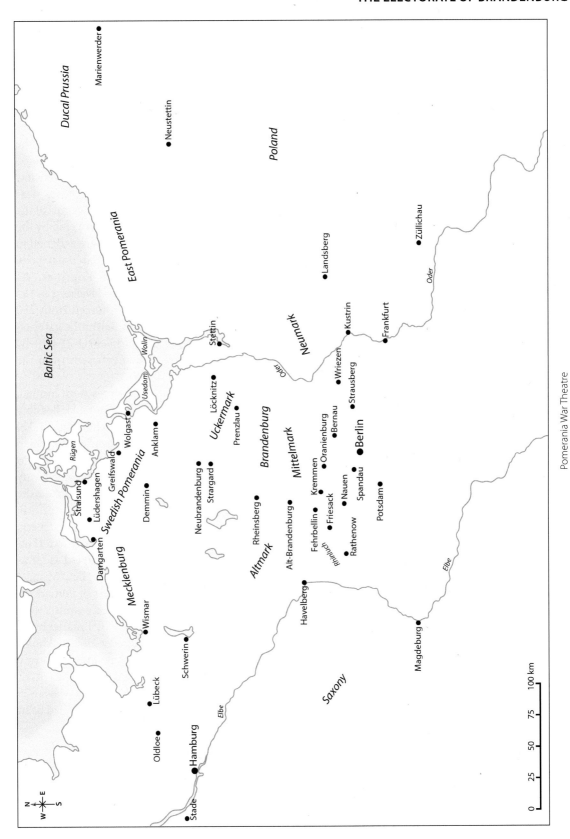

Pomerania War Theatre

In Berlin there were only 500 aged soldiers, left behind due to their limited fighting ability, and 300 new recruits.[178] The recruitment of new troops had therefore to be enforced immediately. The governor issued a general call up to the rural population and the towns and cities, in order to compensate for the lack of regular soldiers. On 20 May, while the main army was still marching in Germany, Friedrich Wilhelm ordered the militia to carry out guerrilla warfare against the Swedes.

Without further reinforcements the regions of the Neumark east of the Oder and the whole of Pomerania could not be held, except at a few fortified locations. The Mittelmark, by contrast, could be manned with relatively few troops, because to the north there were only a few easily defended passes, near Oranienburg, Kremmen, Fehrbellin and Friesack, through the swamps of the Havelland Luch and the Rhinluch. In the east, the march was covered by the course of the Oder. The few available Brandenburg soldiers were assigned to the fortified locations. In this way, as a result of the strategic circumstances, Brandenburg's defences were formed along the line from Köpenick, via Berlin, Spandau, Oranienburg, Kremmen, Fehrbellin and Havelberg to the River Elbe. In addition, the garrison of Spandau was reinforced from 250 to 800 men; it also had 24 cannon of varying calibres. In Berlin the garrison was increased to 5,000 men, including the *Leibdragoner* (BrD-7) sent by Friedrich Wilhelm from Franconia, and the reinforcements sent from the Westphalian domains already in January.

Musketeer with swinesfeather and artillerymen, 1670s, by Richard Knötel.

However, even the Swedish forces were limited, the exact number of troops still disputable. Possibly Wrangel's army numbered approximately 13,000 men at the beginning of the invasion,[179] which had fallen to 12,000 after four months due to desertion, since the soldiers did not receive any salary from December.[180] This drawback made the Swedish invasion even more phlegmatic. By April, Swedish troops had occupied Stargard, Landsberg, Neustettin, Kossen, and Züllichau in order to recruit there as well. East Pomerania was occupied as far as Lauenburg and several smaller places. Then Wrangel settled the Swedish army into quarters in Pomerania and the Neumark, and some advanced outposts were settled on the River Havel and Alt-Brandenburg, west of Berlin. The French envoy in Stockholm demanded on 20 March that the Swedish army extend its occupation to Silesia and conduct itself in agreement with French plans. In early May 1675 the Swedes began the spring campaign that had been

---

178 Jany, *Geschichte der Königlich Preußischen Armee*, p.230.
179 According to the *Theatrum Europaeum*, p.566, the Swedes were 7,620 infantry and 6,080 cavalry with 15 guns. Concerning this latter figure, Hesse, *Charles XI's War*, p.58, gives for the artillery 38 guns.
180 Hessen, *Charles XI's War*, p.58.

THE ELECTORATE OF BRANDENBURG

strongly urged by the French. Wrangel and his officers had been recruiting soldiers, but suffered further losses due to disease and desertion. The Swedish plan was to cross the Elbe to link up with Swedish forces in Bremen-Verden. The Swedish army entered the Uckermark, passing through Stettin; although the capability of it was not comparable to that of earlier times, the former view of Sweden's military might remained. This led, not least, to rapid early success. The first fighting took place in the region of Löcknitz, where on 5 May 1675 the fortified castle held by a 180-man garrison surrendered after a day of shelling of the Swedish artillery, in return for free passage to Oderburg.[181] Following the conquest of Löcknitz, the Swedes advanced south and occupied Neustadt, Wriezen and Bernau. Their next objective was the Rhinluch, which was only passable in a few places. These had been occupied by the Brandenburg *Landjäger* militia, armed peasants and volunteers. Learning about the Swedish offensive, Anhalt-Dessau sent troops from Berlin and six cannon as reinforcements under Major General Sommerfeld in order to coordinate the defence of the passes at Oranienburg, Kremmen and Fehrbellin. On 14 May, the Swedes advanced on the Rhine line in three columns: the first against Oranienburg; the second against Kremmen; and the third, which at 2,000 men was the strongest, against Fehrbellin. There was heavy fighting for the river crossing which lasted several days in front of Fehrbellin. Because the Swedes did not succeed in breaking through here, the column diverted to Oranienburg where, thanks to advice from local farmers, a crossing had been found which enabled about 2,000 Swedes to press on to the south. As a consequence the positions on either side at Kremmen, Oranienburg and Fehrbellin had to be abandoned by Sommerfeld. Shortly thereafter, the Swedes mounted an unsuccessful storming of Spandau. However, the whole of Havelland was now occupied and Wrangel established his headquarters in the town of Alt-Brandenburg, but after the capture of Havelberg the command moved to Rheinsberg on 8 June. Field Marshal Wrangel, who left Stettin on 6 June to follow the army, only made it as far as Neu-Brandenburg because a severe attack of gout left him bedridden for 10 days. The command passed to his half-brother Lieutenant General Wolmar Wrangel. Sick and borne on a chair, Carl Gustav Wrangel finally reached Neuruppin on 9 June. He immediately ordered reconnaissance detachments to be sent towards Magdeburg. On 11 June, he left with an infantry regiment and two cavalry regiments for Havelberg, which he reached the next day, preparing to occupy the Altmark the following summer. To this end he had all available boats gathered on the Havel River to build a pontoon bridge across the Elbe.[182]

Because of the cold weather and the losses suffered in Alsace, and after learning of the enemy's poor progress in the opening phase of the invasion, the Prince-Elector decided that he would not deploy his main army immediately on a new campaign in Pomerania, and remained in Schweinfurt

---

181 Jany, *Geschichte der Königlich Preußischen Armee*, p.238. As a result, Götz was later sentenced to death by a court-martial and executed on 24 March 1676.

182 Friedrich Ferdinand Carlson, *Geschichte Schwedens: Bis zum Reichstage 1680* (Gotha, 1885), p.605.

91

until late May. Friedrich Wilhelm had to negotiate before he left the Upper Rhine. For this purpose, on 9 March he went for talks at The Hague, which he reached on 3 May. The negotiations and necessary appointments with the friendly powers gathered there lasted until 20 May. As a result, Holland and Spain declared war on Sweden at the urging of the Prince-Elector. Apart from this, he received no concrete assistance from the *Reich* or Denmark. On 22 May 1675, the Great Elector held a military parade in the quarters on the River Main, the day after he divided the army into three columns and headed north. Between 27 and 28 May, after a march through Meiningen, Erfurt and Merseburg, the columns crossed the western border of the Electorate at Halle. After some days of rest, the army reached Magdeburg on 11 June. Despite having crossed the formidable Thuringian Forest, which was still relatively barren of resources, the Brandenburgers moved rapidly, covering nearly 200 miles in 20 days. The march was celebrated as a remarkable operation in Berlin and by the Allies, since the difficult march had not affected the army, who still numbered 14,000 men.[183] In Magdeburg, Friedrich Wilhelm learned that the enemy had dispersed to forage for supplies.[184] The War Council examined the strategic situation and focused on the roads that connected the Swedish outposts and the main army. Among these, one road passed through the village of Rathenow, where the River Havel could be crossed. Despite receiving intelligence that the Brandenburg army was on its way, the Swedish commanders neglected reconnaissance.[185]

On the evening of 14 June, a Brandenburg strike force of 5,000–6,000 cavalry, 800 dragoons and 1,350 infantry supported by 15 light guns,[186] marched undetected under *Feldmarschall* Georg von Derfflinger to Rathenow, where the vanguard arrived early in the morning. Inside the village, about 500 Swedish horsemen were quartered. Since Derfflinger had served in the Swedish army in the 1640s he spoke some Swedish, and therefore managed to persuaded the enemy picket to open the gates to him and his dragoons. As the Brandenburg dragoons entered the village they took the enemy by surprise. About 390 Swedish soldiers were killed and a further 192 captured, including the commander and his wife. The successful action brought to Derfflinger and his men 500–600 horses, six standards and a pair of kettledrums.[187]

That same day the Swedish main army marched to Havelberg, intending to cross the Elbe, but the strategic scenario had changed dramatically after the capture of Rathenow. Upon hearing of the unexpected event, the Wrangel

---

183 Jany, *Geschichte der Königlich Preußischen Armee*, p.237.

184 Carlson, *Geschichte Schwedens*, p.603. To make matters worse, disputes broke out amongst the Swedish officers, resulting in discipline being lost and serious plundering and other abuses by the soldiery occurring against the civil population. Furthermore, the lack of supply forced the Swedish commander to disperse the army over a wide area to be supplied with the necessary food and provision. As a result, the Swedes lost two valuable weeks crossing the Elbe.

185 Hessen, *Charles XI's War*, p.59. Standard Swedish practice since the Thirty Years' War was to follow up an intelligence report with further questions to the reporting officers, and to send out cavalry patrols to gather further information in the area. After the failure of the campaign, a commission was appointed by King Carl XI for an enquiry, which found that neither practice had been followed.

186 Jany, *Geschichte der Königlich Preußischen Armee*, p.239.

187 Pelet-Narbonne, *Geschichte der Brandenburg-Preußischen Reiterei*, p.51.

The arrival of the Brandenburg army at Magdeburg in June 1675 in a nineteenth century print. (Author's Collection) The Great Elector is dressed more or less correctly, while the bourgeoisie are shown wearing very anachronistic clothing.

brothers, shocked by the surprise, incorrectly estimated the enemy numbers. Judging the Brandenburg strike force to be much greater in strength than it actually was, Wrangel opted to withdraw. This was exactly what Friedrich Wilhelm had expected. He was already ordering Derfflinger to cut off the Swedish retreat, but Derfflinger opposed the plan, arguing that his men were too exhausted from the march and the assault on Rathenow. The Great Elector, backed by Prince Friedrich of Hessen-Homburg, overruled him, stressing the need for a decisive campaign.[188] A loyal soldier, Derfflinger dropped his objection and set out at once.

The ensuing separation of the Swedish armies, who were caught entirely by surprise, meant that a crossing of the Elbe was no longer possible. Wrangel, who was in Havelberg without supplies, now ordered the main Swedish army under Wolmar Wrangel to join him via Fehrbellin. In order to facilitate the task for his half-brother, Carl Gustav left for Neustadt on 16 June. The Brandenburg vanguard found the Swedes spread out for four miles along the Havel River from Havelberg in the north to Alt-Brandenburg in the south. To the Swedish rear lay a large swamp: a certain disadvantage

---

188 Förster, *Friedrich Wilhelm, der Grosse Kurfürst*, p.165.

The Great Elector and General Derfflinger the day before the Battle of Fehrbellin depicted in a nineteenth century German print. (Author's Collection)

should a sudden, hurried retreat be necessary. According to local spies, the Swedes again had no idea that the Prince-Elector's army had drawn so close. Oblivious to the circumstances, the Swedish army concentrated solely on garrison duties and the brutal business of suppressing the numerous peasant uprisings in the area.[189]

The Great Elector's target was Waldemar's contingent, which had left Alt-Brandenburg and was heading east for the small town of Fehrbellin, on the Rhine. Aware that Fehrbellin was the only suitable place to cross the marshes, Derfflinger knew exactly which route the younger Wrangel would take. The Brandenburg cavalry raced forward, hoping to cut off Waldemar at Nauen; a Brandenburg corps of 1,200 cavalry and dragoons under *Obrist Lieutenant* Sydow had moved to this town on 16 June, where the two armies engaged in the first field encounter of the war.[190] Nauen was only accessible via a narrow embankment on the lake side extending to the south. At the most profitable point, two companies of Swedish infantry with some guns were entrenched awaiting for the enemy. However, they refrained from resisting when they discovered the large number of enemy horsemen, threw the cannons into the nearby lake and hastily retreated. The fleeing troops were pursued by Sydow and his cavalry to the outskirts of the town. Most of the Swedish army had already retreated, crossing a stream behind the town. A battalion of Swedish musketeers inside Nauen was pressed by the Brandenburgers who engaged

---

189 Jany, *Geschichte der Königlich Preußischen Armee*, p.241.
190 This episode has often been neglected by German historians, since Rathenow and Fehrbellin were the most resounding actions, but the battle revealed the strategic disposition of the two sides: the Brandenburg army on the offensive to the bitter end, and the Swedes instead trying to avoid any confrontation.

THE ELECTORATE OF BRANDENBURG

in a fierce fight. Even before reinforcements arrived, 200 Brandenburg cavalrymen managed to drive off 1,000 of the enemy forming Waldemar's rearguard. Running out of ammunition, the Swedish infantry inside Nauen hastily abandoned the position under pressure from the Sydow's cavalrymen. However, the latter were unable to cross the stream. On the other bank, the Swedes had placed a battery with several cannons. Their fire forced the Brandenburgers to retreat. Meanwhile, the Swedish army had formed up in full battle order. Derfflinger managed to cross the stream with his cavalry on the bridge, which had been damaged by the Swedish artillery, and despite the enemy fire managed to place three cannons which successfully responded. Realising that Waldemar's position was still favourable, Derfflinger assessed that continuing the attack was too risky. He was therefore given the order to retreat to Nauen and make camp for the night.[191]

At Nauen the Swedes had managed to thwart the enemy plan. It would be up to another force, speeding towards Fehrbellin itself, to block the Swedish escape. Led by Colonel Joachim Henniges von Treffenfeld, the Brandenburgers consisted of a mere 130 horsemen. Their purpose was to avoid the enemy, enter the town and destroy the bridge, thus severing the Swedish retreat.[192] Upon reaching its destination the raiding party immediately set the bridge afire, but the destruction had barely commenced when the Swedes began arriving early on 28 June. Waldemar found the bridge smouldering yet still very much intact, and it needed only minor repairs before it could be crossed. Friedrich Wilhelm had no intention of providing the time necessary for them, declaring confidently, 'We are so close to the enemy, that he must lose his hair or his feathers.'[193] Waldemar now knew that the main Brandenburg army was close, but he did not fear an imminent attack. He correctly surmised that the only way Friedrich Wilhelm could possibly reach him before the bridge was repaired was with cavalry alone, and he believed such an assault without infantry support would be far too risky. At least one man on the field, however, already knew that the Great Elector intended to roll the dice. That man was Henning, who, along with his horsemen, was already hiding inside Fehrbellin, hoping to delay the Swedes as long as possible. The wait was brief. Shortly after Waldemar's arrival, the vanguard of the Brandenburg cavalry under Hessen-Homburg arrived on the scene. Friedrich Wilhelm, still en route, ordered the Prince to await his arrival, but Hessen-Homburg was impatient, and determining the Swedes to be on their last legs, ordered an immediate charge through the pouring rain. Initially, the Brandenburg cavalry was successful in pushing the defenders back, but the Swedes fought tenaciously and quickly brought the offensive to a halt. Waldemar was determined to retreat across the bridge, no matter what.

Friedrich Wilhelm, Derfflinger, and the rest of the Brandenburg cavalry arrived at noon, raising the Elector's total strength to roughly 7,000 horsemen

---

191 Alois Straka, *Schlacht bei Fehrbellin, 18. Juni 1675* (Fehrbellin: Rat der Stadt, 1987), pp.77–78.

192 Ernst Friedrich Christian Müsebeck, *Die Feldzüge des Grossen Kurfürsten in Pommern 1675–1677* (Marburg, 1897), p.65.

193 Förster, *Friedrich Wilhelm, der Grosse Kurfürst*, p.166.

against the equally numerous Swedes. Unlike the Great Elector, Waldemar also possessed infantry and he considered this a decisive advantage. Rather than exploit his advantage with an immediate counter-attack, inexplicably the Swedish commander ordered his troops to stay in position. Waldemar soon realised his error when the rest of the Brandenburg cavalry reached the field and soon occupied the hills opposite the Swedish right. This exposed the Swedes to the danger of being outflanked. Waldemar had no choice but to attack, only now he would be forced to make an exposed uphill charge. The Prince-Elector positioned his 13 light guns atop the hill in preparation for an enemy assault. Of the Swedish 38 cannons, only seven were operational, and would be unable to assist in the assault. Furthermore, the Swedish left, hindered by the marshes, would be unable to add any additional weight to the action. Already the Brandenburg artillery was raining hell down upon the Swedes, forcing them to move. On Waldemar's command a wave of Swedish infantry, followed by cavalry, stormed up the hill. Despite the cannon fire searing through their ranks, the Swedish assault progressed well, putting the battle's outcome in doubt; the infantry reached the hill's summit and captured the Brandenburg artillery, and it appeared that the gambling Prince-Elector was about to be routed. But Friedrich Wilhelm had no intention of meekly accepting defeat. Rallying his men, he raced to the front of the line, crying: 'Forward! Your prince and captain will conquer with you, or die like a soldier!'[194] In his zeal, the Elector suddenly found himself surrounded by enemy soldiers. His master of stables, Emanuel Froben, was struck down, supposedly on account of his riding the Prince-Elector's grey horse: an exchange in mounts having been made to help ensure the Elector's safety. The situation was dire, but to Friedrich Wilhelm's great fortune, some dragoons pierced the enemy ranks and extracted him from harm. Meanwhile, the Elector's bravery had inspired his men, and the Brandenburg troops began to drive back the Swedes.[195] They recaptured their guns, which to everyone's amazement had not been spiked, and poured furiously down the opposite slope of the hill. With their cannons blazing, the Brandenburg cavalry smashed into the remnants of the disordered Swedish right and sent it fleeing into Fehrbellin.

The Brandenburg officers urged Friedrich Wilhelm to burn the town, but he rebuked them, stating, 'I am not come to destroy my country, but to save it.'[196] Instead, the Prince-Elector ordered his horsemen to storm the Swedish infantry. The ensuing charge failed, and the desperate Swedish soldiers held firm; Friedrich Wilhelm called off further offensives and was content to allow the remaining Swedes to withdraw. Exhausted by days of hard riding and fighting, the Brandenburg cavalry declined to pursue. Waldemar, satisfied to cross the now-repaired bridge, crossed the River Rhin in good order, leaving behind eight of his cannons.

---

194 Förster, *Friedrich Wilhelm, der Grosse Kurfürst*, p.167.
195 Melle Kinkenborg, *Fehrbellin: Nach Berichten und Briefen der Führende Männer* (Leipzig, 1913), p.81.
196 Müsebeck, *Die Feldzüge des Grossen Kurfürsten*, p.67.

THE ELECTORATE OF BRANDENBURG

The Battle of Fehrbellin; the fourth tapestry of the series *Kriegstaten des Großen Kurfürsten* ('The Great Elector's Deeds of War') focusing on his campaigns against the Swedes between 1675 and 1679. Here, the Elector is depicted as a victorious commander who reaffirms his territorial claims, as the territories he conquered in Western Pomerania were awarded back to Sweden in the interests of European balance at the Peace of Saint-Germain-en-Laye of 1679. Until well into the eighteenth century, tapestries were regarded as an effective means of displaying princely power. The city and landscape views in the backgrounds are based on drawings by the Dutchman Abraham Jansz Begeijn, who was appointed court painter to the Elector of Brandenburg in 1688. Through the contributions of the artists Rutger von Langenfeld, Paul Carl Leygebe and the brothers Jean-François and Alexander Casteels, who demonstrably designed the cartons for this series, this is a very precious source illustrating military clothing of the Brandenburg army in the last quarter of the seventeenth century.

The Brandenburg victory at Fehrbellin came at the cost of only 500 men. Swedish casualties were slightly higher, between 500 and 600 dead and wounded, and they would lose still more as a result of incessant peasant raids. At the close of the campaign, Carl Gustav Wrangel had 13,500 men at his disposal, but his army found themselves back on Swedish territory, from where they had started the war.[197] Nevertheless, both sides claimed victory. Friedrich Wilhelm celebrated his driving off the Swedes from Pomerania, while Waldemar Wrangel insisted that his bloody assault had delayed the enemy long enough to save the bulk of his force. Strategically, however, the triumph belonged to the Great Elector and his army, which earned Brandenburg the distinction of being the first German state to deal such a stunning blow to a major European power.

Sweden's overall strategic situation deteriorated further when, between June and July, the Holy Roman Empire and Denmark declared war on Sweden. King Carl XI was now in a difficult situation, attacked on several fronts and isolated from his French ally by Dutch–Danish naval superiority. The Allies estimated that Sweden would not be able to gather a field army capable of taking the offensive into enemy territory for the rest of the year. The opportunity had to be exploited without delay. Between June and July,

---

197 Hessen, *Charles XI's War*, p.64.

Detail of the monument to the Battle of Fehrbellin, built in 1875 for the two hundredth anniversary (Author's Photograph). Countless myths surround the battle – a major Brandenburg success achieved thanks to the courageous fighting of the Prince-Elector's soldiers. After the victory, Friedrich Wilhelm actually became 'The Great Elector'. Although the Brandenburg victory at Fehrbellin on 18 June 1675 resulted in no real territorial gains, it was significant for its propaganda value, because it was the first major defeat of a Swedish army in a considerable time. As a consequence, every episode that occurred during the battle became iconic in the German Empire, and augmented the myth of the Great Elector as the founder of the Prussian military tradition.

the combined Brandenburg and Imperial army that faced the Swedes consisted of some 20,000 men, and was growing towards 30,000. To this force, the Danish army added a further 18,000 troops for the campaign against Wismar on the German Baltic coast, where Sweden had its largest port and which was also the most suitable starting point for an attack on Denmark.[198] The Allies also prepared another contingent for seizing the Swedish territory of Bremen-Verden with troops from Habsburg Austria, Münster and Brunswick duchies.

By early August 1675, the Brandenburg army marched into Swedish Pomerania. Thirty days later, the Danes led by King Christian V advanced on Oldloe and joined the Brandenburg army. A council of war met in September 1675 a few miles from Stralsund, and the Danish King and the Great Elector decided to postpone the conquest of the city and agreed to besiege Wismar as soon as the Danish fleet could support the Brandenburg army. The Danish fleet therefore sailed to Wismar. As the Swedish fleet threatened a naval relief, the island of Poel – the granary of the fortress of Wismar – was conquered by 2,000 Brandenburg soldiers. The Allies' Great Elector and King Christian V of Denmark agreed that Wismar would pass to Denmark after its capture, and on 4 October Wismar was blockaded by the Danes under the command of Major General Sandberg with 5,000 men. The Duke of Mecklenburg, whose territory had been crossed by Danish and Brandenburg troops, protested unsuccessfully, and had to pay for the supply of the troops. The blockade of the harbour, which began on 24 October 1675, proved to be a very effective measure. The main Danish army headed to Damgarten and joined the Brandenburg troops in front of Wismar on 29 October. There were up to 18,000 men, with an artillery train of 76 cannons; inside Wismar, Carl Gustav Wrangel, the defeated governor of Swedish Pomerania, had 1,344 infantry, 200 dragoons and 1,000 militiamen.[199]

Meanwhile, in late September, the Brandenburg corps under *Generalwachtmeister* Schwerin entered Swedish Pomerania from the east,

---

198 Hessen, *Charles XI's War*, p.67.
199 Müsebeck, *Die Feldzüge des Grossen Kurfürsten*, p.68.

across the River Oder. According to the plan issued by the War Council, in early October, Schwerin seized by surprise the weakly garrisoned islands of Usedom and Wollin. On 21 October, having penetrated the enemy defences under Mardefelt in eastern Pomerania, the Brandenburg troops laid siege to the fortress of Wolgast. The fortress guarded the access to the Baltic Sea from the River Oder, and therefore had a relevant strategic value, and for this reason Wolgast had been reinforced with soldiers and improved with additional defences since 1660. The Swedes offered a strong resistance, but on 31 October, after the explosion of the gunpowder magazine, the garrison surrendered. With this conquest of Wollin and Usedom the Allies could control this vital sector, which also meant that the Swedish fortresses of Demmin, Anklam and Stettin no longer could be supplied by sea. However, although these places were exposed, they had strong garrisons and winter was approaching.

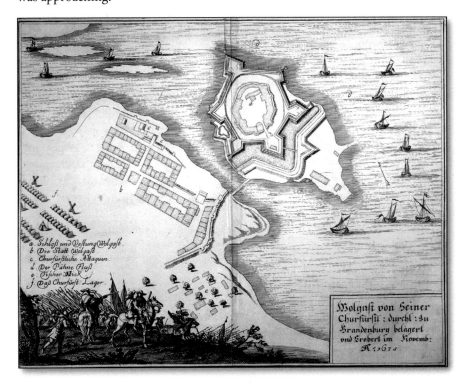

The strongly fortified position of Wolgast in a contemporary print. (Author's Collection)

In early November, at Wismar, the besiegers threw up the redoubts of the city gates and stepped up their attacks. Because of the severe frost and the resulting consolidation of the marshy ground, Wrangel considered surrender, but when the weather changed at the end of November he decided to continue the resistance, and as a result the Brandenburg–Danes intensified the pressure. A Swedish attempt by Count Königsmarck to relieve Wismar from Stralsund failed. Despite the stubborn defence of the Swedes and bad weather with rain and snow, the besiegers under Lieutenant General Niels Rosenkrantz succeeded in storming the city on 13 December. Together with representatives of the council and the tribunal, the Swedish governor Wrangel agreed favourable surrender conditions with Rosencrantz. Wrangel surrendered on 14 December with free right of departure to Stralsund; 500 infantry and 150 dragoons left the city.

In the winter 1675–76, the Allies discussed the plan for the next campaign. Friedrich Wilhelm agreed to continue the campaigns in Swedish Pomerania, and to support the German operation in the principality of Bremen-Verden. The goals were the Swedish fortresses of Stettin and Stralsund. In early 1676, some 2,000 Brandenburg soldiers moved from Minden heading to Bremen. In spring, Friedrich Wilhelm assembled the troops for the campaign in Swedish Pomerania: the field army numbered 12,000 men including Danish and Imperial cavalry. As usual for the Great Elector, he did not start the operation before gathering all the troops and storing enough provisions and fodder in the magazines, and this delayed the beginning of the campaign until June. On 17 August the Allies seized Anklam, and on 30 September Demmin also surrendered. Only then did the Great Elector turn to Stettin, which had already resisted an Imperial–Brandenburg siege in September–November 1659.[200] This time the siege lasted for about a month, but once again, the Great Elector was forced to leave the siege due to poor weather, and march back to winter quarters.

In July 1677, the Allies besieged Stettin again with 20,000 Brandenburg and allied troops supported by a powerful siege artillery. Inside the city, Major General Wulfen had no more than 2,300 regular soldiers and possibly a further 2,000 militiamen.[201] In an attempt to bend the garrison by a blockade, Stettin was targeted by intense artillery fire, and the Allies only performed the first direct assault on 10 December. By then the defenders were almost out of ammunition and supplies, and no relief force could be expected, since the Danish and Dutch fleet had closed access to the city by sea. On 11 December Wulfen opened surrender talks, and 15 days later he left Stettin with some 700 soldiers permitted to carry away their weapons.[202]

Meanwhile, following the Swedish defeat at Malmö and Landskrona, the Great Elector agreed to support Denmark with 1,500 cavalry and dragoons for the incoming campaign against Stralsund. The plan was to conquer the island of Rügen in order to also isolate the city from the sea, and to deprive the Swedes of their primary source of fodder for the cavalry. On 3 September 1677, the Danish and Dutch fleet sailed to the island of Rügen and landed the troops without encountering resistance. The allied army, under King Christian of Denmark, numbered 7,300 men including troops from Denmark and Brandenburg, as well as Habsburg Austria, Hessen-Kassel, and Münster. This invasion force crossed the island to seize the *Altefähr* and the *Neuefähr*, the two fortified connections with Stralsund on the south side. The island had a small garrison of just 200 infantry, while in Stralsund 5,800 men were quartered. Caught by surprise by the enemy landing, the Swedish commander of Stralsund, Otto Wilhelm von Königsmarck, concentrated

---

200 See Mugnai, *Wars and Soldiers*, vol. 2, pp.135–141.

201 Müsebeck, *Die Feldzüge des Grossen Kurfürsten*, p.78.

202 According to Friedrich Thiede, *Chronik der Stadt Stettin: Bearbeitet nach Urkunden und den Bewährten Historischen Nachrichten* (Stettin 1849), p.754, during the siege 2,443 civilians also died.

THE ELECTORATE OF BRANDENBURG

Tapestry of the siege of Stettin, (Oranienburg Palace Museum). In the right foreground, the Prince-Elector Friedrich Wilhelm and his heir Prince Friedrich follow the explanations of a general standing to their left, who is presumably the Prince of Homburg. In front of them, a young page or officer raises a plan to which their conversation refers. Derfflinger appears to the right of the group with his left arm raised. Scenes of the siege are depicted vividly and in great detail in the foreground: the embroidered saddle cover and pistol holsters on the left, and the page on the right with the plan looks to his side, where two men are rolling a barrel. While Stettin can be seen in the background on the left and the wide flowing Oder on the right, the middle ground is dominated by the detailed depiction of the Brandenburg artillery. The perspective has been shifted in favour of the visibility of detail. The artillery constables on the left wear a blue coat with red cuffs, while servants and other artillerymen are dressed in grey, brown and even green. In the background, the infantry wear coats of blue, grey and red.

the few island troops in Neuefähr, which had stronger fortifications. King Christian, unaware of the enemy weakness and receiving information about a major Swedish cavalry force on the island, did not assault either bastion, but contented himself with establishing an outpost as observation point. Only when the cavalry landed did he move out of the outpost occupying the islands, but he left *Neuefähr* in Swedish hands. In October Christian returned to Copenhagen, leaving the command at Rügen to his second in command, Rumohr. The expeditionary corps on Rügen soon began to suffer from attrition, in particular from disease. Moreover, one of the Brandenburg regiments of cavalry was called back from the ongoing siege of Stettin, and replaced by poorly trained horsemen.

Detail from the landing at Rügen in 1677, with the fortress of Neuefähr in background, engraving by Romeyn de Hooghe (Rijksprentenkabinet, Amsterdam). Although the artist depicted the event in heroic tones, the action was far from bloody, as the small Swedish garrison avoided battle, preferring to barricade themselves in the fortress of the island.

The Swedish, aware that with the loss of Rügen there was no hope of holding Stralsund, attempted to regain the control of the island in the winter. On the evening of 7 January some 3,800 Swedes, mostly cavalry, had landed on the promontory of Prosnitz on the southern coast of the island, where Swedish troops still retained the fort of *Neuefähr*. The next day, the sentinels saw the enemy approaching from the south. The army which faced the Swedish numbered approximately 2,000 cavalry and 3,000 infantry and moved to occupy a strong position north-west of the village of Gustow, opposite the Warskow Manor. The Brandenburg cavalry and dragoons, under *Obrist* Hülsen numbered 970 men in all.[203] In the morning at about 9:00 a.m. the battle began with an artillery duel. The Swedish artillery prevailed, and to make matters worse for the German–Danes, Major General Rumohr was hit by a roundshot which shattered his left arm, leaving him mortally wounded. Hereupon Königsmarck ordered his troops to advance; the attack was met by Brandenburg cavalry and dragoons from the left wing, but the Swedes succeeded in driving the enemy cavalry apart. Even after the Brandenburgers had regrouped and were reinforced by reserves, they were driven back again by the Swedish cavalry supported by the artillery fire, which was very effective. The German troops rallied once more, but received no effective support from the Danes on the opposite wing, so were driven back by numerical superiority. Then the Swedes pressed the Danes on their flank and rear who, demoralised, were chased apart in wild flight. After four hours of fighting the Swedes succeeded in capturing almost all the Danish infantry. Königsmarck occupied Bergen, pursuing the enemy who had fled to Jasmund and Wittow, where the several German troops surrendered. The expeditionary corps had lost some 400 killed and had been almost entirely

---

203 Jany, *Geschichte der Königlich Preußischen Armee*, p.258.

THE ELECTORATE OF BRANDENBURG

captured. Swedish losses were reportedly no more that some 50 dead and 120 wounded.[204] Some of the captured soldiers entered the Swedish army and were garrisoned in the Neuefähr. Rügen became Swedish again for a short time.

The serious defeat at Warskow did not deter the Allies. In the spring and summer of 1678, the Danish fleet targeted Rügen several times. Meanwhile, by mid-July the Brandenburg field army was ready in Western Pomerania. However, the start of the campaign was delayed by the prolonged absence of the Brandenburg naval squadron led by Benjamin Raule, who did not arrive until August. The command of the allied fleet was taken over by the Danish Nils Juel, second in command of Admiral-General Cornelis Tromp. The Brandenburg expeditionary corps was commanded by Field Marshal Derfflinger and comprised 1,440 cavalry, 300 dragoons and 5,500 infantry, a total of 7,240 men. In addition, Derfflinger had a field artillery force comprising four guns of 6lb and 14 of 3lb with 76 artillerymen. The Danish corps strength was 1,800 men.[205]

Between 3 and 4 August the fleet landed both contingents not far from Stralsund. On the night between 5 and 6 August 500 Brandenburg infantrymen entered a suburb of Stralsund, plundered it and took 14 prisoners. As in the previous year, the fall of Stralsund depended on the control of Rügen. Once the circumvallation of Stralsund was completed, the allied war council planned a new expedition to retake the island. The invasion began on 12 September 1678, when the Dutch and Danish fleet covered the 2,500 Brandenburg troops who landed on Rügen and they recaptured the island within two days.[206] The German prisoners of the Battle of Warskow, who had been pressed into Swedish service, immediately surrendered the fortress of Neuefähr.

With the island under allied control, Stralsund's turn had come. On 24 September Friedrich Wilhelm began to ship his troops from Rügen to the mainland, and on 30 September the siege of Stralsund began. The Great Elector moved to his headquarters in Lüdershagen, awaiting further troops from Brandenburg, which increased the besieging army to 21,500 men and 80 guns. Stralsund's Swedish garrison had 3,000 regular soldiers and 3,000 militiamen. The city had a well-supplied arsenal and many provisions, but there was little hope of receiving any relief, as the Allies were pressing the Swedish army on all fronts. The besiegers advanced with trenches in front of the city, despite the tenacious Swedish resistance. In early October the Brandenburg and Danish artillery targeted the city and the harbour for days; between 5 and 9 October, Friedrich Wilhelm ordered a pause, and made an attempt to prevent the imminent destruction of Stralsund by opening surrender negotiations. However, the city authorities and the Swedish commander refused. On 10 October 1678 the besiegers received a ship

---

204 Hessen, *Charles XI's War*, p.195.

205 Jany, *Geschichte der Königlich Preußischen Armee*, p.266. Brandenburg provided a total of 10 warships, seven of which had been armed by the Great Elector himself. Jany, *Geschichte der Königlich Preußischen Armee*, p.259.

206 Jany, *Geschichte der Königlich Preußischen Armee*, p.266.

WARS AND SOLDIERS IN THE EARLY REIGN OF LOUIS XIV – VOLUME 7 PART 1

Tapestry of the landing at Rügen, 12 September 1678 (Oranienburg Palace Museum). With his baton raised, the Great Elector on a grey horse supervises the deployment of his troops on the island of Rügen. On the right, the electoral ship can still be seen, which had recently landed the Prince-Elector and Field Marshal Derfflinger. Behind the group of officers positioned on the headland, the landing of troops from the Brandenburg fleet can be seen in a bay. Densely loaded with soldiers and horses, the fleet approaches the coast. In some places, the water is still too deep and the horses and soldiers have to swim. Even if all these scenes did not take place at the same time, the tapestry accurately depicts the overall events. In background the cavalry are wearing buff coats, while officers have red coats and a kettledrummer and trumpeters have coats of blue cloth. On the right, the infantry is dressed in blue or red. On the extreme right, in blue and white, is presumably the *Garde zu Fuss* regiment. Note the battle formation with musketeers and pikemen.

loaded with ammunition and gunpowder from Stettin, which also delivered 1,000 incendiary grenades. On the same day, the Brandenburg artillery began to shell the city with these projectiles. Fire spread quickly, facilitated by the large stocks of hay and straw stored in the city. On the morning of 11 October 1678 the siege was suspended for new, fruitless negotiations, but the disastrous effect of the bombardment persuaded Königsmarck to then reopen the negotiations for surrender. With the remaining 2,543 soldiers of the garrison, the brave Swedish general left Stralsund on 18 October and embarked for Sweden. On the same day, the allied troops occupied the city and the local council took an oath of homage to the Prince-Elector of Brandenburg.[207]

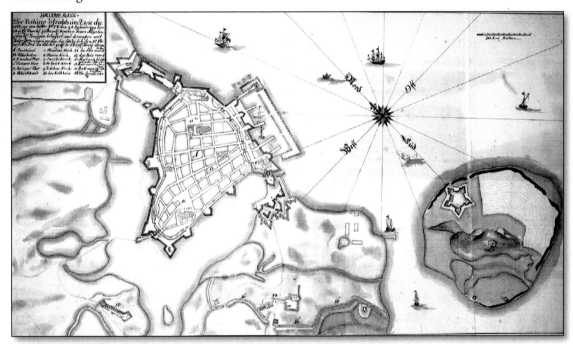

Plan of the fortification of Stralsund. The defenders could take advantage of the wide channel surrounding the town, but the blockade from the sea by the Danish and Dutch fleets deprived the defenders of any outside support and, together the heavy artillery fire, this forced the Swedish commander to surrender after 48 days.

Friedrich Wilhelm did not stay long in Stralsund. On 25 October he turned his attention to Greifswald, the last remaining Swedish possession on the German coast. The town was defended by a small garrison of 460 men, and like Stralsund, they had no hope of relief. On 15 November, after a few days of bombardment, Greifswald could no longer be defended and surrendered on 17 November.

The peace negotiations at Nijmegen changed the strategic scenario in Northern Europe, allowing Sweden to plan a full-scale invasion into enemy territory, and the objective of the offensive was East Prussia. After a long preparation, in late November 1678 Swedish General Henryk Horn crossed the border with 11,200 men and headed to Königsberg.[208] News of the invasion reached Friedrich Wilhelm in December 1678, while he was still in Swedish Pomerania. With his usual attitude for aggressive warfare

---

207 Herbert Ewe: *Geschichte der Stadt Stralsund* (Weimar: Böhlau, 1984), p.319.
208 Hessen, *Charles XI's War*, p.214.

the Prince-Elector decided to drive the Swedes out of East Prussia with a surprise action, despite the freezing cold, delaying the winter quartering as he had done four years earlier. On 30 December the field army left Greifswald and Stralsund and by 10 January 1679 had reached Marienwerder in East Prussia. The Swedes were on the Pregel River, near Königsberg, defended by 3,000 Brandenburgers under Joachim Ernst von Görzke. The task that Friedrich Wilhelm had set himself was to reinforce the Königsberg garrison with half of his troops and to evade the Swedes with the other half. Then Görtzke was to assault the Swedes from behind on his way out of Königsberg, while the Prince-Elector himself was to cut off the their retreat in order to destroy them with a full engagement. However, what had enabled success in the campaign of 1675, namely secrecy, was not repeated. Horn received news of the approaching enemy army and therefore withdrew to Tilsit. Since it was no longer possible to encircle and capture the Swedes, the task was to reach the enemy and force them into a battle under conditions unfavourable to them. The Brandenburgers marched to Braunsberg and Heiligenbeil on foot, and then – to save time – by sledge commandeered through the Frische Haff. On 16 January, Friedrich Wilhelm reached Königsberg, and after a day's rest the Brandenburg troops marched against the Swedes, who had in the meantime occupied Tilsit and quartered in the town. The Prince-Elector's army was divided into three columns: a vanguard of 1,000 cavalry, followed by another 3,000 infantrymen a few hours later, and finally the main force of around 5,000 men. Joachim Henniges von Treffenfeld led the vanguard,

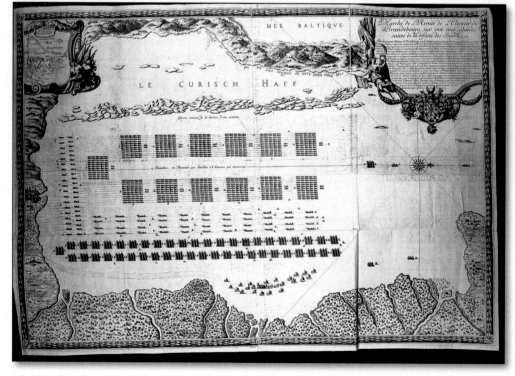

Print entitled *Marsch des Brandenburgischen Heeres über das Kurische Haff im Jahre 1679*, illustrating the Brandenburg army in order of battle heading in pursuit of the Swedes in January 1679. The winter campaign turned into a series of inconclusive encounters fought in dramatic weather conditions.

THE ELECTORATE OF BRANDENBURG

Derfflinger and Friedrich Wilhelm commanded the other two columns. The troops always crossed the frozen Kur lagoon between Labiau and Gilge on sledges; on 15 January the proximity of the enemy did not allow the use of sledges, and the soldiers crossed the frozen ground marching in column. At Tilsit, Horn seemed determined not to leave Prussian territory without a fight and deployed his troops in order of battle. On 20 January there was a first battle near Splitter, which engaged Treffenfeld's vanguard. The next day, near Heydekrug, Görtzke pressed the enemy and routed the rearguard. After this clash, the Swedes retreated north towards Riga.

Friedrich Wilhelm was undecided whether or not to pursue the enemy, but chose the first option to drive the Swedes out of the theatre of war. The pursuit was to be conducted across the snowy moors in extremely cold temperatures, the task being entrusted to Major General Johann Adam von Schöning with 1,600 cavalrymen. The Brandenburgers found an ally in the Lithuanian population, who were openly hostile to the Swedes.[209] Colonel Truchsess von Waldburg, whom Schöning had sent to Königsberg to deliver a message to the Elector, arrived at headquarters and reported that 'our soldiers did not need maps to pursue the enemy, because the road is covered with dead Swedish soldiers'.[210] At the end of January the cold became very intense, causing frostbite and death by frostbite. At the cost of great suffering the Swedes reached Telschi (today Telšiai in Lithuania), a small town halfway between Tilsit and Riga, only five kilometres from the Swedish border. Horn, who estimated that the approaching enemy was much weaker than he was, decided to take it on. On 7 February, unexpectedly Schöning and his men were faced with an opponent deployed in battle order on frozen ground that hindered cavalry movement. Horn had about 3,000–4,000 men with the artillery still intact. Schöning deployed the cavalry on high ground in two wings in front of the Swedes. The dismounted dragoons, on the other hand, occupied two small woods to the left and right of the high ground to target the Swedes on both flanks at the appropriate time. Realising that the Swedes were at the limit of their resistance, Schöning ordered Colonel Joachim Balthasar von Dewitz, Derfflinger's son-in-law, to engage the enemy by advancing lined up with pistols and carbines in hand. The Brandenburg cavalry executed the action according to seventeenth century tactical manuals, but failed to break through, and the Swedes for their part counter-attacked. Schöning responded to the threat with the dragoons, who were mounted and advanced on the flanks of the enemy. The battle took place under prohibitive conditions but none of the sides abandoned their positions, as everyone realised that fleeing would certainly be fatal, while continuing to fight gave them a chance of survival.[211] However, the intense cold rendered the firearms ineffective and many shots misfired due to the damp gunpowder. The two sides avoided coming into close contact, and the battle came to a halt only at nightfall, without either side prevailing. The Swedes retreated in good order into the

---

209 August Riese, *Friedrich Wilhelm's des Grossen Kurfürsten Winterfeldzug in Preussen und Samogitien gegen die Schweden im Jahre 1678/1679* (Berlin, 1864), p.97.

210 Riese, *Friedrich Wilhelm's des Grossen Kurfürsten*, p.97.

211 Riese, *Friedrich Wilhelm's des Grossen Kurfürsten*, p.98.

darkness; losses were minimal on both sides. The Brandenburgers claimed 28 dead and 30 wounded; Schöning, at the head of his dragoons, was saved by a captain of his cavalry who took the pistol from a Swedish cavalryman who was about to fire at the Brandenburg general. Over the next two days Schöning continued the pursuit of the Swedes in small patrols all the way to Riga. Finally, on 9 February, he gave orders to return to Königsberg to take the news of the retreat of the Swedish army to the Prince-Elector.

In May 1679, under the threat of a strong French corps assembled on the west bank of the Rhine, close to Brandenburg's possessions, Friedrich Wilhelm was forced to join the peace negotiations. After the Treaty of Saint-Germain en Laye, signed on 29 June 1679, the Great Elector had to return almost all of his conquests to Sweden, except the eastern bank of the River Oder which was ceded to Brandenburg, but retaining the towns of Gollnow (today Goleniów in Poland) and Damm (Dąbie). The balance of the war was ultimately modest, but Brandenburg had now definitively established itself as a major power in Europe.

Uniforms and Equipment

Gemeiner Musketier and *Schallmeienpfeiffer* depicted in a nineteenth century illustration. (Author's Collection) The *Schalmei* or chalumeau was a precursor of clarinet and in some German armies was an alternative to the fife. Richard Knötel reproduced this figure with a few differences. Probably the coat and waistcoat are reproduced incorrectly. In a contemporary source, the uniform is described as: black hat with red and white edging; dark blue coat laced with white and red; natural leather breeches; scarlet red stockings; tin buttons. In Brandenburg, as in all Western European armies, the *liberey* (livery) of drummers and fifers was at the whim of the commanders, just as this was also expressed on the flags, on grenadiers' caps, ammunition bags and, in the cavalry, the edge and the monogram on saddle covers and on the standards, kettledrums and trumpets. Lace or livery lace in the colours of the regimental commander's coat of arms were applied to the drummers' coats, especially on the sleeves and the back, the pockets, and sometime ran above the sleeves in the form of cross bars or chevrons and incorporated cloth strips hanging from the back of the shoulders, which had developed from the false sleeves from the early seventeenth century. This kind of 'sleeves' disappeared from the Brandenburg infantry in the late 1690s.

THE ELECTORATE OF BRANDENBURG

The study of the uniforms of Brandenburg-Prussia constitutes an iconic chapter in German military history. In the nineteenth century, amidst the general enthusiasm aroused by the acquired Imperial dimension, a multitude of works were published on the army of the Great Elector, regarded as the founder of the German military tradition. Although many of these works are questionable from a scientific point of view and show an obvious approximation in the style of the illustrations accompanying the text, they derived from items that have now largely been lost. Other contributions were published in the 1930s, and with few exceptions are embarrassing works due to their propagandistic meaning and unreliable reconstructions. Against this deplorable scenario, Carl Röchling and Richard Knötel's works emerge from the general mediocrity and stand, though far from complete, as the best iconographic sources on early Brandenburg uniforms.

However, even in the post-Second World War period, further works continued to be published that derived from these sources and very little research has been conducted in the archives. As a result, some recent works have contributed to 'poisoning the wells' on this matter, since any in-depth research has yet to be carried out.[212] However, the enterprise promises to be very complex, considering that most of the documentation concerning the purchase of military clothing is scattered in the private archives of the families that had a Colonel Proprietor: at least until 1685 the state administration delegated the purchase of uniforms to the regiments' commanders, with a few exceptions represented by the Household units or the regiments belonging to the Prince-Elector or his relatives.

As for the years before 1700, the primary sources for the Brandenburg army are very rare and these are even more limited if the search moves to the 1660s. A notable exception is the series of tapestries depicting the victories of the Great Elector in the war against Sweden of 1674–79.[213] This remarkable series was the basis of the research carried out by Richard Knötel for the illustrations published in his works.[214] From several details and particulars, it seems that the artists who drew the illustrations did extensive research and did not use conventional models, and even though the preparation of the tapestries began many years after the episodes took place, there is a reasonable certainty that these works can be relied upon for the style and colours of the Brandenburg army uniforms and equipment in the late 1670s. The soldier's coat no longer had the former tails, but the more fitted cut of the *Leibrock* (*justaucorps*), usually with a low collar, a row of buttons down the front, wide

---

212 Among these works, the booklet of Manfred Fürst, *Brandenburg-Preussische Uniformen 1630–1713* is illustrative of this nefarious trend. This work is an arbitrary reconstruction of uniforms and flags of the Brandenburg army, drawn from heterogeneous sources with manifest errors in dating military clothing. In addition, the history of many units is incorrect and contributes to the incomprehensibility of many of the alleged reconstructions.

213 The series consists of six tapestries manufactured by the French atelier of Pierre Mercier, today preserved in the Museum of the Oranienburg Palace. Two tapestries, illustrating the battle of Warsaw (1656) and the conquest of Anklam (1676), were lost between 1786 and 1891.

214 In *Die Grosse Uniformenkunde* (Rathenow, 1890), Knötel places his reconstructions of Brandenburg soldiers in the early 1680s. However, Knötel depicted the same subjects in Fedor von Köppen, *Preussens Heer in Bild und Wort*, and Gerhard Pelet-Narbonne, *Geschichte der Brandenburg-Preußischen Reiterei*, dating these to the 1670s.

The tapestry depicts the siege of Stralsund by Brandenburg troops in the autumn of 1678. The Prince-Elector on his white horse is leading the operation. He is accompanied by Elector Friedrich and General Derfflinger. To their left, a mounted officer of infantry with colours and drums steers his horse in the direction of the commanders. The centre ground is dominated by a train of 14 horses, harnessed in pairs, pulling a massive mortar. In the background, the Brandenburg artillery is shelling the city of Stralsund, which is already in flames. On the left, a musketeer, dressed in dark blue and white, belongs to the *Garde zu Fuss* regiment, as do the troops in the centre. The tapestry also shows in great detail the uniform of a drummer in the Prince-Elector's livery.

sleeves with rather large round cuffs, and pockets with large buttoned pocket flaps on both sides. Classical scholars of the German uniforms outline the changes in the waistline (sword belt, scarf) as characteristic. In 1672 the waist was quite high, in 1675 normal (as today), from 1680 to 1686 it was low, from 1688 to 1695 normal again, but then low below the navel.[215]

All major authors who have dealt with the Brandenburg army report that the colour chosen for the cloth of infantry uniforms was dark blue as early as the 1620s.[216] In 1659 the Brandenburg infantry in Schleswig-Holstein wore

---

215 Richard Knötel and Herbert Sieg, *Handbuch der Uniformkunde* (Leipzig, 1896), p.9.
216 Martin Lezius, *Die Entwicklung des Deutschen Heeres von Seinen Frühesten Anfängen bis Ansere Tage in Uniformtafeln* (Berlin, 1936); Richard Knötel, *Handbuch der Uniformkunde* (Leipzig, 1896); Klaus-Peter Merta, *Das Heerwesen in Brandenburg-Preußen von 1640 bis 1896. Die Uniformierung* (Berlin: Brandenburgisches Verlagshaus, 1991). How much this was due to Swedish influence is debatable, not least because Gustav II Adolph's infantry also wore clothing of other colours.

THE ELECTORATE OF BRANDENBURG

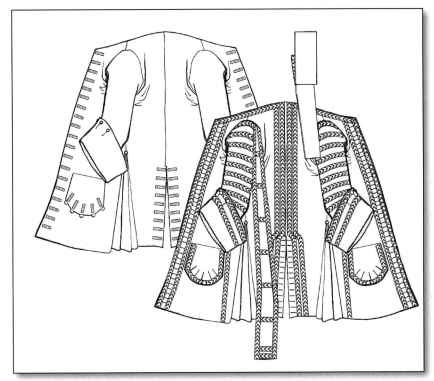

Coat pattern of the *Garde zu Fuss'* musketeer and drummer after the tapestry of the taking of Stralsund.

blue coats,[217] however, it is certain that at least until the 1680s the Brandenburg infantry also wore grey and red coats. For the latter, the illustration depicting the auxiliary corps for Hungary in 1686 clearly shows that out of eight regiments, three are wearing red coats.[218] However, it is noteworthy that in the same year, a letter from an officer states that the fame of the *blauen Wölker* became a matter of honour for the Great Elector's troops.[219]

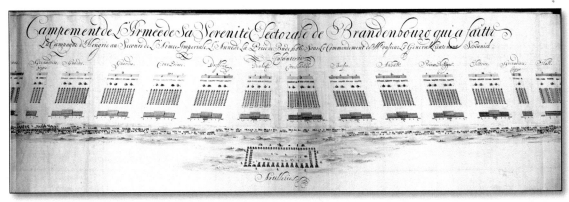

Detail from the *Brandenburg Feldzugs der Kaiserlichen Armee in Ungarn zur Einnahme von Buda, 1686* (Hessische Staatsarchiv, Marburg), depicting the Brandenburg corps assembled for the upcoming campaign against the Ottomans. Although the figures are only a few millimetres high, the colours of the coats and other details are recognisable.

---

217 Jany, *Geschichte der Königlich Preußischen Armee*, p.341.
218 Regiment *Kurfürstin* (BrI-57), *Derfflinger* (BrI-60) and *Barfuss* (BrI-2). Hessische Staatsarchiv, Marburg, WHK 6/19: *Plan vom Feldlager der Armee des Kurfürsten von Brandenburg* (1686).
219 Jany, *Geschichte der Königlich Preußischen Armee*, p.341.

All contemporary sources show that after 1660 the Brandenburg infantry's style of dress was that typical of northern Germany, with the knee-length coat (*Rock*) and the broad-brimmed hat of felt, possibly black or very dark grey. The cravat shows the modern pattern with the edges falling on the breast. The soldiers wrapped the cravat around the neck and tied it with a ribbon of different colour. In 1657, as a sign of recognition on the field once the alliance with Sweden was overthrown, red cravats were distributed to infantry and cavalry.[220] The orders concerning the equipment state that by 1655 the musketeers received 'a good bandolier with 20 cartridges'. A year later, the Prince-Elector ordered the distribution of a *Schweinsfeder* to each musketeer to replace the fork (musket rest), but this could be completed only in the early 1660s for lack of means to manufacture them.[221] The same coat worn by the musketeers is also worn by the pikemen, who, according to the sources, continued to wear breastplate armour until the next decade.[222] As in other German armies, from the early 1670s military clothing began to be stably codified, and the iconographic sources for the period confirm the adoption of the French–Dutch style in the matter of uniforms. The muster regulations of 1672, according to which the muster commissioners had to report, dealt with 'the colour of the flags, livery and clothing, including the company officers', and in the case of the cavalry, 'the colour of the saddle covers and cloaks', prove that the troops had received items of the same colour and pattern.[223] In the infantry, clothing allowances had been introduced in the 1660s, and half a thaler per man was monthly detracted from the salary for this purpose.[224]

The *Kamisol* (waistcoat) was not yet part of the uniform, but the private infantryman often wore a doublet under the coat, just as he did for ordinary labour service. He also wore natural-coloured calfskin breeches, double white or coloured stockings in cold weather, and sturdy shoes with buckles and fringes. The headgear was made of grey, sometimes pale coloured felt, with black being the most widespread colour.

The grenadiers wore the *Mütze* instead of the brimmed headgear of felt, it was originally a wide-brimmed hat bearing a leather or metal plate on which the colonel's name or coat of arms was painted. The bag of the grenadier cap ended in a tassel which hung down backwards or sideways. In addition to the cap, the grenadier also had the usual hat.

In the last decade of the Great Elector's reign, clothing was usually issued every two years in the garrisons. The clothes were to be purchased in the Electorate of Brandenburg, also by the regiments quartered in Prussia and Cleves, and the officers had to

Hautbois of the grenadier company of the *Garde zu Fuss*, 1690s. Dark blue mitre cap with gold edgings and monogram; embroidered white eagle and red-white-black Elector's cap, red tassel and gold grenades on the back; red cravat; dark blue coat laced with gold; carmine red scarf, breeches and stockings; gold buttons.

---

220 Crouzas, *Die Organisationen des Brandenburgischen und Preußischen Heeres*, p.13.
221 Jany, *Geschichte der Königlich Preußischen Armee*, p.176.
222 Crouzas, *Die Organisationen des Brandenburgischen und Preußischen Heeres*, p.13.
223 Jany, *Geschichte der Königlich Preußischen Armee*, p.341.
224 Jany, *Geschichte der Königlich Preußischen Armee*, p.342.

THE ELECTORATE OF BRANDENBURG

report their sources of supply. On 23 January 1685 the Elector ordered that each regiment should be given a certain *Couleur* for ensigns and clothing. The commissioners had to report 'the colour of both', but unfortunately these documents have not been preserved, except for a few, and therefore the regimental colours are known from individual details. After the death of the Great Elector, most infantry regiments were dressed in dark blue coats with red cuffs and lining, and tin or brass buttons, with the exception of the *Garde zu Fuss* (BrI-9) regiment, which continued to have white facings.[225]

In the 1680s the musketeers began to replace their bandoliers with cartridges and ammunition pouch, and the waist belt for the sword as introduced in French, Swedish and Dutch armies. Reports from 1681, 1683 and 1684 already mention *Leibgurtel* (waist belts) or *Leibriemen* (waist straps), which were stretched over the ammunition pouch belt to keep it in position.[226] Again in imitation of the Swedish army, between the end of the 1670s and the beginning of the following decade the infantry received rain cloaks, certainly a useful item to cope with the rigours of the climate in north-central Europe, and to save many soldiers from sickness caused by the cold.

In foreground, a musketeer of the early 1680s with *Schweinsfeder*, wearing a sword on a waist belt and with an ammunition pouch after the Swedish and Dutch models; drawing by Richard Knötel. (Author's Collection)

---

225 Karl Redlin, 'L'Armée Brandebourgeoise' in *Le Bivouac*, n. 12 – April 1984, p.21. Another exception was the regiment *Markgraf Philipp Wilhelm* (BrI-65), which maintained orange facings.
226 Redlin, 'L'Armée Brandebourgeoise', p.344. The Regiment *Garde zu Fuss* (BrI-9) wore waist belts at the funeral of the Great Elector in 1688. On the other hand, in 1687 Prince Ferdinand of Courland ordered 'broad boudriers' for his regiment.

By 1672 the infantry received flintlocks to replace the matchlock musket.[227] In the campaign of 1674 in Alsace, muskets with rifled barrels were also distributed, following the example of the *fusil rayée* of the French infantry.[228] Sources are elusive regarding the number of flintlocks distributed to the regiments. In 1674 the main arsenal in Berlin received 3,000 matchlocks, 1,000 *Dragonermusketen* and 500 *Hollandische Musketen*, namely flintlocks. The next year, an expenditure account relates the delivering of 1,050 matchlocks, 889 muskets for dragoons and 58 *lange Musketen mit Feuer und Luntenschlössern* (long muskets with fire and matchlocks).[229] This information provides clues as to the percentage of flintlocks compared to the matchlock muskets, and the use of rampart muskets in the fortresses. In 1675, the newly raised marine battalion *Bolsey* (BrI-54) received flintlocks, and by 1677 the *Lippstädtischer Flinten* were also distributed to the grenadiers.[230] In 1681 the first order concerning the distribution of flintlocks to the infantry regiments was finally issued by the Great Elector, who ordered that 25 men in every company had to be trained with the new firearm. Two years later the same number is registered in the regiments *Kurfürstin* (BrI-57) and *Anhalt-Dessau* (BrI-39) which, however, had received the new muskets for the first time.[231] In 1682, instead, the regiment *Spaen* (BrI-26) was already armed mostly with flintlocks, and all the musketeers of *Leibcompagnie* had received the new *Lippstädtischer Flinte*.[232] Between 1687 and 1688 all the infantry would receive flintlocks to replace the old muskets. In the early 1680s, plug bayonets were also distributed to the infantry.

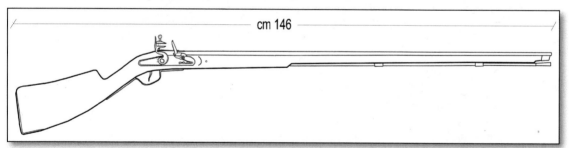

Lippstädtischer or *Hollandische* flintlock. (Author's Reconstruction)

An examination of existing iconography reveals that in the late 1670s the infantry introduced the custom of identifying different ranks by their stockings. In a contemporary source dating to 1678, the private infantrymen of the *Leibregiment* wear white stockings, while the drummers have the same in red.[233] The use of stockings as a sign of rank became a permanent feature in the following decades.[234] The *Plan* of 1686 shows, even with approximate

---

227 Redlin, 'L'Armée Brandebourgeoise', p.329.
228 Köppen, *Preussens Heer in Bild und Wort*, p.7.
229 Jany, *Geschichte der Königlich Preußischen Armee*, p.330.
230 Jany, *Geschichte der Königlich Preußischen Armee*, p.330. The name derived from the arsenal of Lippstadt, where these weapons were produced.
231 Jany, *Geschichte der Königlich Preußischen Armee*, pp.330–331.
232 Jany, *Geschichte der Königlich Preußischen Armee*, pp.330–331.
233 Tapestry illustrating the siege of Stralsund, Museum of the Oranienburg Palace.
234 Redlin, 'L'Armée Brandebourgeoise', p.23.

THE ELECTORATE OF BRANDENBURG

details, that officers, NCOs, *Spielleute* and private soldiers wore stockings of different colours, and the officers wore red coats in six out of nine regiments.[235]

In the 1660s the cavalry were actually only represented by the cuirassiers. They wore back and breast armour, buff *Koller* and over these a blue coat.[236] Cavalry clothing included leather breeches and high boots with spurs, an iron gauntlet – later only leather cuff gloves – and the universal lobster helm. A wide cloak of coarse grey cloth completed the equipment of the cavalrymen. In the 1670s the lobster helm was gradually replaced by the broad-brimmed hat with two iron bands laid crosswise to protect against blows to the

The death of Prince Alexander of Courland during the siege of Buda, 26 June 1686, by Richard Knötel. It is not known whether the regulations on distinctive colours intended in 1685 was actually carried through, because the choice of details was still at the discretion of the regiment's Colonel Proprietor. In this regard, Prince Ferdinand of Courland, who replaced his brother as Colonel Proprietor of the regiment, wrote to his second in command in 1687: 'I would like the private soldier's coats to have red or blue facings (...) with white lace on the cuffs.' The Colonel was to choose the colour for the cuffs that best matched the white lace.

---

235 Hessische Staatsarchiv, Marburg, WHK 6/19: *Plan vom Feldlager der Armee des Kurfürsten von Brandenburg* (1686).
236 Köppen, *Preussens Heer in Bild und Wort*, p.6.

Portrait dated to 1656-60 of *Oberst* Pful (or Pfuel), artist unknown. (Author's Collection). Pful was colonel of cavalry twice between 1656 and 1672. He wears the conventional buff coat and a blackened back and breast. Note the buff coat's sleeves piped and laced with silver.

head. In the 1670s the existing iconography depicts the Brandenburg cavalry wearing a peculiar buff coat with piped sleeves, similar to the models in use in the previous decade in Northern Europe. Other contemporary iconography shows some cavalrymen of the regiment *Spaen* (BrC-28) in 1678 wearing lobster helms and possibly breastplates under their cloaks.[237] In the late 1680s some cavalry regiments would have ceased to wear the buff coat, replacing it with a cloth *justaucorps* in French style worn over a leather waistcoat, a feature which was also common in other German armies. According to the classical authors, only the *Leibregiment* should continue to wear leather *Koller*, breastplate and lobster helm until the end of the century.[238] However, a detailed description of the uniform issued to regiment *Anhalt-Dessau zu Pferde* (BrC-29) in 1688 seems to confirm that the buff coat was distributed to the troopers in the subsequent years too. The uniform consisted of black headgear with silver edging, white cravat with black strap, leather *Koller* with blue cuffs turned back to half arm, grey cloak with blue lining and collar, natural leather breeches, black waist scarf with orange and silver fringes, blue saddle cover with red-white edge and a silver 'A' and Electoral hat embroidered on the corner.[239] The trumpeter and kettledrummer wore a dark blue cloak with red collar and lining. Whether this equipment was actually worn in battle is disputable.

As for the officers and NCOs: 'Unlike the troopers, they wore blue coats, richly decorated with gold and silver trim and embroidery. NCOs also had gold and silver-embroidered buttons, buttonholes and saddles cover laced of gold and silver. The uniforms of captains, lieutenants and *Kornett* were uniformed as the non-commissioned officers but with more laces and embroideries.'[240] As usual, in the Brandenburg army too, officers could dress as they chose, and some data confirms that armour and helm remained common, especially in action.

---

237 Romeyn de Hooghe's print, *Slag bi St Denis, 1678*.
238 Crouzas, *Die Organisationen des Brandenburgischen und Preußischen Heeres*, p.14.
239 Pelet-Narbonne, *Geschichte der Brandenburg-Preußischen Reiterei*, p.19.
240 Pelet-Narbonne, *Geschichte der Brandenburg-Preußischen Reiterei*, p.19.

THE ELECTORATE OF BRANDENBURG

Cavalry officers wearing *Kollet* and *justaucorps*, 1675–80, by Richard Knötel. The great German military artist draw these figures after the horsemen embroidered on the tapestries preserved in the Oranienburg Palace. The laced sleeves of the buff coat were typical in the 1660s and originally intended to replace metal protections for the arms, but in the late 1670s their use was decisively out of fashion.

Detail from the print of the Battle of Saint-Denis, fought on 14 August 1678, by Romeyn de Hooge (Author's Collection). In the background, some horsemen identified as belonging to the Brandenburg cavalry regiment *Spaen* (BrC-28) are wearing 'lobster-pot' helmets and cloaks.

WARS AND SOLDIERS IN THE EARLY REIGN OF LOUIS XIV – VOLUME 7 PART 1

'Lobster-post' helmet and armour belonging to Major General Joachim Hennings von Treffenfeld, German manufacture, 1670–80, preserved in the Deutschen Historischen Museum, Berlin.

Horse bits and bridle accessories, illustration from Gerhard Pelet-Narbonne's *Geschichte der Brandenburg-Preußischen Reiterei, Teil I. Die Alte Armee* (Berlin, 1905).

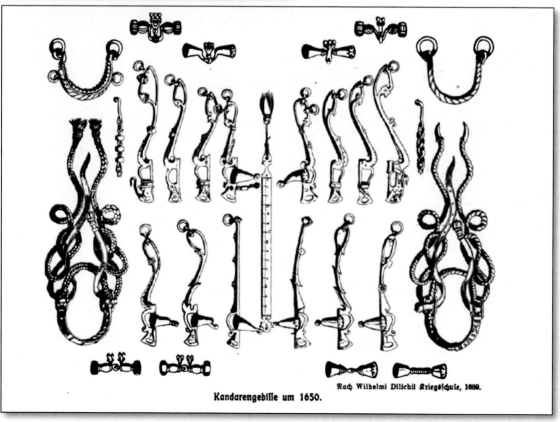

As a side weapon the horsemen carried a long strong sword with basket hilt, a carbine with cross belt, and two pistols inside the holsters. Saddle covers were in the regiment's distinctive colours, but in at least one case, these items identified the companies within the regiment. In the aforementioned *Anhalt-Dessau* regiment, saddle and pistol holsters covers of blue, yellow, red and green are mentioned in 1683.[241]

The dragoons wore the same coat as the infantrymen – dark blue for the *Leibregiment* – the broad-brimmed hat, leather gloves, and leather breeches like the cavalry, and light – so-called Brandenburg – boots. Waistcoats of cloth or leather were also worn since the 1670s. Regarding weapons, the dragoon carried a short musket hanging on the strap over the shoulder and later from a large belt, a couple of pistols and during the campaigns against the Ottomans, a shorter sword like that issued to the infantry, which replaced the cavalry sword.[242] In 1686, cavalrymen and dragoons of the auxiliary corps in Hungary received buff coats to be worn over the *justaucorps*.[243]

Artillery uniforms were usually of blue cloth, but contemporary sources of the late 1670s also depict servants and other artillery crewmen in grey or red.[244] According to other sources, during the campaign of 1686 in Hungary, the artillery wore brown coats.[245]

The use of *Feldzeichen* was another typical feature of the German Armies. In 1656 the Brandenburg troops fastened a bunch of straw to the headgear, while in 1674 the troops in Alsace adopted the oak twig like the Imperialists.[246]

Stücknecht (mattross) wearing a brown *Rock* and red waistcoat, 1670s. Illustration by Carl Röchling.

---

241 Jany, *Geschichte der Königlich Preußischen Armee*, p.348.
242 Köppen, *Preussens Heer in Bild und Wort*, p.6.
243 Pelet-Narbonne, *Geschichte der Brandenburg-Preußischen Reiterei*, p.65.
244 Tapestry illustrating the battle of Fehrbellin, Museum of the Oranienburg Palace.
245 Pelet-Narbonne, *Geschichte der Brandenburg-Preußischen Reiterei*, p.65.
246 Pelet-Narbonne, *Geschichte der Brandenburg-Preußischen Reiterei*, p.18.

4

The Electorate of Bavaria

In the seventeenth century, Bavaria was the largest and most populous state of Germany. It is estimated that at the end of the century, about 1.5 million people lived in 34 cities, 93 market towns, 4,700 villages, and 104 monasteries distributed in 41,290.5 square kilometres.[1] The Electorate included barely half of the modern day *Land*, divided in Upper and Lower Bavaria, and the Upper Palatinate, this latter being a third of the overall extension of the state.[2] The Electoral domains included enclaves in Swabia and Franconia. As in other parts of Germany, Bavaria greatly suffered for the consequences of the Thirty Years' War. However, the depopulation of the countryside had diverse effects in the different parts of Germany. In Bavaria the nobility, whose income consisted of peasant dues and rents, became impoverished and dependent upon money-lenders. Even the properties of the wealthier families were burdened with heavy debts, and only a minority were still able to live according to their custom and to send their children abroad 'to learn the noble exercises.'[3] Those of the less well-to-do often came into the hands of speculators who invested their capital in real estate. The Bavarian peasants, on the other hand, benefited from this situation. Because of the scarcity of tenants the landlords were forced to grant them better terms. Serfdom disappeared and labour services were often commuted into quit-rents. The depopulation of the Thirty Years' War could not lead to a revival of the manorial system, and in Bavaria the peasants' position continued to improve. These considerable differences in social development can be illustrated by the figures of population density. In the late seventeenth century Bavaria had about 73 inhabitants per (English) square mile, while the average in Germany was about 50 or less.[4] In spite of the poor economic scenario in Germany at

---

1   Laurence Spring, *The Bavarian Army During the Thirty Years' War 1618–1648* (Solihull: Helion & Company, 2017), p.xii.

2   Until 1779 the Electorate also comprised the *Innviertel*, ceded to Austria with the Treaty of Teschen, which concluded the War of the Bavarian Succession.

3   *New Cambridge Modern History*, p.436. The nobility strongly complained about the buying-up of noble estates: 'if any came on the market the religious foundations offered the best price; their ready cash was pushing aside the nobility. Only a minority were still able to live according to their custom and to send their children abroad 'to learn the noble exercises'.

4   *New Cambridge Modern History*, p.437.

Bavaria in 1648

121

Prince-Elector of Bavaria, Ferdinand Maria von Wittelsbach (1636–1679). In his youth he studied political science with the Jesuits, but upon the sudden death of his father in 1651 he was called to succeed him with his uncle, Albert VI of Bavaria, and his mother as tutors until 1654. The most important goal of his government was the reconstruction of the state after the devastation of the Thirty Years' War. His 30 year rule was an essential prerequisite for the consolidation and development of Bavaria. He introduced several economic and financial reforms favouring the peasants and raised a new class of officials for the government of his territories. Following the example of France, he also initiated the development of Jean-Baptiste Colbert's economic theory of mercantilism, which enabled him to bridge the economic gap with the rest of Europe much earlier than other German states. His marriage to Enrichetta Adelaide of Savoy developed his interest in Italian and French culture, especially in their architecture and music. The couple opened up many career opportunities in civil administration and the army to professionals from France and Italy. For his virtues as a wise and impartial ruler, the Italian historian Gualdo-Priorato called him 'The Solomon of our century'.

that time, the Bavarian subordinate classes enjoyed arguably better conditions than the other German subjects.

The house of Wittelsbach had ruled in Bavaria as Dukes since 1180, and in 1623 had gained the status of Prince-Electors of the Holy German-Roman Empire.[5] This occurred when Emperor Ferdinand II secretly transferred power from Friedrich V, Prince-Elector of the Palatinate to Maximilian of Bavaria, as a reward for defeating Friedrich's Protestant army in 1618 and recovering Bohemia. As a member of the *Reich*, the Elector of Bavaria held a place in two Imperial circles: those of Bavaria and Swabia. The Wittelsbachs of Bavaria had no expansionist aims comparable to those of other German princes and no noteworthy territorial claims either, with the exception of sovereignty over some Imperial cities, notably Ulm, and the Austrian Tyrol, both achieved, for a short time, in the early eighteenth century.

The princes who ruled Bavaria in the second half of the seventeenth century were very different from each other, but in a way they were complementary in transforming Bavaria into a modern military-fiscal state. Ferdinand Maria (1636–1680) laid the basis for the creation of a standing army, and despite the lack of resources he gave impetus to the rationalisation of armaments, and the technological development of weapons and military engineering. He also favoured the introduction of modern administrative theories, and tried to bring the army under the control of the state, especially in the matters of equipment and clothing. However, he only succeeded in limiting the dominance of the colonel-proprietors, who in Bavaria as elsewhere held a monopoly on recruitment and ultimately on military affairs. As a result,

---

5   The Bavarian branch of Wittelsbach even provided an Emperor, Ludwig IV, who ruled from 1314 to 1347.

even in Bavaria until the 1680s, there was no instrument comparable to a general staff, not even in the embryonic state like that introduced in Brandenburg.

On the other hand, Ferdinand Maria succeeded in relegating the estates to a marginal position, and despite the opposition he faced in order to implement his absolutist policy, in 1669 he was powerful enough to no longer meet the provincial diets: a decision that even the Great Elector Friedrich Wilhelm of Brandenburg had never managed to impose. Among the first German supporters for the agreement with France, in foreign policy he maintained a prudent policy that focused on the needs of his own state to recover from the tragedy of the Thirty Years' War. Bavaria remained far from the disputes that characterised the rise of France between 1667 and 1679. However, Ferdinand Maria did not remain inactive on the diplomatic front. In the initial months of the Franco-Dutch War, sincerely persuaded of the possibility of reaching a ceasefire, he tried to negotiate with Emperor Leopold I for a peace agreement with Louis XIV. He testified his will in a letter to Leopold I, describing him as a 'lover of the common welfare', but to the Imperial diplomat Königsegg he added as a conclusion: 'If the Emperor wants to go to war, he must ask God if he has honestly done his duty to prevent it.'[6] Although the talks did not succeed, and Bavaria was tied even more closely to France by receiving subsidies until 1679, Ferdinand Maria exploited this resource to increase the army, and managed to pursue a politic of equilibrium in order to maintain the neutrality of the Electorate.

Maximilian II Emanuel (1662–1726) in a youthful portrait by Petrus Schenk. (Author's Collection) Throughout his reign Max Emanuel patronised the arts. The first half of his reign was still dominated by his parents' Italian court artists, but following his politic trajectory he turned to the French taste in matters of architecture and music, becoming the originator of the Bavarian Rococo.

The political parabola of his son and successor, Maximilian II Emanuel (1662–1726), followed a very different direction. When he inherited the Electoral mantle in 1680, he brought Bavaria back onto the Habsburg side, and fought against Louis XIV as a member of the League of Augsburg, but later he became one of the most resolute allies of France during the War of the Spanish Succession. Like his father, Max Emanuel worked to modernise his state, and the army was also a target of his principal reforming actions, but unlike Ferdinand Maria he was not only a prince interested in military matters but was himself a soldier, beginning his career as a commander at the age of 21.

---

6   Staudinger, *Geschichte des Kurbayerischen Heeres*, vol.I, p.221.

In 1688 Max Emanuel's fame as a courageous officer was assured when he seized Belgrade from the Ottomans. The 'Blue King', so called because of the colour of his soldiers' uniforms, was the true founder of the Bavarian standing army, establishing a modern organisation of command and administration, as well as an efficient militia and technical corps.

The Centres of Command

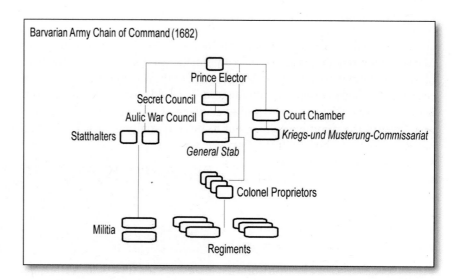

The Bavarian Chain of Command

As is obvious, the command of the army was a privilege that in Bavaria fell exclusively to the Prince-Elector, who no less obviously appointed his own *Lieutenant*. The latter held de facto the command of the army on campaign, but this event occurred rarely during the reign of Ferdinand Maria, while his successor Max Emanuel exercised field command himself on several occasions, both of his own troops and even when the army included allied contingents. The centre of all military affairs in Bavaria was the War Council (*Kriegsrat*), sometimes also called the Aulic War Council (*Hofkriegsrath*) like that existing in Vienna, and to which it referred as a model. And exactly as in Austria, military balance was administered by the central treasury, the Aulic Chamber (*Hofkammer*). Although in the event of war this organisation made the conduct of military affairs difficult, it was nevertheless a way of avoiding the financial disruptions that had characterised the Bavarian military during the Thirty Years' War. Moreover this constituted a novelty, as the Aulic War Council had been established in 1651, a few months after Ferdinand Maria's accession to the throne. Although he did not prove to be a ruler with the military aptitude of his predecessors, the Elector was a conscientious ruler to whom history gives credit for conducting a policy of state restoration. He preferred to appoint as presidents of the War Council able administrators, albeit experts in military affairs. In 1651, after the short presidency of his uncle, Duke Albert VI, the office went to Count Prospero d'Arco, a veteran of the Thirty Years' War who belonged to a family which had served the

THE ELECTORATE OF BAVARIA

Bavarian Wittelsbach since the early 1600s. After him the position passed to Duke Philipp von Sulzbach, who held the office until 1675, replaced by Baron Hannibal von Degenfeld until 1683.[7] The succession of presidents during the reign of Max Emanuel was now more focused on military-technical skills, but the personalities who held the office worked well, especially when working under a centralising personality like the Prince-Elector. They were in succession Count Giovanni Carlo Sereni, a former Imperial general and veteran of the Franco-Dutch War, replaced in 1689 by Adam Heinrich von Steinau.[8]

After the War Council and the Aulic Chamber, another centre of control of the Electoral army was the Secret Council (*Geheim Rath*): in which, as

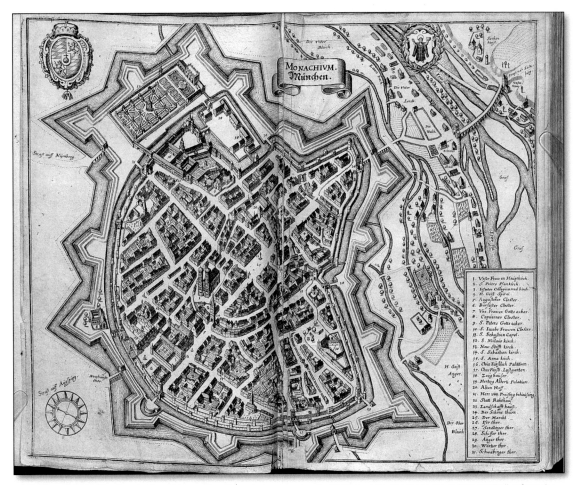

München and its fortifications in the mid-seventeenth century, engraving by Matthäeus Merian the Elder and Martin Zeiller, from the *Topographia Bavariae* (Frankfurt am Main, 1644).

---

7   In November 1683, Degenfeld, whose family had served in the Venetian army during the Cretan War, entered the service of the Most Serene Republic as senior commander for the incoming war against the Porte. He also acted as military entrepreneur in the recruitment of German mercenaries.
8   Friedrich Münich, *Geschichte der Entwicklung der Bayerischen Armee seit zwei Jahrhunderten (1618–1818)* (München, 1864), pp.3–4 and 510.

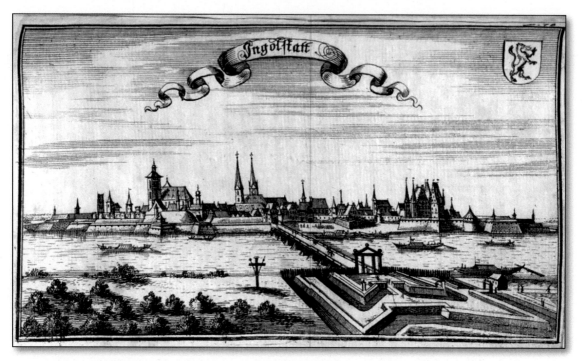

Ingolstadt in a late seventeenth century print in Anton Wilhelm Ertl, *ChurBayerischer Atlas* (Nürnberg-Oettingen, 1687).

Amberg, the major town in the Upper Palatinate, in a print dating to the mid-seventeenth century, from Anton Wilhelm Ertl, *ChurBayerischer Atlas* (Nürnberg-Oettingen, 1687).

usual, the president of the War Council also participated, in view of sensitive strategic matters such as foreign policy, and of course military policy. Musters and payments were under the control of the commissioners, who belonged to the *Kriegs-und Musterung-Commissariat*, with – until 1648 – a *General-Commissar* as senior officer. In peacetime all the commissioners served under the supervision of the military governor, or *Statthalter*, of the province. These latter had their residence in Münich, Ingolstadt, Amberg and in the other major garrisons of the Electorate. In wartime too, a war chancellery was raised, dependent on the field army headquarters and consisting of a variable number of personnel who dealt with the military correspondence between the senior commanders and the court. For this reason, the War Chancellery had its own office in Münich, where a *Kriegs-Registrator* and five chancellors operated.[9]

In 1682, Max Emanuel improved the conduct of military affairs with the establishment of a general staff (*General Stab*), consisting of the highest ranking generals and other officers such as the *Quartiermeister General*, the *Lieutenant Adjutants-General*, and the *Ober-Proviantmeister*, who headed a structure that included the senior provost (*Obergewaltiger*), *Auditor*, *Stabsfourier*, physician, conductors and servants. Max Emanuel also reformed the War Chancellery, instituted a supply general staff (*Proviant General Stab*), and modified the structure of the War Commissariat, providing it with its own directional office based in Münich, with staff and employees specifically trained for that task and, above all, independent from the military governors' control.[10]

The Army under Ferdinand Maria

During the Thirty Years' War the Bavarian army was reputed as the most efficient and redoubtable force of Germany, able to field up to 24,000 men in different phases of the conflict. However, between 1649 and 1651, from the 20,000 professional soldiers still in arms in the last year of that war, only one company of mounted guards (*Leibgarde zu Ross* or *Korbiner Garde*), two garrison companies in Münich and Ingolstadt (*Stadtquardia*), an incomplete infantry company in the Upper Palatinate, and the palace guards of foot (*Trabanten*) still remained: in total, 760 men.[11] In August 1655, one year after his definitive assumption of the state's government without the tutelage of his mother and uncle, Ferdinand Maria took his first decision regarding the army. 1655 was not a random date: by that year, Swedish troops were to leave the quarters they still occupied in Bavaria and the Upper Palatinate.

---

9   Münich, *Geschichte der Entwicklung der Bayerischen Armee*, p.5.
10   K.u.K. Kriegsarchiv, *Feldzüge des Prinzen Eugen von Savoyen*, p.445.
11   Staudinger, *Geschichte des Kurbayerischen Heeres*, vol. I, p.113.

Bavarian *Trabant* mid-seventeenth century (Bavarian Staatsarchiv – Kriegsarchiv BS I/68). Black hat with white and blue feathers; white and medium blue doublet and breeches, white stockings; red leather baldric; red waist scarf.

The Prince-Elector asked the War Council for its opinion on the means and number of a military force for facing possible enemies, assessing with concern what was happening in Poland after the Swedish assault. Ferdinand Maria ordered an accurate budget calculation to be prepared, which was to include the following items: recruiting, equipping and maintaining an army with the strength of that of 1629; the cost of an army corps sufficient for the simple defence of the squares; the cost for a number of soldiers capable to expel 'the most illustrious plagues', namely the foreign occupation. In this latter case, a project on how to use the *Landvolk* (militia) was also required.

The Council submitted two proposals. The first assumed an *Armada* of 21,000 soldiers subsequently able to operate as a field force both offensively and defensively. This army comprised 7,500 horsemen or *Archibusieren* and 500 Croats as cavalry; 12,000 infantrymen divided into eight regiments of 10 companies each; 1,000 dragoons, and the artillery with a train of 1,090 horses and 545 conductors. The second proposal was, instead, only a defensive army of 10,000 soldiers, including 7,500 infantry, 2,000 cavalry, 500 dragoons and an artillery corps with 250 draw animals and 125 conductors. For each army, the War Council calculated the expense for recruitment, equipment, and maintenance with five months of 'winter rations' and seven of 'summer rations'.[12] The latter proposal included the distribution of the soldiers in 13 garrisons, supported by 6,900 men of the territorial militia.[13] The Aulic Chamber cooled the Council's spirits by presenting an economic budget that was far from covering the budget required for armies of such proportions. For its part, the Secret Council expressed its concern about the mobilisation of the militia, stating that the mobilisation of so many peasants would ruin the state's economy.[14] Ferdinand Maria suspended the implementation of the projects until further notice. German historians outlined the decision of Ferdinand Maria in clear terms:

---

12 Staudinger, *Geschichte des Kurbayerischen Heeres*, vol. I, p.167.
13 Staudinger, *Geschichte des Kurbayerischen Heeres*, vol. I, p.167. These were München with 2,000 infantry, 2,000 militiamen, 150 cavalry; Ingolstadt: 2,000 infantry, 1,000 militiamen, 100 cavalry; Straubing: 400 infantry, 600 militiamen, 50 cavalry; Landsberg: 300 infantry, 300 militiamen, 50 cavalry; Rain: 400 infantry, 300 militiamen, 50 cavalry; Kelheim and Wafferburg : 300 infantry, 300 militiamen; Burghausen, Branau and Schärding: 150 infantry, 300 militiamen; Amberg: 1,200 infantry, 600 militiamen, 150 cavalry; Neumarkt: 500 infantry, 300 militiamen, 50 cavalry; Cham: 150 infantry, 300 militiamen. A later project for the defence force proposed only 9,400 infantry, 6,900 militia and 750 cavalry, distributed between München, Ingolstadt and Amberg.
14 Staudinger, *Geschichte des Kurbayerischen Heeres*, vol. I, p.168.

THE ELECTORATE OF BAVARIA

His country's difficulties, his love of peace and his firm will to maintain neutrality at all costs prevailed over foreign policy. However, the plan to form a standing army was a sign that he had decided to resist the temptations of France, which had offered him the possibility of being elected Emperor. But he did not want to cede his country's title at the price of a costly empire obtained through the wiles of France.[15]

The Prince-Elector returned to the matter in 1657, when the sudden death of Emperor Ferdinand III, the dispute with Karl Ludwig of Wittelsbach, Prince-Elector of the Palatinate, for the possession of Weiden and Parkstein, and the appointment as *Reichsvikar* forced Ferdinand Maria to raise 4,000 infantry and 1,500 cavalry. This force was organised in four infantry regiments-battalions of five companies of 200 men, plus two autonomous companies. The command of the largest unit was entrusted to the most experienced captains who had served under the previous Prince-Elector. They were *General-Feldzeugmeister* Count Maximilian Willibald Truchsess zu Waldburg-Wolfsegg, already *Statthalter* of Amberg (Upper Palatinate); *Generalwachtmeister* Count Franz von Fugger-Kirchberg; *Generalwachtmeister* Franz von Royer, and *Obrist* Ferdinand von Puech.[16] The final strength of the infantry was 4,384 men, just 16 less than expected. As for the mounted troops, the 1,547 horsemen mustered in June formed two regiments-squadrons of three companies with 100 men under colonels Truckmüller and Kolb, one company of life guards (*Leibgarde zu Ross*), and a further nine free companies, one of which was dragoons.[17] This figure did not include the *Stadt Quardia* of München and Ingolstadt, who had 100 and 150 men respectively.

Maximilian Willibald of Waldburg-Wolfegg (1604–1667), in an engraving by Wolfgang Kilian dated 1663. (Author's Collection) He was governor of the Upper Palatinate and is best remembered as an art collector and for having founded the Wolfegger Kabinett. Maximilian was well educated in the liberal arts and spoke, aside from his native German, French, Italian and Latin. A chronicle of the house of Waldburg-Wolfegg from 1785 describes him as a 'great lover of the secret and natural sciences like medicine, chemistry and alchemy'.

---

15 Staudinger, *Geschichte des Kurbayerischen Heeres*, vol. I, p.169.
16 Staudinger, *Geschichte des Kurbayerischen Heeres*, vol. I, p.169. The *Freykompagnien* were under *Obrist Lieutenant* Culer and Leoprachting.
17 See Appendix II: Bavaria: Standing Troops under Ferdinand Maria (Late Spring 1657).

Forced to move between what was his desire and what was possible, at the beginning of 1658 the Prince-Elector made detailed enquiries to his councillors about the foreign situation, and in particular about the possibility of licensing all the professional troops. Without exception, all the councillors stated that a disarmament was out of the question; the War Council also suggested that the Elector should be satisfied with the 'state of war', namely the current state of his army, but recommended the re-establishment of the *Landfahnen* (militia companies) in order to use them if necessary. If financial constraints dictated the disbanding of the 'Military' or at least a reduction in its size, political considerations favoured the retaining of the troops, and for a time it was still the decisive factor in maintaining a core of professional soldiers. However, after the Treaty of the Pyrenees between Spain and France on 7 November 1659, and six months after the Peace of Oliva on 3 May 1660, when the tension in Europe had eased somewhat, Ferdinand Maria decided to lighten the economic burden by retaining 19 companies of foot, and 13 companies of horse, one of which was a company of dragoons.[18] Ultimately the reduction was more apparent than substantial, as almost all the troops established in 1657 remained in service, with just a saving of 300 foot and 300 horse. With the professional troops still in service, a field corps as *reserve* was to be raised, comprising 600 infantry and 400 cavalry.[19]

The need to deal with the army again emerged in 1661, when Ferdinand Maria, pressed by the *Reichstag*, adhered to the 'crusade' against the Porte in support of Emperor Leopold I. On 14 May 1661 the Elector promised to raise a *Hilfskorp* of 1,200 foot and 300 horse as contribution to the circle of Bavaria and to join with the army that *Generalleutnant* Raimondo Montecuccoli was gathering in Hungary. In mid-July, eight infantry companies and three cavalry companies left Münich and headed to Hungary via river. Before the end of the month a further cavalry troop took the same destination, increasing the strength to 400 horsemen. The contingent was carefully prepared, and according to the judgement of an eyewitness turned out to be made up of good-looking and well-built people.[20] The infantry formed a regiment under the *Generalwachtmeister* Puech (BvI-4), the less aged of the Bavarian senior commanders. Each company comprised:[21]

1 *Hauptmann*
1 *Lieutenant*
1 *Fähnrich*
1 *Feldwebel*
1 *Führer*
1 *Fourier*
1 *Musterschreiber*

---

18   Staudinger, *Geschichte des Kurbayerischen Heeres*, vol. I, p.177; 14 infantry companies were distributed as garrison in Bavaria and another five in the Upper Palatinate; the cavalry was distributed with 11 companies in Bavaria and two in the Upper Palatinate.
19   Staudinger, *Geschichte des Kurbayerischen Heeres*, vol.I, p.177.
20   Archivio Segreto Vaticano, Segreteria di Stato 1026, Avvisi, *Avvisi di Germania*, 4 May 1661.
21   Staudinger, *Geschichte des Kurbayerischen Heeres*, vol. I, p.182.

THE ELECTORATE OF BAVARIA

1 *Feldscherer*
8 *Korporale*
4 *Spielleute*
18 *Gefreite*
112 *Gemeine*

The cavalry, in turn, formed another regiment under the *Obrist* Nikolaus von Höning (BvC-3), and each company received the following organisation:[22]

1 *Rittmeister*
1 *Lieutenant*
1 *Kornett*
1 *Wachtmeister*
1 *Quartiermeister*
1 *Musterschreiber*
1 *Feldscherer*
1 *Trompeter*
2 *Korporale*
87 *Gemeine Reiter*
3 *Gemeine zu Fuss* (as servants of the officers)

The corps included the artillery, consisting of two 3-pdr light guns, each served by four *Konstablern*, and a train of 16 horses with six conductors. The ammunition included 300 projectiles of iron, 50 boxes of canisters, powder, matches and 200 hand grenades.[23]

The drawbacks experienced by the Bavarian contingent bear testimony to the critical condition of the Hungarian war theatre. After the first campaign, the infantry had lost through illness the equivalent of two companies, which were replaced in the winter 1661–62, but by the end of the year the regiment had been further reduced to seven companies. As a result of the replacements sent to Hungary, the garrisons in Bavaria and in the Upper Palatinate numbered just 40–50 men. In February 1663, the infantry regiment deployed six companies with 800 men in all.[24] The condition of the cavalry did not seem any better, since by the beginning of 1664 the overall strength was reduced to two companies with fewer than 300 men. From the garrisons of the Electorate, reinforcements were once again drawn for Hungary. When, in October 1663, news arrived of the Tatar incursion into Moravia and Silesia, the Münich court feared for the safety of the state. In this gloomy climate, government officials received orders from the Elector to send 1,600 infantrymen to defend the country, and soon afterwards another 1,400 men headed to the border: in all 3,000 foot in 15 companies. Together with the infantry, nine cavalry companies were mobilised, each of 100

---

22 Staudinger, *Geschichte des Kurbayerischen Heeres*, vol. I, p.182.
23 Staudinger, *Geschichte des Kurbayerischen Heeres*, vol. I, p.292.
24 Staudinger, *Geschichte des Kurbayerischen Heeres*, vol. I, p.184. The author, who investigated the military archives in Münich, reports that another source claims the regiment was reduced to just three companies, and therefore disbanded in the early months of 1663.

horse, and a further 200 dragoons were recruited. The enlistment of recruits concerned not only the Electorate, but also the neighbouring states, not only in Germany, but even in Italy.[25] In February 1664, the infantry fielded seven companies of 150 men, later increased to nine.

By March, the contingent in Hungary had been restored to 1,200 infantry and 300 cavalry. Regiments *Puech* and *Höning* participated in Zrínyi's winter campaign, culminating in the siege of Pécs and the conquest of Kanisza, but the consequences of five months of hard operations became apparent in the summer. On 1 August 1664 when the Bavarians, together with the Imperial troops, those of the *Kreise*, the *Deutsche Allianz* and the French corps sent by Louis XIV, fought in the victorious battle of Szentgotthárd, the contingent fielded a fighting force of just two infantry battalions and one cavalry squadron.[26] The participation in the war against the Porte was celebrated in Bavaria as an extraordinary event, above all because it was the first military action performed by the troops of the Electorate since 1648. The return home of the contingent was preceded by a letter full of gratitude that on 29 November 1664 the War Council, on behalf of the Elector, sent to Puech and Höning:[27]

> By the grace of God, now that there is no doubt about the peace that the Empire has concluded and ratified with the Grand Turk, and with our people, who are safe in our lands, as well as with the soldiers who are under your command in Hungary. And since we still have five infantry companies of 200 men each, and two horse companies of 100 men in our service, all now experienced men of your regiments, whom you, by their qualities and courage, were able to lead in the recent campaign, and who are still well suited for war service, will remain in our service.

Less prosaically, the letter gave further instructions to the two commanders to select officers, NCOs and soldiers. Those who for reasons of age, physical condition or other serious illness were no longer able to serve, should be discharged; however, as a reward, the Prince-Elector assigned to them a full month's salary, and to the horsemen accorded the right to retain the horses, 'if still available'.[28] Before the end of 1664 the war councillor and *Ober-Kommissar* Georg Willesohn passed on to the garrison commanders the order of the Elector to restore the companies under their command to 200 men each with new recruits. The final result was a significant decrease of the professional troops, which were reduced to six companies of infantry and three of cavalry.[29]

Whenever the state felt threatened, like a toad the army increased in size. In 1667, during the French invasion of the Spanish Low Countries, followed

---

25   Staudinger, *Geschichte des Kurbayerischen Heeres*, vol. I, p.186.

26   Kurt Peball, 'Die Schlacht bei St. Gotthard-Mogersdorf 1664', in *Militärhistorische Schriftenreihe*, III-1964.

27   Staudinger, *Geschichte des Kurbayerischen Heeres*, vol. I, p.187.

28   Staudinger, *Geschichte des Kurbayerischen Heeres*, vol. I, p.194.

29   Staudinger, *Geschichte des Kurbayerischen Heeres*, vol. I, p.194.

THE ELECTORATE OF BAVARIA

by the crisis with Vienna, Ferdinand Maria ordered the raising of new 14 infantry, six cavalry and two dragoon companies. Before the end of the year, the infantry increased by a further four companies; the overall strength was 4,000 infantrymen and 1,328 horsemen. The company organisation was also modified. Each infantry company now comprised:

1 *Hauptmann*
1 *Lieutenant*
1 *Fähnrich*
1 *Feldwebel*
1 *Führer*
1 *Musterschreiber*
1 *Fourier*
1 *Feldscherer*
1 *Gefreiter-Korporal*
6 *Korporale*
4 *Spielleute*
18 *Gefreite*
163 *Gemeine*

The cavalry companies received the following organisation:

1 *Rittmeister*
1 *Lieutenant*
1 *Kornett*
1 *Wachtmeister*
1 *Quartiermeister* (Fourier)
1 *Musterschreiber*
1 *Feldscherer*
2 *Trompeter*
1 *Schmied*
1 *Sattler*
2 *Korporale*
87 *Gemeine Arquebusieren*

As for the dragoon companies, these comprised:

1 *Hauptmann*
1 *Lieutenant*
1 *Fähnrich*
1 *Wachtmeister*
1 *Feldschreiber*
1 *Fourier*
1 *Feldscherer*
3 *Korporale*
6 *Gefreite*
2 *Spielleute*
92 *Gemeine*

The distribution of the companies in the garrisons was a clear sign that the Electorate wanted to maintain a defensive attitude. The following year, however, the War Council submitted to the Prince-Elector a project to raise one 'field battalion' of six infantry companies and one squadron of three cavalry companies. In February 1669, after receiving support from France, Ferdinand Maria ordered a new reduction of the professional troops. Five infantry companies were disbanded and the others reduced to 125 men.[30] The cavalry was reduced to four companies and the two dragoon companies joined into one. The reduction of troops offered the opportunity for an economic return, since with 10 dismissed companies a field regiment under *Obrist* Bühren (BvI-7) was formed, and hired to Venice for the defence of Candia with the *Vertrag* signed on 13 March.[31] However, the reduction of the professional soldiers continued on 22 March, when all the infantry companies in the Electorate were reduced to 100 men.

In June 1669 the regular troops numbered 2,400 foot and 200 horse, of which 1,650 foot and all the cavalry were quartered in the Upper Palatinate.[32] These figures did not include the *Leibgarde zu Ross*, and the *Stadt Quardia* companies, the latter now becoming actual static garrisons, composed by aged veterans and invalids. The diminishing role of both the *Stadt Quardia* companies is confirmed by their gradual decline of strength. In Münich there were about 100 men, while in Ingolstadt the company numbered in some periods up to 200 men, but strongly decreased in the 1670s.[33] In 1669 this latter still deployed 185 men, comprising some *Gefreite* as the professional infantry. In Münich the strength remained at 100 men, not including the officers.[34] Another company comprising aged soldiers had been formed in the Upper Palatinate with 74 infantrymen, 58 of which were privates, and quartered in Rothenberg.[35] These companies continued their activities without receiving any new recruits, with the exception of soldiers dismissed from the professional infantry because they were unable to serve in the regular units. They could enter the *Stadtquardia* as a reward, and only on the Prince-Elector's decision. The companies of Münich and Ingolstadt were finally disbanded between 1681 and 1682 under the rule of Max Emanuel.

---

30 Staudinger, *Geschichte des Kurbayerischen Heeres*, vol. I, p.194, p.304. One company had only 75 infantrymen.

31 Staudinger, *Geschichte des Kurbayerischen Heeres*, vol. I, p.194, p.562.

32 Münich, *Geschichte der Entwicklung der Bayerischen Armee*, p.24.

33 Staudinger, *Geschichte des Kurbayerischen Heeres*, vol. I, p.204. In April 1559, the Stadt Quardia of Ingolstadt comprised one *Hauptmann*, one *Lieutenant*, one *Wachtmeisterlieutenant*, one *Feldwebel*, four *Büchsenmeister*, 10 *Gefreite*, two *Statthaltertrabanten*, four *Spielleute*, eight *Korporale*, and 153 *Gemeine*.

34 Staudinger, *Geschichte des Kurbayerischen Heeres*, vol. I, pp.205–206. In February 1668 the company of Münich, under *Generalwacht-und Zeugmeister* Franz von Royer, comprised one *Obrist* as Lieutenant, one *Fähnrich* with three *Korporalenschaft* of 25 men each under a *Korporal*. Another list registers an overall strength of 100 men, with one *Hauptmann*, one *Lieutenant*, one *Fähnrich*, one *Feldwebel*, four *Korporale*, two *Spielleute*, 14 *Gefreite* und 76 *Gemeine*.

35 Staudinger, *Geschichte des Kurbayerischen Heeres*, vol. I, pp.205–206.

From 1669 to 1672, the Bavarian military scenario was similar to a 'still life' painting;[36] however, Ferdinand Maria did not interrupt to deal with the security of his state. Like other German princes he turned to France, and in 1670 concluded with Louis XIV a treaty of *subsidia*, with which the parties agreed reciprocal support in case of war, which meant a significant French payment for raising an army. In the spring of 1672 the peace in Europe was shattered by the French invasion of the United Provinces of the Netherlands. The winds of war had already blown across Bavaria in the first month of the year. On 11 January, awaiting the French subsidies after the new treaty with Louis XIV, the Prince-Elector had demanded funds in order to strengthen his small army by recruiting 1,550 infantry, 600 cavalry and 200 dragoons. A second request established the recruitment of 3,400 infantry, 500 cavalry and 100 dragoons.[37] On 26 November Ferdinand Maria had increased the professional army to 6,400 infantry divided into 32 companies of 200 men; 1,200 cavalry with 12 companies of 100 men; 400 dragoons with four companies of 100 men. Before the end of the year, a further infantry company was raised. Moreover, with eight companies were formed two 'field regiments' under *Generalfeld und Obristlandzeugmeister* Prospero d'Arco and *General-Feldzeugmeister* Johann Berlo. In May 1673 two more infantry regiments were formed, now with five companies each, followed by a further four, including one with four companies. In 1673, the infantry fielded 51 companies of variable strength.

A young Max Emanuel portrayed in the 1670s by Paul Mignard (Bayrisches Nationalmuseum, München). The Prince is dressed in a cavalry officer's outfit consisting of a leather *Koller* with sleeves of red velvet and full embroidered cuffs. The blue silk scarf with a gold edge is typical for high-ranking Bavarian officers of this period.

---

36 Staudinger, *Geschichte des Kurbayerischen Heeres*, vol. I, p.210.
37 Staudinger, *Geschichte des Kurbayerischen Heeres*, vol. I, p.212.

General Johann Berlo de Coquier (1600?–1683), senior commander of the Bavarian army and Governor of Ingolstadt in a print dating to the mid-1670s. (Author's Collection)

Each standing regiment of infantry established its *Stab*, comprising:

1 *Obrist*
1 *Obristlieutenant*
1 *Obristwachtmeister*
1 *Adjutant*
1 *Oberfourier*
1 *Kriegsauditor* with his men
1 *Kaplan*
1 *Sekretär*
1 *Proviantmeister*
1 *Profoss* with his guards

The organisation of the regiments included a tactical repartition with two *Feld-Bataillonen*, which included:

1 *Kommandanten* (*Obristlieutenant*)
1 *Major*
1 *Fourier*
1 *Kaplan*

Each company now comprised 120 men, with one *Hauptmann*, one *Lieutenant*, one *Fähnrich*, one *Feldwebel*, one *Führer*, one *Fourier*, one *Musterschreiber*, one *Feldscherer*, one *gefreiten Korporal*, four *gemeine Korporale*, three *Spielleute*, 12 *Gefreite* and 92 *Gemeine*.[38] There remained another nine *Freykompagnien* numbering between 150 and 200 men.[39] After 1672, in some musters, one *Kapitän d'Armes* is also registered in the regiment's staff.[40]

The cavalry did not form regiments, and continued to field single companies with the usual staff and 89 horsemen.[41] In November 1672 there were 800 horsemen divided into eight companies. In the same month the dragoons numbered 400 men with three companies, while a fourth company of 200 men was raised in December. The dragoons retained the organisation established in 1667.[42]

The European political scenario, ever in ferment, offered Ferdinand Maria the opportunity to test his troops in the field. This happened in the summer of 1672, when his brother-in-law Carlo Emanuele II of Savoy requested an infantry corps to be deployed in the ongoing war against the Republic of Genoa.[43] Meanwhile, after the *subsidia* concluded with France in 1670 and 1672 another treaty, now valid for 10 years, followed on 14 January 1673: by this the Prince-Elector, in return for a French payment of 100,000 florins and a monthly indemnity of 16,000 *Reichsthaler*, agreed 'to defend the Peace of Westphalia', and above all to increase his troops to 8,000 infantry and 3,000 cavalry. This treaty was followed on 10 February and 12 June 1673 by defensive alliances with Württemberg and Pfalz-Neuburg 'against foreign troop who could cross, quarter and impose extortions of war'.[44] Recruitment progressed so well thanks to French money that the Prince-Elector was able to form an observation corps in the Upper Palatinate, in order to guarantee the neutrality of his state against possible crossings by belligerents, namely the Imperial troops, or against any gathering of soldiers from other states. However, the Prince-Elector's will to maintain Bavaria's neutrality did

---

38   Staudinger, *Geschichte des Kurbayerischen Heeres*, vol. I, p.216.

39   Staudinger, *Geschichte des Kurbayerischen Heeres*, vol. I, p.216. The free companies of 200 men had the same organisation as the companies in the regiments, but with seven *Korporale*, four *Spielleute*, 18 *Gefreite* and 163 *Gemeine*.

40   Staudinger, *Geschichte des Kurbayerischen Heeres*, vol. I, p.364. From 1674, in the *Berlo zu Fuss* (BvI-9) there were some cadets or aspiring sons of officers who served in the companies and received double the pay of the private soldiers.

41   Staudinger, *Geschichte des Kurbayerischen Heeres*, vol. I, p.217. Since 1674 there was also one *Vice-Korporale* in some cavalry companies.

42   Friedrich Münich, *Geschichte des Königlich-Nayerischen I. Chevaulegers-Regiments Kaiser Alexander von Rußland. 1: Die Stämme des Regiments (1645–1682): Gleichzeitig ein Beitrag zur ältesten Bayerischen Heeres-Geschichte von 1611–1682* (Münich, 1862), p.47.

43   See Bruno Mugnai, *Wars and Soldiers*, vol. 6, part 2, p.85.

44   Staudinger, *Geschichte des Kurbayerischen Heeres*, vol. I, p.217.

not prevent him from sending troops to his cousin Maximilian Heinrich, Prince-Bishop Elector of Cologne, who had entered the war against the Dutch Republic together with France, England and Münster. In July 1673 the Bavarian army could field 8,400 infantry, 2,500 cavalry, and 500 dragoons, not including the mounted Life Guard company and the *Stadt Quardia*.[45] This figure did not take into account the 10 infantry companies of the regiment sent together with two companies of dragoons to Cologne. In autumn the strength increased by 1,200 foot after the enlistment of a regiment from Mecklenburg.[46]

In October, *General-feldzeugmeister* Berlo took command of the observation corps in Upper Palatinate, comprising 27 companies of infantry,[47] 16 of cavalry and three of dragoons, for 7,725 men in all.[48] However, the duties of the observation corps requested more cavalry, and above all a command staff able to lead the units on the field. This necessity persuaded Ferdinand Maria to reform the cavalry organisation. On 1 August 1673 the War Council was invited to discuss with Lieutenant General Charles de Haraucourt, commander-in-chief of the cavalry, the formation of five cavalry, and one dragoon regiment, 'and in addition to designate colonels and staff officers, as well as the size of companies to assemble.'[49] The decision was postponed until the following year, when five *Arquebusieren* regiments were finally raised between March and June.

In 1674 the infantry regiments were established to seven companies of 200 men. The free companies were also joined in *offene Regimenter* (open regiments) for tactical use. A decisive impulse was given to matters concerning training and discipline; in this regard, the War Council had prepared detailed *Instruktion* to colonels and commanders, which referred in particular to the administration of justice and the drill of the infantry. In 1674 a *Kriegs-Exercitien-Manual* was issued to the infantry officers, the regulations inspired by the most modern theories introduced in France, and focusing on manoeuvres and intensity of fire. The drill for the musketeers comprised 39 motions, which simplified many of the outdated procedures for training the soldiers to use the heavy muskets with fork rests. The exercise of the pikemen still maintained great importance and comprised 59 motions.[50] The proportion of pikes had almost changed towards the end of the Thirty

---

45 Staudinger, *Geschichte des Kurbayerischen Heeres*, vol. I, p.220. In the autumn, the overall force was 12,360 men, comprising 9,600 infantry, 2,300 cavalry and 460 dragoons.

46 Staudinger, *Geschichte des Kurbayerischen Heeres*, vol. I, p.220, *Regiment Bibow zu Fuss* (BvI-15). During those same months, the attempt to raise a further infantry regiment with the battalion under *Obrist* Jean-Louis de la Perouse, coming from the campaign in Italy, had a short life.

47 Staudinger, *Geschichte des Kurbayerischen Heeres*, vol. I, p.236. These were seven companies from *Culer zu Fuss*, four from *Puech zu Fuss*, three from *Berlo zu Fuss* and 13 free companies.

48 Staudinger, *Geschichte des Kurbayerischen Heeres*, vol. I, p.236. The Amberg arsenal delivered artillery and ammunition to General Berlo, who was gathering the troops near Neumarkt. The guns were two iron *Doppel-Falconettes*. Berlo had initially requested three 12-pdr and six 3-pdr guns, 'but due to the lack of draught horses he had to be satisfied with that number'.

49 Staudinger, *Geschichte des Kurbayerischen Heeres*, vol. I, p.221.

50 Münich, *Geschichte der Entwicklung der Bayerischen Armee*, pp.25–30.

THE ELECTORATE OF BAVARIA

Years' War in favour of firearms, so that the ratio changed to the traditional one pikeman for every two musketeers.[51]

Pikemen, from *Precetti Militari*, by Francesco Marzioli (Bologna, 1670). This military treatise was dedicated to Prince-Elector Ferdinand Maria of Bavaria. Although there is no certainty that the figures depicted are actually Bavarian soldiers, the work is a very fine sources relating the military clothing in a period of transition between old and new fashions.

Ferdinand Maria was very interested in technological development, and with regard to armaments he favoured the improvement of artillery. The state's inventories provide interesting information on the different types of weapons existing in Bavaria. Among the inventories of the München *Zeughaus* (arsenal), that of 1662 is probably the most accurate, and registers the following weapons and calibres:

2 *doppelte Kartaunen* (96lb)
8 *ganze Kartaune* (48lb)
2 *dreiviertel Kartaune* (36lb)
4 *halbe Kartaune* (24lb)

---

51 Staudinger, *Geschichte des Kurbayerischen Heeres*, vol. I, p.361. This proportion did not change at least until 1679, when the disbanded companies each delivered 120 muskets and 60 pikes to the arsenals.

3 *Singerinnen* (50lb)
7 *Schlangen* (18lb)
4 *Notschlangen* (9lb)
20 *Falkonen* (6lb)
10 *doppelte Falkonette* (3lb)
8 *einfache Falkonette* (1lb)
14 *Haubitzen* (9lb)
25 *Scharfedinlein* or *Serpentinen* (½lb)
41 *Kammerstücke* (guns with chamber)
8 *Böller* (petards)
5 *kleine stücke* (unspecified light guns)
4 *Stürzenbrecher* (curtain breakers)
5 *Regimentstücke* (light regimental guns, possibly of 4lb)

This classification of the guns is the classic one used in southern Germany and Austria in the seventeenth century, and reveals more than a clue about the interest in experimentation offered by the more updated inventions

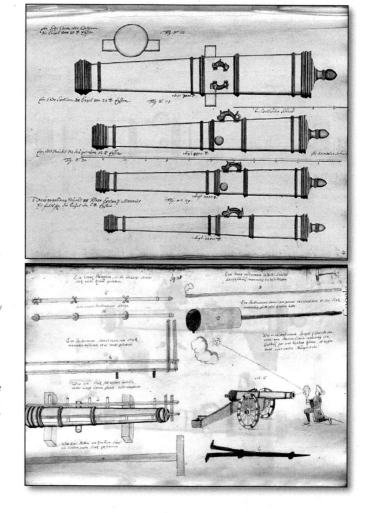

Heavy guns classifications, and guns testing from Anton Faulhaber's *Artilleriekunst*, written and illustrated between 1680 and 1702 (Bayerischer Staatsbibliothek, München). The *Artilleriekunst* is a manuscript comprising four parts relating artillery production, fortification and engineering in seventeenth century Germany and it is possibly the best source on this subject. Each part is fully illustrated with plans of fortresses, and drawings of cannons, howitzers and mortars. Gun and mortar production had already started during the reign of Ferdinand Maria. Most of these weapons were presented to the Prince-Elector, often in the presence of the entire court, and tested several times at the München firing range in front of the Neuhauserthor. According to Bavarian historians, local manufactured cannon were the most common in the electoral army.

in matter of artillery.[52] Apart some ancient guns, the field guns of 24, 18 and 12lb, as well as the regimental pieces had been cast during the reign of Ferdinand Maria and some were of iron. The arsenals were located in Münich, Ingolstadt, Amberg, Burghausen, Braunau, Schärding, Wasserburg, Landshut, Straubing, Deggendorf, Kelheim, Rain, Cham and Rothenberg. Of these, the first three were well provided for, but the others poorly equipped.

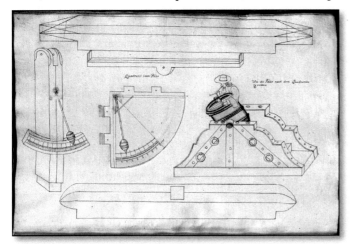

Mortar and carriage, from Anton Faulhaber's *Artilleriekunst*. Between 1676 and 1679, Münich carpenters and blacksmiths produced a large number of new shafts for the double, whole, and half *Kartaune*, as well as for mortars, single and double falconets, and other light guns.

Even the personnel who dealt with artillery were subject to reforms. The constables, who before 1660 were indifferently denominated *Büchsenmeister*, *Feuerwerker*, and even *Granadieren*, were now identified as *Konstabler*, and administered directly by the Aulic Chamber. In 1668 there were 81 artillerymen that could be used on campaign; this number increased further when, at the beginning of the 1670s, the Prince-Elector issued an order to train the most skilled private soldiers as constables. Thus, according to a decree of 3 July 1673, 60 civilians were sent to Münich, Braunau and Amberg, and another 40 privates were sent to Ingolstadt for the instruction in use of artillery. From 1671 to 1674 the arsenal of Münich received a 'firework master' and a 'patented' *Büchsenmeister*, alongside 120 citizens and private soldiers, who received training as artillerymen, some as constables and artificers and others only as constables or gunpowder makers.[53]

Under Ferdinand Maria, Bavaria became self-sufficient in matter of powder, produced by the mills in Münich, Grünwald, Aibling, and Wolfratshausen, which could supply 52.5 *Zentner* (2,940kg) of powder per month.[54] Although the formation of a standing army was hindered by the scarcity of resources, the Prince-Elector never ceased to plant the foundations for a war industry. Improvements were also experimented with in the army train, above all for introducing regulations to avoid the multiplication of the

---

52   Staudinger, *Geschichte des Kurbayerischen Heeres*, vol. I, pp.278–280. In addition to the 170 guns made in Bavaria, there are also about 80 foreign weapons captured in battle which, based on their names and calibres, almost correspond to the Bavarian calibres. The guns produced in Bavaria were mostly from an older era, but they were all still usable and, with the exception of a few, were equipped with accessories and loading tools.
53   Staudinger, *Geschichte des Kurbayerischen Heeres*, vol. I, p.288.
54   Staudinger, *Geschichte des Kurbayerischen Heeres*, vol. I, p.288.

wagons that inevitably occurred when the troops marched on campaign. The spread of the number of wagons was reminiscent of the Thirty Years' War, and the contemporary documents offer an exhaustive picture about this problem. The reports show that from 1661 onwards, when marching on campaign or during a transfer, each company of foot or horse was regularly equipped with two 'commissary wagons' with four horses for the provisions, and another for transporting tools and the sick. Within the border or inside the Electorate, the peasants always had to transport the baggage with their wagons and animals. After the troops were taken over by the foreign commissars, as occurred in Savoy-Piedmont and Cologne, they were responsible for transporting and supplying the troops. However, the number of commissary wagons was never sufficient, and troops marching to Piedmont and to the Netherlands brought with them much larger convoys of wagons, including vehicles requisitioned locally. The regiment and the companies of dragoons on their march to the Netherlands added 24 other wagons for the troops' baggage; in addition there were also another 40 wagons for the transport of 140 women and 144 children, and even this was not sufficient for the needs of the contingent.[55]

Production of gun powder from Anton Faulhaber's *Artilleriekunst I, Pulverbereitung und weiter.*

In July 1674 the War Council prepared a new plan for increasing the professional army. The decisive influence on this decision was the secret negotiations that took place on 19 June between the Bavarian Minister, the Landgrave Hermann Egon von Fürstenberg, and the Vice-Chancellor Kaspar Schmid on the one hand, and the French extraordinary envoy, the Duke of Vitry, on the other. The agreement was confirmed by Louis XIV on 5 July, with which France financed the Prince-Elector to maintain neutrality. In addition to the *subsidia* already paid in 1673, Ferdinand Maria received a further payment of 75,000 German florins for the recruitment and equipping

---

55 Staudinger, *Geschichte des Kurbayerischen Heeres*, vol. I, p.311.

of 1,500 cavalrymen, and another 12,500 *Reichsthaler* per month for their maintenance. The French money permitted the increasing of the cavalry to 30 companies of 100 cavalrymen in five regiments, and four dragoon companies of 125 men. In 1675, the infantry regiments were reduced to six companies, in order to raise further regiments, and increasing the number of regiments to nine, with additionally just two free companies.[56]

In 1675, the size of the army could permit the establishment of a *Feldarmee* with its own battle order comprising 14 infantry battalions, 20 squadrons of cavalry, two of dragoons, and six light guns, deployed in two lines, a reserve, and regular centre and wings. The army trains required 144 horses for the troops, 47 for the senior commanders, 10 for the *Generalkommissariat*; while the artillery train received 40 horses for the guns and a further 44 for the ammunitions. Both trains were assisted by 138 drivers and *Fussknechte* (Assistants).[57] The overall strength was 7,200 infantry, 2,700 cavalry, and 250 dragoons. Proudly, Prince-Elector Ferdinand Maria occupied the first position in the command assisted by his senior commanders: *General-feldzeugmeister* Graf Berlo, as *Ober-Kommandant*, held the command of the centre; *Generallieutenant* d'Harancourt the right wing; *Generalwachtmeister* Puech the left; *Generalwachtmeister* Montfort the second line, and *Obrist* Bibow the *Reserve*.

However, this superb deployment was short-lived, as the Peace of Nijmegen ended the Franco-Dutch conflict and consequently reduced the military needs of Bavaria. All regiments were disbanded and autonomous companies reconstituted. Between May and June 1679, 35 infantry companies were dismissed, 27 in Bavaria and eight in the Upper Palatinate; 20 cavalry companies, 15 in Bavaria and four in the Upper Palatinate, and one dragoon company in the Upper Palatinate followed the same fate. This left a total of only 22 infantry, 10 cavalry and three dragoon companies overall; the professional troops decreased to 5,000 foot and 1,000 horse. The infantry companies now numbered 18 *Gefreite* and 155 *Gemeine*, but new ranks were introduced, such as the four *Fourierschützen* and three *Zimmerleute*. A core of specialists for the technical corps was retained in München, including one *Ingenieur*, one *Wachtmeisterlieutenant* and two *Zeughausbeamte* (arsenal conservators). Furthermore, emulating the French army, four *Karabiners* were introduced in each infantry company.

It was the last act concerning the army taken by Ferdinand Maria, who passed away on 26 May 1679, leaving the destiny of the state in the hands of the promising prince heir.

---

56 Staudinger, *Geschichte des Kurbayerischen Heeres*, vol. I, p.250. According to the author, the aim of decreasing the infantry was to increase the cavalry, since indeed new horsemen were recruited for this purpose, and even a 'specification' issued in 1675 shows the five cavalry regiments 'with the new addition' of eight companies of 100 men. However, other sources show that the old formation with six remained unchanged, and that the new recruits were probably only recruited to strengthen the existing companies.

57 Staudinger, *Geschichte des Kurbayerischen Heeres*, vol. I, pp.253–254. Ammunition requirements included 50 quintals of match, and 50 quintals of musket balls; reserve ammunition was calculated at 10 musket balls for each infantryman, cavalryman and dragoon, and 600 projectiles for the artillery.

The Army Under Max Emanuel

Bavarian pikeman and musketeer, late 1690s, from Anton Hoffmann, *Das Heer des Blauen Königs. Die Soldaten des Kurfürsten Max II. Emmanuel von Bayern. 1682–1726* (Münich: Manfred Göbel, 1909). According to the most authoritative Bavarian army's scholars, the pikemen had discarded armour in the 1660s. Note the detailed bandolier with cartridges, pouch and match carried by the musketeer.

Although the new Prince-Elector's military policy marked a significant turnaround compared to the one under his father, in the early 1680s the economic conjuncture had not yet been overcome. Moreover, the end of the French subsidies made any rearmament policy uncertain. In 1682, on the eve of the war between the Porte and the Austrian Habsburgs, the Bavarian army was still at its lowest point. However, the emergency caused by the worrying news coming from Constantinople forced the Electorate, like many other German states, to intervene to face the threat. Extraordinary contributions, and the funds from the Pope favoured the raising of a new army. With the *Dekret* issued by Max Emanuel on 29 June 1682, seven regiments of infantry and four of cavalry were raised, joining the free companies with new recruits from the Electoral domains.

The infantry regiments now had eight companies. In detail, each company comprised:

1 *Hauptmann*
1 *Lieutenant*

THE ELECTORATE OF BAVARIA

1 *Fähnrich*
1 *Feldwebel*
1 *Führer*
1 *Fourier*
1 *Feldschreiber*
1 *Feldscherer*
1 *gefreiten Korporal*
6 *gemeine Korporale*
4 *Fourierschützen*
3 *Trommler* [drummers]
1 *Pfeiffer* [fifer]
16 *Gefreite*
111 *Gemeine*

The latter were 24 pikemen and 87 musketeers; the *Fourierschützen* were armed with flintlocks. With the *Generale* issued on 22 October 1682, the Prince-Elector ordered the captains to select eight *Grenadiere* in each company.[58]

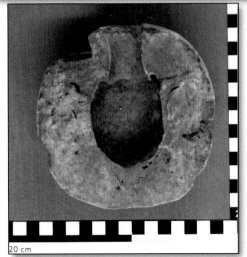

Left and centre, pottery and glass hand grenades, late seventeenth century (Bayerishes Armee Museum, Ingolstadt); Right, pottery hand grenade discovered in 1983 at Ingolstadt during the construction of the underground car park at the former Feldkirchner-Tor-Bastion.

---

58 Münich, *Geschichte der Entwicklung der Bayerischen Armee*, p.41.

Cavalry regiments were reconstituted to six companies each with 100 rank and file as follows:

1 *Rittmeister*
1 *Lieutenant*
1 *Kornett*
1 *Wachtmeister*
1 *Quartiermeister* (Fourier)
1 *Musterschreiber*
1 *Feldscherer*
2 *Trompeter*
1 *Schmied*
1 *Sattler*
2 *Korporale*
87 *Gemeine*

Max Emanuel's goal was to create an army of 12,000 men within a year, and in this regard the War Council pointed out that only four generals were still in service, and field officers were also few.[59] A certain number of officers were therefore examined to select a core of commanders capable of successfully directing the troops on campaign. However, while recruits for the rank and file could be enlisted within the Electorate, and senior commanders with military experience could be obtained from other states, it was much more difficult to find competent officers with the rank of major and above. Together with the NCOs they were the ones who provided the backbone of the army, but in 1682 the military career was not very attractive in Bavaria, and for reasons of prestige army service enjoyed low popularity and was never as high as it was in other German states. However, among many merits, Max Emanuel succeeded in reversing this trend and gradually managed to raise a corps of native officers, restoring to the army the prestige lost in previous years.

Initially, the Prince-Elector committed to gather a corps of 5,000 foot and 3,000 horse, which were to be joined with the Imperial army which Duke Charles V of Lorraine was assembling in Austria. On 6 August the contingent was modified to 4,800 infantry and 3,400 cavalry and dragoons, with 20 field guns, 28 light guns and four heavy mortars. The army and artillery trains comprised 1,022 horses, 287 conductors and 225 assistants. Only two infantry regiments remained in the Electorate, alongside the garrison company Schrenth headquartered in Rothenberg and one free company of cavalry.

A further three free companies of cavalry were raised in summer: that of *Rittmester* Schwinghamer, with 91 horses and 93 men, *Rittmeister* Ulm, 62 and 97, and *Rittmeister* Pappenheim, 97 and 97. On 3 September, the three companies formed a field squadron and then headed to Austria, where the horsemen were distributed among the cuirassier regiments. In

---

59   Münich, *Geschichte der Entwicklung der Bayerischen Armee*, p.39.

April, eight dragoon companies of 125 men were raised by amalgamating the new recruits with the men of the existing four companies. With these, two squadrons or 'half-regiments' of four companies were created under *Feldmarshall-Lieutenant* Hannibal von Degenfeld.[60] In September, two new cavalry regiments were raised, *Harancourt Cuirassieren* (BvC-15) and *Löbell Cuirassieren* (BvC-16), each of six companies of 100 men, which after the muster numbered 447 horses and 548 men, and 529 horse and 560 men respectively.[61]

Between 1683 and 1688, the Bavarian army maintained its strength to significant numbers, although each year the Hungarian campaigns consumed whole companies. Every year, at the end of the campaign, the commissioners' reviews transmitted the list of losses suffered by the troops, and consequently the War Council issued the licences to enlist new recruits. Nevertheless, in 1684 Max Emanuel raised the funds to increase the Bavarian relief corps to 13,000 men. This contribution, although paid at a good price and never reached on the field, gave Max Emanuel the title of the Emperor's best ally, at least in the first phase of the war against the Porte. However, the losses sustained and the difficulty of maintaining a company at full strength forced the Prince-Elector to decrease the number of men in the infantry companies. In April 1685, apart from the *Leibregiment* the regiments in Hungary deployed eight companies of 125 men, with the same number of officers, and four *Korporale*, eight *Gefreite*, four *Fourierschützen*, four *Spielleute* and 97 *Gemeine*. For tactical purposes the grenadiers from all the infantry regiments were joined in a company of 125 men under a grenadier *Hauptmann*. In September the cavalry and dragoon regiments were also reformed into nine companies of 62 men.[62] Before the end

Bavarian cuirassier, late seventeenth century, illustration by Anton Hoffmann. (Author's Collection) The celebrated work of Hoffmann provides a great deal of information about the army under Prince-Elector Max Emanuel, but mainly focusing on the years 1700–1726. The talented artist researched among the items preserved in the Bavarian Army Museum of Ingolstadt as well as in private collections. Sadly, many of these items were destroyed during the Second World War, and others had been lost over time. Although the figures depicted by Hofmann belong to a more recent age, weaponry and other items are consistent with an earlier period.

---

60 Staudinger, *Geschichte des Kurbayerischen Heeres*, vol. II, p.43. In January 1684, both the 'half-regiments' formed the regiment *Sachsen-Eisanach Dragoner* (BdD-2).
61 Staudinger, *Geschichte des Kurbayerischen Heeres*, vol. II, p.45.
62 Staudinger, *Geschichte des Kurbayerischen Heeres*, vol. II, p.55.

WARS AND SOLDIERS IN THE EARLY REIGN OF LOUIS XIV – VOLUME 7 PART 1

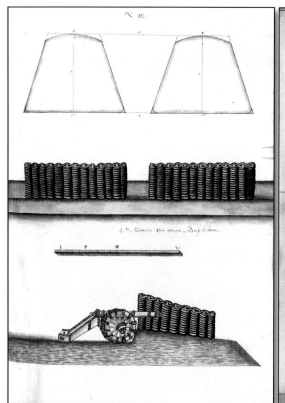
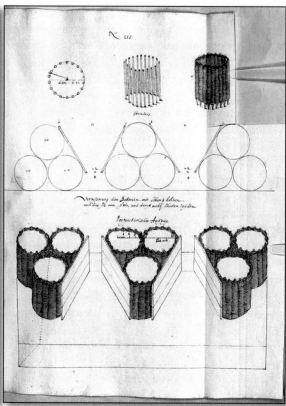
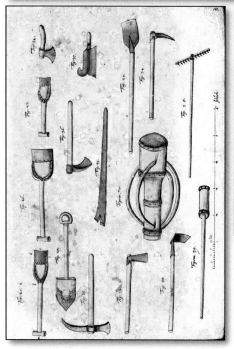

Artillery position, gabions, pioneers' tools, and siege workers from Anton Faulhaber's manuscript of 1680–1702 (Bayerischer Staatsbibliothek, Münich). According to Karl Staudinger's *Geschichte des Kurbayerischen Heeres Insbesondere unter Kurfürst Ferdinand Maria, 1651–1679* (Münich, 1901), there were a number of infantry officers with knowledge of siege techniques. Among them was Captain Tobias Anders, who served in the *Beltin* infantry regiment during the Savoy-Piedmont war against Genoa in 1672. The most important of the Bavarian military engineers was the *Oberingenieur* Christoph Heidemann, author of the *Architectura Militaris* published in 1664.

of the year, a new dragoon regiment of 600 men was raised with volunteers recruited in Hamburg.[63]

The Bavarians fought in Hungary until 1688, when they took part in the conquest of Belgrade under their Prince-Elector. This was the last major action performed in the Hungarian war theatre, since in September the French invasion of the Palatinate called the German Prince to join the League of Augsburg.

In 1683, a new regulation of the infantry's drill was issued, which improved that of 1673, introduced under Ferdinand Maria. In 1687, Max Emanuel convened the War Council to discuss a new regulation concerning the military administration. The *Verpflegungs-Ordonanz* was completed before the end of the year,[64] and established the details of payment, food and horses for every rank from the generals to the private soldiers, overcoming the antiquated separation of summer and winter pay and treatment inherited from the Thirty Years' War, by conferring to the army a status of a stable, state-integrated body. One year after, the War Council issued a new regulation which dealt with supply and the army train, inspired by the French magazine system.[65]

Like his father, Max Emanuel invested many resources in the education of a corps of artillerymen, engineers and miners, and the measures sometimes had the touch of originality. Initially, he assigned the best constables to teach the basics of artillery to the children of farmers, who paid a modest sum to the school. The state arsenals provided the teaching instruments, including cannons and projectiles. For the instruction in the use of these weapons, as well as fireworks and grenades, young people had to pass an exam and pay an

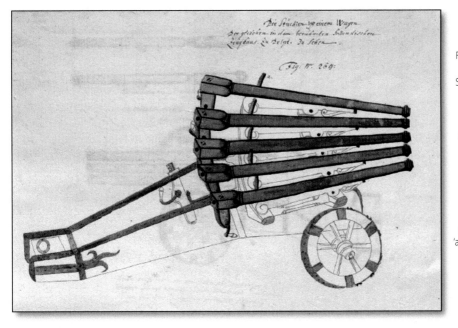

Five barrelled gun with chamber loading for rapid fire from Anton Faulhaber's manuscript of 1680–1702 (Bayerischer Staatsbibliothek, München). Multiple similar light guns are recorded in the Bavarian artillery arsenal in the 1670s and 1680s. Staudinger again describes these 'organ guns' as consisting of five more barrels, either side by side, or on top of each other, or even permanently connected 'and comparable to today's *mitrailleusen*'.

---

63 Staudinger, *Geschichte des Kurbayerischen Heeres*, vol. II, p.55, regiment *Bielke Dragoner* (BvD-4).
64 Münich, *Geschichte der Entwicklung der Bayerischen Armee*, pp.58–62.
65 Münich, *Geschichte der Entwicklung der Bayerischen Armee*, pp.54–55.

additional fee. These schools were also open to soldiers, who were instructed free of charge.[66] According to Bavarian historians, The Electoral troops that took part in the defence of Candia in 1669 and those who fought for Savoy-Piedmont and Cologne in 1672 included excellent artillerymen. In the 1680s, *Constables* were sent to Venice to testify to the high efficiency of the Bavarian school.

Already in the 1670s, the War Council had discussed the idea of establishing a regular organisation for the field artillery. Several proposals had been studied for this purpose, among which that of 1676 which provided a complete picture of the contemporary field artillery corps introduced in the European armies.[67] Max Emanuel also improved the train service, which was divided according to genre, into horse or ox train, or by type, into supply, artillery and bridge train. Particular care was taken to establish a corps of trained personnel including corporals and baggage masters, which was very advanced in comparison to what existed in other armies not only in Germany, but even in Europe. The bridge train was associated with the artillery train and was therefore directed by officers of this corps.

Pursuing his father's plan for the production of uniforms and equipment, Max Emanuel established a factory in München which supplied everything the troops needed, while the armament was produced in the state arsenals.[68]

Certainly, among the merits that historians can ascribe to Max Emanuel, his commitment to improve the living conditions of soldiers was among the first. Greatcoats – *Kaputrock* – were issued to the infantry to better cope with the winter, especially in Hungary, and beer or wine had to be provided to help the soldier to serve in the colder months. The improvements also included military justice. According to some contemporary testimonies, criminal laws and punishments were rather mild in the Bavarian army. Capital punishments

Musketeer with *Kaputrock*, 1686–88. (Author's reconstruction in the style of Anton Hoffmann) The greatcoat must have contributed significantly in mitigating the harshness of the soldiers' living conditions. The instructions for Commissioner General of War Pelkhover issued on 6 March 1674, state that for an army strength of 12,000 men, an approximate loss through illness and desertion of 1,000 men per year was assumed.

---

66   K.u.K. Kriegsarchiv, *Feldzüge des Prinzen Eugen von Savoyen*, vol. I, p.448.
67   Staudinger, *Geschichte des Kurbayerischen Heeres*, vol. II, p.297.
68   K.u.K. Kriegsarchiv, *Feldzüge des Prinzen Eugen von Savoyen*, vol. I, p.450.

were rare, and even the most serious crimes incurred at most a ban from the state. As a rule, the sentences inflicted on soldiers consisted of corporal punishment such as beatings, or fatigue duties. Even the laws against duels between soldiers, enacted several times by Max Emanuel, were prosecuted mildly. In the opinion of contemporaries, it was emphasised that 'despite such mildness, the Bavarian soldiers had distinguished themselves for discipline and obedience during the campaigns against the Ottomans in Hungary from 1683 to 1688, nevertheless, towards the population of that country, whether friend or foe, they committed often exorbitant excesses.'[69]

Household Troops

The history of the Bavarian guard units followed a pattern quite similar to those existing in other German states. The soldiers dealing with the person of the Prince-Elector were of the company of the *Trabanten*, who essentially served as palace foot guards. They were not exactly a military corps since they did not perform military duties. This was the main difference that marked them from the *Leibgarde zu Ross* or *Arquebusieren Garde* (bvc-i), which was a company of mounted lifeguards in charge of providing an escort to the Prince-Elector when he travelled through the state or led the army on campaign. In 1658 *Leibgarde zu Ross* were 100 horsemen under a captain who received the salary of colonel.[70] However, it seems that the low status of the company no longer responded to the daily needs of the court service, since by an ordinance of 10 July 1660, issued immediately after the reduction of the army, Prince-Elector Ferdinand Maria ordered the increase of the company to 48 horsemen, excluding officers and NCOs, and subsequently added another 28 horsemen and two corporals, though dismissing eight of the oldest among the rank and file. This reinforcement was undoubtedly also influenced by the Prince-Elector's desire to retain for the future a core of veterans already experienced in military matters. In 1661, however, the company was reformed and its numbers decreased to 80 horsemen and 16 *Provisioner* (lance-corporals who served without pay but received food rations). The resulting company was composed of one *Hauptmann*, one *Lieutenant*, one *Kornett*, one *Wachtmeister*, one *Fourier*, six *Korporale*, two *Trompeter* and 67 *Korbiner* (carabineers).[71] In the 1660s the company is sometimes designated as *Korbinereitern*, after the firearms carried in service. Even if the Elector did not take part in military actions, in 1661 he sent a captain, the Scottish-Irish Count Hamilton, and two corporals as *supernumerari*, to join the Bavarian cavalry in Hungary. This internship, risky but necessary to test the value of the men who had the delicate function of protecting the sovereign's life, resolved positively, since they distinguished

---

69   K.u.K. Kriegsarchiv, *Feldzüge des Prinzen Eugen von Savoyen*, vol. I, p.452.

70   Staudinger, *Geschichte des Kurbayerischen Heeres*, vol. I, p.151.

71   Staudinger, *Geschichte des Kurbayerischen Heeres*, vol. I, p.152.

themselves for their exceptional courage demonstrated in action against the Ottomans.[72]

In 1664 the number of the *Korbiner* was still 80 horsemen and 12 *Provisioner*, but the strength fell to 68 in 1665. In 1668, immediately before the reform of the company, it numbered 64 men and nine *Provisioner*, including officers and NCOs. On 13 April 1669, the mounted life guards of the *Archibusier* or *Korbinerreiter* were transformed into the company of the *Hartschiere* (bvc-ii), which formed a new unit under the personal command of the Prince-Elector. Three days before, Ferdinand Maria had already decreed that only horsemen who were actual 'knights' could serve among the *Hartschiere*.

Alongside the *Hartschiere* a new company was raised, denominated *Leibquardia von leichten Pferden* (bvc-iii), which shortly afterwards took the name of the disbanded *Korbiner* horse guard. This company comprised half of the *Reiterkompagnie* of the *Rittmeister* Friedrich Beinns headquartered in München with 55 men, including one *Hauptmann*, one *Kornet*, one *Fourier*, four *Korporale* and 47 horsemen.[73] On 29 March 1670 the new *Korbinergarde* received detailed instructions about their service inside and outside the Prince-Elector's residence in München. The two horse guards had precedence over the foot guards – the *Trabanten* – and the *Korbinergarde* preceded the other mounted guards. Members of the two new companies received the same salaries as the previous lifeguards. The first commander of the *Korbinergarde* was the Savoyard Jean-Louis de la

Hartschiere (mounted Life Guard) in parade dress, 1671. (Author's reconstruction in the style of Anton Hoffmann) Black hat with azure and white plumes; medium blue tunic laced in white and black; medium blue coat with black cuffs laced in silver; silver buttons: medium blue saddle cover trimmed white and black and with a silver monogram.

---

72 Staudinger, *Geschichte des Kurbayerischen Heeres*, vol. I, p.152.
73 Staudinger, *Geschichte des Kurbayerischen Heeres*, vol. I, p.154. This company continued to be denominated *Die Gewest Fritzsche Kompagnie*.

THE ELECTORATE OF BAVARIA

Perouse.[74] The appointment, promotion and dismissal of officers, such as the *Hartschiere* and the *Korbiner*, were carried out by the Elector himself, while the oath of loyalty was sworn to the captain-commander. The commanders of the three lifeguards carried a black ebony cane, the *Spanish Rohr*, as a symbol of their position as senior officers. The two companies showed themselves in all their splendour for the first time in the spring of 1670, on the occasion of the passage of the Prince-Bishop Elector of Cologne in Münich, and again on 31 June 1671 at the reception of Prince-Bishop Maximilian Gandolf of Salzburg.[75]

The strength of the two mounted lifeguards remained unchanged from 1669 until the death of Ferdinand Maria, although small fluctuations occurred. In 1680 the *Hartschiere* and *Korbiner* numbered 55 men each, and a few weeks before the start of the 1684 campaign, both horse guards were scrupulously inspected especially regarding the health of their men. The horsemen found still able were placed in the *Hartschiere*. On 18 August the *Korbinergarde* was then disbanded, leaving the Mounted Household with just one company, which continued to exist until the following century. Of the disbanded company, one *Wachtmeister*, one *Fourier*, four Korporale and 48 *Korbiner* remained in service forming a half-company of aged veterans, while 30 men joined the *Hartschiere*.[76] They accompanied Prince-Elector Max Emanuel in all the military campaigns from 1683 to 1688. Most of the members of the *Hartschiere* were originally from Bavaria but some names indicate that entry was

Hartschiere, mounted Life Guard, in campaign dress 1683–88 (Author's reconstruction in the style of Anton Hoffmann). Blackened iron 'lobster' pattern helmet and armour; medium blue coat with black cuffs and lining laced in silver; medium blue breeches; Medium blue saddle cover with white and black trim and a silver monogram.

---

74 Staudinger, *Geschichte des Kurbayerischen Heeres*, vol. I, p.155.
75 Staudinger, *Geschichte des Kurbayerischen Heeres*, vol. I, p.155.
76 Staudinger, *Geschichte des Kurbayerischen Heeres*, vol. II, p.27. The documentation relating the inspection of the life guards in 1684 includes notices about the career of some horsemen. Among these, there is the story of *Korporal* Johann Walchen, aged 61, 'who had fought bravely in many battles and skirmishes during his 45 years of service, asked for a waiting allowance and justified his request by saying that in the Thirty Years' War he had captured a Swedish kettledrummer together with his instruments and taken him away prisoner, an episode for which, he stated, the witnesses were still alive.'

not denied to foreigners. In 1685 the company was augmented with two *Korporale* and 22 lifeguards. On 11 April 1687 an order of the Prince-Elector increased the *Hartschiere* with one *Korporal* and one horsemen taken from each company of the cuirassier regiments: the horse guard now numbered 200 men. Each year, 100 guards in turn joined the army on campaign. In 1688 a report registers the *Hartschiere* divided in five brigades of 20 men each, then in 1689, 150 lifeguards escorted the Prince-Elector during the campaign on the Rhine against the French.[77]

In 1684 Max Emanuel also raised his own *Leibgarde* of foot, attributing this title to the regiment *Mercy zu Fuss* (BvI-17). Apart from the exterior symbols and a clothing of better quality, the foot guards received the attention of an actual elite corps, and in 1685 they retained a different strength, with 150 men per company, while the companies of the ordinary regiments had decreased to 125.[78]

Militia

Although the militia had a long history in Bavaria, during the Thirty Years' War, it lost much of its importance. After 1688 the economic conditions of the Electorate made it difficult to maintain an efficient service. At the beginning of 1651, the last year of his reign, Maximilian I ordered all *Landfahnen* (militia companies) to be disbanded 'for the economic relief of the country', with the exception of those belonging to strategically important places.[79] In total, 29 companies were to be disbanded. The Prince-Elector's councillors did not pronounce on the matter, but after the death of Maximilian I they considered maintaining the still-existing companies and gave orders to fill the gaps in the ranks. According to them, in order to maintain an acceptable level of efficiency, the companies were to be trained every Sunday for at least two to three years, while the militia of the larger towns were to start training again without further delay.[80] During Ferdinand Maria's tutelage, Duke Albert VI pursued the project to disband the militia but the intention remained a dead letter. In Bavaria in 1654, a total of 11,237 men were still available on paper, divided between Münich, Landshut, Straubing, and Burghausen. In the Upper Palatinate, under the orders of 28 *Landlieutenants*, there were 5,936 men divided into 1,970 *Doppelsöldner* (pikemen), 3,670 *Musketiere*, and 296 *Schützen*. The Prince-Elector ordered that service in the militia was only to be required from the town burghers. The renunciation of the employment of peasants was confirmed in 1655, when the War Council proposed a *Landesdefension* of 6,900 men in all.

---

77 Staudinger, *Geschichte des Kurbayerischen Heeres*, vol. II, p.28.
78 Staudinger, *Geschichte des Kurbayerischen Heeres*, vol. II, p.54.
79 Staudinger, *Geschichte des Kurbayerischen Heeres*, vol. II, p.54.
80 Staudinger, *Geschichte des Kurbayerischen Heeres*, vol. II, p.54.

On 10 October 1663, the War Council issued the Prince-Elector's order through an *Instruktion* for the militia companies of Ötting, Branau and Schärding in Bavaria. The order established the duties of the militiamen, their number and training sessions. Before the end of the year, after an accurate registration of the families of the Electorate, another *Instruktion* followed. The document established the number of companies for each province, for 15,802 men in all; in detail:

Münich	14 *Landfahnen*	5,556 militiamen
Landshut	7 *Landfahnen*	2,912 militiamen
Straubing	6 *Landfahnen*	2,177 militiamen
Burghausen	6 *Landfahnen*	2,065 militiamen
Upper Palatinate	11 *Landfahnen*	3,092 militiamen

Moreover, in the major towns further four *Stadtfahnen* were established with 1,700 militiamen in all; in detail:

Münich	2 *Stadtfahnen*	683 & 400 militiamen
Landshut	1 *Stadtfahnen*	250 militiamen
Straubing	1 *Stadtfahnen*	323 militiamen

In the same year, the *Primaplana* of companies was established, comprising one *Hauptmann*, one *Lieutenant*, one *Fähnrich*, one *Feldwebel*, one *Führer*, one *gefreiten Korporal*, 6–10 *Korporale* (one for every 40 men), three drummers and one fifer.[81]

In 1672 the Prince-Elector and the War Council turned again to the matter, when the news coming from Poland caused concerns in Münich: the government feared that the Ottoman and Tatar raids could extend as far as the Inn and Danube. On 26 June 1672 an extraordinary council formed by the provincial authorities convened in Landshut, to discuss the matter. In addition to the supply requested by the mobilisation of 4,000 militiamen, to be replaced every two months by another 4,000, the service was to be remunerated by a reward. The economic burden was considered too high, and most of the provinces decided against it; consequently, the War Council shelved the project and finally abandoned it.[82]

The muster of the Bavarian *Landfahnen* executed in the summer of 1672 registered 5,563 foot militiamen in Münich, 2,925 in Landshut, 2,115 in Straubing, and 2,052 in Burghausen, totalling 12,655 militiamen in all. Four years later the figure had not changed, and the muster details specified 7,496 musketeers. The absence of data concerning the Upper Palatinate was the consequence of the suspension of the service between 1669 and 1674.[83] The

---

81   Staudinger, *Geschichte des Kurbayerischen Heeres*, vol. I, pp.319–320.
82   Staudinger, *Geschichte des Kurbayerischen Heeres*, vol. I, p.321.
83   Staudinger, *Geschichte des Kurbayerischen Heeres*, vol. I, p.323. Before 1674, the last information about the Upper Palatinate militia is from 1669. There were 11 *ruhenden* (literally, 'sleeping')

regular service in the Upper Palatinate started again in 1675, as confirmed in the *Exerziere* for the militia of Amberg. Each Sunday, 38 militiamen with one *Feldwebel*, one *Korporal*, and five *Gefreite* met to receive the training from their officers. The next Sunday a further 38 militiamen and NCOs followed for the same duty, which was to be repeated after six Sundays.

In 1680, a new regulation was issued to the militia by Prince-Elector Max Emanuel. The foot militia, now denominated *Landausschuss*, consisted of three classes. The first comprised the younger subjects and was therefore regarded as an elite militia, while the second class, identified by the term *Landwehr*, comprised the older subjects. A final class, the *Landsturm*, constituted the mass conscription of all the subjects in the Electorate. Each militia class was divided into the traditional companies of *Landfahnen* and enjoyed a good reputation among commentators at the end of the seventeenth century, who emphasised the skill of Bavarian peasants as marksmen. At the end of the century, there were about 1,200 first class militia.[84] The mounted militia was not introduced until the following century, and in those years it remained the custom for nobles to provide one or more mounted militiaman depending on the extent of their possessions. The Prince-Elector's intentions included turning the elite militia into a reserve for the completion of the professional army, and to facilitate this he offered volunteers the possibility of enlisting for only two years, and afterwards being discharged from the militia service for life. However, enrolment always remained voluntary, and like other German princes, Max Emmanuel also had to resort to volunteers from other parts of Germany to complete his professional army.[85]

The Bavarian Army on Campaign

Bavaria had been the only state to have fought throughout the Thirty Years' War, first as part of the Catholic League and then with an independent army. However, after 1648 the Electorate maintained a rigid policy of neutrality, which before 1683 offered little occasion to involve the Bavarian troops in military action. At least with single units, the Electorate joined its troops with those of the *Reich* in 1661–64 against the Ottomans in Hungary and Transylvania, and always against the same enemy; five years later, the Prince-Elector hired an infantry regiment to Venice for the defence of Candia.[86] In 1669 the *Bühren zu Fuss* (BvI-7) marched to Italy after the agreement with

---

Landfahnen which disposed of 400 halberds and partisans, 2,276 muskets, 2,229 bandoliers, 2,240 forks for muskets, 425 pikes, 639 *Wischer* (scrub brushes), and four drums.

84   K.u.K. Kriegsarchiv, *Feldzüge des Prinzen Eugen von Savoyen*, vol. I, pp.447–448.
85   K.u.K. Kriegsarchiv, *Feldzüge des Prinzen Eugen von Savoyen*, vol. I, pp.447–448.
86   Bavaria had already hired troops to Venice in 1649, when a regiment of 1,000 foot had served in Crete until 1652 or 1653, under the 'brave colonel Crossen (or Closen)'. In 1659, another regiment recruited in Bavaria sailed to Candia under the Venetian colonel Negron, usually denominated in the sources as *Reggimento di Baviera*. See Bruno Mugnai, *The Cretan War – The Venetian-Ottoman Struggle in the Mediterranean* (Warwick: Helion & Company, 2018), pp.111, 185.

the Republic signed on 13 March for 1,000 musketeers in 10 companies.[87] Venice paid the cost for eight companies, and the Prince-Elector, to testify his solidarity with the Republic in the war against the Porte, assumed the expense for two.[88] Volunteers and artillery constables joined the regiment, increasing the Bavarian contingent to 1,050 men. On 19 April they were quartered in Verona and mustered by the Venetian *Inquisitori di Stato*. Some drawbacks delayed the arrival to Venice, since the cash needed to pay the troops had not yet been delivered. For this, Colonel Bürhen was forced to declare that he would not leave Verona until the Republic had fulfilled its obligations. Finally, on 24 April, thanks to the intervention of *provveditore* Contarini, a courier brought at least part of the money; payment of the remaining balance was secured for arrival in Venice. Thus, on 27 April, the regiment could be embarked on 22 boats to sail down the Adige River the following day. On 31 May, after four weeks spent in the quarters located at the Lido of Venice, 450 men sailed to Crete on the vessel *San Nicolò*, followed by the rest of the contingent the day after on eight tartans. The Bavarians landed at Candia on 29 June, having left six sick men at Cephalonia. Inside Candia, Colonel Bühren and his men were assigned to the reserve corps at the bastion of Sant'Andrea, one of the most exposed sectors, where the besiegers had managed to advance and break through the curtain after months of relentless fighting. The events which involved the Bavarians are little documented,[89] however, it is certain that they experienced the dramatic final phase of the siege. According to the report of Colonel Bürhen, written on 12 July, he was immediately ordered by Morosini to place his men in the other most threatened sector, the Forte San Demetrio, close to the bastion Sabbionera, and in the 'crowned work' of Santa Maria, with the order to keep the ravelin of San Nicolò at all costs. Days after, the regiment also manned the fort of Palma with one company and Santa Maria with the others, then placed a guard of 50 men in the ravelin San Nicolò, located between the two fortified sectors, where they remained night and day for two weeks. In late July the Bavarians managed to repel a furious enemy assault on the Sabbionera bastion; then in August and early September, they joined the German infantry in the extreme defence of Sant'Andrea. Again specific information is rare.[90] The review carried out in September on the islet of Standia, after the surrender of Candia, does not help in forming a comprehensive picture either. The muster registered 137 men fewer than the number landed in June, and this would be an extraordinarily low casualty rate compared to that suffered by the other contingents in Candia. However,

---

87 Staudinger, *Geschichte des Kurbayerischen Heeres*, vol. I, p.562.

88 Staudinger, *Geschichte des Kkurbayerischen Heeres*, vol. I, p.564.

89 Staudinger, *Geschichte des Kurbayerischen Heeres*, vol. I, p.583. The author points out: 'Here is where our account should begin, with a broader consideration of the singular events; unfortunately, the circumstances are such that our sources provide only weak evidence of the Bavarians' participation in the struggle. A diary of the siege, such as still exists today for other contingents, may have been swept away by the waves of the Adriatic on the return voyage; but the foreigners mostly thought only of themselves in their accounts and our knowledge of the events is based on only a few fragments of documents.'

90 Staudinger, *Geschichte des Kurbayerischen Heeres*, vol. I, p.592.

when in mid-November the Bavarian regiment was mustered again in Corfu, only 230 men survived.[91] This might suggest that the September review in Standia included a large number of wounded and sick who did not survive the sailing to Corfu. The same number landed at the Lido on 29 November, the surviving companies numbered between 21 and 38 men.[92]

The suffering of the Bavarians was not over: their return home was hindered by the prohibition of the Imperial authorities in Vienna to cross Austrian territory, a treatment in return for Ferdinand Maria's support for Louis XIV, and the same prohibition came from Milan. The return was delayed until January 1670 when, after much negotiation, the Republic of Venice embarked the Bavarians on a vessel which circumnavigated the entire Peninsula as far as Nice. The sailing cost the lives of six men, while one captain on board another ship, was captured by corsairs from Tripoli and lived there as a slave until 1671, when finally Ferdinand Maria paid the ransom for his freedom.[93]

Prince-Elector Ferdinand Maria of Wittelsbach and his wife Enrichetta Adelaide of Savoy in a hunting party, portrayed by Jan Miel in 1658–63. (Venaria Reale Palace, Turin) The Prince-Elector is wearing a fashionable coat in dark blue laced in silver. Note the details of the horses' bit and bridle.

---

91 Archivio di Stato di Venezia, *Senato Mar – Provveditori da Terra e da Mar, Dispacci*, b. 670, dated 29 November 1669.
92 Staudinger, *Geschichte des Kurbayerischen Heeres*, vol. I, p.594.
93 Staudinger, *Geschichte des Kurbayerischen Heeres*, vol. I, p.597.

In Savoy-Piedmont Service, 1672

In September 1672 Carlo Emanuele II of Savoy, the Italian brother-in-law of Ferdinand Maria, asked for 2,000 infantrymen through his representative in Münich Jean-Antoine du Chastel de Bertrand de la Perouse. The Duke of Savoy had approached Ferdinand Maria with regard to hiring soldiers in anticipation of the new offensive he was preparing against the Republic of Genoa, after the unsuccessful outcome of the one begun in June. Ferdinand Maria's relations with his relative in Turin were excellent, and many of Savoy's subjects as well as Italians from other states had served and still served at court or in the Electoral army. Given these premises, no obstacles or political compromises prevented Ferdinand Maria from supporting Carlo Emanuele II's war effort. On 16 September 1672, 10 companies each of 120 infantrymen joined in a regiment under Colonel Wilhelm Beltin, alongside a field battalion of four companies of 125 foot, under *Obristlieutenant* and captain of the *Leibgarde der Hartschiere*, Jean-Louis de la Perouse, a nephew of the Savoy-Piedmontese diplomat. The 1,700 Bavarian infantrymen were all musketeers, since pikes had proved to be completely useless on the Ligurian battlefields. The contingent left Münich on 23 September; the Duke of Savoy obtained permission for the troops to pass through the territory of the Swiss confederation and the Valais Republic, thus avoiding any interference with Austrian and Spanish territories. The Bavarians took part in the last major action of the conflict, the siege of Ovada, in the *Oltregiogo* of Genoa, a strategically important territory straddling the Ligurian Apennines. On 8 October Ovada was seized, but the campaign ended in disaster for the besieging troops who were caught up in the explosion of the city's arsenal. The Bavarian infantry concluded the campaign with the occupation of Rossiglione on 10 October.[94] In late November the Bavarians took winter quarters in Turin, and in January 1673 they left Piedmont heading to Münich along the route travelled months before. Upon departure, 288 men were registered as casualties;[95] upon arrival in Münich, on 3 March 1673, the regiment numbered 852 men and the battalion 325. The return march and the crossing of the Alpine passes in the winter season had caused considerable inconvenience and further soldiers had died from diseases or had deserted.[96]

Campaigns in the Netherlands, 1672–74

Parental links favoured the hiring of further contingents, and almost simultaneously with the contingent sent to Italy, Prince-Elector Ferdinand Maria raised a corps for his cousin Maximilian Heinrich von Wittelsbach, Prince-Bishop Elector of Cologne. However, this kind of aid was of a very

---

94   See also Mugnai, *Wars and Soldiers*, vol. 6, part 2, pp.187–189.
95   Staudinger, *Geschichte des Kurbayerischen Heeres*, vol. I, p.604.
96   Staudinger, *Geschichte des Kurbayerischen Heeres*, vol. I, p.606.

different nature from that provided to the Duke of Savoy. In 1671 Prince-Elector Ferdinand Maria had already signed a treaty with France: this did not prevent him pursuing a policy of neutrality, however, this time he would be militarily sustaining an ally of Louis XIV. And Cologne was not a marginal ally. The alliance with the Prince-Bishop Elector allowed Louis XIV the possibility of advancing along the Rhine to invade the Dutch Republic without crossing Spanish territories. This opportunity was the cornerstone of the French war cabinet's strategy for the campaign of 1672. In München, everyone knew that since 1669 the architects of the Franco-Bavarian agreement, the three brothers Wilhelm, Franz and Hermann Egon von Fürstenberg, had endeavoured to persuade Ferdinand Maria to provide indirect support to his cousin in Cologne in the event of a war against the Dutch. In the autumn of 1671, the Cologne councillor Friedrich Wilhelm von Bockhorst, entrusted by the Prince-Bishop Elector with a mission to the German courts, repeatedly appealed to München for armed assistance, emphasising Cologne's difficulty in maintaining its neutrality in the face of a Dutch provocation, which was being aired as increasingly probable. The demands Bockhorst presented to Ferdinand Maria were not insignificant: a 'well-dressed' foot regiment, equipped with all primary and secondary armament, comprising 18 companies of 2,000 men, of which at least 1,200 had to be 'veterans and proven', under the command of a 'valiant and experienced colonel as well as good captains and other well-trained officers'.[97] In addition, six cavalry troops totalling 400 men under Colonel Höning and two companies of dragoons under Colonel de Martin were requested, to which three Cologne companies of 86 men each would then be subordinated under a lieutenant colonel appointed by the Prince-Bishop Elector. In order to take command of the army of Electoral Cologne, Major General Berlo, who at the time had entered the service of Bavaria precisely on the recommendation of Maximilian Heinrich, was asked to make himself available.[98] The troops of the Bavarian auxiliary corps were to remain in the service of Bavaria, but were not to be recalled until Cologne had agreed a peace with the Dutch Republic. Maximilian Heinrich offered to cover all expenses for the recruitment and transfer of troops from Bavaria, as well as the payment of allowances for dead soldiers and all other expenses in exactly the same way as for the Cologne troops, from the day of their arrival in the Electorate until their return to Bavarian territory.

When Cologne's head of foreign affairs, Wilhelm Egon von Fürstenberg, travelled to München in person at the beginning of April, he explained the proposals of Prince-Elector Max Heinrich in detail and focused attention on the alliance between France and Cologne, which had been kept secret since January. Now, after further negotiations lasting several weeks, München and Cologne reached an agreement, which was signed by the two sovereigns on 25 April 1672. In the meantime, the senior commanders requested by Bockhorst did not leave Bavarian service, and Maximilian Heinrich had

---

97   Staudinger, *Geschichte des Kurbayerischen Heeres*, vol. I, p.608.
98   Staudinger, *Geschichte des Kurbayerischen Heeres*, vol. I, p.608.

THE ELECTORATE OF BAVARIA

considerably reduced his demand, cancelling the 400 horsemen and reducing the strength of the foot regiment to 1,200 or 1,500 men at maximum.[99]

With this agreement Ferdinand Maria promised to deliver to Cologne a regiment of 1,200 men on foot with the senior officers and NCOs 'for the defence and insurance of the Elector and the Archbishopric of Cologne', and to pay the transfer costs until the soldiers reached the place where Cologne would take charge of them, which was established as Wertheim am Main. In turn, Maximilian Heinrich promised that if Bavaria ever needed that regiment it would be returned immediately without any objection, nor would he disband it without Ferdinand Maria's knowledge when peace came, pledging to replace as soon as possible the human losses suffered during the time it had been in his service.[100]

Naturally, there was still a long way to go before the auxiliary corps was ready to march. Ferdinand Maria insisted on a definition of the French protection. The offers made by Louis XIV on this matter did not give the desired certainty for all possible events to come, and then further negotiations were necessary. These lasted until 27 May 1672, when the French guarantee treaty was finally signed by the Prince-Elector. With this agreement France undertook, in the event that Ferdinand Maria was attacked by an ally of the Dutch Republic because of the military support granted to Cologne, to send troops to rescue Bavaria 'at the first call for help and without loss of time, and if necessary to intervene on behalf of the Elector's state with all its military might'.[101] Furthermore, in the event of an assault, further support in the form of troops or in money was to be regulated by a special agreement between France and Cologne on the one hand, and Bavaria on the other. The treaty was signed on the same day that Cologne declared war on the Dutch Republic. On the same day, Ferdinand Maria informed Maximilian Heinrich that he had arranged for both the infantry regiment and the two dragoon companies to meet in time to arrive in Wertheim on 9 or 10 June.

Although recruitment started late, on 2 February, the new regiment was completed in a short time and consisted of 11 companies of 125 men. After the appointment of the officers of the existing four companies on 5 March, those for the seven new companies were also appointed by decree on 14 March.[102] The command of the regiment was entrusted to *Obrist* Johann Wilhelm von Culer (BvI-10). The companies gathered in Münich left Bavaria on 29 May; a day later they were joined by those from Ingolstadt. Culer arrived to take command on 2 June, together with the companies from the Upper Palatinate and de Martin's dragoons. The dragoon company Dubelier was still on the march from Wilshofen with the horses of both the companies. The following day, *Generalwachtmeister* Puech examined the regiment and declared that it was complete and 'composed of fine and brave people'.[103]

---

99   Staudinger, *Geschichte des Kurbayerischen Heeres*, vol. I, p.609.
100 Staudinger, *Geschichte des Kurbayerischen Heeres*, vol. I, p.609.
101 Staudinger, *Geschichte des Kurbayerischen Heeres*, vol. I, p.610.
102 Staudinger, *Geschichte des Kurbayerischen Heeres*, vol. I, p.611. The officers included a Frenchman, *Obristlieutenant* Claude de Bronne, and a Tuscan, the *Hauptmann* Cosimo Compagni.
103 Staudinger, *Geschichte des Kurbayerischen Heeres*, vol. I, p.612.

On 4 June the troops departed from Wending, together with the commissioner in charge of handing them over to his colleagues from Cologne. However, the poor state of the roads and the unusual heat of the summer of 1672 considerably delayed the march of the troops. French war preparations were well known and had understandably aroused the anxious concern of the population. The irritation that dominated public opinion against Cologne did not help to give the Bavarian troops a benevolent welcome. Only the territory of Ansbach made an exception; while in Königshofen, in the state of Mainz, whose Elector was on very good terms with France, the Bavarians received 'more than just a roof over their heads'. Even Wertheim, residence of the Count of Löwenstein, brother-in-law of the Landgraves of Fürstenberg, closed its doors to the Bavarians, who were forced to camp outside the town.[104] In Wertheim the Cologne commissioners took over the Bavarian troops and led the infantry by river to the assembly point at Kaiserswerth on the Rhine, while the two companies of dragoons – Dubelier had just joined them – continued by land. But the departure of the Bavarian commissioner made the troops nervous. Rumours that the regiment had been sold to France found credence, but on 10 June Culer's prudence and reputation succeeded in completing the embarkation without further inconvenience. Twenty-four boats were used to transport the infantry. When the companies crossed the border of the Electorate of the Palatinate between Lorch and Bacharach, the local authorities refused the passage, even though two captains offered to stay as hostages for the time necessary to cross the territory of that state. The troops had to abandon their ships and continue on land to circumvent the border with the Palatinate, which was heavily guarded by soldiers and militia, and thus reach the Electorate of Cologne.[105] On 17 June the infantry marched to Reuss, where there was the second major encampment of the French army, and then, after a short pause for rest, headed to Kaiserswerth, the gathering point for the troops of the Elector of Cologne, between Düsseldorf and Duisburg. On 19 June, the infantry regiment and the dragoon companies left for the theatre of war together with the troops of Cologne.

The Bavarians participated in the campaigns in the province of Overijssel and Drenthe, which succeeded in a series of easy conquests. On 29 June, after 10 days of campaign in the Netherlands, Maximilian Heinrich informed his Bavarian cousin that the infantry regiment was 'solid and in good condition'.[106] On 11 July, the strong fortress of Coevorden surrendered after a six-day siege. Then on 18 July the campaigns encountered their first serious obstacle, before Groningen, where the military fortunes of Cologne and Münster turned into a painful retreat. In August, after the disastrous outcome of the siege, the regiment numbered 650 men.[107] The army of the prince-bishops rallied out in the entrenched camp between Coevorden and Shoonebeek, and remained inactive until September, awaiting reinforcements. At this date the Bavarian infantry numbered 769 men still able to fight, but the companies were

---

104 Staudinger, *Geschichte des Kurbayerischen Heeres*, vol. I, p.613.
105 Staudinger, *Geschichte des Kurbayerischen Heeres*, vol. I, p.613.
106 Staudinger, *Geschichte des Kurbayerischen Heeres*, vol. I, p.615.
107 Staudinger, *Geschichte des Kurbayerischen Heeres*, vol. I, p.628.

decreased to 10.[108] The dragoon companies, instead, were disbanded and the rank and file joined the army of Cologne. In late September the infantry regiment was transferred to Deventer for garrison duties, and remained there until November 1673, when it moved to Zwolle. On 15 November a detailed muster registered the regiment's strength. Alongside three field officers, six among *Quartiermeister, Auditor, Adjutant*, chief surgeon, drum-major, and secretary, eight *Knechten*, and 38 servants of the officers, there were 28 company officers, 10 NCOs, nine surgeons, 50 corporals, three *Kadetten*, 112 lance-corporals and 413 private infantrymen.[109]

After the peace agreed with the Allies on 15 November 1673, the Prince-Bishop Elector of Cologne returned the regiment to Ferdinand Maria within the terms established by the contract stipulated in 1672.

Vienna, Buda and Belgrade, 1683–1688

Increasingly alarming news about the Ottoman offensive against Austria began to circulate in München in the summer of 1682. The initial consternation of the Bavarian court found in the young prince Max Emanuel a personality not easily overwhelmed by bad news. Above all, the court found a resolute commander, who wanted to prove to the whole of Europe that his family's traditional good qualities as soldiers had not died out. Although he had never held an independent command, the Prince-Elector had excellent theoretical knowledge and a great desire to exploit what he had learned about tactics and military strategy. With this in mind, it was no surprise that he wanted to contribute to the war against the Porte by leading a large and well-equipped contingent. Enlistment licences were therefore issued by the War Council and agreements were renewed with the free cities of the Empire where the Bavarian army traditionally sought volunteers. In January 1683, while the Bavarian representative at the Diet of Regensburg was discussing the formation of a league with the other states of the Empire, the Court Chamber authorised an expenditure budget for the army to raise an expeditionary corps of 8,000 men.[110] On 26 January an agreement was signed with the Emperor and the other states of the circle of Bavaria to coordinate efforts in the creation of a contingent capable of embarking on campaign. The Prince-Elector proposed to join the troops of the circle with those of his own army, in order to make the conduct of operations and the supply easier. For this task, Max Emanuel appointed *Feldmarschall-Lieutenant* Degenfeld, who received instructions from the War Council.[111]

---

108 Staudinger, *Geschichte des Kurbayerischen Heeres*, vol. I, p.637. The sources do not say whether the casualties were the result of fighting, or more probably, to desertion, since the shortage of supplies suffered by the armies of Cologne and Münster caused many soldiers to abscond.

109 Staudinger, *Geschichte des Kurbayerischen Heeres*, vol. I, p.638.

110 Ludwig Hüttl: *Max Emanuel. Der Blaue Kurfürst 1679–1726. Eine Politische Biographie* (Münich: Süddeutscher Verlag, 1976), p.122.

111 Staudinger, *Geschichte des Kurbayerischen Heeres*, vol. II, p.158.

The enlistment of new troops lasted until the beginning of the summer, particularly because money was slow to come. Moreover, some cases of plague among the troops forced the Bavarian authorities to impose quarantine, increasing the delay. In addition to the difficulties caused by these circumstances, the country had suffered greatly from the devastating storms of the spring of 1683. The Upper Palatinate, ravaged by 'cruel hailstorms and torrents of water', was barely able to provide fodder for the 10 cavalry companies quartered in the provinces. It came as welcome news that on 17 March the quarantine period was declared sufficient, and after a report of approval by the *collegium sanitatis*, the troops were allowed to move from their quarters at the beginning of April.[112] Notwithstanding these concerns, Max Emanuel intensified the efforts to raise his army, and in May ordered an improvement to the cavalry armament, replacing the old wheelock carbines with more modern weapons.[113]

On 21 July, orders were finally issued to the commanders to march with their men to the assembly places. The infantry was to concentrate in Straubing by 23 July, followed the next day by the cavalry; the contingents from the Bavarian Circle were to assemble in Branau by 30 July. The infantry continued its journey on boats along the Danube, while the cavalry marched overland towards Linz, followed by the artillery and the supply train. During the march, the Electoral troops learned that on 29 July the Tatars and their Hungarian allies under Thököly had been defeated at Pressburg (Bratislava) by the Duke of Lorraine.

On 16 August, the Bavarian contingents met the Imperial corps under General Leslie on the right bank of the Danube. Two days after, the Bavarian cavalry joined the Imperial cavalry under Dünnewald. The Bavarian infantry and artillery laid the camp before Krems under the senior commander with the highest rank, Hannibal von Degenfeld, with the *Generalwachtmeister* Louis de Beauvau as second in command. Here, at the town gates, the Bavarian troops saw the spiked heads of 70 Ottomans. Up to then, the Bavarians had lost 24 infantrymen and 16 horsemen through disease or desertion.[114] On 21 August, the Electoral infantry and that of the Bavarian Circle headed to Passau to join the contingents of Swabia and Franconia, which were assembling under the command of the *Reichs-Generalfeldmarschall* Prince Georg Friedrich zu Waldeck.

On 29 August the march resumed, and stopped again on 3 September. A camp was set up in Tulln, the point of assembly for the Polish army, and where King Jan Sobieski installed his headquarters. The Bavarians left Tulln on 6 September, heading for the slopes of the Wienerwald. On 7 September Sobieski and Charles of Lorraine established the order of battle: the Bavarian infantry, together with the Saxons and the Empire contingents, were placed on the left wing, while the cavalry was in reserve behind them. During the night of 8–9 September, the Prince-Elector Max Emanuel, accompanied by his *General Stab*, arrived at Tulln. After the King of Poland, he was the

---

112 Staudinger, *Geschichte des Kurbayerischen Heeres*, vol. II, p.59.
113 Staudinger, *Geschichte des Kurbayerischen Heeres*, vol. II, p.61.
114 Staudinger, *Geschichte des Kurbayerischen Heeres*, vol. II, p.161.

THE ELECTORATE OF BAVARIA

highest in the hierarchy of princes together with Johann Georg III of Saxony. As was customary in that age, he met the two army leaders, and 'graciously placed himself at their disposal'.[115]

The allied commanders received the appeals from Vienna and discussed assaulting the enemy as soon as possible. Max Emanuel was among the commanders who expressed opposition to advancing without reconnaissance.[116] On 10 September the Imperial–German–Polish troops advanced into the hills of Sauberg, next to Kahlenberg; by dusk the German infantry and cavalry had encamped by the village of St Andra on the western edge of the Wienerwald, while the Poles, arriving late in the day, bivouacked a few miles to the west. On 11 September reconnaissance discovered that a few Ottoman infantrymen had occupied the two high points at the end of the ridge, but only as observation posts. The enemy had recently dug some ditches and might be about to strengthen the position further, but they had not occupied the ridge and built actual field fortifications. A party of volunteers from the allied army, including the Bavarian *Hauptmann* Houchin, chased the enemy outposts during the night.[117]

Bavarian cavalry at Vienna, 12 September 1683; detail from the painting *Belagerung und Entsatz der Stadt Wien im September 1683* (Heeresgeschichtliches Museum, Vienna). Although the Bavarians performed a secondary role in the battle, they are shown in a close combat against the Ottomans. Prince-Elector Max Emanuel led them in the action. The painting shows cuirassiers with 'lobster' helmet, armour and buff coat, and trumpeters and kettledrum wearing medium blue coat with yellow sleeves and blue cuffs.

---

115 John Stoye, *The Siege of Vienna* (Edinburgh: Birlinn, 2006), p.264.
116 Staudinger, *Geschichte des Kurbayerischen Heeres*, vol. II, p.178.
117 Staudinger, *Geschichte des Kurbayerischen Heeres*, vol. II, p.178.

In the Battle of Vienna, at Kahlenberg on 12 September, the Bavarians were deployed together with the Empire troops in the centre of the allied battle order. They faced the difficult task of assaulting the *Türkenshanze*, which was defended by the Janissaries who stubbornly defended themselves before abandoning their position due to the collapse of resistance on their right. In the final phase of the battle, the Bavarian cuirassiers supported the action of the cavalry under general Enea Silvio Caprara, and received praise from the Austrian commander. Since there was a low rate of casualties, however, the Bavarians did not play a decisive role in the battle. The muster of 1 October registered that the infantry had lost 34 dead, 1,221 sick, two 'who had left the army' (deserters) and another 394 were in Austrian hospitals north of Vienna, for a total of 1,651 casualties. As for the cavalry, 30 were dead, 680 sick, 13 in the hospitals, leaving 2,535 men still available; more than 700 horses had died.[118] The cavalry regiments were quartered at Kroatish-Wagram (later Wagram an der Donau) but on 10 October had decreased to 1,951 able horsemen. The artillery was quartered at Komárom.[119] In the subsequent engagements, the Bavarian infantry participated at the siege of Esztergom with 3,816 men, claiming the loss of 36 men.[120]

For the campaign of 1684 Max Emanuel managed to increase the Bavarian contingent, but the 13,000-man goal remained unattained. On 27 April, under Duke Charles V of Lorraine, 39,000 Austrians, Swabians, Franconians, and Bavarians gathered around Esztergom to move against Buda, the capital of the *Beglerbeg* of Hungary. The Bavarians did not take part in the double encounter of Visegrad and in the ambush of Vac, since they formed the reserve corps that joined the main army before Buda on 23 June. Although the Allies had relatively easily occupied the site of Pest, the resistance of the defenders inside Buda was fiercer than expected. In late June the allied plan was complicated by a night raid of the Ottomans, who succeeded in breaking the siege and entering the city with supplies and reinforcements. The siege continued, and in August the Bavarian infantry had lost 400 men. Casualties must have been considerable when, alongside the infantry of the Swabian Circle, they fought a series of hard encounters facing the relentless enemy sorties against the approaches. Before the end of the campaign, six squadrons of Bavarian cuirassiers and three of dragoons participated at the encounter of Erd, and the assault on Osjek. On 13 September Max Emanuel, as commander-in-chief of the allied army in place of the sick Charles of Lorraine, offered the surrender to Buda on behalf of the Emperor, but received a negative response. Disagreements between the Imperial and German commanders, combined with the rains, the stubborn resistance of the Ottomans, and the impending frosts, prompted the Allies to break off the siege at the end of October.

Little is known about the overall casualties suffered by the Bavarians during the campaign, but it is possible to form a picture from the information dating back to January 1685. By that date, the cavalry deployed just 133 officers

---

118 Staudinger, *Geschichte des Kurbayerischen Heeres*, vol. II, p.177.
119 Staudinger, *Geschichte des Kurbayerischen Heeres*, vol. II, p.178.
120 Staudinger, *Geschichte des Kurbayerischen Heeres*, vol. II, p.178.

and 1,353 cavalrymen, with only 892 horses. A further 402 horsemen were sick, while 842 were registered as 'remained behind'.[121] The colonels claimed that in just two years the cavalry had lost 3,000 men, and warned the War Council to urge the arrival of reinforcements 'otherwise it will be impossible to enter on campaign'. As for the infantry, in the muster of 12 January the six regiments numbered 93 officers and 1,322 privates, of which 407 were without equipment and weapons. There were 1,119 sick and a further 1,021 were registered as 'absent'; the regiment *Montfort zu Fuss* (BvI-21) had only 27 rank and file.[122] At the beginning of May, 1,562 infantry recruits and a further 1,716 cavalrymen and dragoons were sent to Pressburg, where the Bavarians had their winter quarters; 500 horses were purchased. In June, the Bavarian contingent had increased to 7,000 men instead of the planned 8,200.[123] The campaign of 1685 began with the violent raids of the Ottoman and Tatar cavalry against the allied outpost along the Danube. Meanwhile, news circulated about the gathering of an Ottoman army of over 80,000 men under the new Grand Vizier Ibrahim Paşa, the same who had led the successful relief action in Buda the year before. In late summer, the Duke of Lorraine moved his composite army with the aim of besieging the Ottoman garrison at Érsekújvár (now Nové Zámky in Slovakia), which had already been blockaded for months. The force included 33,000 Imperial soldiers and 22,000 consisting of Bavarians, Saxons, and men from the circles of the Empire, as well as 25,000 of the Hungarian *Adelige Insurrektion*: the feudal Magyar militia.[124] On 7 July Lorraine began the siege of the enemy fortress, but at the same time the Grand Vizier, covered by the screen of raiding parties before him, had led his army to Esztergom, which was invested on 26 July. Despite the brilliant manoeuvre with which he had outflanked the Allies, Ibrahim Pasha was surprised on 16 August just below Esztergom by the Duke of Lorraine, and suffered a severe defeat. Three days later Érsekújvár surrendered and once inside the city the besiegers committed a brutal massacre of the defenders, in which not even the civilians were spared. The Bavarians took part in all the major actions and casualties were again considerable, since in October the *Leibregiment zu Fuss* (BvI-17) numbered just 667 men.[125]

In late May 1686 the army under Charles of Lorraine, now consisting of 32,350 Imperial soldiers, 16,000 Hungarians, 8,000 Bavarians, 7,800 from Brandenburg and 4,700 from Saxony, as well as Swabians, Franconians, Croats and at least 1,000 volunteers from all over Europe, headed to Buda, defended by 10,000 men under the elderly but resolute Arnavut Abdurrhaman Paşa. Max Emanuel had again prepared his troops with great care. The *General Stab* included the *General-Feldzeugmeister* Sereni, the *Feldmarshall-Lieutenant* Steinau, and the *Generalwachtmeister* Arco, Rummel and Latour. With them two *Generaladjutanten*, one interpreter, one physician, one surgeon, three

---

121 Staudinger, *Geschichte des Kurbayerischen Heeres*, vol. II, p.215.
122 Staudinger, *Geschichte des Kurbayerischen Heeres*, vol. II, p.215.
123 Staudinger, *Geschichte des Kurbayerischen Heeres*, vol. II, p.216.
124 Payer, *Armati Hungarorum* (Münich: Korösi Csoma Sándor, 1990), p.124.
125 Staudinger, *Geschichte des Kurbayerischen Heeres*, vol. II, p.226.

captain-engineers, one captain and one lieutenant of miners accompanied the army. The infantry deployed 10 battalions from regiments *Steinau* (BvI-22), *Rummel* (BvI-23), *Gallenfels* (BvI-19), *Seyboltdorff* (BvI-20) and *Leibregiment* (BvI-17). The cavalry comprised 12 squadrons of cuirassiers from regiments *Arco* (BvC-11), *Salburg* (BvC-13), *Latour* (BvC-15), and *Bielke* (BvC-17), and six squadrons of dragoons from regiments *Arco* (BvD-2) and *Schier* (BvD-3); the company of the *Hartschiere* escorted the Prince-Elector as had occurred the previous year. The artillery comprised 30 *halbe Kartaune*, 10 mortars, of which one was 60lb, two *Falconen*, two *Quartierschlagen* and 16 light guns for the regimental artillery.[126]

Alleged portrait of Count Johann Baptist d'Arco (1660?–1715), by Wolfgang Pulver (Private collection). He was son of the Aulic War Council's president Prospero. The d'Arco family came from Trento and had several branches in Austria and Savoy-Piedmont. Johann Baptist d'Arco followed his father's career in the Electoral Army as cavalry officer and later joined the Imperial Army, after his father was disgraced at court in 1675. Eight years later, he came back to Münich and was appointed Colonel Proprietor of a Bavarian cuirassier regiment (BvC-11). Johann Baptist d'Arco was celebrated as a valiant commander and fought in all the campaigns against the Ottomans between 1683 and 1688.

Before the beginning of the campaign, Max Emanuel had joined the allied troops, and was appointed as commander of the cavalry vanguard by the Duke of Lorraine. On 18 June the Imperial–German army laid siege to Buda. As the siege proceeded, on 14 July the Imperialists and Germans repulsed an attempt by Grand Vizier Süleyman Paşa near Bia to bring relief to the city. Having conquered some strategic positions in June and early July, the resistance of the Ottoman garrison succeeded in slowing the allied progress, however, the explosion of the city arsenal during the first phase of the siege was decisive for the outcome of the operation. On 27 July, two combined assaults were prepared. On the west side, against the trenches and the roundel defending the artillery on the *cavaliere* erected by the defenders, the Bavarians were ready to enter the action. The formation included two assault parties with a frontage of 10 men, comprising one lieutenant and 20 musketeers protected by metal helms; one sergeant with six volunteers and 10 grenadiers were followed by a corporal with six pioneers to destroy the enemy palisade. To support the action, 100 infantrymen with one captain, two lieutenants and one sergeant were deployed in the trenches to ensure that the volume of fire was constant and as

---

126 Staudinger, *Geschichte des Kurbayerischen Heeres*, vol. II, p.231.

THE ELECTORATE OF BAVARIA

intense as possible. Two platoons comprising 25 infantrymen with shovels, under the orders of a lieutenant, were ready to go into action, along with two others comprising 75 men with sandbags, led by a captain and a sergeant. Lastly there was a reserve corps under one lieutenant colonel, one major, one captain with 50 corporals armed with partisans. One lieutenant with 30 grenadiers, followed by two captains, two lieutenants and 200 musketeers, had the task of penetrating the trench at the right moment. The corps comprised mainly officers and privates from the *Leibregiment* and with them one Imperial and one Saxon battalion accompanied the assault, securing the flanks.[127]

At 4:00 p.m., three artillery volleys gave the signal for the operation to begin; the fighting lasted until evening and was extremely fierce. The defenders threw grenades and other incendiary weapons, and even stones, against the assault columns. The Bavarians captured a mortar and eight cannons, but were hit by a rain of bombs from the battery positioned on the cavalier. In the middle of the action Max Emanuel himself rushed in, followed by his generals, all of whom showed great disregard for the danger.[128] By evening the besiegers controlled a large sector of the trench, but the roundel, the breach and the entrance to the palisade were still in the hands of the defenders. The Bavarians claimed 117 dead and many wounded, including a lieutenant colonel, two majors and two captains. The assault carried out by the Imperialists and Brandenburgers against the breach of the arsenal on the opposite side of the city was also very bloody and achieved modest results.[129]

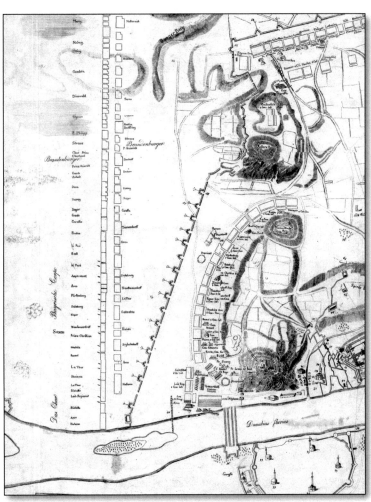

Detail from the plan of the Siege of Buda in 1686, by Charles de Jouvigny, showing the deployment of the Bavarian troops on the west side of the city. (Hungarian national Library, Budapest)

---

127 Staudinger, *Geschichte des Kurbayerischen Heeres*, vol. II, p.236.
128 Staudinger, *Geschichte des Kurbayerischen Heeres*, vol. II, p.236.
129 Raoul Gueze, 'La Liberazione dell'Ungheria dal Turco (1683–1699) nelle fonti conservate in alcuni fra i principali Archivi di Stato Italiani' *in OSZK – Rivista di Studi Ungheresi* (Rome–

In the following days, the allied artillery constantly targeted the enemy trenches. On 1 August the Bavarians prepared a new assault against the breach on the left side of the castle wall, with a party consisting of 40 volunteers and 400 infantrymen. The assault achieved no appreciable results, but cost few casualties. A new assault on 3 August was repulsed with the loss of three officers and 10 soldiers killed and six officers and 20 soldiers wounded.[130] On 10 August, news about the approach of the enemy persuaded the allied command to improve the defences on the circumvallation line. On 13 August the vanguard of the Ottoman relief army approached the allied circumvallation, but was repulsed by the Imperialists. On 22 August a new assault on Buda managed to achieve some progress, but the enemy resistance remained very strong, and the Ottoman sorties succeeded in repulsing the enemy from key positions. However, the fate of Buda was sealed. The death of the brave Ottoman commander, Arnavut Abdi Abdurrhaman Paşa, and the collapse of a large section of the curtain wall weakened resistance. After 77 days of fighting, three offers of surrender rejected, and a tormented 36-hour council of war, the Duke of Lorraine ordered the final assault on Buda on the morning of 2 September 1686. The arrival of about 8,000 fresh troops brought a welcome support for the upcoming action. The assault began at 2:00 p.m. About 3,000 Imperialists and Germans moved to assault the city from the east, while a mixed corps of 1,500 Bavarians, Saxons and Brandenburgers, with a further 1,500 infantrymen on reserve, tried their

Budavár Visszavétele (the recapture of Buda Castle) by Benczúr Gyula, painted in 1896 (Hungarian National Gallery, Budapest). The painting represents the Romantic version of the conquest of the Ottoman Hungarian capital; however, it is interesting to note that Max Emanuel occupies a prominent position among the allied commanders being portrayed just behind Charles V of Lorraine.

Budapest, 1986), p.50.
130 Staudinger, *Geschichte des Kurbayerischen Heeres*, vol. II, p.236. Among the dead was Captain Pontevico of the Gallenfels Regiment.

THE ELECTORATE OF BAVARIA

luck on the other side. Two more corps began feint assaults in the centre. The action was supported by all the artillery, which targeted the enemy positions with a storm of projectiles. The Bavarians, Saxons and Brandenburgers were repulsed with heavy losses, but with a second assault managed to seize a bastion and 16 guns. The Imperialists and Germans were also successful and finally entered the city, and in the late afternoon, after a bitter fight inside, all resistance ceased. After months of deprivations and suffering, the allied troops could not be stopped and massacred most of the enemy: about 3,000 soldiers and civilians were killed and a further 2,000 taken as prisoners and slaves. The victorious Allies plundered the properties of the residents until night.[131]

On 2 October, the Bavarians marched to their winter quarters. The muster executed on 24 September registered 73 officers and 1,505 private cuirassiers, but this figure included only three regiments. As for the dragoons, the regiment *Schier* still had 24 officers and 472 privates.[132] Once again it was the infantry which was most severely damaged by the campaign. By December, the *Leibregiment* had only 245 able soldiers, and a further 98 were registered as sick, convalescent and 'commanded' or assigned to recruiting pickets in the Electorate. Regiment *Steinau* had 260 soldiers on the field and a further 150 sick; *Seyboltdorff* 252 and 66, *Gallenfels* 352 and 85.[133] At the end of the year, 411 soldiers returned from the hospitals to the regiments, however, half of this number died during winter quartering due to the exceptionally cold winter of 1686–87.[134]

The following year, Max Emanuel gathered 9,133 soldiers instead of the planned 11,025, but his efforts were rewarded with the assignment to command a mixed Imperial–Bavarian corps of 12,875 men. The campaign began in May, and the Allies were able to advance with almost no resistance along the Danube heading to Belgrade, but the plan to besiege the city – considered the 'gateway to Hungary' due to its position straddling three major rivers – was ended by the news of the imminent arrival of a strong enemy army gathering at Edirne under Sari Süleyman Paşa. Despite difficulties due to the extension of supply lines, Charles of Lorraine regained the initiative and on 12 August 1687 anticipated the enemy moving to Siklós, because the position and the wooded and rough ground at Edirne made it an unfavourable battlefield for the Ottoman cavalry. Lorraine disposed approximately 40,000 men, facing an estimated enemy force of 60,000–65,000. The allied right wing, moving westward, began to march through the densely forested area. By relying on numerical superiority, the Ottoman commander ordered an attack with the entire army on the Imperial army's left wing, which under Max Emanuel was still in its earlier position and according to the battle plan was also to start marching west. The Ottoman army caught the Imperial

---

131 Jean Berenger, 'Le Siège de Buda de 1696', in *Dix-Septième Siècle*, n. 229 (2005/4), p.609.
132 Staudinger, *Geschichte des Kurbayerischen Heeres*, vol. II, p.245. *Bielke Cuirassieren* (BvC-17) with 25 officers and 502 horsemen; *Arco* (BvC-11) with 24 and 499; *Latour* (BvC-15) with 34 and 504.
133 Staudinger, *Geschichte des Kurbayerischen Heeres*, vol. II, p.246.
134 Staudinger, *Geschichte des Kurbayerischen Heeres*, vol. II, p.246.

army near the village of Mohács and the nearby Nagyharsány Hill, with its steep and heavily wooded slopes. The Ottoman cavalry, consisting of 8,000 *sipahis*, tried to outflank Max Emanuel from the left. The Prince-Elector immediately sent a courier to the Duke of Lorraine, informing him that the wing was under threat. Orders were given and sent quickly and positions taken immediately to repulse the Ottoman assault. The allied infantry held their position, and Imperial General Enea Silvio Piccolomini with some of his cavalry squadrons successfully counter-attacked and repulsed the advance of the Ottoman horsemen, while the rest of the army could not get through the dense forest. Fortunately for the Allies, the Grand Vizier was surprised by the unexpected enemy resistance and stopped the attack. The Ottoman artillery continued to shell the allied positions with little result, and infantry and cavalry were ordered to hold their positions. This pause in the fighting gave the right wing of the allied army enough time to return to its original deployment. The Duke of Lorraine initially thought to defend the positions, which might have led to a relative standstill, but the Prince-Elector and Baden persuaded him to order a large-scale counter-attack. The deployment of the allied army lasted until the afternoon, when at 3:00 p.m. Sari Süleyman Paşa decided to attack again. The *sipahis* supported the Janissaries' frontal attack by attempting to outflank the allied army; the Prince-Elector successfully resisted the attack with his infantry and then the whole allied army moved against the Ottoman positions. The fighting lasted hours and was very fierce, and Max Emanuel himself was injured by a musket ball in the left hand. In

The Battle of Mohács, fought on 12 August 1687, engraving of Charles de Juvigny and Justus van der Nyport (Staatsarchiv of Baden-Württemberg, Karlsruhe). Juvigny placed value on having been an eyewitness of the battle. The engraving shows the decisive moment of the battle before the Ottoman commander's tent, which is surrounded on the eastern side by the approaching Allied troops. Throughout the first phase of the battle only the left wing under Max Emanuel saw the main action. There was a dense forest in front of the allied army's right wing that prevented it from attacking. Despite this, the Duke of Lorraine attempted an outflanking manoeuvre to force the enemy to withdraw, but his battalions and squadrons lost their way in the forest. However, in the afternoon, the rash Ottoman new assault failed and the Duke of Lorraine managed to annihilate the enemy army. The casualties of the Allies were very light, about 600 men, while the Ottoman army suffered huge losses, with an estimated 10,000 dead, as well as the loss of most of its artillery (about 66 guns) and much of its train. The splendid tent of the Grand Vizier and 160 Ottoman flags fell into enemy hands. It is reported that the value of the share of the bounty that was given to the Elector of Bavaria exceeded two million golden ducats.

THE ELECTORATE OF BAVARIA

the late afternoon the Ottoman assault collapsed, as did its resistance, and Sari Süleyman Paşa's army retreated in a wild flight. For the Porte, the defeat was of a proportion comparable to that suffered at Vienna.

The battle casualties were very low, but the climate of the Danube region severely affected the allied army. In October the Bavarian corps headed to its winter quarters in Buda, Neuttra and in the Zips region. The infantry numbered 2,226 men; cavalry and dragoons were 2,446 in all.[135] In the spring of 1688 Max Emanuel, newly appointed as commander-in-chief of the main army replacing the convalescent Charles of Lorraine, gathered 33,500 Imperial and German troops, of which 9,900 were Bavarians. This was the weakest force to take the field since 1683, but on 16 May the troops moved to complete the conquest of the other Hungarian towns still in Ottoman hands. In the centre of the country, the important fortress of Székesfehérvár surrendered on 19 May, while Transylvania came under the control of the Imperialists under General Antonio Carafa. In mid-July, Ujlak and Peterwardein were also seized by the Allies. On 9 August the allied army crossed the Sava River and three days later began the siege of Belgrade, securing three more bridgeheads over the Sava to the west with the conquest of Dubica, Gradiska, and Brod. Approach trenches were opened, but the siege's operations were delayed by the presence of strong Ottoman cavalry corps a few miles from Belgrade. Max Emanuel ordered the Margrave of Baden to guard the routes coming from the south, securing the besieging army from behind. On 5 September the Margrave defeated an Ottoman corps under the Pasha of Bosnia, near Derbent. At Belgrade the siege continued until 6 September, when, after fierce fighting, the Allies took control of the island in front of the Old Town, and on the same day penetrated inside the curtain, forcing the Ottomans to take refuge in the citadel, which finally surrendered the following morning. As occurred years before, a massacre began and soldiers and civilians were killed without distinction.

Max Emanuel before Belgrade, 1688, oil painting by Henry Gascar (Bayerische Staatsgemäldesammlungen, München). Note the page wearing the Prince-Elector's livery.

---

135 Staudinger, *Geschichte des Kurbayerischen Heeres*, vol. II, p.247.

The victory was widely celebrated in Vienna, as well as in Münich and other German capitals, but before the end of the month there came the unexpected news that the French army had invaded the Palatinate and was threatening the Empire's territories. This act meant war again against Louis XIV, forcing the Bavarians and the other German contingents to hastily return west to face the new threat.

Officer and Trooper of Hussars of Regiment Lidl von Borbula, 1689-89, by Anton Hoffmann's Das Heer des Blauen Königs 1682-1726. After the Hungarian campaigns, in 1688 Max Emanuel raised a mixed corps of 690 hussars and Serbian infantry, and entrusted it to *Obristlieutenant* Johann Baptist Lidl von Borbula. Von Borbula joined the Bavarian cavalry in 1686 with the *Gränitz-Ungarn zu Pferd* and a Serbian Free Corps participating in all of the major campaigns until the conquest of Belgrade in 1688. A contemporary painting in the Bavarian Army Museum in Ingolstadt shows him in a mix of Hungarian and Ottoman dress. The squadron had a short life, since it was disbanded after a few months, but the legacy of the Hungarian campaigns found an unprecedented aftermath. Johann Baptist settled '1,500 Serbian and Greek [Orthodox] men and women' on his estates of Hart on the River Inn, where they started families and made their home. In 1689, Johann Baptist was appointed as *Generalkriegskommissar*, just before his death later in the same year.

Uniforms and Equipment

In Bavaria, the distribution of uniform equipment and clothing to soldiers began as early as the mid-1660s. Although the administration of these issues was managed by captains in the companies and colonels in the regiments, the instructions of the War Council for the infantry officers indicated that at least as far as headgear, coats, breeches and stockings were concerned, all these

THE ELECTORATE OF BAVARIA

items were of the same colour and model.[136] In 1671, the first ordinances were issued establishing a supply service at the expense of the state, run by a commissioner appointed by the Court Chamber, in order to introduce 'the uniformity of dress and armament' in the infantry.[137] In fact, after 1671 the sources increasingly often provide information on the expenses for soldiers' clothing, and from then, the items that soldiers could keep after their discharge are also recorded. Unfortunately the sources do not offer much information concerning colours and accessories, but they testify to a regular administration of the military clothing that Bavaria was managing with updated instruments. This process was also supported by the fact that Ferdinand Maria, in order to revive the domestic woollen cloth and clothing industry, ordered the regiments and companies to meet their needs from local manufacturers. In 1672 he even had a factory built in the Au, near Münich, to facilitate the procurement of cloth for uniforms and other items for the army. In 1677, 3,000 new *bandeliers* were ordered, each with 11 cartridge straps and a *Korporal* (powder flask). These new bandoleers had 'blue-white silk fringes.' In addition, there were also 742 new and old *Patronentasche*, each with a powder flask decorated with the golden globe.[138] The regiments continued to resort to this supplier channel until 1678, but from 1679 several deliveries of cloth from merchants in Münich and Regensburg were paid for directly by the Court Chamber, and not by the colonels or captains. This regulation was also a way to put an end to the regular abuses some officers committed, in order to procure illicit gains through arbitrary deduction from the soldiers' salaries.

Just how far the Prince-Elector was aware of the importance of a regular supply of clothing for his soldiers is confirmed by the report of *Generalalkriegsfommissärs* Pelkhover, in an inspection executed in 1675, in which he describes the state of the army. He wrote: 'the cavalry is so well clothed and mounted that it can easily be ascertained', but with regard to the foot troops he added: 'the colonels themselves and their officers, such as lieutenant colonels and majors must take more care of the soldiers, so that their equipment and clothing are better maintained than these are at present.'[139]

The first iconographic sources depicting Bavarian soldiers are approximately dateable to 1656–60.[140] The images show the typical transitional style with the officers dressed according to the canons of the time, including both coats tailored on the pattern of Dutch–French *justaucorps*, or petticoat

---

136 Münich, *Geschichte der Entwicklung der Bayerischen Armee*, p.34.

137 Staudinger, *Geschichte des Kurbayerischen Heeres*, vol. I, p.348. The oldest account concerning the requirements for manufacturing military clothing dates to 1671, and concerns the expense for the dress issued to the company of Captain Flemming. It includes 300 *Ellen* of cloth for *Röcke* (coats), 400 *Ellen* of *Boy* for the lining, 400 dozens of tin buttons, 80 items of headgear, 40 *Lot* of silk (for the headgear trim?), and 26 *Ellen* of black linen for the cravats. The list also includes the cost for manufacturing 72 *Musketier-Röcke*.

138 Staudinger, *Geschichte des Kurbayerischen Heeres*, vol. I, p.362.

139 Staudinger, *Geschichte des Kurbayerischen Heeres*, vol. I, p.351.

140 This is a series of six black and white prints representing officers and private infantrymen preserved in the Federal German Army Library in Münich.

pourpoint with *Rhingraves* breeches. Private soldiers wear short coats, more akin to the outdated Thirty Years' War jackets than the *Rock* introduced in Western Europe. Pikemen carry no metal protections and wear the conventional broad-brimmed hat. The pike was between four and five metres long, usually made of ebony, and had not changed significantly over the years. Musketeers carried the matchlock without a fork rest. In the 1650s the gun stock and barrel had been lightened, and the fork had fallen into disuse after 1665. However, the calibre could vary considerably, although the *Puech* regiment in the Hungarian campaigns of 1661–64 carried only medium-calibre matchlocks.[141]

Bavarian officers, mid- to late 1650s (Bavarian Staatsarchiv – Kriegsarchiv).

Another primary source depicts a Bavarian musketeer of the early 1670s.[142] As for the previous iconographic source, this is also in black and white, but a description of a Bavarian infantryman in 1674 seems to refer to the aforementioned figure, since the items, shape and cut of the dress correspond perfectly to it. The musketeer should wear a medium blue *Rock* and breeches, brown leather shoes with red ribbons, grey-white stockings and black broad-brimmed hat with a large blue feather; on the right shoulder

---

141 Staudinger, *Geschichte des Kurbayerischen Heeres*, vol. I, p.356.
142 Staudinger, *Geschichte des Kurbayerischen Heeres*, vol. I, p.348. The figure on the cover of the *Exercitien* or drill manual of 1674.

THE ELECTORATE OF BAVARIA

of the coat red tassels are fastened.[143] The style of the uniform is now that codified in France and Northern Europe, however the most authoritative Bavarian military scholar points out that for a very important detail, Italian influence was also decisive.[144] After Ferdinand Maria's marriage to Henrietta Adelaide of Savoy, many Italians had arrived at München from Piedmont and other regions. The Italian connection would have been behind the choice of the typical Bavarian army colour in the years to come, namely the Bavarian blue (or *Kornblau*). This would have happened in 1673: when the Duke of Savoy dismissed the Bavarian infantry that had fought with his army against the Republic of Genoa in 1672, he had given orders for them to be completely dressed with new clothing before returning home. The soldiers received new clothes manufactured with the same blue cloth as the Duke's *Gardes*. When the soldiers of the *Beltin* regiment (BvI-11) and *Perouse* battalion arrived in München in their new blue uniforms, they caused quite an impression at court. It was the Savoy envoy to the Bavarian court, Francesco Rica, who described

Bavarian pikeman, mid-late 1650s. (Bavarian Staatsarchiv – Kriegsarchiv, BS I/70)

this event in a letter sent to Turin in March 1673. According to the diplomat, the general satisfaction had been so great that 'Ferdinand Maria declared to him that from henceforth his infantry would always wear uniforms of that colour.'[145] Until 1672, the most common colour for the infantry coats was grey or blue, but the latter seems to take over after 1673. However, blue coats had been already distributed in 1669 to the regiment *Bürhen* (BvI-7) before it sailed to Crete, and also the *Culer zu Fuss* (BvI-10), which marched to Cologne in 1672, is described wearing blue uniforms.[146] The anecdote of the Italian diplomat is almost certainly authentic, however in subsequent years, the Prince-Elector's wish was not respected: even in the last years of his rule there were not only blue uniforms for the infantry. This is clearly stated by an order issued by the War Council to a captain in 1679, in response to the request for new uniforms, in which he was ordered to take for the soldiers 'coats of grey cloth, which would be more durable and more suitable for service'. Moreover, at the beginning of 1679 the regiment *Wagenseil* (BvI-8)

---

143 Staudinger, *Geschichte des Kurbayerischen Heeres*, vol. I, footnote at page 351. The author quotes the work of Theodor Heinrich Topor von Morawitzky, *Materialien zu Einem Künftigen Landtage in Bayern* (Regensburg, 1800), vol. IV, p.16.
144 Staudinger, *Geschichte des Kurbayerischen Heeres*, vol. I, p.312.
145 Carlo Merkel, *Adelaide di Savoia, Elettrice di Baviera* (Torino 1892), p.312. The blue coat with red cuffs delivered to the regiment *Beltin* is also confirmed in Archivio di Stato di Torino, *Patenti, Controllo Finanze*, 1672.
146 Staudinger, *Geschichte des Kurbayerischen Heeres*, vol. I, p.352.

was assigned a company wearing grey coats with yellow facings.[147] Reasons of 'good economy' prevailed and therefore the cheaper grey cloth was not entirely set aside, reserving the medium blue mainly for the Household's uniforms.[148] In addition, other indications suggest that full uniformity within the regiments was also far from being achieved, and indeed, the constant assembling and disbanding to which the Bavarian infantry was subjected must have contributed to frustrating the plans.

However, it is certain that in the 1670s the clothing and equipment of the Bavarian infantry were just as modern and up-to-date as those introduced in Western Europe.[149] Pikemen no longer wore corselets, which definitely disappear from the arsenals' inventories, and only officers used metal protection, especially the gorget, as a distinction of their rank. Through this period, the Bavarian military dress became gradually more similar to French fashion, and the *justaucorps* of the officers as well as those of rank and file followed the same pattern. Usually, the clothing of the officers and NCOs was of better quality and also distinguished by the ribbons fixed on the right shoulder which, according to some authors, could be regarded as the precursors of epaulettes.[150] The feathers on the headgear also denoted status.

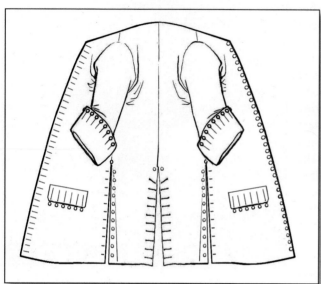

A reconstruction of a coat based on an engraving from 1675 by Carl Gustav Amling, depicting the Bavarian Commissioner Pelkhover, shows a *justaucorps* with a long row of buttons. The Commissioner wears a rich lace cravat around his neck with wide ends falling down over his breast. From the right shoulder to the left hip runs a wide brocade bandolier with a heavy fringe, probably of gold silk. Pelkhover has long hair, naturally flowing and uncombed, in the so-called style *allonge*; no headgear is visible.

In the 1680s the infantry continued to be dressed in grey or blue, and even in green, as in the case of regiment *Puech* (BvI-18) in 1682.[151] Gradually, the medium blue became the most common colour of the Bavarian infantry at least in the late 1680s. A durable feature of the Bavarian infantry was the cravat of black linen for private soldiers and corporals, which lasted until the end of the century. The grenadiers, introduced in 1682 in each company, carried flintlock, grenade bag and after 1685 axes; however they did not receive particular uniform or headgear, and until 1695 they wore the same broad-brimmed hat of the musketeer and

---

147 Staudinger, *Geschichte des Kurbayerischen Heeres*, vol. I, p.355.
148 Staudinger, *Geschichte des Kurbayerischen Heeres*, vol. I, p.351.
149 Jürgen Kraus (ed.), *Vom Bunten Rock zum Kampanzug* (Ingolstadt: Bayerischen Armeemuseums, 1987), p.20.
150 Staudinger, *Geschichte des Kurbayerischen Heeres*, vol. I, p.352.
151 Anton Hoffmann, *Das Heer des Blauen Königs. Die Soldaten des Kurfürsten Max II. Emmanuel von Bayern. 1682–1726* (München: 1909), p.10; and München, *Geschichte der Entwicklung der Bayerischen Armee*, p.41.

THE ELECTORATE OF BAVARIA

pikemen.[152] Probably, individual grenadiers could have worn a slouch hat or other headgear to facilitate their duty.

According to the reconstructions of the major Bavarian army specialist, in 1682 the infantry regiments received coats with lining and cuffs of different colour. As for the breeches, these were in natural leather for the summer, and cloth for the winter.[153] Even the colour of the stockings cannot be determined with certainty. In other armies of the time, soldiers wore different coloured socks than NCOs and officers. In Bavaria at the turn of the century, infantry soldiers are depicted wearing striped socks of various colours: a typical feature also in Austria. In Max Emmanuel's army, infantrymen wore coloured socks, sometimes coinciding with the colour of cuffs and lining.[154]

The pike, which fell into disuse on the Hungarian front after 1686, was replaced by the bayonet, or more often the *Schweinsfeder*. However, as early as 1677, sources refer to 'muskets with pikes or with new model swords', which in both cases could allude to bayonets. As for side weapons, in 1669 a Münich blacksmith had supplied the troops destined for Candia with '202 half swords', presumably the dagger to be used as a defensive weapon in the hand-to-hand combats that were very common during the siege.[155] After 1679, reports increasingly mention the *Springstock*, or jumping pole, an item intermediate between a weapon and a tool. The *Springstock*, about two metres long with an iron base and tip, was used on campaigns to facilitate marching in the mountains, or even for jumping over trenches. Sometimes it appeared as a distinctive weapon of some NCOs, especially in Austria, where it was used by *Führer* and *Fourier*, so much so that in the following century its shape became similar to a partisan. In Bavaria the *Springstock* was also used by the *Fähnrich*, just as in the Imperial army. Of some interest is the fact that in 1661 the regiment *Puech* received 60 *Springstocks* with strong metal spikes four *Schuh* (30.48cm) long, so that they could be used 'in combat as well as on the march over steep terrain to avoid falling'. Some details suggest a use very close to the *Schweinsfeder* that would appear later. In 1677, sources also mention a new *Springstock* model with screws, removable fittings and a metal roundel at the base. Two years later, the inventory of an infantry company records 121

Plug bayonets, before 1700 (Bayerishes Armee Museum, Ingolstadt)

---

152 Hoffmann, *Das Heer des Blauen Königs*, p.10.
153 Hoffmann, *Das Heer des Blauen Königs*, p.10.
154 Staudinger, *Geschichte des Kurbayerischen Heeres*, vol. I, p.355.
155 Staudinger, *Geschichte des Kurbayerischen Heeres*, vol. I, p.363.

muskets and 60 pikes for soldiers, eight polearms for officers and NCOs, and two new model *Springstocks*.[156]

The inventory also included three drums, because after 1675 each company had three drummers. Together with the fifers they formed the 'music' of the infantry. In Germany the fifer was also known as the *Schalmeipfeifer* if he played the *Schalmei* (chalumeau), and no matter which instrument they played, they were usually employed as servants of the officers and remained at their disposal in quarters. Contemporary accounts relate that, like the drummer, he wore clothing with laces, and usually of colours different from those of the troops.

The introduction of the uniform in the cavalry was less problematic. In the 1660s, cavalry recruitment was usually accorded to volunteers who presented themselves 'fully clothed' and equipped with their own horse.[157] Cavalry dress in southern Germany had long been codified and consisted of the 'universal' *Göller* or *Koller* in buffalo or sheepskin of natural colour. Gradually the clothing of the cavalry was improved to make the companies more homogenous, as recommended to the captains, who were obliged to purchase clothing, equipment and accessories established by the War Council. In this way the cavalry also introduced a regular uniform, however it did not always include metal protection or helms. In 1675 the War Council, in accord with the Aulic Chamber, established a budget for the purchase of clothing and equipment as had occurred in the infantry. In the same year the *Rittmeister* Malleloi received 1,000 florins 'for the complete uniform of his company', which

Bavarian cuirassier field officer, late seventeenth century/ early eighteenth century, by Anton Hoffman.

---

156 Staudinger, *Geschichte des Kurbayerischen Heeres*, vol. I, p.364.
157 Staudinger, *Geschichte des Kurbayerischen Heeres*, vol. I, p.355.

THE ELECTORATE OF BAVARIA

included buff coat, with back and breast armour and steel lobster helm, probably painted in black.[158] This introduction gave good results, since before the end of the year chief commissioner Pelkhover praised the cavalry, but he had to reprimand the behaviour of a captain of the regiment *McKay*, because he deducted part of his men's salary to pay for the 'yellow saddle cover and holsters' purchased in Münich according to the new orders, while his men claimed that the costs 'had already been reimbursed at least three times with the deductions already paid'. The investigation by the commissioner found that the arbitrary deductions had been used to purchase the 'livery' uniform of a third trumpeter, who had been enlisted into the company as supernumerary for illicit gain on the part of the officer; although the state had pledged to reduce this kind of fraud, there was always another way to bypass the regulations.[159]

Since 1675 cavalrymen regularly received a cloak, usually of grey cloth and wide enough to cover both horsemen and horse. The high, wide boots, that reached to the knees, were of leather of natural colour, but from the 1680s tended to be darker if not completely blackened. Through the 1670s, and until 1682, the uniform of the Bavarian cavalry changed little. The breeches could be of cloth or of natural leather as for the buff coat. Above the

Left: 'Lobster' helmet and back and breast plates, late seventeenth century (Bayerishes Armee Museum, Ingolstadt); Right: Officer's 'Lobster' helmet, southern German manufacture, 1670–80 (Czech Army Museum, Prague). Metal protection was usually worn by the Bavarian cavalry from the 1660s. A *Votivtafel* depicting Captain Pendler von Penfelden, an officer of the Höning regiment, is preserved in the sacristy of the Karmeliterkirche in Münich, and depicts him in 1664 while serving in Hungary. He wears a simple back and breast over a leather *Koller*. A metal vambraces gauntlet is worn on the left arm, and the same protection is visible on the arm of a cuirassier in the background, an indication that this was probably a standard item.

---

158 Staudinger, *Geschichte des Kurbayerischen Heeres*, vol. I, p.356.
159 Staudinger, *Geschichte des Kurbayerischen Heeres*, vol. I, p.356.

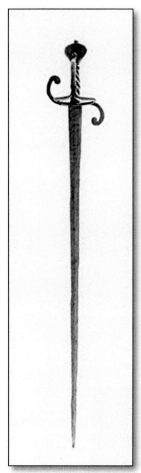

Cavalry sword, dated 1660 (Bayerishes Armee Museum, Ingolstadt). This kind of sword was widely issued to cavalrymen of southern Germany armies before the introduction of the Pallash.

latter, the private horsemen wore the bullet-proof iron corselet. In general breastplates were very unpopular among the troops and sometimes even among officers, but the War Council insisted on their use on campaign. The common headgear was the iron *Zischägge*, also called *Sturmhaube*, with the characteristic adjustable steel bar for protection of the face. The private cuirassiers wore the black cravat as for the infantry, with the ends at the front, above the buff coat and secured under the breastplate. Major changes occurred in 1682, when the buff coat was replaced by the *Rock* similar to the infantry model, and of grey cloth for all the regiments.[160]

As occurred in the contemporary German armies, the dragoons had the same clothing as the infantry, except for the boots. There are no iconographic sources depicting Bavarian dragoons from the 1660s–1680s, except for later reconstructions. Valuable information comes from the research of the late nineteenth century scholars, who confirm that differences between infantry and dragoon uniforms were minimal. In July 1674, 24 private infantrymen had been selected to be transferred to Dublier's company of dragoons; they asked to be 'completely mounted as dragoons', but they only meant the horse and weaponry (since they received a musketeer's pay, whereas dragoons received a higher salary), and indirectly this should confirm the substantial ambivalence of both modes of dress.[161]

Unfortunately, the same source provides little knowledge about artillerymen and engineers, or whether *Büchsenmeister* and *Konstabler* wore special clothing or distinctions. The most authoritative scholars suggest that only after 1682 did artillerymen receive grey coats with medium blue facings.[162]

In addition to the weaponry, which was provided by the arsenals of the Electorate, the militia was also subject to regulations concerning clothing. The decree of 23 June 1673 ordered that all members of the *Landfahne* should come for training with their weapons, swords and headgear. A subsequent decree, issued on 1 September 1673, prescribed the distribution of 'regular clothing' to the companies, without, however, specifying any details as to which colours and which items. However it is probable

Pallas, cavalry broadsword, late seventeenth century (Bayerishes Armee Museum, Ingolstadt), Black leather scabbard with brass fittings, dark brown wooden grip with brass guard and pommel.

---

160 Hoffmann, *Das Heer des Blauen Königs*, p.40.
161 Staudinger, *Geschichte des Kurbayerischen Heeres*, vol. I, fn p.358.
162 Hoffmann, *Das Heer des Blauen Königs*, p.60.

THE ELECTORATE OF BAVARIA

that the Prince-Elector only issued a *Rock*, almost certainly of grey or coarse brownish cloth.[163] More recent iconographic sources show the Bavarian artillerymen wearing grey coat with medium blue cuffs and lining.[164]

---

163 Staudinger, *Geschichte des Kurbayerischen Heeres*, vol. I, fn p.324.
164 Hoffmann, *Das Heer des Blauen Königs*, p.63.

5

The Electorate of Saxony

No other princely dynasty in Germany epitomised the relationship between state and ruling house like the Wettins. After the western part of Saxony reverted to the main Wettin line following the death of Duke William III in 1482, Saxony became the second power in the *Reich* next to the Habsburg domains. Moreover, the family network expanded to include members who became ecclesiastical dignitaries in Magdeburg, Halberstadt and Mainz, with additional claims to duchies on the Lower Rhine. They secured the continuity of the dynasty with their sons and asserted themselves as heirs to the Saxon Electoral privilege. The Wettins ruled further Saxon territories, as a consequence of the fragmentation between Ernestine and Albertine lines, extending the house's influence through marriages in all Germany, although not always harmoniously. Alongside the political prestige, Saxony increased its importance in the sixteenth century, becoming the focus of European attention, since it was there that the first phase of the Protestant Reformation was anchored. In 1547, Prince-Elector Moritz succeeded in clearing the way for the recognition of the new faith in the *Reich*, and under Wettin rule, the Electorate of Saxony more than any other power in Germany protected the Protestant faith. The Saxon electors became leaders of the Protestant German states, a primate consolidated in 1654, when the Regensburg Diet's *Corpus Evangelicorum* confirmed them in this status.[1] In the *Reich*, Saxony was the one of the only states, together with Mainz, the Palatinate and Bavaria, to enjoy the right which placed it outside the jurisdiction of the Imperial courts – the so-called *privilegium de non appellando* – while among the Hohenzollern domains this right was in force only for Brandenburg.

---

1   The title lasted until 1697, when after the election to the Polish throne, Friedrich August adhered to the Catholic faith, leaving the leading of the *Corpus Evangelicorum* to Prince-Elector Friedrich III of Brandenburg.

THE ELECTORATE OF SAXONY

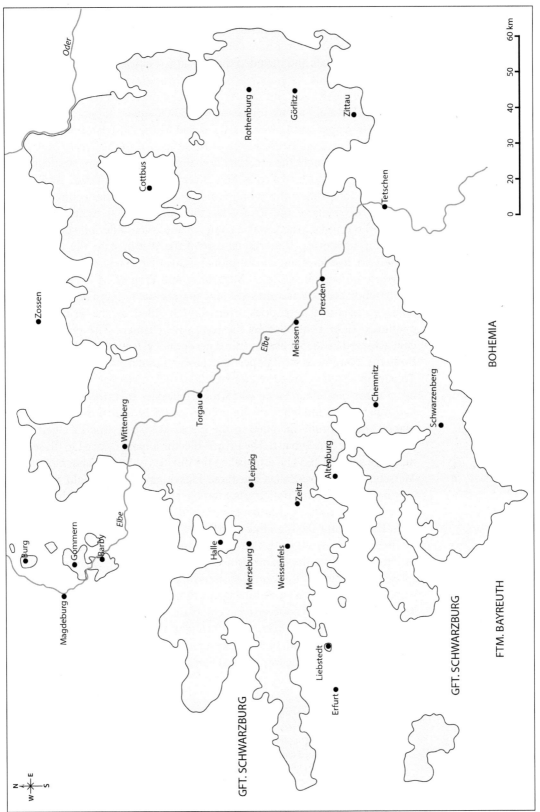

The Electorate of Saxony after the Treaty of Westphalia

In the seventeenth century, the Electoral branch of the Wettin family ruled a relatively homogeneous group of territories, compared to other German states. The Electorate comprised the Duchy of Saxony, which was the core of the state and included the two largest cities, Dresden and Leipzig. The Electoral rule extended across the Landgraviate of Thuringia, the Margravate of Meissen and the exclave of Gommen and Burg to the north. In 1635, Electoral Saxony increased by 13,000 square kilometres with the addition of Upper and Lower Lusatia, ceded by the Austrian Emperor when the Prince-Elector sided for him against Sweden with the Treaty of Prague. Although at first sight the Electoral domains seemed to compose a compact state, in fact they formed a collection of very different territories. As in other German principalities, the ruling family was the only connecting element. This, in theory, gave the Prince-Elector some judicial rights within the domains, but in fact there was a complex and often differing status among the Saxon territories. The original core of the Wettin state, the Margravate of Meissen, had laws and constitutional rights that characterised it from the bishopric of Naumburg-Zeitz, Merseburg and even of Meissen itself until this latter bishopric was annexed to the margravate in the sixteenth century. Some ecclesiastical territories, even though ruled by the Prince-Elector, continued to be controlled by the respective chapters. The vast territorial gain achieved in 1635, Lusatia, added new political features to the Electorate. Both the Margravates of Upper and Lower Lusatia had been fiefs of the Bohemian Kingdom, and therefore retained their own constitution. This was not a secondary affair, since when their delegates met, the general estates had much more influence in the process of decision making, and neither margravate was fully included in the Electoral system. The Electorate also included three fiefs entrusted by Prince-Elector Johann Georg I to his second marriage sons. In 1654 he established the duchies of Saxe-Weissenfels, Saxe-Merseburg and Saxe-Zeitz. The three Dukes enjoyed the right to control internal and economic policies, but foreign affairs were still held in Dresden for the whole country. Moreover, the Dukes had no seats in the *Reich's* diet. The expense for the large courts and art collections had to be borne by the secundogenitures, which in turn reduced the tax revenue available to Dresden. While the Saxon Prince-Elector had to pay for one court, his successors had to pay for four. Decisions made by the Prince-Electors for the whole country were seen as tutelage in these semi-autonomous territories, becoming a source of concerns and complaints.[2]

Though the Thirty Years' War brought an increase of the Electoral domains, which totalled 34,537 square kilometres, it marked the end of the 'Saxon Golden Age'.[3] The war affected Electoral Saxony especially badly in the

---

2   Frank Göse, 'Von der "Juniorpartnerschaft" zur Gleichrangigkeit. Das Brandenburgish-Sächsische Verhältnis in 16. und 17. Jahrhundert', in F. Göse (ed.), *Preussen und Sachsen. Szenen einer Nachbarschaft* (Dresden: Sandstein Verlag, 2104), p.51. The Dukes' delegates to Vienna and Berlin, complained about the weakening of the Electorate as a whole. With disgust, the Electoral ambassador in Berlin had to report in 1688, how displeasing it was to hear the cousins of Merseburg and Zeitz speaking of his Electoral Serenity as a *Caput Familia*.

3   In 1623, Prince-Elector's relations with the Emperor began to deteriorate. Saxony's neutrality was minimally respected by the Imperial troops, which on several occasions looted the border

west.[4] In the 1650s, the Electorate had approximately 650,000 inhabitants, half compared to 1618. Most of the decrease in Saxony's population due to the war came about indirectly through epidemics and economic factors related to the stagnation of trade, but troop movements and wartime occupations also caused considerable loss in both urban and village populations.[5] The losses were mitigated to a large extent by religious refugees, about 150,000 of whom came to Saxony from Bohemia and Silesia.[6]

The devastation caused by the Thirty Years' War nevertheless continued, as battles against the Swedes went on for more than 10 years. Electoral Saxony left the direct fighting provisionally with the armistice of 1645 and permanently through a 1646 treaty with Sweden. However, after 1648, Swedish troops were slow in leaving Electoral Saxony: only after payment of a stipulated tribute of 276,600 thalers agreed on

Left, Prince-Elector Johann Georg II in a portrait by Johann Fincke from 1665, together with, right, Friedrich Wilhelm of Brandenburg (Staatliche Kunstsammlungen Dresden). The Saxon Wettin and the Brandenburg Hohenzollern were the only Protestant Prince-Electors of the Empire. The Wettin held the leadership of the reformed German princes.

---

areas of the Electorate. In 1631, Prince-Elector Johann Georg I finally felt compelled to enter the war against the Emperor on the side of Sweden. The decisive factor for the radical change in policy was the military situation, since Swedish troops were already on Saxon soil at the time.

4   The Battle of Breitenfeld took place near Leipzig in 1631, as did the Battle of Lützen the following year. Leipzig was besieged several times, and its population declined from 17,000 to 14,000. Other urban centres, notably Dresden and Meissen, were spared, while Chemnitz was severely damaged and lost its earlier importance. However, after the complete devastation of Magdeburg, its importance as a metropolis in the east of the Holy Roman Empire passed to Leipzig and Dresden. Many smaller towns and villages fell victim to massive looting, especially after General Wallenstein gave free hand to his second in command Holk. From August to December 1632 the Croatian light cavalry raided numerous villages, plundering them, maltreating and killing the inhabitants and leaving a swathe of destruction in its wake.

5   Karlheinz Blaschke, *Bevölkerungsgeschichte von Sachsen bis zur Industriellen Revolution* (Weimar: Bohlau, 1967), p.96. According to the author, Saxony's population was reduced by about half as a result of the war. Other authors point out that such a large decrease may have been true in individual regions, but that it cannot be applied to the entire population.

6   Günther Franz, *Der Dreißigjährige Krieg und das Deutsche Volk. Untersuchungen zur Bevölkerungs- und Agrargeschichte* (Stuttgart: Lucius & Lucius, 1979), p.17.

30 June 1650 did the last of the Swedes leave the Electorate. Life increasingly returned to normal after the hired mercenaries were also released. When Johann Georg II (r. 1656–1680) succeeded his father, Electoral Saxony was still suffering from the economic consequences of the war. It was not until the reign of Johann Georg III (r. 1680–1691) that the damage and dire social welfare situation were overcome. Resettlement of village farms and urban households proved to be the most difficult problem. The first sign of recovery was an increase in tax revenues. Mining, metallurgy, crafts, trade and transportation recovered slowly but steadily. The Saxon estates of the realm had regained influence during the war due to the territorial princes' great need for money. In the second half of the seventeenth century, contrary to what happened in Brandenburg and Bavaria, the electors had to convene the state parliament far more frequently than before, and in 1661 the Saxon estates were able to assert their right to self-assembly. Discussion, compromises, and tiring negotiations marked the policy scenario of the Electorate, and the principle matter of these was almost always the raising of a permanent army.

Though the Electoral branch of the Wettin family had no interest in expanding its domains, some of the neighbouring princes pursued different politics, and this could not be eluded. However, in this period, the Saxon Prince-Electors had no territorial interest near their border, since they already controlled the most important cities of the region and dominated the few tiny duchies bordering the *Reich*. Claiming new territories far away was nearly impossible. Even the submission of Magdeburg in 1668 by Brandenburg, and the succession crisis in Saxe-Lauenburg in 1689, did not persuade the Prince-Electors to sustain their prerogative with arms. Since Saxony could not cross territorial boundaries, it was practically forced into a low-profile geostrategy, at least for the remaining years of the seventeenth century. Feeling itself to be like 'a fish in a barrel', the Electorate of Saxony maintained a rigid neutrality, which Louis XIV exploited for his plans, since together with other German princes, notably Bavaria and Brandenburg, Johann Georg II received French subsidies in 1679.[7] However, the French

Prince-Elector Johann Georg III portrayed by an unknown artist in 1680. He ruled for 11 years from 1680 to 1691, during which time he established a standing professional army.

---

7   Wilson, *German Armies*, p.63.

connection lasted only a few months, since Johann Georg III, succeeding his father in 1680, did not join the alliance with Louis XIV and sided with the Austrian Habsburgs.

The Saxon Mars

Uninvolved in wars for territorial expansion, Johann Georg II saw no need to increase the size of the professional army, or consequently the tax burden for his subjects. The substantial inoffensive attitude of Saxony appears intrinsic in its military organisation at higher levels. The Prince-Electors had no actual 'secretary' and ministers who dealt with the Military, and this matter was discussed among the members of his Secret Council, who in turn formed the Secret War Chancellery (*Geheime Kriegrsatskanzlei*), chaired by a *Secretarius*. The Prince-Elector met this body in Dresden and requested its opinions about recruitment, militia, appointment of officers, disbanding of units, and dismissing of soldiers, NCOs and officers. The members of the chancellery were also required to advise on the disbandment of garrisons, their strength, the introduction of new regulations, and the examination of disciplinary cases concerning officers. However, the responsibilities of the War Chancellery were limited and only the secretary was retained in post in peacetime. Every topic that required money was discussed together with the director of the Court Chamber (*Kammerdirektor*), who managed the finances.

The Court Chamber supervised the work of the commissioners in charge of mustering the troops. In this regard, the Electoral domains were divided into seven circles (*Kreise*) both for administrative purposes and recruitment; these were *Kurkreis*, Meissen, Leipzig, Erzgebirge: Thüringen and Vogtland, each with its own commissioner. They were the source of several complaints, because – according to contemporary reports – the provinces' authorities accused them of all sorts of corruption. In all the Electorate 'many grievances accused the commissioners, because they ignored tax norms and tables when billeting troops and extorting seven thalers a month from their own hosts', also because the commissioners did not receive regular pay from the

Dresden, in an early eighteenth century print. (Author's Collection) The fortifications of the Electoral capital had been much improved during the seventeenth century and further works were completed during the reign of Prince-Elector Johann Georg II.

state.[8] The troubles continued, forcing Prince-Elector Johann Georg II in 1676 to order that only locals with good knowledge of the province should be recruited as commissioners.[9] In 1678 the Prince-Elector appointed two commissioners for the circle of Vogtland and Thuringia, and one for the others. A regular salary was also introduced and this reduced the need, if not the possibility, to extort money from the citizens. In each circle also operated the *Kreishauptmann*, a rank usually entrusted to a couple of nobles who had the task of leading troops and recruits marching through the Electorate.

Johann Georg II appointed a commander-in-chief who dealt with the training and service of the troops, with an unknown number of adjutants managing supply, train, ammunition and other logistical matters. Under him, a small number of senior commanders served in the army, according to their rank which followed the traditional denomination introduced in Germany since the beginning of the seventeenth century, with *Feldmarschall, Feldzeugmeister*, and *Generalwachtmeister*, although the former rank was appointed only in wartime. The highest ranking officer during the reign of Johann Georg II was the *Hofmarschall* Christian Ernst von Kanne, who also held the command of the Electoral cavalry until 1677.

This architecture lasted until 1681, when in November a project for a new organisation was submitted to the Prince-Elector by the *Kammerdirektor* Christian Dietrich von Bose. His plan provided for the creation of a stable War Chancellery, to be denominated *Geheime Kriegskanzlei*. The proposal was implemented, and the following January Bose became the first director of the War Chancellery. While a decree of the Prince-Elector announcing its formation was issued on 4 March, the unexpectedly urgent mobilisation of the army for the campaign of 1683 in Austria delayed the works for its establishment. It was only after the return from Vienna that a commission was created on 14 November to examine the problems that had emerged during the campaign.

Baron Christian Ernst von Kanne (1617–1677). He was a member of a family which had served the Wettin princes since the sixteenth century. His father, Bernhard Ludolph Kanne, was the Court Chamberlain and owned the two manors of Klöden and Löwendorf. Christian Ernst entered the service of the Prince-Elector Johann Georg I of Saxony at an early age and later became, Governor of Gräfenhainichen in 1671 and later also of Schweinitz, Schlieben, Seyda and Annaburg.

---

8   Walter Thenius, *Die Anfange des Stehenden Heerwesen in Kursachsen unter Johann Georg III. und Johann Georg IV* (Leipzig, 1912), p.29.

9   Thenius, *Die Anfange des Stehenden Heerwesen in Kursachsen*, p.29.

Plate A – Electorate of Brandenburg, infantry 1660s–1670s.
1 - *Schwerin zu Fuss*, Musketeer 1657–60
2 - Unknown unit, Pikeman, early-1660s
3 - *Markische Leibgarde*, Ensign 1664

See Colour Plate Commentaries for further information.

Plate B – Electorate of Brandenburg, Infantry 1680s.
1 – *Bolsey Marine Regiment*, Marine 1676–80
2 – *Spaen zu Fuss*, Musketeer 1685
3 – *Doenhoff zu Fuss*, Company Officer 1680–85
See Colour Plate Commentaries for further information.

Plate C – Electorate of Brandenburg, Cavalry 1670s.
1 – Cavalry Regiment *Markgraf Ludwig von Brandenburg*, Pauker (Kettledrummer) 1678
2 – Cavalry Regiment *Markgraf Ludwig von Brandenburg*, Trooper 1678
a-b-c: liveries, 1660–1690

See Colour Plate Commentaries for further information.

iii

Plate D – Electorate of Brandenburg, Cavalry and Dragoons, 1670s–1680s.
1 – Cavalry Officer, 1678
2 – *Leibdragoner* Regiment, Dragoon 1685
3 – *Du Hamel zu Pferde*, Trooper 1688
See Colour Plate Commentaries for further information.

Plate E – Electorate of Brandenburg, *Trabantengarde*, 1675–78.

See Colour Plate Commentaries for further information.

Plate F – Electorate of Bavaria, 1660s–1670s.
1 – Infantry Regiment *Puech*, Musketeer 1661–64
2 – Cavalry Officer, 1670–75
3 – Infantry Regiment *Wagenseil*, Musketeer 1679
See Colour Plate Commentaries for further information.

Plate G – Electorate of Bavaria, 1683–85.
1 – Dragoon Regiment *Schier*, Dragoon 1684
2 – Unknown Cuirassier Regiment, Trumpeter 1683
3 – *Leibregiment zu Fuss*, Grenadier 1685
See Colour Plate Commentaries for further information.

Plate H – Electorate of Saxony, 1660s–1670s.
1 – Unknown infantry unit, Pikeman 1660
2 – Musketeer, 1666
3 – *Leibregiment zu Pferde*, 1676–78
See Colour Plate Commentaries for further information.

Plate I – Electorate of Saxony, 1680–86.
1 – Cuirassier, Trooper 1680
2 – Artilleryman, 1683
3 – Musketeer, 1686

See Colour Plate Commentaries for further information.

Plate J – Prince-Bishopric of Münster Infantry, 1670s.
1 – NCO, 1672
2 – Musketeer, 1672
3 – Senior Officer, 1670

See Colour Plate Commentaries for further information.

Plate K– Prince-Bishopric of Münster, Cavalry 1672–73.

1 – *Leibgarde zu Ross*, Trooper, 1673

2 – Unknown cavalry unit, Trooper, 1672

3 – Dragoon Regiment *Wolframsdorf*, Dragoon, 1672

See Colour Plate Commentaries for further information.

Plate L – Brandenburg Infantry Colours
1 – *Leibfahne* regiment *Garde zu Fuss* (BrI-9), 1678
2 – *Kompagniefahne* possibly regiment *Belling zu Fuss* (BrI-1), 1684
3 – *Kompagniefahne* regiment *Derfflinger zu Fuss* (BrI-51), 1674
4 – *Kompagniefahne* regiment *Dönhoff zu Fuss* (BrI-43), 1680s
5 – *Leibfahne* and *Kompagniefahne* Regiment *Zieten zu Fuss* (BrI-62), 1677
See Colour Plate Commentaries for further information.

Plate M – Brandenburg Cavalry and Dragoon Colours
1 – Standard of the *Trabantengarde* (BrC-i), 1670s
2 – *Leibstandarte* regiment *Croy zu Pferde* (BrC-39), 1674–79
3 – *Compagnie Standarte* regiment *Spaen zu Pferde* (BrC-28), 1680s
4 – *Compagnie Standarte* regiment *Briquemault zu Pferde* (BrC-43), before 1700
5 – *Compagnie Standarte* regiment *Markgraf Ludwig* (BrC-31), 1682–87
6 – Life Guidon, *Leibdragoner* regiment (BrD-15) 1678–88

See Colour Plate Commentaries for further information.

xiii

Plate N – Bavarian Infantry and Cavalry Colours
1, 2 and 3 – Infantry Company Colours, 1688–90
4 – Company Standard, cavalry regiment *Höning* (BvC-3), 1663–64
5 – Leibstandarte for cavalry, 1670s

See Colour Plate Commentaries for further information.

Plate O – Saxon Infantry and Cavalry Colours
1 – Standard of the *Leibtrabanten Garde zu Ross*, 1676–77
2 – Company Colours of the *2. Leibgarde zu Fuss* (Sal-2), 1683
3 – Company Colour, regiment *Sachsen-Weissenfels zu Fuss* (Sal-4)
4 – Infantry Company Colour of an unknown regiment, 1680–90
5 – Company Guidon of an unknown dragoon regiment, late seventeenth century
See Colour Plate Commentaries for further information.

Plate P – Münster Infantry Colours
1 – Infantry Life Colours of an unknown Regiment, 1677–78
2 and 3 – Infantry Company Colours of an unknown Regiment, 1677–78
4 – Coat of Arms of Münster

See Colour Plate Commentaries for further information.

THE ELECTORATE OF SAXONY

The commission included the High Court Marshal Friedrich Adolph von Haugwitz, and all the senior commanders. They renewed the request for a formation of a stable War Chancellery, which was finally approved by Johann Georg III on 24 January 1684, and definitively installed on 14 February with the title of *Geheimes Kriegsratkollegium*. It became the body through which the Prince-Elector controlled all branches of the army. In wartime, a member of the War Council would join the army on campaign. The composition of the council changed throughout the years and the number of members was not established until the 1690s. Subordinated to the new council, a new War Chancellery was also established, comprising a war councillor, secretary, administrator, clerk and servant.[10] While the Secret War Council did not have a seat, because its members had other official duties, the War Chancellery was located in the Taschenbergpalais of Dresden. The office had the task of dealing with musters and the payment for the troops, and the issuing of the recruiting patent or *Werbung*. The War Chancellery also supervised the work of the General War Payment Office (*Generalkriegszahlamt*), comprising of the general war paymaster, one *Kopist*, and one field-accountant with aids. The chief of the office had the delicate task of receiving the contribution in the Upper Saxon Circle.[11]

The original project of 1681 included the raising of a field postal service

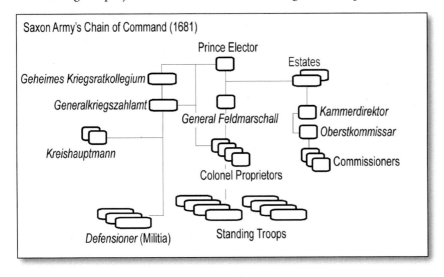

Saxony Chain of Command

(*Feldpost*), which dealt with the writing, copying and transmission of military correspondence, similar to one introduced in Bavaria. The postal service provided the delivery of the correspondence between the commanders, the War Council and the court twice a week.[12] In the 1680s the office served on

---

10 Oskar Schuster and Friedrich August Francke, *Die Geschichte der Sächsische Armee von der Errichtung bis in die neueste Zeit: Unter Benutzung Handschriftlicher und Urkundlicher Quellen*, vol. I (Leipzig, 1885), p.111.
11 Querengässer, *The Saxon Mars and His Force*, p.42.
12 Querengässer, *The Saxon Mars and His Force*, pp.42–43. Because in the *Reich* the postal service was an Imperial right, there were inevitable conflicts with other services when the army operated abroad. In the 1680s, the Saxon field post's activity caused immediate protest from

campaign under the *Feld-Postmeister* Wilhelm Ludwig Daser, who had his base in Leipzig.

The War Commissariat continued to operate under the supervision of the *Kammerdirektor* until 1688. In 1681, as part of the reforms undertaken by Johann Georg III, the rank of *Oberstkommissar* was reintroduced. Two years later the Prince-Elector established two commissioners in each circle and the territories belonging to the secundogenitures also had commissioners sent from Dresden. The salary increased remarkably after 1684, as a sign of the new duty required of the commissioners, who not only supervised every quartered regiment and company, but now mediated between the military and civilians, and dealt with the same matters in the territories of the vassal Dukes. By 1 January 1688 the commissioners were subordinated to the new War Chancellery, in charge of the control of the troops on the march, in order to organise the billeting, and sending to the regiments the letters to obtain food and quarters from the provinces of the circle. It was a complex task, because the Saxon army had no barracks except the few in some fortresses and in Dresden, and then the soldiers were billeted in among the citizen's houses. The commissioners issued the billets to the troops, who with the bed also received from the civilians salt, pepper, candles and wood. Between 1683 and 1686, the commissioner in charge of the affairs in the Duchy of Saxe-Merseburg twice forwarded his resignation because of continuous conflict with Duke Christian, 'who disliked him for his vigorous handling of the duties'.[13]

In 1681 the Prince-Elector reintroduced the rank of *Generalfeldmarschall* with the appointment of Joachim Rüdiger von der Goltz, a former Brandenburg general, in order to exploit the skills of this experienced veteran for the organisation of the new standing army. As during the reign of Johann Georg II, the *Generalfeldmarschall* was always the Prince-Elector's Lieutenant, acting on behalf of the ruler from whom his authority derived. As a regular member of the War Council, he received all the regiment's muster reports and petitions for leave, promotion or retirement, as well as reports concerning judicial matters. Because of his age, Goltz was forced to relinquish the rank in November 1683. His successor, the former *Generalfeldmarschall-Lieutenant* Heino Heinrich von Flemming, was appointed on 15 February 1684, but it was not until Goltz's death that Flemming received his full rank, on 8 September 1688. Like his predecessor, Flemming belonged to the Brandenburg nobility, and had joined the Saxon service in 1682.[14] The employment of senior officers from the army of the Great Elector indicates that the influence of Brandenburg on the newly raised Saxon army was decisive. However, in the 1680s Saxony was not devoid of officers, who in fact were in great number and the majority of them could be

---

the Austrian *Oberst-Generalpostmeister* Count von Paar, the Thurn und Taxis family and even the Imperial court: 'The Austrian ... hampered Saxon communications, because he felt his privileges threatened. However, because neither the Emperor nor the Reichstag, where other princes put forward similar proposals for the organisation of military postal services, could settle the matter, John George III was finally successful.'

13 Thenius, *Die Anfange des Stehenden Heerwesen in Kursachsen*, p.31.

14 In 1691 Flemming resigned and returned to Brandenburg's service.

considered experienced veterans. In 1682 there were 267 officers who served in the army; about 90 percent had served before for more than 10 years and only a minority in foreign armies. Some officers went through different careers, on average they had served two Prince-Electors before 1682, and about a fifth came from the Brandenburg army, while another considerable percentage also served in the Imperial and Dutch armies. Their service varied between six months and 38 years for a Saxon and between one and 32 years for foreigners.[15]

Joachim Rüdiger von der Goltz (1620–1688). A native of Prussia, he entered the Imperial army in the 1640s, but from 1648 to 1654 he was *Maréchal de Camp* in the French army during the war against Spain and later during the civil unrest of the *Fronde*. In 1653, the young Louis XIV awarded him the three Bourbon lilies as an heraldic augmentation and French nobility for his family in recognition of his services during the *Fronde*. In 1654, Goltz left France and entered the service of Brandenburg as a colonel. From 1674 he was General of Infantry and Governor of Berlin. In 1675, he entered Danish service as a Field Marshal while retaining his Brandenburg rank. In 1680, with the authorisation of the Great Elector, he entered the service of the Electorate of Saxony as Field Marshal General, and was considered a talented organiser, but in 1681, he was already a sick man and unable to take the field. In 1683, he was relieved from command, but officially kept the position until his death in 1688.

Heino Heinrich von Flemming (1632–1706). Flemming was born in Martenthin into an old noble Brandenburg family. After an education at German Universities, Flemming fought the Ottoman Turks as a colonel of auxiliary troops in the service of Brandenburg. Friedrich Wilhelm sent him to Poland in 1672 as commander of the Ducal Prussian contingent against the Ottomans. After serving William III of Orange, Flemming eventually returned to Brandenburg. Because of his skill and courage he received many offers to change service, and in 1682 became *Feldmarschall-Lieutenant* in the Saxon army. He accompanied Prince-Elector Johann Georg III and the Saxon auxiliary troops in 1683 to the relief of Vienna. On 8 September 1688, he was appointed Field Marshal after the death of Joachim von der Goltz. The following year, he commanded the Saxon troops on the Rhine under Johann Georg III. However, he was suspended for multiple personal offences, accused of corruption. He left the Saxon army and entered the Brandenburg army again. Flemming successfully commanded in Flanders and retired in 1698 due to his poor health.

---

15   Querengässer, *The Saxon Mars and His Force*, p.56.

Historians outline that military service never enjoyed favour in Saxony comparable to other German states, and for various reasons the military career was never regarded as high as it was, for instance, in Brandenburg.[16] As a result, the Saxon officers belonged to the less wealthy nobility of the Electorate, and poor resources often meant poor consideration which frustrated the attitude for sacrifice. Furthermore, military careers were hampered by the modest size of the army, which offered little opportunity for improvement. Although the Saxon officer class was composed almost entirely of nobles, the best careers were often those of wealthy nobles and high-salaried foreigners. In 1681 Johann Georg III tried to forbid his noble subjects from serving in foreign armies, but the estates protested, because – they said – the nobility had no access to, and nearly no resources from the Prince-Elector's army, and therefore they followed the path of war outside the country, training themselves in a foreign army.[17] With their opposition, the estates declared that the majority of the Saxon nobility lacked the financial means to take service as colonels or captains. The resistance did not diminish and Johann Georg III renounced his intention to abolish military service abroad.

In the same year, the Prince-Elector established a hierarchy among the senior officers, introducing the rank of *Feldmarschall-Lieutenant* expressly for Flemming, which was later changed to *Generalleutnant*. Apart from the highest ranks, native officers held all the posts of subordinates, such as the Quartermaster General and the Auditor, which were appointed as permanent members of the *General Stab*. In the field, surgeon, staff quartermaster, staff courier, guide, general wagon master and two field couriers were usually added to the army.

As for every German state in the second half of the seventeenth century, the main problem in maintaining an army of significant proportions was how to procure the necessary money. Although Saxony did not pursue a hegemonic policy comparable to that of neighbouring Brandenburg, the political prestige of the Electorate could not be sustained without an army, and this became a sensitive matter under the ambitious Prince-Elector Johann Georg III. With the new military organisation, Johann Georg III provided the army with a modern administration, but it did not serve the raising of funding and supply, but their proper distribution. The main source of funding was taxes, and these were not paid on a regular basis because taxes being under the control of the estates, the Prince-Elector had to negotiate with them for any further resource. In this regard, the relations between the sovereigns and the Saxon estates led to a completely different outcome than in Brandenburg, but as occurred in Berlin, Dresden also had to deal with the composite nature of the Electoral territories. While the taxes were voted by the estates as representative of the whole Electorate, the heterogeneous nature of the governance meant it was not always easy to get revenues out of some provinces. The major problems came from the three vassal duchies. While the Prince-Elector argued he had a right to raise taxes for the army because

---

16 Querengässer, *The Saxon Mars and His Force*, p.56.
17 Göse, 'Von der "Juniorpartnerschaft" zur Gleichrangigkeit', p.74.

he was master of all the state, the Dukes countered with the argument that they enjoyed sovereignty over their territories. However, the *jus de belli et pacis* held by the Prince-Elector not only included the right to sign alliances, but also quarter and the raising of recruits, as well as collecting money for the maintenance of troops. Moreover, the local estates had their own traditions which were much older than the institution of these territories as fiefs. In the 1680s, disputes between the Prince-Elector and Duke Johann Adolph of Saxe-Weissenfels focused on the fiscal policy of the Electorate. Since Johann Georg III had won the upper hand by 1681, on 29 June Johann Adolph signed an agreement with his cousin and granted revenues, provisions and quarters for the Saxon troops. In 1684 another agreement was signed, obliging the Duke to pay annually further contributions, but in 1686 Johann Georg III reminded the Duke about the default he had accumulated. Further negotiations followed, and in 1687 the Duke finally sent money, which the Prince-Elector used for the salaries of his mounted life guards and two regiments of infantry. However, Johann Adolph complained about the burdens of quartering Electoral troops, especially because his territories were located along the main roads leading from Electoral Saxony to the Rhine, so troops heading west had to transit his major towns.[18] The scenario was similar in Saxe-Zeitz, where the Duke had arbitrarily modified his contribution, and only in 1682 and 1683 did he make a sizeable contribution.

Portrait of Johann Lämmel (1644–1705), the skilled and influential chief of the Saxon military administration, in a print from the 1680s. (Staatlichen Kunstsammlungen, Dresden) Presumably through the mediation of his father-in-law, Benedict Thomae – a Swedish regimental quartermaster, Johann Lämmel obtained a position in Saxony in 1680, where he was appointed as accountant in the War Chancellery. In 1682 he passed to the General War Payment Office as a paymaster, a position he held for more than 20 years. In 1686 he increased his influence when he was appointed general paymaster, and became an important figure in providing funds, and especially credit, for the army, much of which came from his own resources. But he seems to have lined his own pockets while doing so and after his death, it was calculated that he might have 'acquired' as much as 300,000 thalers. Such cases show that the early modern state needed the private clientele networks of its officials, because the administrative organisation was all too small for its tasks.

The Empire's constitution could be exploited to raise more funds, since Saxony, as one of the major members of the *Obersächsischer Kreis*, could use its leading position to exchange the provision of troops for subsidies. Therefore, the Prince-Elector offered to provide his troops on behalf of the circle and then collect money from the unarmed principalities in compensation. Johann Georg II had already tried to exploit this opportunity in 1673, but it did not bring many benefits, since the *Kreis* was little involved in the war against France. Furthermore he had been a great admirer of

---

18   Querengässer, *The Saxon Mars and His Force*, p.30: 'John George countered with the argument, that the Duke had other debts too, which were not related to his contribution for the army. In the years following this was fixed at 7,000 thalers which were rarely paid in full.'

Louis XIV, and in Germany there were not a few who viewed his actions with suspicion.[19] However, Saxony, like the other major states of the Reich, exploited this scenario on several occasions, such as in September 1677 when the Saxon cavalry corps on the Upper Rhine commandeered the Swabians' field artillery.[20]

It was only by the 1680s that Saxony managed to sign actual agreements with smaller states, which agreed to pay contributions in return for exemption from billeting. Agreements were signed between 1682 and 1688 with the princedom of Schwarzburg, the baronies of Schönburg, Blankenheim and Kranichfeld, the counties of Reuss, Stollberg, Barby and Mansfeld, and the Abbey of Quedlinburg. These contributions were collected with the permission of the Emperor, who granted the Prince-Elector this right for the defence of the *Reich* from his major enemy, notably France.[21] The Prince-Elector began looking for additional funds and a very profitable opportunity came in 1682 with the upcoming Ottoman campaign against Austria. In November, Emperor Leopold I negotiated with the Prince-Elector one *Hilfskorp* from Saxony to be used against the Ottomans. The talks took time, because Johann Georg III was looking to the Dutch Republic for subsidies in return for troops. A three-year contract was finally signed with the Emperor on 7 June 1683, when the Ottomans were already marching to Vienna. In 1685 another agreement was signed with the Republic of Venice for the hiring of three infantry regiments. In January 1686 Johann Georg III agreed a new contract with the Emperor for another auxiliary corps, for three regiments of infantry and two of cavalry for 4,700 men in all.[22] In 1688 a last contract was agreed for a single infantry regiment.

The Standing Army

While the Treaty of Westphalia guaranteed Electoral Saxony the *jure de armi et pacis*, by 1651 the army was disbanded to a large extent. One year after, the professional troops still serving in the Electorate comprised one company of *Einspänniger* (cuirassiers) of 121 horsemen and 143 artillerymen; the infantry consisted of Dresden's *Unterguardia*, a civic corps composed of militiamen, and 678 veterans distributed to the state as sedentary garrisons: 1,452 men in all.[23] Modest changes in strength occurred in the following years: in 1656 the new Prince-Elector Johann Georg II raised a cavalry *Leib-Eskadron* of two companies with 205 horsemen, a company of Swiss musketeers of 200 foot, and a company of Croats with 132 light cavalrymen, this latter employed as life guards.[24] In the same year another mounted company of

---

19   See also Mugnai, *Wars and Soldiers*, vol. 2, pp.117–118.
20   Wilson, *German Armies*, p.50.
21   Thenius, *Die Anfange des Stehenden Heerwesen in Kursachsen*, p.11.
22   Schuster and Francke, *Die Geschichte der Sächsische Armee*, pp.110–111.
23   Schuster and Francke, *Die Geschichte der Sächsische Armee*, p.82.
24   The Croats were raised following the fascination for the exotic typical in the Baroque age, especially to a personality like the flamboyant Johann Georg II.

THE ELECTORATE OF SAXONY

life guards, denominated *Leibgarde zu Ross*, was established as the personal escort of the Prince, but the unit did not perform actual military duties and served as 'palace corps' alongside the Croats. Before the end of the year, the pompous Johann Georg II recruited another life guard, this time of infantry, trusting to Lieutenant-Governor de Magny, until then commander of the cavalry troop, to recruit a company of Swiss Guards. However, the company was 'Swiss' in name only, because it was composed of Germans, although they wore Swiss style dress. Alongside the *Primaplana*, in 1659 the company numbered 108 halberdiers.[25] A further company of Life Guard of foot, the *Hochdeitsche Trabanten*, was also raised with 56 men in all.[26] On 14 February 1657 the former cavalry troop of the Life Guard was abolished, replaced by a new company with the name *Deutsche Leibgarde zu Ross*. It consisted of one *Obrist*, one *Obristlieutenant*, one *Rittmeister*, one *Kornett*, one *Lieutenant*, four trumpeters, one kettledrum, one *Wachtmeister*, six *Korporale*, 14 noblemen with 14 servants and 61 *Einspänniger*, in total 105 men with 105 horses.[27] In subsequent years the company increased to 256 men, enlisting further horsemen as well as noble cadets and volunteers.

In 1658 a company of *Leibgarde Dragoner* of 120 men was also raised, then in October 1663 Prince-Elector Johann Georg II mobilised the newly formed *Leibregiment zu Fuss*, under the *Obrist* Brand von Lindau to join the auxiliary corps gathered by the German princes to support the Austrian Emperor in the war against the Porte. The regiment numbered 1,174 men with six companies, and on 16 September, in Torgau, the Prince-Elector carried out the inspection, declaring himself a Colonel Proprietor. On 26 September the regiment marched from Dresden to Hungary through Bohemia, together with four field guns and 300 *zentner* of gunpowder to join the Imperial corps in Upper Hungary under *Feldmarschall* Louis Raduit de Souches.[28] In addition to the regiment, the Circle of Upper Saxony had voted

Saxon *Schweizerleibgarde* from an eighteenth century manuscript preserved in the library of the *Kunstsammlungen* in Dresden. A small unit of 20 men entitled *Oberguardia* was originally raised in 1555. In 1656 the company was established to 108 men. This number increased to 112 men in 1669, but one year later the strength was reduced by half for economic reasons. In the 1680s the company was increased again and comprised 1 *Hauptmann*, 1 *Hauptmann-Lieutenant*, 1 *Lieutenant*, 1 *Unter-Lieutenant*, 1 *Fähnrich*, 1 *Secretarius*, 1 *Wachtmeister-lieutenant*, 1 *porte-enseigne* (standard-bearer); 1 surgeon, 1 *Fourier*, 6 *Rottmeister* (corporals), 3 fifers, 3 drummers, 96 guards, 4 carpenters, 2 *Fourier-Schutzen* for the captain and 8 hautbois. Essentially, this court dress had changed little compared to the previous century, and consisted of black broad-brimmed hat edged of white with blue and white plumes, Swiss style doublet and breeches of yellow and blue laced of silver, yellow cloak lined in blue, silver buttons, white stockings with blue tassels and bows on the shoes.
Halberd of the Electoral Swiss Guard, late seventeenth century. (Basel City Museum) Iron with gilded engraving, and crimson red tassel.

---

25 Schuster and Francke, *Die Geschichte der Sächsische Armee*, p.84.
26 Schuster and Francke, *Die Geschichte der Sächsische Armee*, p.84. The duties of this guard included police duties within the prince's residence and guarding of the entrances to the palace.
27 Schuster and Francke, *Die Geschichte der Sächsische Armee*, p.84.
28 Friedrich von Beust, *Feldzüge des Kursächsischen Armee* (Homburg, 1803); vol. II, p.4. One *zentner* is equivalent to 51.4kg.

for a contingent *in triplum* in accordance with the *Reich*'s resolution, for which Electoral Saxony was to provide a further cavalry regiment of three companies with 309 men. The command was entrusted to *Obrist* Wolframsdorff, but the formation of the cavalry companies which was to be formed with recruits from 11 different states of the circle, encountered so many obstacles that the regiment could not be gathered until 27 August 1664, by which time the Emperor and the Sultan had already agreed on an armistice. Since the Imperial delegates had declared at the Diet in Regensburg that the Emperor no longer needed these troops, Saxony refrained from sending troops to the Upper Saxon contingent.[29] Of the three cavalry companies, two companies, as well as the artillery assigned to the auxiliary contingent in Hungary, were dismissed at the beginning of 1665, but one cavalry troop under Wolframsdorff remained in service.

In 1666, Prince-Elector Johann Georg II still had 1,404 infantrymen, 663 horsemen and 150 artillerymen of professional troops, 188 foot of the Household troops, 501 other infantrymen of the Dresden *Unterguardia*, and 6,000 militiamen 'on paper'. The discipline of these troops left much to be desired. For this reason, by 1660 the Prince-Elector had issued the *Reiterrecht* (Equestrian Law), which consisted of a regulation to improve service, discipline and military justice for the cavalry.[30]

On 1 July 1667, Obristlieutenant Schweinig received a patent for the establishment of a new dragoon company of 100 men for the Prince-Elector's lifeguard, which was mustered on 4 December 1667. In addition, Johann Georg II ordered that the infantry *Leibregiment* be increased to the 'old force' of six companies. As recruitment proceeded slowly, the regiment could not be gathered in Dresden until April 1670; the

Pikemen from the *Kurtze Iedoch Deutliche Beschreibung Des Pique-Spielens* (1660), by Johann Georg Pascha. (Niedersächsische Staats- und Universitätsbibliothek, Göttingen) The author published his works in Leipzig and the majority were dedicated to Prince-Elector Johann Georg II. Everything therefore suggests that the soldiers depicted belong to the Electoral Saxon army or at least to the areas of Upper and Lower Saxony.

---

29 Schuster and Francke, *Die Geschichte der Sächsische Armee*, p.85.
30 Schuster and Francke, *Die Geschichte der Sächsische Armee*, p.87.

THE ELECTORATE OF SAXONY

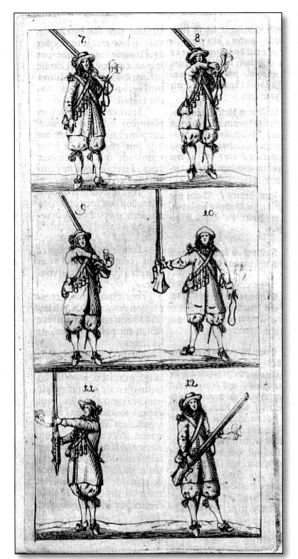
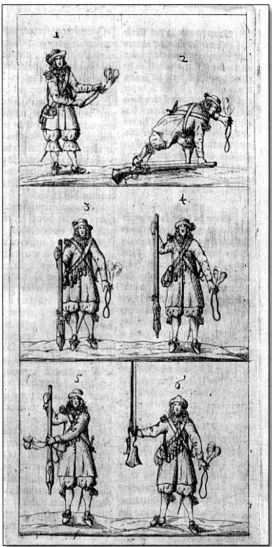

Musketeers from the *Deutliche Beschreibung, Von dem Exerciren in der Mußquet* (1666), by Johann Georg Pascha.

Obristlieutenant Johann Kuffer was appointed as colonel. In October 1668 a regiment of horse was formed under *Obrist* Christian Ernst von Kanne with the five cavalry companies already existing and a sixth company recruited in 1669; the companies numbered between 70 and 100 men.[31] Due to economic shortages the company of Swiss musketeers was disbanded before the end of the year, but in 1671 the resulting savings enabled the raising of a further two companies of 76 men for the *Leibdragoner*, which increased the strength to a squadron. In 1673 a fourth company was added.[32] In 1671 French influence pushed the Prince-Elector to raise another Household company of 24 horsemen and five officers and NCOs, which took the name of *mousquetaires*. The company was formed by noblemen and dismissed officers and had the

---

31 Schuster and Francke, *Die Geschichte der Sächsische Armee*, p.87.
32 Schuster and Francke, *Die Geschichte der Sächsische Armee*, p.87.

precedence in the escort service for the Prince-Elector; like their French counterpart of the first company, the Saxon *mousquetaires* mounted only white horses. In 1676 the *Leib-Trabantengarde* (sac-iv), formerly *Deutsche Leibgarde zu Ross*, had 335 horsemen divided into three companies and six *Korporalschaft* under *Generalwachtmeister* Reitzichitz. On 1 January 1677 a fourth company was raised, increasing the strength to 374 *Trabanten*.[33]

As for the infantry, three free companies were raised in 1673, each with 234 men.[34] By 1675 the infantry *Leibregiment* had 10 companies, but once returned from the Rhine in April, it was divided into three regiments, two of which were denominated 1st and 2nd *Leibregiment* (SaI-1 and SaI-2), while the third – short-lived – regiment was assigned to *Obrist* Hannibal von Degenfeldt (SaI-3). By 1679, after the Peace of Nijmegen, all the infantry regiments had been reduced to a few companies, while all the cavalry regiments had been disbanded. On 24 May 1680, the standing force numbered 1,740 infantry, included the palace guards with 65 men, and 391 cavalry and dragoons.[35] This was the last demobilisation of the Saxon professional army. In November 1680, soon after his accession to the Electoral throne, Johann Georg III decided to raise an actual standing army. This wish was not completely new: a few months before he died, Johann Georg II had prepared a *memorandum* to be presented to the estates, asking for an increase of military expenditure in order to increase the artillery and the standing garrisons, and to raise a field force of 1,000 cavalry, 3,000 infantry, with a modern field artillery. In the thoughts of the Prince-Elector, this modest and relatively less expensive force might meet the estates' approval. To save more funds, Johann Georg II dismissed some of the expensive but militarily useless palace guards and diminished the size of the Swiss Guard.[36]

However, because most of the Electorate, including Dresden and the court itself, was still under the threat of the plague to which his father had fallen victim, the new Prince-Elector Johann Georg III did not manage to achieve significant results in 1680. The estates failed to meet for the *memorandum*, and just a few delegates assembled in Meissen in November approved the funds for the repair of the fortresses and the money to pay the troops still in service. However, the Prince-Elector did not wait for better times for the raising of the standing army: he enlisted Colonel Ulrich von Premnitz, again from Brandenburg's army, in order to organise recruitment and drill of the troops.

In November 1681, Johann Georg III finally presented his plan to the estates. Aware of the continuing weakness of the Electorate in the aftermath of the plague, he first argued that his domains with the usual taxation could not maintain a standing army. Therefore, he demanded the establishment of magazines with resources to supply a field army of 8,000 men. For this purpose, the estates had to grant 1,000,000 thalers per year. Additionally,

---

33 Schuster and Francke, *Die Geschichte der Sächsische Armee*, pp.31–35.
34 Schuster and Francke, *Die Geschichte der Sächsische Armee*, p.87.
35 Schuster and Francke, *Die Geschichte der Sächsische Armee*, pp.87, 93.
36 Querengässer, *The Saxon Mars and His Force*, p.26. The company of the Swiss Guard was reduced to 96 halberdiers.

THE ELECTORATE OF SAXONY

the militia had to be raised to defend the borders in case the army left the Electorate. Because the existing troops lacked payment, the estates should also grant the money and more taxes to pay them off.[37] After examining the Prince-Elector's project, the estates replied harshly. The negotiations give an impressive example of the comparably strong constitutional position of the Saxon estates and the weak position of the Prince-Elector. In their grievances, presented to Johann Georg III on 22 November, the estates demanded an investigation into the management of the domains and questioned why more debts had not been settled in recent years. They strongly rejected the request to raise the militia, arguing that the civilians could be trained anyway, but keeping them under arms would have deprived the treasury of 3,000 good taxpayers. They also complained about lax discipline and the excesses of the professional troops, especially regarding billeting. The estates accused the military commissioners of quartering the soldiers without consulting municipal authorities. The universities of Leipzig and Wittenberg, in particular, complained that soldiers were quartered in the surrounding villages, so these did not generate the income needed to pay the professors. The cities, drawing the darkest picture of the general state of the territory, finally protested about the fact that soldiers took additional work, depriving citizens of their jobs. The billeted soldiers also pressed money and foodstuff illegally from the civilians and so reduced the tax income. In the words of Alexander Querengässer, 'Regarding the small size of the existing forces, the [estates] grossly overstated their case as a first step for negotiations between prince and estates, giving the assembly the feel of an Oriental bazaar.'[38] Consequently, the estates were only willing to grant the country and drink tax (the oldest and most important ones), the meat money and other expenses, while at the same time they halved the funds for the troops, and insisted Johann Georg III not raise more soldiers than he could maintain. Magazines and money for the repair of the fortifications were not granted.[39]

It was clear that Johann Georg III could not achieve any great success, and therefore he declared that he could not maintain an army and magazines with less than 800,000 thalers. He also wanted to establish an indirect tax which other states, such as Brandenburg, introduced to cover the costs of the 'Military'. This was another awkward topic, because once established, the exercise could become a financial instrument beyond the control of the estates – which only could affect direct taxation. On 15 February 1682 the estates finally approved most of the requests, but in return Johann Georg III reduced his demands for the army to 700,000 thalers. This sum had to be negotiated again and again through subsequent assemblies but did not change until the early eighteenth century. Another quite sensible request of the estates to use the army as a police force against increasing brigandage was refused by the Prince-Elector. On 5 March 1682, Johann Georg III and the estates found a compromise and new taxes were issued to maintain a

---

37   Thenius, *Die Anfange des Stehenden Heerwesen in Kursachsen*, p.11.
38   Querengässer, *The Saxon Mars and His Force*, p.28.
39   Thenius, *Die Anfange des Stehenden Heerwesen in Kursachsen*, p.12.

force of approximately 10,000 men. The estates even granted the grain for the magazines.

In January 1681, the Prince-Elector issued his first order regarding the new organisation of the Saxon army. He ordered the two Life Guard infantry regiments and the *Leib-Freicompanien* to be joined into a single unit under the command of *Obristlieutenant* Hans Heinrich Escher. The regiments had now nine companies, but soon increased to 12. In 1682 the regiment was entrusted to Joachim Rüdiger von der Goltz, while a new lifeguard regiment with eight companies was raised. Goltz, became *Generalfeldmarschall*; in turn, Promnitz was promoted *Generalwachtmeister*.

With the question of funding settled, extensive recruitment started in the spring of 1682. The Prince-Elector was finally able to raise four regiments of infantry with eight companies, and four of cavalry with six, with an additional dragoon regiment of six companies. For his personal guard, he raised just one company of horse and one of foot and a further two infantry companies quartered at Wittenberg. The overall force numbered 7,157 infantry, 2,608 cavalry, 614 dragoons and 142 artillerymen.[40] By as early as May 1682, Johann Georg III could muster his new army. The infantry increased to six regiments. The cavalry regiments were cuirassiers, while the dragoons consisted of the conventional mounted infantry. Nevertheless, the organisation of all the five mounted regiments was the same, and consisted of six companies of 100 horsemen, while the infantry regiments were formed of eight, except for the 1st Regiment of Life Guards, which had 12 companies.[41] As under Johann Georg II, each infantry company comprised two-thirds of musketeers and the rest of pikemen, totalling 147 men including officers and NCOs. The field artillery was established at 24 guns – although there were many more available in reserve in the arsenal at Dresden – and 64 wagons. By 1683 a grenadier company was added to each regiment. In the 1st *Leibregiment* it became the 13th company, in the other regiments the 9th. Each grenadier company consisted of 60 men.[42]

The Saxon army seemed small if compared to those of the major states of Germany, but Johann Georg III had succeeded in creating a modern professional force, which restored political influence to his state. The number of troops enabled him to meet the requirement of the estates that he not recruit more troops than could be paid for. Interestingly, under Johann Georg II's successors, especially Friedrich August, the size of the army was increased until the eve of the Great Northern War in 1700. This was achieved even though the basic budget of 700,000 thalers never changed, and obviously this was possible with great difficulty and by diverting other resources. As occurred in other German states, the increase of the fighting force occurred after external subsidies became available.

Though the resources remained limited, Johann Georg III did not cease to improve his army. In 1684, the Prince-Elector issued a regulation entitled *Wie*

---

40 Schuster and Francke, *Geschichte der Sächsischen Armee*, p.98.

41 Frank Bauer, 'Zur Organisation und Struktur der Kursächsischen Armee an der Wende vom 17. zum 18. Jahrhundert', in *Sächsische Heimatblätter* Nr. 5 (1983), p.225.

42 Schuster and Francke, *Geschichte der Sächsischen Armee*, p.112.

Wir es bei Unsern Truppen und Militär-Etats in Einem und Andern Woollen Gehalten Haben.[43] It contained provisions on the rank of the regiments among themselves, the delivery of the guards of honour for the Prince-Elector and other official duties. The regulation dealt with sensitive matters, including the strict control of the captains by the colonels and field officers because they paid the salaries to their soldiers without deductions. As early as 1684, following another Electoral decree, the colonels of the regiments of foot and horse had to draw up precise lists of all men in their companies, which were submitted 'in sealed rolls' to the Secret War Chancellery, and to provide proof of differences of strength or changes every months. Officers had to become aware of their prerogatives, since military service was a matter of honour. As for the ranking of the regiments within the army, the *Trabantengarde* was senior within the cavalry, followed by the cavalry *Leibregiment*. The *Leibregiment* of foot ranked senior to all others, followed by the regiments of the senior commanders and other generals. The dragoons were considered as a separate specialty and without rank in the hierarchy.[44]

In 1685, the army moved to a training camp for the first time; the various regiments arrived on 22 June at the town of Torgau, the place chosen for the gathering. In 1687 an ordinance was issued that specified that a new *exercitium* would be introduced in the infantry, and for this purpose a *Lehrrabtheilung* (training section) was established in Dresden. The infantry was organised in companies of only musketeers and grenadiers; from each regiment, one adjutant and one NCO from each company had to go to Dresden to be instructed in the new regulation, and the Italian *Hauptmann* Alberti acted as instructor.[45]

Johann Georg III also tried to improve discipline inside the army. Since the Saxon army consisted to a considerable degree of foreigners without connection to the Saxon population, the relationship between soldiers and civilians was often problematic. Already in 1683, the Prince-Elector had to note with regret that '[in] our Military, especially in the cavalry, and the regiment of dragoons all kind of disorders, insolences and excesses are going on by not alone ruining their horses but riding back and forth inflicting damage to the grain in the fields, and otherwise causing many mischiefs and complaints'.[46] Another serious problem was the rampages of soldiers against their hosts, and the clientele inside the army. Since colonels often sold officer positions to incompetent people, in 1687 the Prince-Elector ordered that officer appointments should only be made upon presentation by the senior commanders, or according to indication of the colonels but only for lower ranks.[47]

There were many complaints about recruitment of volunteers; it was not unknown for recruiting officers to use force, or scams, to achieve their ends.

---

43   Schuster and Francke, *Geschichte der Sächsischen Armee*, p.111: 'As we want to maintain our troops and our military budgets in the one and the other, as we want it to be preserved.'

44   Querengässer, *The Saxon Mars and His Force*, p.80.

45   Schuster and Francke, *Geschichte der Sächsischen Armee*, p.111.

46   Querengässer, *The Saxon Mars and His Force*, p.68.

47   Schuster and Francke, *Geschichte der Sächsischen Armee*, p.111.

In August 1687, Saxon subject Andreas Küchler complained that while on a trip to Leipzig his son Samuel was dragged from his coach by the soldiers of Hauptmann Alenbeck, treated to a bloody beating and forcibly enlisted. However, cheating men into military service against their will was not welcome, because these recruits tended to undermine discipline and desert. Because of that, the ordinance of 1682 forbade recruiting by force, getting men drunk or using other tricks. On the other hand, the order forbade the discharge of soldiers in return for payment. Recruiting officers were asked to take care not to enlist the sons of citizens and peasants if the fathers were dependent on their labour, and if a man was recruited illegally he should be released. However, the recruitment parties continued to be a feared presence in Saxony.[48]

The army raised by Johann Georg III was a typical force of this age, and there was nothing particularly different from the Western and Central European armies of the late seventeenth century. Though the infantry could be regarded as relatively modern, training and drill followed the rigid classical doctrines. The tactical organisation of 1682 established for the infantry battalion a six-rank formation still with two-thirds musketeers and one-third pikemen. Each file consisted of five private soldiers and one *Gefreiter* (lance corporal).[49] This was the typical tactical organisation of Western European infantry in this age. The experience matured during the campaigns against the Ottomans in Hungary and Greece served as an impulse for the adoption of an armament consisting mostly of muskets, replacing pikes with the *Schweinsfeder* as early as 1683.[50] On the battlefield of Hungary and Greece the Saxon soldiers won recognition and earned a good reputation throughout Europe.

The Militia

The Saxon militia had been established in regiment-sized units since 1615. In this year, two regiments of foot formed by eight large companies of 520 men, and two regiments of horse, or *Ritterpferde*, with 902 and 690 horsemen were established. The infantry was provided by the cities depending on their population, the cavalry by the noble families depending on the income of their properties. The militia exclusively performed a defensive role, as indicated by its denomination – *Defensioner* – even though this was not explicitly mentioned in the regulations. The Saxon militia proved not very reliable during the Thirty Years' War and was reduced to little more than a reserve for the field army.[51] After 1648 the militia never found a satisfactory

---

48 Querengässer, *The Saxon Mars and His Force*, p.61: 'In May 1689 ... the municipal council of Laubau wrote to the Alderman of Upper Lusatia in Bautzen and told him, that the one sergeant's recruitment squad was not only operating during the weekly market, but also on Sundays and holidays so that the populations of the nearby villages were now too afraid to venture into town.'
49 Querengässer, *The Saxon Mars and His Force*, p.90.
50 Schuster and Francke, *Geschichte der Sächsischen Armee*, p.112.
51 Querengässer, *The Saxon Mars and His Force*, p.16.

organisation. However, also after the creation of a regular standing army, Prince-Electors Johann Georg II and above all Johann Georg III tried to reform the militia system and exploit its military potential. Between 1681 and 1683 the Prince-Elector repeatedly asked the estates to raise the militia but received nothing but complaints, leaving the matter suspended. Only when almost the entire regular army left the Electorate for Hungary the summer of 1683, did the militia became a topic which could not be ignored. However, an actual call to arms was avoided because of the additional costs this would create.

In 1684 Prince-Elector Johann Georg III prepared another proposal for a new organisation of the militia which once more was rejected by the estates. In their opinion, the militia had never been very effective but only expensive, and it seemed doubtful even to try a reorganisation 'now that a formidable standing army had been established'.[52] The Prince-Elector did not reply, but to demonstrate that the militia was still not officially disbanded, he issued patents in order to maintain the companies of cavalry in readiness and asked for 1,500 horsemen and another 1,500 to be held in reserve. Militiamen should be offered tax incentives, but because there never a serious threat from a foreign power there was no need to call them to arms. In 1688 the Prince-Elector once more called up the militia, after the army left the Electorate

A view of Dresden in an engraving by Gabriel Tschimmer, depicting the *Unterguardia* in 1678 with its ensign (with thanks to Alexander Querengässer for this picture).

---

52. Ernst von Friesen, 'Das Defensionwesen im Kurfürstenthume Sachsen', in *Archiv für die Sächsische Geschichte*, 2 (1864), p.223.

for the Rhine. The militiamen would be provided with new ammunition pouches and weapons like the regular troops.[53]

Similar to the Bavarian *Stadtquardia*, but formed by civilians serving on a voluntary basis, there was also a municipal guard in the capital called the *Unterguardia*. Between the 1660s and 1670s it deployed a strength between 770 and 501 foot militiamen;[54] their service was limited to guarding the entrances to the capital and controlling public order at city fairs and markets. Like a military unit worthy of the name, the *Unterguardia* had its own field officers and ensigns.

The Saxon Army on Campaign

The contemporary commentaries are proof of the good discipline of the Saxon troops; there is also a mass of documented complaints about bad behaviour in the home quarters, but this is typical for this age. Shortage of food was a bitter and recurring eventuality in the seventeenth century, and the Saxon army did not represent an exception. Already during the Rhine campaign, the shortage of supply for the troops demonstrated that Saxony was only poorly capable of providing enough rations and other supply for the army on campaign. This caused more than one concern in 1674, and again in 1683 when the Imperial Aulic Chamber had to provide for the Saxon troops in Hungary.[55]

In July 1673 Emperor Leopold I turned to Prince-Elector Johann Georg II to hire troops, to increase the army he was gathering in Bohemia to support the Dutch Republic against France. On 13 August the two sovereigns signed an agreement for 3,000 horse and foot, to be presented in Eger before the next winter. The contingent to be sent to the Rhine initially comprised a cavalry regiment of six companies, an infantry regiment of 10 companies, and a small field artillery corps. *Hofmarschall* Christian Ernst von Kanne was entrusted as commander. With him, the prince heir Johann Georg von Wettin held the command of his cuirassier regiment.

Prince-Elector Johann Georg II gathered the troops in early November at Zwickau and personally mustered them: they numbered 1,179 infantry,

---

53 Friesen, 'Das Defensionwesen im Kurfürstenthume Sachsen', pp.223–224.
54 Schuster and Francke, *Geschichte der Sächsischen Armee*, p.82.
55 Wilson, *German Armies*, p.185. The situation went to a bitter escalation in the 1690s. Johann Georg III was determined that the services of his 12,000 soldiers provided to Emperor Leopold I, whose numbers exceeded his formal obligations, should not be at the expense of ruining Saxon finances. He particularly wanted the soldiers to winter close to the front in southern Germany, to spare him the cost of billeting and transit home each spring and autumn. Treaties to this effect were made with Vienna in March 1690, and again at Torgau the following year, endorsing the continued exploitation of the unarmed Upper Saxons in addition to assignations on Hanau, Frankfurt and Franconia. Leopold was trapped: he appreciated the importance of retaining the lesser territories' confidence and loyalty, but he was powerless to oppose Saxon demands. He did seize the opportunity of Johann Georg III's death on 22 April 1691 to throw doubt on the validity of the Torgau Treaty, but the Saxon commander, Adam von Schöning, seized four Frankfurt villages and blockaded the city until it paid its share of the contributions.

THE ELECTORATE OF SAXONY

1,648 horsemen and four field guns, totalling 2,841 men, not including general staff and servants.[56] In detail:

Infantry: *Leibregiment* (SaI-1), 10 companies for 1,179 men
Cavalry: *Leibregiment* (SaC-2), 6 companies for 621 horsemen; *Kurprinz Cuirassieren* (SaC-3), 6 companies for 600 horsemen
Dragoons: *Leibdragoner* (sad-ii), 4 company for 419 dragoons
Artillery: 1 Stückhauptmann, 1 *Zeugdiener*, 5 *Büchsenmeister* and 15 *Knechte*

In early March 1674, the Saxons joined the Imperial army in the Upper Rhine. They were assigned to the corps under the Imperial *Feldmarshall-Lieutenant* Enea Silvio Caprara, quartered between Schifferstadt and Maubach. Near the latter location, on 14 March, the Saxons sustained the first encounter with the enemy and it was not a fortunate action. In the night, an outpost of cavalry comprising 50 Saxon dragoons was surprised by 600 French from the garrison of Landau under the *colonel general des dragons* Louis François, Marquis de Boufflers. The French routed the Saxons and caught by surprise the Imperial headquarters of Rheingönheim. The Imperial–Saxon side claimed the loss of 300 men either dead or wounded and 82 prisoners, including two officers.[57] On 31 March the Imperial Diet declared war on France. Although reluctant to join the *Reichskrieg*, Johann Georg II did not gather his contingent for the Upper Rhine Circle; not all of his objections were unjustified. The army of the Empire announced itself to be a force of troops from all over Germany, whose reliability was little to be expected. Like Friedrich Wilhelm of Brandenburg, Johann Georg II did not join the troops of the circles but maintained them as an autonomous corps, even under a commander-in-chief designated by the Empire's diet.

The Saxon troops followed the march of Caprara's corps on the Rhine, and on 3 June, 150 horsemen assigned to guard the boat pontoon near Philippsburg were ambushed by a superior force of French cavalry and infantry. The Saxon horsemen held the position with remarkable bravery, but 113 soldiers were killed and the rest taken prisoner.[58] This encounter was the prelude to the defeat suffered by Caprara at Sinsheim on 16 June, when the 6,000 Imperial and allied troops were routed by 15,000 French under Turenne. During the battle General Kanne was in great danger, and Prince Johann Georg also risked capture by the French. He was rescued by the dragoons, who under the second in command, Prince Heinrich of Saxe-Gotha, charged the enemy and succeeded in repulsing them.[59] Both the Saxon cavalry regiment and the dragoons suffered heavy casualties, including three officers dead and three wounded; the artillery lost three cannons, while the infantry managed to limit its losses. As a result, in July the cavalry and dragoons marched back

---

56   Schuster and Francke, *Geschichte der Sächsischen Armee*, p.88.
57   Friedrich von Beust, *Feldzüge des Kursächsischen Armee*, vol. II, pp.20–21.
58   Friedrich von Beust, *Feldzüge des Kursächsischen Armee*, vol. II, p.21.
59   Friedrich von Beust, *Feldzüge des Kursächsischen Armee*, vol. II, p.24.

to Saxony while the infantry was quartered in the Palatinate. In October the artillery was reinforced with two mortars of 16lb and six light guns of 6lb.[60] Assigned as garrison in Heidelberg, the Saxons did not join the allied army in Alsace, since Prince-Elector Johann Georg III did not allow his troops to cross the Rhine, because their duty was only to defend the *Reich*. This saved them from the bitter defeats suffered at Mulhouse, Entzheim and Türkheim during the celebrated Turenne's winter campaign of 1674–75.

That winter was very bitter for the Allies, since in December 1674 the news of the Swedish invasion of Pomerania further thwarted their plans. In June 1675, pressed by Emperor Leopold I, the Prince-Elector agreed to gather two contingents. The first was to support Brandenburg in the Upper Saxony Circle and comprised the newly formed regiment *Degenfeld zu Fuss* (SaI-3) and the regiment *Maltzan Dragoner* (SaD-1). In August they joined the corps under the prince of Anhalt-Dessau on the River Oder, and in October participated in the operation between Stettin and Damme with the Brandenburg troops. The second contingent comprised three companies of infantry, 17 companies of cuirassiers, and 10 companies of dragoons, which joined the Imperial army under Montecuccoli on the River Neckar.[61] This time the campaign was a success for the Imperial side. The Saxon cavalry took part in the major encounters of the campaign, culminating with the battles of Salzbach and Altenheim, fought on 29 and 31 July 1675. There is little information about the casualties suffered by the Saxons in 1675, but they, as the other troops, suffered more from shortage of supplies than from enemy fire.

In May 1676, the prince heir Johann Georg accompanied the 1,200 cavalry troops of the *Leibregiment* (SaC-2) and *Kurprinz* (SaC-3) during the march to the Upper Rhine. On 2 June he was 'graciously appointed' as Imperial *Feldmarschall-Lieutenant* by Emperor Leopold I, but days later he fell sick and returned to Dresden. He would rejoin the allied army in August during the siege of Philippsburg, where the Saxon cavalry was guarding the circumvallation line under the Margrave of Baden-Baden. The next month, the Saxons took winter quarters in Franconia.[62] In January 1677 the contingent sent against the Swedes joined the Imperial corps under *Generalwachtmeister* Cob in the Lower Saxony Circle, but in March the Saxons returned to the Electorate, where both regiments were disbanded.[63]

In February 1677 the newly appointed Imperial general Johann Georg met his contingent of 1,200 horsemen quartered in Nurnberg; the Saxon cavalry was assigned to the cavalry corps under the command of the Prince himself. In mid-April the Imperial field army entered Alsace with about 26,000 men under the Duke Charles V of Lorraine. After leaving 4,000 men under Johann Georg on the Seille River to secure the road to Strasbourg,

---

60 Schuster and Francke, *Geschichte der Sächsischen Armee*, p.89.
61 Friedrich von Beust, *Feldzüge des Kursächsischen Armee*, vol. II, pp.39–40. The infantry companies belonged to the *Leibregiment* (SaI-1), the cavalry troop were four from the *Leibregiment* (SaC-2), six form *Kurprinz* (SaC-3) and seven were free companies; the dragoons came from the *Leibdragoner* (sad-ii) and five were free companies.
62 Schuster and Francke, *Geschichte der Sächsischen Armee*, p.90.
63 Friedrich von Beust, *Feldzüge des Kursächsischen Armee*, vol. II, p.70.

THE ELECTORATE OF SAXONY

Lorraine marched north for the Moselle. The Saxon and Imperial cavalry engaged in a series of encounters with the French between 29 May and 5 June, however, the Imperial advance was stopped by the French at Pont-à-Mousson, and Lorraine was far from joining the Dutch-Spaniards for the common objective of besieging Charleroi. By mid-July the Imperial and allied army was spread out between the villages of Gengenbach and Lahr, with a forward outpost at Denzlingen; in August the campaign seemed destined to fail, and Lorraine, distressed by the lack of troops, was unable to prevent the enemy from joining part of its forces with those in Alsace to attack Johann Georg on 7 September. The Prince and his cavalry fought a rearguard battle but were outnumbered by the French, and were forced to retreat from the Seille to Strasbourg pursued by the enemy. On 21 September, before the arrival of Charles of Lorraine, Johann Georg was surprised again by the French and defeated near Gengenbach by the Marquise of Créquy. Then the French crossed the Rhine to repair to Alsace, eluding Lorraine, who could only engage the enemy rearguard with his cavalry, at Klockersberg, on 7 October. Weeks later, the allied army was preparing winter quarters behind Strasbourg and did not prevent the French advance into Breisgau, leaving a free hand to Créquy for an assault on Freiburg, which surrendered on 16 November.

In 1678, notwithstanding the chronic shortage of supplies and funds and with the army far from complete, Lorraine began the operation earlier than usual. The plan agreed with the Dutch-Spaniards provided that the Imperialists would operate a diversion in Lorraine, to besiege Thionville or other forts in French hands, to threaten the enemy in the Low Countries from the south. The offensive also served to divert French attention from Charleroi, an objective that the Dutch-Spaniards wanted to achieve as soon as possible. By April the Saxons participated in the major events of the campaign as part of the cavalry corps under Prince Johann Georg. Having seized Bitche and Saarbrucken, after the destruction of the French magazines in the city Lorraine was forced to wait for supplies, and soon the French led by Créquy succeeded in taking the initiative. The attempt to retake Freiburg failed and shortage of supply forced Lorraine to repair to the right bank of the Rhine. On 23 July Prince Johann Georg achieved a good success at Tavendorf against a strong enemy party which tried to cross the River Kinzig, but the French, having received reinforcements from Flanders, outnumbered the Imperialists and their allies. This allowed Créquy to seize the strategic town of Kehl, and then destroy the bridges of Strasbourg on both sides of the Rhine between 27 July and 8 August. In September the Imperial field army had no money, and turned to the states close to the war theatre to collect resources and billets, with serious consequences for the local population. Prince Johann Georg returned to Saxony before the end of the year and the cavalry followed him the following spring, after the Peace of Nijmegen had ended the Franco-Dutch War.

Between 1663 and 1678, Saxon participation in the wars was limited to small contingents, but a significant exception occurred in 1683 when Johann George III, now the new Prince-Elector, promised to gather 4,700 men for the auxiliary corps hired by Austria for the war against the Porte. The agreement was signed on 21 June 1683 in Dresden, and soon the Prince-Elector appointed his staff, which included *Feldmarschall-Lieutenant* Flemming and three major generals with their adjutants. With them a considerable number of people and servants of the court were also added: overall 377 persons with 373 horses with an indeterminate number of wagons.[64] However, the Prince-Elector was less prompt at gathering his soldiers, because the cost for the organisation of the army supply train and baggage climbed to unexpected figures. The artillery alone needed money for horses, wagons and drivers, and only a third of the funds were then available. The number of guns was reduced from 24 to 16 pieces. Even more critical was the organisation of supplies. Before the summer, Johann Georg III had sent his representative the Duke of Saxe-Lauenburg to Passau in Austria to negotiate the details of the agreement, and demand that the Saxon troops would be supplied in the Austrian territories. He also demanded overall command of all the German troops in the army which was gathering under Duke Charles of Lorraine. While the first request could be discussed, the latter demand encountered some resistance from the German allies. Emperor Leopold I remained vague and gave to Johann Georg III some inconclusive promise, but soon the Imperial delegates explained that the contribution of Saxony was no more substantial than that offered by other German princes, notably Bavaria. The Prince-Elector was forced to renounce his request without further discussion, but the affair had again delayed the departure of the Saxon troops. Because the negotiations with Austria still produced no results, the estates of Saxony pressed the Prince-Elector to not join the campaign personally, but the warlike attitude of Johann Georg III meant he could not avoid participating in an event which could bring glory and honour to his dynasty.[65]

Finally the army was assembled between June and July near Dresden. The contingent consisted of the Life Guard company, six infantry, four cavalry, and one dragoon regiments, with 16 guns and two petards; in detail:[66]

General Stab: *Generalfeldmarschall-Lieutenant* Heino Heinrich von Flemming, *Generalwachtmeister* Saxe-Weissenfels, Neitschütz and Trauttmansdorff

Infantry: *Leibregiment* (SaI-1); *Schönfeld* (SaI-2); *Herzog Christian* (SaI-4); *Kuffer* (SaI-6); *Flemming* (SaI-7); *Löben* (SaI-8), with 52 companies divided in 12 field battalions

Cavalry: *Leibgarde-Trabanten* (sac-iv); *Leibregiment* (SaC-2); *Trauttmansdorff* (SaC-3); *Plotho* (SaC-4); *Goltz* (SaC-5), with 27 companies divided in 15 squadrons

Dragoons: *Reuss* (SaD-2), 6 companies divided in 3 squadrons

Artillery: 173 artillerymen and drivers with 16 light guns and 36 wagons.

---

64 Schuster and Francke, *Geschichte der Sächsischen Armee*, p.101.
65 Querengässer, *The Saxon Mars and His Force*, p.102.
66 Schuster and Francke, *Geschichte der Sächsischen Armee*, p.102.

With the artillery, the whole contingent numbered 7,037 infantrymen and 3,194 horsemen, much more than the number established in the agreement of June.

On the morning of 18 July the army was mustered by the Prince-Elector, and under its officers performed a manoeuvre with the infantry in the centre and the cavalry on the wings. Four days later the army left the camp, heading to Vienna. After a first stop in Dohna, the march continued in small stages of 15–20 kilometres per day; the following week, the Imperial commissioners met the Saxon columns and begged the Prince-Elector to accelerate the march because for weeks Vienna had been under siege. The commissioners

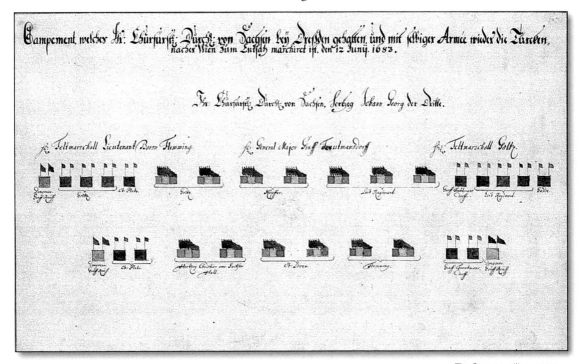

The Saxon auxiliary corps gathered in Dresden for the 1683 campaign against the Ottomans (*Aufstellung des Feldlagers der Armee des Kurfürsten von Sachsen bei Dresden vor dem Zug Gegen die Türken nach Wien, 12. Juni 1683*, Hessisches Staatsarchiv, Marburg).

also informed Johann Georg III that the Imperial magazines had no provision for his troops.[67] The march stopped every three or four days to rest the troops, and at this rate the Saxon contingents crossed the Bohemian border on 10 August. After a pause near Meissenau, the march resumed on 15 August, when a letter of Emperor Leopold I informed the Prince-Elector that the issue of supply would be soon solved.[68] After crossing the Austrian frontier the infantry marched in readiness to engage in the fight, while the cavalry was deployed in vanguard with pickets which constantly took turns. On 16 August the Saxon contingent camped near Krems on the Danube. The next week the allied columns approached to Dürrenberg, where they received the salute of Emperor Leopold I and then continued their march to Vienna. On 30 August the Electoral troops crossed the Danube and on 2

---

67 Querengässer, *The Saxon Mars and His Force*, p.104: 'It was the first time that this issue would trouble their relationship [between Vienna and Dresden].'
68 Querengässer, *The Saxon Mars and His Force*, p.104.

September stopped at Tulln, where the allied army was concentrating, and the Saxon contingent laid camp not far from the Bavarians. Alarms and other events occurred as the relief army approached Vienna, engaging the enemies in some skirmish. On 28 August, false news that the Ottomans had crossed the Danube and were converging on the flanks of the allied army turned out to be unfounded. Days later, General Flemming informed the Prince-Elector that the Ottomans were plundering the Saxon baggage train. The Prince-Elector with his staff rode to get more information, and on the way learned that the news was a false alarm caused by some Polish cavalrymen who had been mistaken for the enemy.[69] On 5 September the allied war council met under King Jan Sobieski, and Charles of Lorraine agreed to move as quickly as possible to Vienna. At Tulln, the army was deployed in battle order: the Saxons formed the left wing alongside the Imperialists. The Imperial cavalry took the vanguard to clear the way alongside a half-squadron of Saxon cuirassiers.[70] During a skirmish, the Saxons claimed their first battle casualty: the Prince-Elector's groom of the chamber.[71]

On 11 September the allied army reached the forest at the foot of the Kahlenberg mountain; the 6,000 Saxon infantrymen under General Flemming occupied the top. Here, in an ancient monastery, Duke Charles of Lorraine and Johann Georg III took their quarters. In the evening, the noise of skirmishes could be heard, and Flemming brought forward three light guns and some infantry to repulse the enemy scouts. The next day Duke Charles of Lorraine deployed his left wing in three battle lines. Six Imperial and five Saxon battalions stood in the first line; a further 10 Imperial and eight Saxon battalions were in the second, together with five Imperial and four Saxon squadrons of cavalry. The third line, in reserve, was formed of the other Imperial and Saxon infantry battalions and cavalry squadrons. In the early morning, after an hour of prayer, a rocket gave the signal to advance, and the left wing with the Saxon troops marched down the Kahlenberg and came into battle first. The battle chronicle reports that the Saxon infantry engaged the Ottoman infantry deployed between the villages of Grinzing and Nussdorf. The first line under Duke Christian of Saxe-Weissenfels could exploit the natural defences of the ground, but the second and third lines advanced on open ground and met a fierce resistance from the enemy defending the nearby positions on the Schreiberbach stream. As the fight progressed, the situation of the Imperial and Saxon troops became critical, but they received support from the Duke of Saxe-Weissenfels' infantrymen of the first line, who assaulted the Ottomans on the flank. Thus the Duke offered his unprotected right flank to the enemy; this dangerous position was secured by the dismounted dragoons of the *Reuss* regiment alongside the Imperial infantry of the third line, which re-established the front. After an hour of fighting, the Imperial and Saxon infantry increased the pressure and managed to bend the enemy resistance. The allied battalions advanced and invested the enemy who occupied the sunken road north, to

---

69   Querengässer, *The Saxon Mars and His Force*, p.105.
70   Querengässer, *The Saxon Mars and His Force*, p.105.
71   Schuster and Francke, *Geschichte der Sächsischen Armee*, p.171.

the village of Döbling. The Saxons and Imperialists were able to organise a well-coordinated assault, pinning the Ottomans in their front and pressing them on the flanks. Soon, the Saxon infantry broke into the road and pushed back the enemy in disorder; General Flemming was commended for this action.[72] The Ottomans tried to organise a defence on the Russberg hill and the Weinhaus sector, but the day was over for them. The Allies overwhelmed the Ottoman defences and seized the hills at about 8:00 a.m, then exploited the pause to re-establish their front, and Lorraine ordered the advance to resume. The Saxon and Imperial infantry moved south making good use of the regimental artillery. Meanwhile, Johann Georg III with the Saxon and Imperial cavalry left the position on the Kahlenberg to support the exhausted and brave Saxon and Imperial battalions in their fight. It was at least noon when the Polish right wing, after a difficult march through the rugged terrain reached the Ottoman positions. The following events saw the Saxon infantry involved again in the final phase of the battle. At about 2:30 p.m. Flemming performed another assault alongside the Saxon cavalry against the hills north of Währing; shortly after, Ottoman resistance collapsed when the Polish troops routed them in the centre. According to some reports, at the end of the battle Johann Georg III saw a group of Ottomans fleeing across the Danube with their Christian slaves. The Prince-Elector charged them with his *Tranbanten Garde* and freed the slaves.[73]

The day after, the victory celebrations were frustrated by divergence in the allied command. While Sobieski urged pursuit of the defeated enemy, Johann Georg III decided that he would leave the army. He was grievously disappointed about a reputed lack of gratefulness on the part of Emperor Leopold I, who did not mention rewards or privileges for him and his troops. This disappointment resulted as much from ingratitude from the Imperial side, 'as the fact that the Prince-Elector started a campaign in a mix of chivalric thirst for action and political naivety, because he had not fixed any territorial claims in a treaty, before his army left Saxony.'[74] The hasty departure of the Electoral contingent came as a surprise to the Allies. On 5 September the Saxons left Vienna and headed to Neuburg. From here, Johann Georg III wrote a letter to Leopold I, informing him about his decision and telling him that he regarded his duty as fulfilled. The campaign had cost 400 dead,

Christian von Sachsen-Weissenfels (1652–1689). A Duke of the secondogeniture of the electoral branch, he entered the Saxon army in 1672 as infantry officer. In 1680, he became Colonel Proprietor of an infantry regiment and took part in the campaigns against the Ottomans of 1683 and 1686. Reputed to have been a talented and brave commander, in 1689 he was killed during the Siege of Mainz.

---

72 Querengässer, *The Saxon Mars and His Force*, p.107.
73 Beust, *Feldzüge des Kursächsischen Armee*, vol. II, p.85.
74 Querengässer, *The Saxon Mars and His Force*, p.111.

Saxon infantry at Vienna, 12 September 1683, detail from the painting in the collection of Heeresgeschichtliches Museum, Vienna. Note the equipment and weaponry, consisting of flintlock musket and ammunition pouch carried from a waist belt. On the right, an artilleryman in a grey coat with blue cuffs and stockings. The Polish King, Jan Sobieski, left a vivid impression of the Prince-Elector and his troops during the campaign of 1683, writing to his wife: 'Yesterday (10 September), the Elector of Saxony rode with me around the troops, being in his daily red coat; on the horse's bridle three or four spots of silver, no lackey or page (…) even assistants are not around him much, most of them officers'

and about 330 sick and wounded had been left behind in Austria; 445 horses were replaced.[75]

Relations between Dresden and Vienna remained tense and deteriorated further in the spring of 1685, when the troops of the Duke of Brunswick-Lüneburg Hanover asked permission to march through Saxony's Electoral territory to join the Imperial army in Hungary. The Prince-Elector refused, but in response the Duke's troops crossed the border anyway and continued their march. Johann Georg III meditated on using his own army to expel the Hanoverian soldiers, but the idea of engaging in an encounter into his own state frustrated him to desist.[76]

Johann Georg III's resentments lasted until 1686, when finally he agreed for a new auxiliary corps to join the Imperial army in Hungary. The contingent was established at 4,700 men after the payment of a 300,000-thaler subsidy from Vienna. The command was entrusted to his cousin Duke Christian of Saxe-Weimar, newly appointed as *Generalleutnant*, with *Generalwachtmeister* Trauttmansdorff and Röbel as seconds in command. The infantry comprised regiments *Saxe-Weimar* (SaI-4), *Kuffer* (SaI-6) and *Löben* (SaI-8), and the cuirassier regiments *Plotho* (SaC-4) and *Bronne* (SaC-5), with some field

---

75   Querengässer, *The Saxon Mars and His Force*, p.113.
76   For further reading on this topic, see Martin Schröder, 'Die bewegte Bellona Die Kursächsische Durchzug- und Marschorganisation am Beispiel eines Braunschweig-Lüneburgischen Durchzugs von 1685', in *Militärgeschichtliche Zeitschrift*; 77 (2018), 1, pp.1–36.

artillery.[77] The troops left Saxony on 6 April and reached Esztergom on 3 June, from here joining the Bavarian troops and marching to Buda, arriving in front of the city on 17 June. The Saxons were involved in the fighting against the Ottoman relief corps and in the bloody assaults against the city walls. In the great assault of 24 July, the Saxons claimed three officers and 91 soldiers dead; Major General Röbel and a lieutenant were wounded alongside 171 soldiers. On 11 August an Ottoman sortie caused the loss of a further 40 men dead and wounded.[78] The final assault on 2 September involved the Saxons on the west side of the city. The sources did not record the casualties claimed by the Saxon troops, but these were significant, since the action cost 1,500 dead.[79]

The last Saxon campaign in Hungary against the Ottomans occurred in 1688, when the Prince-Elector signed a new contract to provide one infantry regiment. This was formed assembling companies from the other regiments, in order to maintain their number, and entrusted to *Obrist Lieutenant* Cuno Christoph von Birckholz, but assumed the denomination of *Kurprinzlisches Leibregiment* (SaI-11). On 21 April 1688 the 2,000-musketeer regiment was mustered through an Imperial Commissioner and taken into Imperial service. After marching through Bohemia and Austria the regiment reached Osjek, where the allied army was gathering for the planned siege of Belgrade. On 27 August the Saxons participated in the assault which bent the Ottoman resistance; at the end of the action, the regiment claimed the loss of 40 dead and 60 wounded.[80] In October the Saxons took winter quarters in Hungary, where provisions were few and the number of sick increased dramatically. On 26 November Birckholz had just 555 men able to march, 120 were sick and a further 193 sick were left behind in Belgrade.[81] In 1689, the survivors marched back to Saxony.

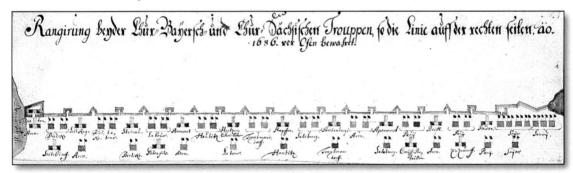

The Saxon corps at Buda, July 1686 (*Schlachtordnung der Bayerischen und Kursächsischen Truppen, die Rechte Seite vor Ofen Gehalten Haben, 1686*; Hessisches Staatsarchiv, Marburg).

The Saxon involvement in the war against the Porte was not limited to Hungary. In December 1684, Johann Georg III left Dresden for Venice, arriving at the lagoon city incognito on 25 January 1685 as 'Count of

---

77 Beust, *Feldzüge des Kursächsischen Armee*, vol. II, p.96.
78 Beust, *Feldzüge des Kursächsischen Armee*, vol. II, p.98.
79 Beust, *Feldzüge des Kursächsischen Armee*, vol. II, p.103.
80 Schuster and Francke, *Geschichte der Sächsischen Armee*, p.113.
81 Querengässer, *The Saxon Mars and His Force*, p.118.

Hoyerswerda.'[82] The presence of the Prince-Elector did not remain hidden, and soon the rumours about his presence for the carnival were present in all the European capitals. Doge Marcantonio Giustinian met Johann Georg III and asked for a Saxon contingent for the upcoming campaign in the Peloponnese; the Republic would take over payment and rations and would also pay a generous sum for hiring these troops. The negotiations had been prepared by a former Saxon officer and military entrepreneur, Hannibal von Degenfeld, who had taken service for Venice in 1684.[83] Before giving a reply, the Prince-Elector asked his own *Feldmarshall* Flemming for advice. The General informed Johann Georg III that several Saxon officers 'might be willing to go'.[84] However, Flemming was sceptical because in his opinion Venice was not a reliable partner, and the troops would have been far away from Saxony while Louis XIV was increasing his army, and therefore he considered it wiser to keep the soldiers at home. On the other hand, he recognised that the Venetian money could bring precious resources for the state treasury, instead of leaving the troops inactive in their quarters.[85] In March, Flemming expressed his views about this matter more pessimistically: His conclusion was that the foreign political scenario was that tense, that the small Saxon army could not spare any troops, and among other things, he outlined that the army had been unable to oppose the march through Saxony of Hannover's troops in the spring of 1685. This latter advice only reached the Prince-Elector after he had signed the contract with Venice on 8 March. In the days following, Johann Georg sent his general adjutant Pflug to Dresden with the orders to prepare the contingent. Two new regiments were to be raised, taking 50 soldiers from each of the existing companies. In all, he ordered the assembly of 3,000 infantrymen in three regiments each with 10 companies of musketeers; the third regiment would be chosen from the existing ones.[86] It was agreed with Venice that the regiments would not be separated and that the corps would serve together. All expenses for the transfer were borne by Venice, both on the outward march and on the return home. Religious matters were also considered, and the Republic guaranteed the Saxon soldiers absolute freedom of religion. A special prize was also issued, consisting in two months' salary for the troops before they marched back to Saxony.[87]

The contingent was mustered by the Prince-Elector on 21 May. It was commanded by *Obrist* Hans Rudolph von Schönfeld, who held the first regiment; *Obrist* Bernhard von Troppau and *Obrist Lieutenant* Kleist assumed the command of the newly formed regiments. After the Prince-Elector recommended that the officers, 'to do their duty well, come back with honour and faithful rendered services, or never put to his presence again',[88] the troops started their march through southern Germany, and crossed the

---

82   Querengässer, *The Saxon Mars and His Force*, p.118.
83   Archivio di Stato di Venezia (ASVe); *Senato, Mar*, b. 1070.
84   Querengässer, *The Saxon Mars and His Force*, p.118.
85   Querengässer, *The Saxon Mars and His Force*, p.118.
86   For this corps, Venice paid Saxony 120,000 thalers. ASVe, *Senato, Mar*, b. 1246.
87   ASVe, *Senato, Mar*, b. 1246.
88   Querengässer, *The Saxon Mars and His Force*, p.120.

THE ELECTORATE OF SAXONY

This drawing is a copy from a little known, and just as little studied, military source for the late seventeenth century. The series is known after the name of the last owner, Filippo Rossi-Cassigoli, a collector from Pistoia who purchased it before 1890. The collection includes 265 drawings by Ignazio Manfroni, a Knight of the Tuscan Order of St Stephen. The work is now preserved in the National Library of Florence, and represents a vivid and fully illustrated chronicle of the Ottoman wars in the Mediterranean during the last quarter of the seventeenth century. Some drawings are augmented by explanatory texts which are an invaluable source for the dress and equipment of the armies in this period. The series starts in approximately 1669 and finishes in 1688, when the Tuscan fleet interrupted its participation in the war as a Venetian ally. This drawing shows an encampment of the Saxon infantry in Venetian service before Modone (Methoni) in Greece in May 1686. The commentary tells us about the operation of the siege and other details: 'Here follows the German Saxon nation, who always goes to war with wives and children. They were four battalions distributed in different places. As they are Lutherans, every evening at 11 pm they make the religious office with the drums in front of their tents with their priest. When they see that the people are all gathered, they begin to pray in their own language and finally they all sing David's psalms in German in a false tune and make a good impression. Then, all kneeling, they receive the blessing from the priests.'

Alps in the good season and without difficulties. With them, 200–300 wives and children followed the expedition towards an uncertain fate. On 18 July the Saxons were quartered at the Lido of Venice. The muster registered the loss of 204 men as dead or deserted, however, the Venetian *Inquisitori di Stato* (commissioners) and the Duke of Brunswick-Lüneburg Hannover, who had his own troops in Venetian service, praised the appearance of the Saxon soldiers.[89] On 4 August, after three weeks of rest, the Saxon infantry was embarked on the convoy led by the *Provveditore* Alvise Marcello and shipped to the Morea, where it arrived six days later off Corone (today Koron). The city had been under Venetian siege since June and surrendered the day

---

89 Querengässer, *The Saxon Mars and His Force*, p.120.

after the arrival of the Saxons.[90] Their presence could not have been more opportune, because with them, Captain General Francesco Morosini could replace the losses suffered in the first part of the campaign. In September the Saxons faced the Ottomans for the first time since their arrival in Greece, in the brief siege of Zarnata and later in the pitched battle of Calamata, where the three Electoral regiments were deployed on the left wing. They bravely sustained the assaults of the Ottoman cavalry, but sustained the main part of the Venetian casualties, who numbered 110 dead and wounded, including a Saxon lieutenant colonel.[91]

In early October Morosini suspended the campaign, and the troops took winter quarters; the Saxons were quartered in Prevesa and Lefkada. By mid-October an epidemic spread in Prevesa, forcing the Venetian commander to move the troops to Corfu. Despite the island's mild climate, the winter caused numerous losses, especially due to poorly treated food and poor hygiene in the quarters. In May 1686 the muster registered 2,202 Saxon infantrymen, namely a loss of over 500 men in less than eight months since their arrival in Greece.[92] The campaign started before the end of the month, and on 3 June the Venetians achieved their first success by seizing the fortress of Old Navarino (today, Pylos). The Saxons joined the field army the day after participating in the siege of New Navarino (Neokastron), which surrendered on 14 June after a heavy bombardment. The next objective of the campaign was the city of Modone (Methoni), under siege from 26 June to 11 July. The Saxons moved alongside the field army under General Königsmarck to Nauplia, which was besieged on 30 July. The Saxons fought during the siege and in the Battle of Argos, which dispersed the Ottoman relief corps on 5 August. The siege was particularly difficult, since the enemy garrison put up a resolute resistance, notwithstanding the heavy bombardment and the terrible conditions inside the city, which exasperated the civilian population who mutinied and asked to surrender. However, the defenders received an unexpected and unstoppable help: a terrible epidemic was spreading in the allied camp. Though it was not clear what the disease was, every day 20–30 people were taken by violent fevers, and many died within a few days. While the besiegers were plagued by the epidemic, the Ottomans appeared again before Modone on 19 August, forcing Königsmarck to face the threat, but this delayed the siege operations. On 29 August the Ottoman relief corps assaulted the Venetian position and engaged in a three-hour battle which was very fierce. However, the Saxons and other Venetian troops held their positions and the failure of the relief corps accelerated the surrender of Nauplia on the day after. Such a conquest came at a high price, and the epidemic continued to ravage the Venetian troops: on 18 September Königsmarck and other allied commanders also

---

90 According to George Finlay, in his *History of Greece under Othoman and Venetian Domination* (Edinburgh: William Blackwood & Sons, 1856), p.213, the Saxon corps numbered 3,300 men. Probably the author includes in this figure the relatives of the soldiers, who had followed their husbands and fathers to Greece.

91 Nicola Beregani, *Historia delle Guerre d'Europa dalla comparsa dell'Armi Ottomane in Ungheria* (Venice, 1698), pp.368–369. He was the *Obrist Lieutenant* Franz Salomon von Freutler.

92 Biblioteca Nazionale Marciana, Manuscript It. VII 2592 (12484), f. 56. Muster executed by the *Inquisitore di Stato* Zorzi Emo on 24 May 1686.

fell sick, and most of the officers implored Morosini to grant them licence to return to Venice. But the Captain General remained firm and decided to take up winter quarters for the troops in Nauplia, and to give a better example he decided to stay there too. However, this certainly did nothing to improve matters, as desertions multiplied. Seeing that the situation was worsening, at the end of September Morosini ordered an accurate inspection of all troops. The sick were to remain in the city, those who were healthy were transferred to the fleet. Despite all the measures taken, from the end of September to the end of October more than 1,000 soldiers died, 227 belonging to the Saxon contingent.[93] Among them was the *Obrist* Schönfeld, while *Obrist Lieutenant* Kleist had to be brought to Venice, because he suffered from consumption.[94]

No reinforcements were expected from Saxony, but in April 1687 the *Zeugwart* (artillery master) Nestvogel with some 'fireworkers' arrived in Venice, where everybody who gave a proof of talent in military matters was taken into Venetian service.[95] During the winter of 1686–87, the Venetian senate discussed with Johann Georg III the possibility of further troops to be used in Greece. On 13 December, the Prince-Elector consented to extend the contract for another year after the payment of 40,000 thalers. The price was considered too high and the senate refused. The response infuriated the Prince-Elector, who on 12 February 1687 informed the Doge of his displeasure and demanded the immediate return home of his contingent. In March the three regiments numbered only 1,006 men able to carry weapons, while 247 were in the hospitals. On 14 May the Saxon infantry, now merged into one single regiment under Colonel Erskin,[96] left Greece and reached Venice a month later. After a quarantine of 50 days, and an additional delay, the regiment began its march back to Saxony under the new commander, the only field officer still alive, *Obrist Lieutenant* Lüttig.[97] On 30 November the Saxons arrived in Nuremberg, where a muster revealed that the strength was further reduced to 761 men.[98] The fate of the soldiers' relatives is unknown.

Uniforms and Equipment

According to the most authoritative scholars who deal with the Saxon army, the distribution of clothing was already being carried out by the State in the first half of the seventeenth century.[99] According to them, in 1613 the foot

---

93   ASVe, *Senato, Dispacci, Provveditori di Terra e di Mar*, b. 1070, d. 89–95. The *inquisitori* reported that 'the spectacle is terrible, since the corpses of soldiers are left unburied'.

94   Querengässer, *The Saxon Mars and His Force*, p.122.

95   Querengässer, *The Saxon Mars and His Force*, p.122: 'Before they left Saxony, they had to promise John George that they would return if ordered, and also that they would only work as gunners and not teach anybody in their art.' However, their contribution was of poor utility, since the Venetian artillery officer did not appreciate the work of the Saxon specialists.

96   Baron Erskin or Erskine was a former officer of the Swedish army.

97   Schuster and Francke, *Geschichte der Sächsischen Armee*, p.110.

98   Beust, *Feldzüge des Kursächsischen Armee*, vol. II, p.94.

99   *Schuster and Francke, Geschichte der Sächsischen Armee*, p.10.

militia received grey cloth jackets with red collars, broad-brimmed hats, cloth breeches in winter and leather breeches in summer, and red stockings.

Five years later a provision was also issued for the 'feudal cavalry', whereby the electoral Prince prescribed that horsemen should present themselves complete with breast and back corselets, and that they could either have them made from new or exchange them for old armour.

Although contemporary iconographic sources relating to Saxon soldiers in the last 30 years of the seventeenth century are rare, the existing ones are of good quality. Among these, it is worth mentioning the *Deutliche Beschreibungen* by Johann Georg Pascha, published between 1659 and 1672.[100] These works probably depict Saxon soldiers, considering that the dedications indicate Prince-Elector Johann Georg II as the dedicatee. Although this type of work used conventional models, the figures show the classic features of the military clothing and equipment in use in northern Germany, initially influenced by Swedish and Dutch patterns, and later by others typically from France. While the illustrations in the texts published before 1666 show a certain variety of styles, including doublets, coats covering up to half a leg, and short breeches, after this date the coats take on the characteristics of the classic German *Rock*-coat, now knee-length, and breeches closed over stockings according to the most widespread style in these years.

Officers with partisan, from the *Deutliche Beschreibung Unterschiedener Fahnen-Lectionen: In Acht Spiel Eingetheilet Nebst dem Piquen-Spiel Pertuisan und Halben Piquen oder Jägerstock*, by Johann Georg Pascha (1673).

There is also an allegedly primary source depicting Saxon soldiers of the late seventeenth century, preserved in the French National Library in Paris. This a collection of 22 plates with Saxon uniforms from 1685 to 1772, of which 13 represent soldiers dated to the earlier period.[101]

The figures are depicted in a very naive style, and some uniforms belong clearly to subsequent decades. Only the infantry uniforms are reliable, although the details appear as very approximate.

Together with these iconographic sources the Saxon archives preserve a fair number of documents, which were thoroughly investigated in the early twentieth century by the authors of the major work on the Electoral army. Thanks to them, it is possible to form a comprehensive picture of the early

---

100 In particular, the *Kurtze Iedoch Deutliche Beschreibung Des Pique-Spielens* published in 1660, the *Deutliche Beschreibung, Von dem Exerciren in der Mußquet* of 1666, and the *Deutliche Beschreibung von dem Exerciren in der Musquete und Pique*, printed in 1672.
101 *Uniformes de l'Electorat de Saxe, 1685–1772*, OB 325 – 4.

THE ELECTORATE OF SAXONY

uniforms of the Saxon soldiers. As in other armies of the time, in Saxony the soldiers' clothing was a matter entrusted to the colonels or captains, who almost always earned additional income from it. In the 1670s the

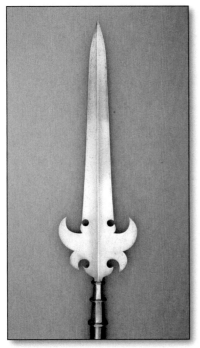

Partisan of an infantry officer, Saxony, c. 1675. Blade length: 60.3cm; overall length 241.3cm. (Collection of the Metropolitan Museum, New York).

Saxon musketeer from the *Uniformes de l'Electorat de Saxe, 1685–1772* (Bibliothèque National de France, Paris). Infantry regiment *Flemming*, 1685: black hat edged in yellow with white and yellow plumes; white cravat; light grey coat with pink cuffs and lining and pink stockings; natural leather breeches; brass buttons.

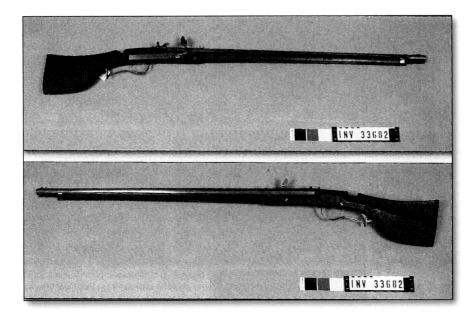

Matchlock musket of Saxon manufacture, probably late 1660s. (Collection of the Armémuseum Stockholm)

221

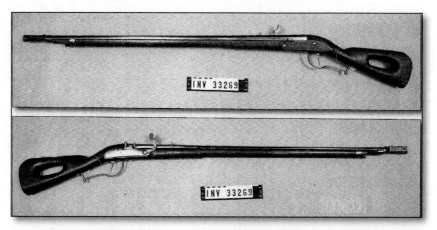

Matchlock musket of Saxon manufacture, 1680s (Collection of the Armémuseum Stockholm). The Saxon weapons industry was improved by Johann Georg III. Muskets and carbines came mainly from the factories in Suhl and Olbernhau. In January 1686, armourer Lorenz delivered 453 bayonets, and in March 1686, 500 muskets complete with bayonets were delivered to Duke Christian of Sachsen-Weissenfels' Regiment. In 1687, many trials were made on the bayonet providing it with grooves, iron and wooden ferrules and grips. In 1688 the first delivery of flintlocks took place, delivered to three non-commissioned officers and 56 soldiers of the infantry regiments Sinzendorf, Sachsen-Weissenfels, Reuss, Kuffer, Flemming and the *Leibregiment*. By 1687 Valentin Möschel in Suhl had already produced the first musket barrels complete with a sight. According to a letter of 3 November 1708, all of the infantry were armed with flintlock muskets as early as 1693–1694. 7,000 matchlocks were still available in the armoury and were to be converted into flintlocks in the Olbernhau arsenal.

infantryman's clothing included coats, breeches, stockings, headgear, shoes, and cravat, distributed by the colonel together with a pair of shirts. In the same period, leather breeches for the summer are mentioned as usual in many German armies of this age.[102] In the next decade, regulations issued by the Prince-Elector Johann Georg III demonstrate the desire to differentiate elite troops from ordinary ones. In this regard, the regiments of life guards received red coats lined of blue or white in 1683, while the other infantry regiments were dressed in grey with facings of different colours. In the same year, grenadiers wore the *Mütze*.[103] Clothing regulations established that the uniform should be changed every three years, but this probably only applied to troops serving in garrisons, since on campaign it could hardly last more than a single year. In 1683, grenadiers and foot guards received *Regenröcke* probably of grey cloth.

The cavalry had received uniforms and regular equipment as early as 1673. This included the universal buff *Kollet* that covered the horseman's body up to the knees. Cuirasses, with breast and back, are recorded in the arsenals as additional protection for all cavalrymen except the *Leibregiment*, who had worn a red uniform since the 1660s. At the same time, metal head protection was just as common and the most widespread model was the traditional lobster helm. Modern reconstructions show Saxon

---

102 Schuster and Francke, *Geschichte der Sächsischen Armee*, p.112.
103 Schuster and Francke, *Geschichte der Sächsischen Armee*, p.112.

THE ELECTORATE OF SAXONY

Saxon grenadier coat, 1683. In the 1680s, regulations issued by the Prince-Elector Johann Georg III demonstrated a desire to differentiate elite troops from ordinary troops. In this regard, the Life Guard regiments received red coats lined in blue or white in 1683, while the other infantry regiments were dressed in grey with facings of different colours. In the same year, grenadiers wore the *Mütze*, which was of blue cloth with white piping for the first *Leibregiment*.

cuirassiers with white metal protection, but some sources and contemporary accounts report that Saxon cuirassiers wore corselets of burnished metal for officers, and black-painted ones for common soldiers.

Saxon artillerymen are represented wearing uniform clothing in 1680, but the sources do not agree about the colours. The painting of the relief of Vienna preserved in the Heeresgeschichtliches Museum shows a Saxon artilleryman wearing a grey coat with dark green facings. This is the source Martin Lezius and Herbert Knötel used for depicting the constable in a grey coat with green cuffs and lining, natural leather breeches, grey stockings,

Helmet and armour belonging to Prince-Elector Johann Georg III, Saxon manufacture c. 1680 (*Turkishe Cammer* of the Residenzschloss Museum, Dresden). Black polished metal with brass fittings, and red velvet straps.

223

black broad-brimmed hat and tin buttons.[104] Other authors represent the same rank wearing a grey coat with red cuffs and brass buttons.[105]

Cavalry parade in Dresden, 1680. Engraving by Sigmund Gabriel Hipschman (Sächsische Landesbibliothek, Dresden). Note on the right trumpeters and a kettledrummer wearing plumed hats.

Saxon artilleryman, detail from an oil painting by an unknown artist, *Belagerung und Entsatz der Stadt Wien im September 1683*. (Heeresgeschichtliches Museum, Vienna)

---

104 Martin Lezius, *Die Entwicklung des Deutschen Heeres von Seinen Frühesten Anfängen bis unsere Tage in Uniformtafeln* (Berlin, 1936), plate 1. The same uniform is depicted by Friedrich Wolfgang in *Die Uniformen der Kurfürstlich Sächsischen Armee, 1683–1763* (Dresden: Beyer, 1998), p.59, but with brass buttons and yellow-black lanyard on the hat.

105 Querengässer, *The Saxon Mars and His Force*, plate iv.

THE ELECTORATE OF SAXONY

Frontispiece of *Sämtliche Schriften von der Fortification* by Georg Rimpler (1636–1683). The famous engineer was a native of Leisnig, in Saxony. Rimpler pursued a military career and joined the Swedish army at the age of 20. Initially serving as a musketeer, Rimpler fought during the campaign of 1656 in Poland, taking an interest in military fortifications. During the 1660s, Rimpler received lessons in engineering in Nuremberg, and in 1669 he accompanied the German troops to Candia in the last campaign of a 25 year long siege by the Ottomans. Rimpler drew inspiration from the effectiveness of the Venetian defences, and upon his return to mainland Europe wrote several works about siege warfare. He also continued his military service abroad, advising the Dutch army against the French. In 1678 he entered service with the Imperial army, overseeing fortifications in Austria and Germany. At the recommendation of Ludwig Wilhelm, Margrave of Baden-Baden, in 1681 Rimpler was appointed Chief Engineer with the rank of Lieutenant Colonel. He planned to further strengthen Vienna and other fortresses on the Hungarian border, which were to become the main obstacle to the Ottoman invasion. During the siege of Vienna, Rimpler oversaw the city's defences until he was mortally wounded by a mine on 25 July, dying in the city hospital on either 2 or 3 August. Rimpler's engineering legacy is controversial, with many of his contemporaries criticising his designs as being overly complicated or expensive. A theory that one of his designs, the 'Rimpler Angle', influenced eighteenth century fortress design was embraced by some historians but remains in dispute. However, his military achievements were well respected, with some of his contemporaries praising his practical skill in battle and the mastery with which he conducted his work.

6

The Prince-Bishopric of Münster

Located in the northern part of today's North Rhine-Westphalia and western Lower Saxony, the Prince-Bishopric of Münster was often held in personal union with one or more of the nearby ecclesiastical principalities of Cologne, Paderborn, Osnabrück, Hildesheim, and Liège. This contributed to making the history of the state particularly varied and complex. Between 1651 and 1688, four Catholic prince-bishops belonging to four different German aristocratic families held the rule of the state. In order, they were the Münster native Christoph Bernhard von Galen, who ruled from May 1651 to September 1678; the Swabian Ferdinand Egon von Fürstenberg, from September 1678 to June 1683; the Bavarian Maximilian Heinrich von Wittelsbach (already Prince-Bishop Elector of Cologne), from September 1683 to June 1688; and finally the Westphalian Friedrich Christian von Plettenberg, whose reign ended in May 1706.

Neighbouring states also marked the history of the prince-bishopric. Münster was bordered by the Dutch Republic and Bentheim to the west, by Cleves, Recklinghausen, and Mark to the south, Paderborn and Osnabrück to the east; to the north and north-east Münster bordered East Frisia, Oldenburg and Hanover.[1] From a geopolitical–confessional perspective, the prince-bishopric appeared as a Catholic outpost in Protestant lands.[2] Despite its relative influence in foreign policy, Münster held patronage over Bentheim, even though the counts were immediate princes of the *Reich*.

---

1   As with all the other prince-bishoprics of the Holy Roman Empire, it is important to distinguish between the Prince-Bishopric of Münster and the Diocese of Münster although both entities were ruled by the same man. Dioceses were generally larger than the corresponding state and in the parts that extended beyond the prince-bishopric, the authority of the Prince was strictly that of an ordinary bishop and limited to spiritual matters. Regarding the borders, until 1648 Münster also ruled the enclave of Wilsharem (Haren) to the north, in the Swedish territory of Bremen. This fief was ceded to Sweden with the Treaty of Westphalia.

2   Alois Schröer (ed.), 'Die Korrespondenz des Fürstbischofs Christoph Bernhard von Galen mit dem Heiligen Stuhl, 1650–1678,' in *Westfalia Sacra* (Münster, 1972), vol. 3, p.53. Christoph Bernhard von Galen stated that he was 'surrounded by Protestant states eagerly seeking to annex the Münster territory'. This suggests that he considered himself to be in a state of permanent danger.

THE PRINCE-BISHOPRIC OF MÜNSTER

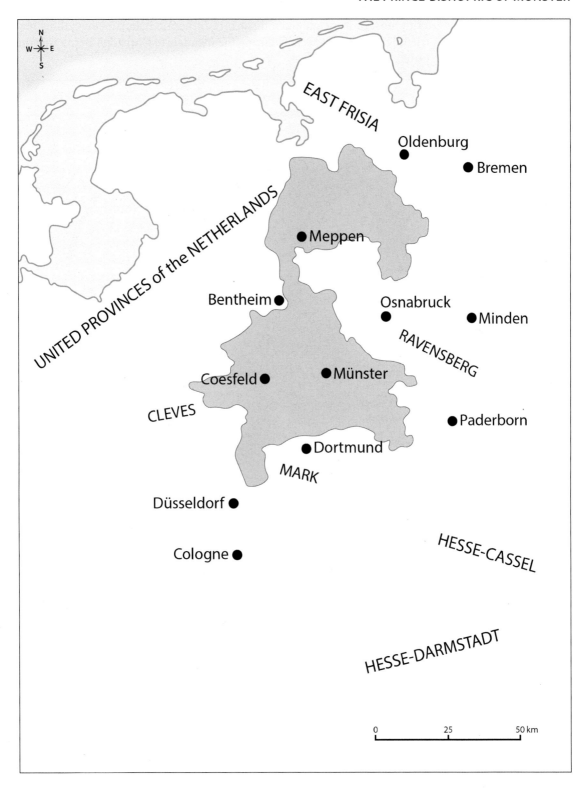

The Prince-Bishopric of Münster in 1648

With most of its neighbours, the prince-bishopric maintained anything but friendly relations, especially during the mandate of Christoph Bernhard von Galen.

Christoph Bernhard von Galen (1606–1678), portrayed together with an allusive hog by Romeyn van Hooghe in 1672 (Print collection of the Rijksmuseum, Amsterdam). Christoph Bernhard was born on 12 October 1606 to an aristocratic Westphalian family. His father, Dietrich von Galen, had estates in the Baltic region and bore the title of Marshal of Courland. Bernard was appointed Prince-Bishop in 1651. After restoring a degree of peace and prosperity to his principality, Galen had to contend with a formidable insurrection on the part of the citizens of Münster; but in 1661 this was solved by the surrender of the city. In 1664, he supported the raising of the *Reich* contingent to support the Imperial army against the Ottomans in Hungary. In 1665, he signed an alliance with Charles II of England in the Second Anglo-Dutch War, until the intervention of Louis XIV and the German Protestant Princes compelled him to make a disadvantageous peace in 1666. When Galen again attacked the Dutch Republic six years later in the Franco-Dutch War, he was now in alliance with Louis XIV. Under the threat of the Triple Alliance, in October 1674 he withdrew his troops from the Dutch Republic and gave up his attempts to restore Catholicism to the Eastern provinces. In 1675 he deserted his former ally, and fought for the Emperor against France. In conjunction with Brandenburg and Denmark-Norway he sent troops against Sweden, and conquered the Duchy of Bremen in the Bremen-Verden campaign. He proved himself anxious to reform the church, although his chief energies were directed to increasing his own power and prestige.

THE PRINCE-BISHOPRIC OF MÜNSTER

In the middle of the seventeenth century the state had an area of 569.58 square kilometres and an estimated population of about 350,000.[3] With his characteristic style, the military historian Galeazzo Gualdo Priorato provides a sweetened relation of the bishopric in the 1660s. Yet, in the balance of some manifest exaggerations, he draws a very accurate picture of the administration and governing bodies. As in other parts of Germany, the estates held political power, and met in the diet – *Landtag* – representing the 12 cities that held the rank of municipality.[4] The diet comprised three orders: the ecclesiastics, the nobility and the cities' deputies. The office of Prince-Bishop was elective and the candidate was nominated by the chapter – or college of clerics – which submitted him to the Pope for approval. The appointment was subject to political dynamics, and candidates were normally chosen from among the local nobility; however, approval was not a foregone conclusion, and in 1683 Pope Innocent XI refused to confirm Maximilian Heinrich von Wittelsbach, already Prince-Bishop of Cologne, Liège and Hildesheim, as Prince-Bishop of Münster. However, although the dispute had a significant political relevance, the Pope's refusal did not prevent Maximilian Heinrich from ruling in Münster until 1688, the year of his death.[5]

The Prince-Bishop managed the government through three councils, the first of which was the Secret Council, consisting of two canonical prelates of the chapter, one nobleman, two legal experts, and one chancellor, headed by a president. The second council was the Aulic Council, divided in ecclesiastical and secular respects. The third council was the Cameral Council, which dealt with economic matters. Moreover, each municipality had its own council formed by 12 senators with the *Stadtrichter* as a president. All these councils also discussed fiscal policy and then military matters, including recruiting, quartering and maintenance. The political scenario was therefore typical of post-Westphalia Germany, with the rigid partitioning of power that severely limited the rule of the prince, both secular and ecclesiastical. As was the case in Brandenburg of the Great Elector, the story of Münster is characteristic of the transformation of the medieval state into a modern, absolutist one, and this transformation again appears explicit in the growth and consolidation of a standing army. However, the final outcome was different: in many respects, Münster could be said to be an unsuccessful Brandenburg.

---

3   K.u.K. Kriegsarchiv, *Feldzüge des Prinzen Eugen von Savoyen* (Vienna, 1876), vol. I, p.84. In the mid-eighteenth century, the estimated population was 380,000 inhabitants.

4   Besides Münster, the other municipalities were Coesfeld, Warendorf, Burcholz, Rheine, Dülmen, Haltern, Werne, Beckum, Halen, Telgte and Vechta. Galeazzo Gualdo Priorato, *Relatione delle Corti e Stati ...* (Leyden, 1668), pp.69–70.

5   Innocent XI's refusal originated from the conflict between the Holy See and Louis XIV, as Maximilian Heinrich belonged to the pro-French faction of the German clergy. Innocent had not forgotten that in 1676 his election as pope had been vetoed by Louis XIV.

229

The *Kanonenbischof* and the Raising of the Standing Army

The formation of a standing army in Münster is linked to the person of the warlike Prince-Bishop Christoph Bernhard von Galen. When in July 1651 the troops of Hesse-Kassel finally completed the long delayed evacuation of the principality, after 18 years of occupation, the regular troops of Münster consisted of just two cavalry companies and a few hundred infantrymen dispersed in the garrisons of the state. This force was under the command of the Walloon *Generalwachtmeister* Johannes de Reumont, a veteran of the Imperial army who had established his headquarters at Coesfeld. In this city, the Prince-Bishop had his residence and his own mounted Life Guard, since political turmoil persisted in Münster. Also residing in the city was the prelate Bernhard Mallinckrodt, who had fiercely opposed Galen's election; the Münster municipality had sided with him and urged the chapter to reformulate the candidature. The city authorities were aware of Christoph Bernhard's authoritarian temperament and his political design, which was aimed at diminishing the powers and privileges of municipalities and estates. The support to Mallinckrodt's cause was also fuelled by other intentions. Münster, which together with Osnabrück hosted the peace negotiations in 1648, was formally subject to the Prince-Bishop, but the city council had long pursued an autonomous policy, and regarded its right as deriving from the aforementioned negotiations, as recognition of the status as an 'immediate' or 'free Imperial' city.

At the start, the dispute was tense but substantially peaceful, and concerned the rights of both the contenders, but gradually the duel became more and more bitter. In this unclear situation, in August 1654, Christoph Bernhard made a decision that seemed an open challenge to the city authorities: he announced that the autumn *Landtag* would gather at Horstmar instead of Münster as had always been customary. The councillors expressed serious concerns, but the Prince-Bishop showed the nature of his temperament,[6] and a consequence of this

Johann von Reumont, alias Johannes van Reumont, (1590?–1672) was a Walloon officer and veteran of the Thirty Years' War. Engraving from *Les Hommes Illustres qui ont Vécu dans le XVII Siècle*, Anselmus van Hulle (Antwerp: 1648).

---

6   Wilhelm Kohl, *Christoph Bernhard von Galen. Politische Geschichte des Fürstbistums Münster* (Münster: Regensburg Verlag, 1964), p.62: 'The decision was bound to cause great bitterness in the city, since it had not committed any legal wrongdoing so far. If the regional parliament

THE PRINCE-BISHOPRIC OF MÜNSTER

determination was that Galen anticipated Mallinckrodt's expected arrest. On 8 September 1654 the Prince-Bishop's life guards, under *Kornett* Finger, received the order to immediately arrest Mallinckrodt in his home, and then lead him out of the city the next day.[7] But moving a prelate from his residence meant violating the extraterritoriality of the churches, and therefore the situation remained in abeyance until 7 October. On that day, breaking the deadlock, the life guards entered the sacristy to seize Mallinckrodt. The prelate boldly faced the soldiers by insisting that they could not enter the church, and threatened to have them hung by their feet. At the same time, a crowd gathered in front of the church forcing the soldiers to desist from their intent.[8] The Prince-Bishop then recalled the officials loyal to him who resided in Münster, so as not to risk becoming involved, in the event of an imposed resolution by force of arms. He deeply regretted this situation, especially since just a few German princes had sided with him: this posed a very serious problem in terms of raising a military force capable of prevailing over the rebellious capital. After 1651 the army had increased to about 1,500 infantry and 200 cavalry,[9] but it was a number too low to bend the resistance of the city. The supply channels for more troops were scarce and numerically insignificant. It was only through the mediation of Cardinal Wilhelm Egon von Fürstenberg in Cologne that Galen could receive 100 infantrymen from Pfalz-Neuburg.[10]

However, the chance to obtain good troops at a reasonable price came with the conclusion of the First Bremen War. In April 1654 the Swedes had besieged the Hanseatic city in an attempt to deprive it of its autonomy and incorporate it into their own territories in Lower Saxony. The Emperor and the German princes had been called upon to intervene to impose a peace, and the siege had ended with a Swedish retreat in July. Consequently, Bremen decided to dismiss for the next winter the mercenaries who had been enlisted to defend the city. Immediately after learning the news, Christoph Bernhard convened the Secret Council to discuss the measures to be taken against Münster. There were three options to choose from: friendly negotiations, surprise action or regular siege. The majority of the councillors would have preferred to punish only the individuals responsible for the riots on 7 October. Hardly anyone thought of an outright siege, because it would have required great means and a lot of money, and it was pointed out to the Prince-Bishop that the treasury was insufficient to recruit even half of the troops discharged by Bremen. Moreover, a siege did not guarantee certain success. Therefore,

---

     had been held in Horstmar, the city could no longer have made concessions on Mallinckrodt or other state affairs.'

7   Kohl, *Christoph Bernhard von Galen*, p.62.

8   Kohl, *Christoph Bernhard von Galen*, p.62: 'The Deacon of the Cathedral was led to Town Hall by the triumphant crowd that celebrated the victory by smashing the windows of the Jesuit College and other places symbolising the power of the Prince-Bishop.'

9   Georg Tessin, 'Beiträge zur Formationsgeschichte des Münsterischen Militärs', *in Westfälische Forschungen. Mitteilungen des Provinzialinstituts für Westfälische Landes- und Volksforschung des Landschaftsverband Westfalen-Lippe*, vol. 32 (Münster: Aschendorffsche Verlagsbuchhandlung, 1982), p.88.

10   Kohl, *Christoph Bernhard von Galen*, p.63.

the councillors suggested to the Prince-Bishop an amicable agreement with the city of Münster. Christoph Bernard agreed with them on some matters, but made it known that he wanted to teach the rebellious city a lesson, and that 'his innermost wishes had not been taken into account by the city authorities'.[11] He also expressed doubts as to whether the Bremen troops should be hired. The day of their dismissal was 26 December; if the decision was in favour of an amicable solution, there was no need to enlist them, but on the contrary, if a military undertaking followed, all that money should not be spent in vain.[12]

Certainly, Galen realised that the emergence of a standing army depended on the Prince's ability to secure more funding from the subjects, since the basic income was always insufficient. As occurred in other German states, the estates of Münster generally opposed demands for increased military expenditure, not because they were insensitive to the presence of external dangers, but due to a mixture of self-interest and political conviction. However, before the end of the year, Galen succeeded in persuading the diet by citing the Swedish threat and getting them to approve an extraordinary taxation of 75,000 *Reichsthaler*, payable in six months.[13] It remains doubtful whether the estates fully believed him, but this was a major success for the Prince-Bishop. In subsequent years the diet's opposition constituted an obstacle to the ambitions of the Prince-Bishop, inducing him to seek other sources of funding.

In late 1654, since the two sides in the dispute could not come to any conciliatory solution, Galen decided to use the military force. He firmly believed he had the right to attack the city. As ruler and Bishop, it was his duty to punish the citizens' insults to his authority, and this persuaded him that a siege was inevitable. Had he acted hastily, he would not have given the rebellious citizens time to prepare for defence and recruit mercenaries and officers capable of sustaining a siege. Military preparations were conducted in the strictest secrecy, but eventually it became clear that Galen was enlisting men throughout the Rhineland and beyond. In January 1655 Galen had increased the army to 3,000 foot and 400 horse,[14] who were assembled at Coesfeld under *Generalwachtmeister* Reumont. In early February the Prince-Bishop's troops blockaded Münster, which had gathered 7,000 men among mercenaries and the city militia. Galen requested that the rebels surrender, but the city council refused, declaring it would rather 'submit to the Turks or even to the devil'.[15] On 4 February the Prince-Bishop felt that the time had come. In the evening, Colonel Dietrich Hermann von Nagel with some horsemen penetrated into Münster to open the doors to the troops waiting outside. However, a servant of a priest revealed to the mayors that the

---

11   Kohl, *Christoph Bernhard von Galen*, p.78.
12   Kohl, *Christoph Bernhard von Galen*, p.78.
13   Kohl, *Christoph Bernhard von Galen*, p.79.: 'When asked by the Bishop of Osnabrück about the passage of a cavalry troop marching from Bremen to Münster, Galen replied that the Swedish danger left no other choice. The Bishop of Osnabrück masked his disbelief by mockingly asking why the Swedes would target Münster among all the German states.'
14   Kohl, *Christoph Bernhard von Galen*, p.79.
15   Hermann Rothert, *Westfälische Geschichte*, (Gütersloh: Prisma Verlag, 1976), vol. III, p.17.

THE PRINCE-BISHOPRIC OF MÜNSTER

Prince-Bishop's soldiers were hiding in the bushes outside the town. Once discovered, Nagel managed to save himself by quickly escaping. The action ended with a bitter failure, and it was the seal to the unsuccessful first siege, which lasted just 20 days.

The city's authorities called the Emperor for a mediation. Negotiations began in March, but were met with resistance from the rebels to accept the presence of a garrison of 1,000 foot and 200 horse in exchange for political autonomy.[16] Furthermore, the city council's request to obtain from the troops the oath of allegiance, like that given to the Prince-Bishop, irritated Galen and caused the interruption of the negotiations. The situation remained pending for almost two years without a shared solution being found, and also due to the unpreparedness of the mediators sent from Vienna. In the spring of 1657, however, a six-month truce was agreed, but the hatred he had accumulated against the city pushed Galen to act before the term expired. In that period, the Prince-Bishop had learned that Münster was looking abroad for help. Therefore on 20 August 1657 Galen ordered Reumont to once again put Münster under siege. This time the besiegers did not resort to bold night assaults, but the siege was preceded by the construction of a regular circumvallation with trenches and embankments. In early September, Galen's artillery began to target the city. The Prince-Bishop was confident that the effect of the new incendiary projectiles fired by mortars and howitzers would be to convince the city to surrender, but the effect was negligible, and his hopes were frustrated; it was on this occasion that Christoph Bernhard received the nickname 'cannon-bishop'. On 17 September, during a 24-hour truce, the city proposed to host a representative of Galen in the city and to accept a garrison of 300 men, but in exchange the Prince-Bishop must recognise Münster's autonomy. To the disappointment of the diplomats, Galen increased his demands to 2,000 soldiers. Even when the city increased its offer to 1,000 soldiers, Christoph Bernhard refused and remained adamant.

Meanwhile, the city council had appealed to the United Provinces of the Netherlands for aid. On 20 October 1657, after the arrival of a Dutch contingent of approximately 4,100 infantry and 2,800 cavalry under Major-General Frederik Magnus of Salm-Neufville, the guns fell silent and slowly Galen's troops took over the blockade.[17] The city council requested a Dutch garrison, which was refused by The Hague; however, the *Raadspensionaris* Johan de Witt opened negotiations, and Emperor Leopold I sent an envoy offering his mediation. This time, too, diplomacy did not achieve appreciable results, especially due to the firm opposition of the Prince-Bishop, who refused any proposals from the rebel city. The resolution of the issue was only postponed, and certainly from this date Christoph Bernhard identified the Dutch Republic as an enemy.

---

16   Kohl, *Christoph Bernhard von Galen*, p.81. For the post of commander Galen proposed General Reumont, who was not unpopular in the city, but in the opinion of the city council Münster could accommodate a maximum of 600 foot and 200 horse.

17   The Dutch troops consisted of 53 infantry and 47 cavalry troops. Olaf Nimwegen, *The Dutch Army and the Military Revolutions, 1588–1688* (English Edition, Woodbridge, Suffolk: Boydell Press, 2010), p.304.

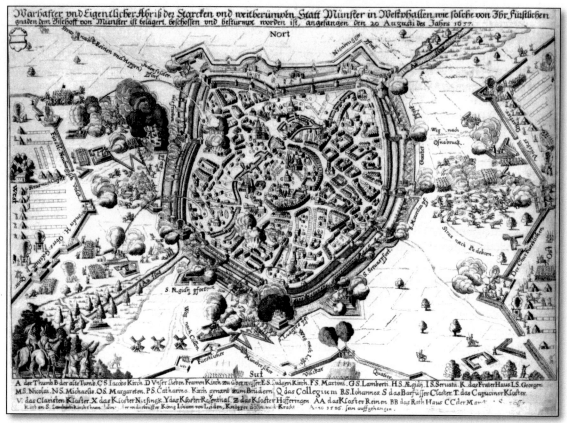

Münster under siege in 1657, engraving by Lukas Schnitzer. (Author's Collection) During the second siege of the city, which began on 20 August 1657, Christoph Bernhard made extensive use of artillery, but the city's strong fortifications withstood the bombardment, which ultimately proved unsuccessful. On 6 September 1657, Christoph Bernhard called on the city to surrender, which it refused. When news spread that a Dutch army with 53 companies of infantrymen and 47 mounted troops was ready to intervene in favour of Münster, the Bishop lifted the siege of the town. The Treaty of Geister of 21 October 1657 was then signed, although this was only a temporary truce.

A propitious occasion to settle accounts was not long coming. In June 1660 the Prince-Bishop moved to take advantage of the loss of influence of the city council, now disliked even by the Emperor, and the absence of the Dutch troops, who had returned to their state in the autumn of 1659. Another decisive motivator was his accession to the Rhenish League, which on the one hand compromised relations with Vienna, but on the other brought him decisive diplomatic advantages. On 12 June his officers received the order to gather their soldiers for a new siege. As commander-in-chief, Galen appointed *Generalwachtmeister* Dietrich Philipp von Wylich. Further troops had been enlisted, including 1,000 Walloon horsemen, who had been assembling in Brussels since the previous year. On 8 July, the infantry was gathering at Borken, Coesfeld, Telgte, Meppen and Dülmen; further soldiers had been taken from garrisons while others were newly recruited. These companies formed three *Brigaden* with 550, 414 (or 512), and 439 (or 500) men.[18] Other newly recruited companies were quartered around Münster.

---

18 Tessin, 'Beiträge zur Formationsgeschichte des Münsterischen Militärs', p.88.

According to a contemporary source, the besieging army consisted of 11,500 foot and 2,600 horse, including the auxiliary troops of the Emperor, Cologne, Trier and Pfalz-Neuburg.[19] If the numbers are correct, this was a significant increase, considering that in March 1660 just 3,373 professional soldiers were registered, of which 479 were cavalry. The same source also reports the presence of 116 artillerymen.[20]

The city of Coesfeld in a print of the late seventeenth century. (Author's Collection) Coesfeld was the main residence of the Prince-Bishop, and had new fortifications built and a strong citadel completed in 1654. Coesfeld had a standing garrison, which included the Household troops. These consisted of one company of Horse Guard and 100 *Heiducken* raised in 1664. The Westphalian historian Theodor Verspohl investigated the archives and found some interesting information about this latter company. He wrote, 'A rather peculiar equipped force was the Life Guard of Bernhard von Galen, as an English envoy, Sir William Temple wrote on his visit in 1668. In a letter sent to Sir John Temple, he said that they were a guard of 100 infantrymen, raised after the campaigns in Hungary, who escorted the Prince-Bishop's carriage. They wore a short brown jacket, a brown cap, and were equipped with a battleaxe, and on their backs a *carabine*.'

The third siege began on 27 July 1660, and was marked by periods of intense bombardment and phases of relative calm. On 12 January 1661, Major General Oswald von Pleuren replaced Wylich, who had died suddenly of natural causes, as field commander. On 26 March 1661, with no hope of receiving help, the city finally surrendered and opened the doors to the Prince-Bishop. He entered escorted by his 200 life guards, which were under the command of Colonel Nagel, and finally they took quarters in the subdued capital.

---

19 Johann von Alpen, *Decadis de Vita et Rebus Gestis Christophori Bernardi Episcopi et Principis Monasteriensis*, (Münster, 1694–1703), vol. I, p.124. The Emperor sent an infantry regiment and another of cavalry just transferred from the Spanish service. Pfalz-Neuburg and Cologne contributed 500 men each.

20 Staatsarchiv Münster, *Fürstentum Münster Landtagsprotokolle* nr. 75; cited by Tessin, 'Beiträge zur Formationsgeschichte des Münsterischen Militärs', p.88.

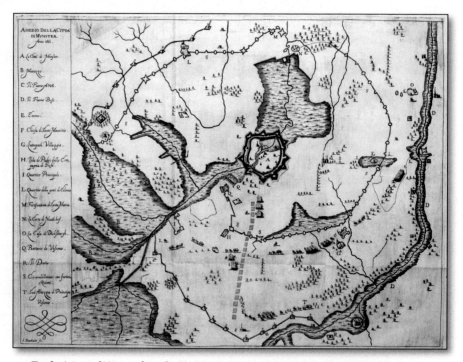

The final siege of Münster, from Gualdo Priorato, *Historia di Leopoldo Caesare* (Vienna: 1670). When, under the influence of Holland, the States General of The United Provinces refused to support the city of Münster, which had been again besieged by Galen from 20 July 1660, it was predictable that the Prince-Bishop would succeed. Soon the city was no longer able to pay its soldiers; furthermore, there were difficulties with supplies. In this desperate financial situation, the city authorities had silver melted down and the council minted an emergency coin. In addition, the council obtained loans from citizens and guilds. At Christmas, Christoph Bernhard had the River Aa dammed to the north, at the exit of the city, so that a basin was formed to flood the northern quarter. Immediately afterwards, the first negotiations for terms began. Galen demanded the handing over of the keys to the city and the admission of a regular garrison. In view of their desperate military situation, the council had no choice and a declaration was signed on 26 March 1661, which ended municipal autonomy.

Army Organisation

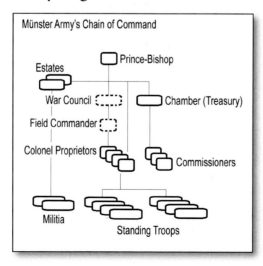

The third siege of Münster marks the actual beginning of the Prince-Bishop's standing army, which now began to raise regiment-size units. Between 1660 and 1661, five 'field regiments' were registered in the muster. Naturally, these were units formed temporarily, given that between 1660 and 1663 most of these were disbanded and then divided again into autonomous companies.

THE PRINCE-BISHOPRIC OF MÜNSTER

However, also in Münster some features were introduced according to the models applied in other countries, and in 1665 an infantry regiment appeared under the same colonel until 1672,[21] while already from 1654 to 1662, the *Reaumont* cavalry regiment was always registered with this denomination. However, for a long time Münster's army continued to more resemble the mercenary contingents of the Thirty Years' War than an instrument administered according to modern systems. With the notable exception of the artillery, and apart from the establishment of a War Commissariat with inspection duties, which was often entrusted to an inadequate number of officials, the Prince-Bishop's army remained under the control of the colonel-proprietors, who negotiated the number of men to be recruited. Although Galen had earned a great reputation by raising a sizeable army, and his experience in the warfare favoured his appointment as main member in the Diet's *Direktorium* for the war against the Porte in 1664,[22] this did not prevent him from being militarily inexperienced in several matters.

As for the provenance of the troops, most of the soldiers were recruited in the Prince-Bishopric and in the Rhenish states, such as Pfalz-Neuburg and Cologne. There are records of soldiers also recruited in Hamburg, Swabia, the Spanish Low Countries and Liège. After all, Galen, like many other princes of Germany, did not care much about the provenance of the troops. When the city of Münster surrendered, 602 infantrymen from the rebel garrison entered the service of the Prince-Bishop after the oath of 5 April 1661; their commander, Colonel Levin, also entered Galen's service. However, due to unknown events, a few weeks later the strength had decreased to 290 men, who were reunited with the garrison under Colonel Oswald Pleuren, and quartered inside the city under strict control.[23]

Living up to his nickname, Galen invested many resources in the formation of a considerable artillery. He attributed the failure of the 1655 siege to the lack of adequate artillery, therefore in the following years bought cannons and mortars abroad and others were manufactured in his own state.[24] In a short time the Prince-Bishop built up a large artillery corps from almost nothing. Cannons, and especially mortars, were acquired in late 1655, the latter included 500lb pieces, stored in Coesfeld together with a great number of projectiles and grenades.[25] In August 1657 the artillery comprised a siege battery of 26 cannons and mortars. In the same year, there are records of light guns for the regimental artillery, and for the first time professional artillery personnel are mentioned in the Prince-Bishop's

---

21 Regiment *Krohne zu Fuss*, see MüI-24 in Appendix II.
22 Gualdo Priorato, *Relatione delle Corti e Stati...*, p.103.
23 Tessin, 'Beiträge zur Formationsgeschichte des Münsterischen Militärs', p.88.
24 Dieter Zeigert, 'Die Artillerietruppe des Fürstbistums Münster 1655–1802. Erster Teil: Errichtung, Organisation und Einsatz der Artillerie unter Fürstbischof Christoph Bernhard von Galen (1650–1678). Ein kurzer Streifzug durch die Geschichte der Artillerie bis zum 17. Jahrhundert', in *Westfälische Zeitschrift*, p.134, (1984), p.18. According to the author, it seems certain that the artillery corps already existed in the Prince-Bishopric. As early as 1652, there are reports of the 'recasting of several artillery pieces', and in 1653–54 of projectiles and grenades, the latter are clearly artillery ammunition for howitzers.
25 Zeigert, 'Die Artillerietruppe des Fürstbistums Münster', p.18.

237

correspondence. In April 1660, 123 artillerymen served as a permanent corps, three years later there were 200. However, at least until 1671 the artillery of Münster retained the typical features of a guild. The personnel were distributed among garrisons according to their importance without having an established strength or organisation. In addition, a large number of craftsmen can be found. Until 1669 there was simply the *Artillerie*, its members being called *Artilleriebediente* (artillery servants/matrosses). The *Stückhauptmann* (captain) appears as first officer during the Hungarian campaign of 1663–64. In September 1672, out of a total field strength of 100 men, there were also 15 craftsmen, increased to 27 in May 1673. There were also still 29 infantrymen as 'henchmen', presumably for lack of available artillerymen to assist regimental pieces, which was generally common in the seventeenth century.[26] Between the 1660s and the following decade, the term *Compagnie* is also used, however this does not mean that it refers to a unit; rather, this term designated the whole artillery corps.

A mortar of the Münster siege artillery found at Groningen with the letters and number 'Ao 62 CBEM' (Year 1662 – Christoph Bernhard Episcopus Monasteriensis) cast on it, and a reconstruction of the mortar with its carriage. (With thanks to Edwin Groot for this information)

Throughout the 1660s Galen managed to increase his artillery, and in 1672, at the eve of the war against the Dutch Republic, he could deploy one of the most remarkable arsenals in Germany.[27] In 1664 Galen's artillery included 81 light cannons ranging from 1.5lb–4lb, 38 field guns of 6lb, 34 of 12lb, seven of 24lb, and two of 36lb. The mortars totalled 27 pieces between 25lb and 100lb, while the howitzers were 60 pieces of 7lb and 12lb. The arsenals included another 63 guns of calibres ranging from 1lb to 37lb, and

---

26 Zeigert, 'Die Artillerietruppe des Fürstbistums Münster', p.21. In a register of the garrison at Meppen from May 1671, the artillery also includes 21 infantrymen employed as assistants, and five carpenters, as well as a clerk, an armourer, a 'bastion master' and other craftsmen, including the widow of a lieutenant, making a total of 32 persons.
27 Zeigert, 'Die Artillerietruppe des Fürstbistums Münster', p.19: 'The fact that the Prince-Bishop paid great attention to his artillery and all inventions and innovations in this field, is confirmed by many documents. Christoph Bernhard – unlike many princes of his time – was an actual patron of artillery.'

another 17 mortars of different calibres. In 1672, the field army that invaded the United Provinces comprised 51 cannons including 31 regimental guns. Another eight pieces of 12lb and eighteen 24lb guns were added as siege weapons. The artillery was completed by 25 howitzers and 61 mortars. The train numbered 600 wagons, carrying tens of thousands of shells of all types, and also gunpowder, an eyewitness reporting that the convoy stretched for miles from the border to the town of Groenlo.[28] The artillery employed in the campaigns of 1672–73 comprised a smaller number of calibres, most of the guns were pieces of 4, 6, 8, 12 and 24lb. This division of calibre in the Prince-Bishop's artillery may have been influenced by the Dutch. Christoph Bernhard obviously took into account the progress of artillery, and Dutch artillery, like that of the French, was technically ahead compared to the German scenario. The use of French terms is documented in Münster as early as 1655.[29]

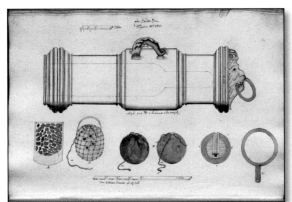
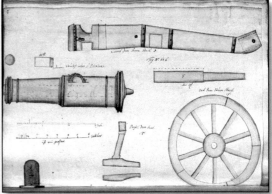

Seventeenth century howitzers with projectiles and carriage from Anton Faulhaber's *Artilleriekunst* (Bayerischer Staatsbibliothek, Münich).

Other features, however, are the result of original experimentation. In 1673, administrative documents refer to artillery companies not only with approximately the same strength, but also joined – before many others in Germany – in an artillery regiment under an *Obrist*, whose total strength was initially established to 600 men, later increased to 775, but only two-thirds completed.[30] In May 1675, the regiment of artillery numbered 729 men, and included a staff comprising two *Adjutanten* (warrant officers), one *Zeugwärter* (arsenal attendant), one *Quartiermeister*, one *Wagenmeister*, one *Feldscherer* (surgeon), one *Gewältiger* (provost marshal), and one *Feldprediger* (priest).[31] The regiment was distributed among Coesfeld, Meppen, Münster, Rheine, Vechta and Warendorf.

---

28 Zeigert, 'Die Artillerietruppe des Fürstbistums Münster', pp.63–64.
29 Zeigert, 'Die Artillerietruppe des Fürstbistums Münster', p.21.
30 Zeigert, 'Die Artillerietruppe des Fürstbistums Münster', p.21. According to Tessin in 'Beiträge zur Formationsgeschichte des Münsterischen Militärs', p.98, in May 1673 the artillery regiment under Colonel Braun had 594 men divided into six companies.
31 Zeigert, 'Die Artillerietruppe des Fürstbistums Münster', p.27. Curiously, there is no mention of intermediate ranks such as blacksmiths, saddlers and other personnel usually present with the

On 2 April 1675 a regulation for the artillery was issued, which established two field battalions of three companies.[32] The regulations provide many interesting details about service on campaign. Probably inspired by the French *Fusiliers du Roi*, each battalion was accompanied by three auxiliary companies in charge of escorting the artillery train.[33] Each auxiliary company included a *Primaplan* of 12 men, three *Spielleute* (musicians), and four pioneers; also 63 *Gemeine* armed with muskets and 12 more with cavalry *Carbienerpistollen*, registered as *Rottmeistern*. This term seems to allude to corporals of the Renaissance German armies. On campaign, the artillery included also the drivers and the personnel dealing with the artillery train, who were enlisted as regular soldiers: a very modern feature for this age.

In 1678, each artillery company had 156 men divided as follows:[34]

1 *Obristlieutenant*
1 *Lieutenant*
1 *Fendrich* (ensign)
3 *Stückjunker*
1 *Veldweibel* (Sergeant)
2 *Führer-Fourier*
4 *Corporalen*
20 *Fewerwercker* (artificers)
38 *Constabele*
6 *Zimmerleuthe* (pioneers)
12 *Rottmeister*
64 *Gemeine*
2 *Tambouren*
1 *Pfeiffer*

Unlike the artillery, which received a regular organisation, a recurrent feature of the Prince-Bishop's infantry and cavalry was the variety of the units' strength. In practice, until 1678 the number of companies in the regiments was never established, and the number of men in each of them also remained subject to considerable variation. As discussed before, colonels were often the first cause of this scenario, since they acted as entrepreneurs who imposed their conditions as to the matter of number of men and companies. Certainly, the variable company strength represented the absence of a rational military policy, and the lack of an organisation capable of maintaining oversight of military affairs. As for the composition of the companies, the sources do not provide details, however, it is likely that they consisted of the conventional proportion of two-thirds musketeers and one-third pikemen, with the usual number of non-commissioned officers and administrative personnel of the

---

artillery.

32 *Regulement Welcher Gestalt die Ordnungh der Artiglerie Eingerichtet Werden Solle*, preserved in Münster State Archive, *Archiv Galen*, LS 539, BI. 7f.

33 *Regulement Welcher Gestalt die Ordnungh der Artiglerie Eingerichtet Werden Solle*. These companies are denominated *Artigl: Neben Compagnien*.

34 Zeigert, 'Die Artillerietruppe des Fürstbistums Münster 1655–1802', p.24.

contemporary German armies. As for the cavalry, only regiment *Post* (MüC-3), raised in 1663, was a cuirassier unit, while the other cavalry comprised unarmoured *Reiter* as was usual in northern Germany.

After the submission of Münster Galen did not stop increasing his army, and he managed to achieve this goal through a policy of rents and loans, turning himself into a kind of military entrepreneur. The intense rotation of units which were then ceded to other states was another feature of Christoph Bernhard's army. Between 1660 and 1665 one infantry regiment entered the Imperial service, another regiment was ceded to the Duke of Pfalz-Neuburg and three more to Spain. In the same period one cavalry regiment joined the Imperial army, one each went to the Palatinate, Sweden and Pfalz-Neuburg, and finally three went to Spain. In the following decade the hiring of regiments was concluded with Denmark, and again with Spain. Furthermore, similar to the measures adopted by Brandenburg and other states, the Prince-Bishop turned to foreign powers to raise his army, as occurred in 1665 with England, and in 1672 with France.

How the regiments were assembled, and how their service was subject to all kinds of rectifications and adjustments for economic reasons is clearly expressed in the *Vertrag* concluded between the Prince-Bishop of Münster and Emperor Leopold I. Shortly before the capitulation of his capital, Christoph Bernhard had promised to send the Emperor 1,000 horsemen and 2,000 infantrymen. The contingent was to serve for two years, and the agreement specified that in exchange for the explicit promise, the Prince-Bishop could recall the soldiers at any time in the event of an emergency. The contingent left Münster in May 1661 and comprised a cavalry regiment of 1,000 men 'on the Imperial size', but which would remain the property of the Prince-Bishop.[35] The regiment had been formed with the autonomous cavalry companies and with soldiers and NCOs from the *Reumont* regiment (MüC-1). The command was awarded to a veteran of the siege of Münster, Lothar Hermann von Post, who served with his men under Montecuccoli in Hungary and Transylvania until 1662. That same year, realising that the maintenance of the regiment would be too burdensome for his state, Galen ceded it to the Emperor. Together with Post's horsemen, Galen had sent two infantry regiments, *Münster* (MüI-5), formed with his own troops, and *Spielberg* (MüI-6), recruited by the Duke of Pfalz-Neuburg but ceded to the Prince-Bishop.[36] Both regiments suffered greatly in Hungary and were disbanded in November 1662. The surviving rank and file entered Imperial service.

In 1663 the infantry of Münster consisted of 1,937 men in 13 companies, four of which, under *Generalwachtmeister* Oswald Pleuren, were quartered in the citadel of Münster, and nine other companies were distributed in the major fortresses of the state. According to Gualdo Priorato these were Coesfeld, Warendorf, Rheine, Dülmen, Lüdinghausen, Ottenstein, Saffenburg, Bevergern, Vechta and Meppen.[37]

---

35 Tessin, 'Beiträge zur Formationsgeschichte des Münsterischen Militärs', p.89.
36 Tessin, 'Beiträge zur Formationsgeschichte des Münsterischen Militärs', p.89.
37 Galeazzo Gualdo Priorato, *Relatione delle Corti e Stati ... del Vescovato e Principato di Munster...* (Leyden, 1668), p.73.

The fortress of Meppen, in an eighteenth century print. (Royal Collection Trust) Meppen was the main fortress guarding the border with the Dutch province of Overijssel.

Before 1663, the only mounted troops were the 200 life guards, and a company under Colonel Nagel, but after that date a further five companies were raised, since the submission of Münster had not quelled Galen's ambitions. In December 1663 he started a territorial dispute with Prince Georg Christian of East Friesland. Although he no longer had the army that had captured his rebel capital, the Prince-Bishop did not hesitate to invade the neighbouring state and occupy some disputed territories with his troops. However, in May 1664 Dutch troops had entered East Friesland to support Georg Christian's cause, forcing the Münster troops to withdraw. It was the second time the Dutch Republic had thwarted his plans. Relentless, Galen did not stop weaving diplomatic plots throughout Germany, and the army was a very useful tool for gaining prestige and consideration. In 1664 the Prince-Bishop sent other troops to Hungary as a member of the *Deutsche Allianz* (the army of the Rhenish League). On 30 August two companies under Hermann von Post, who had returned to Münster service, were formed and sent to Hungary, with a total of 123 horsemen from five different autonomous companies. In addition to the two mounted companies, the contingent under Post included 1,000 infantrymen, two howitzers and 12 light field guns. The infantry sent to Hungary was also drawn from the existing autonomous companies.

In June 1664 two further battalions headed to Hungary, one under Lieutenant General Toller with four companies for a total of 453 men, and the other under General Nitzau with four companies totalling 452 men, both completed with recruits from Hanau; 915 men in all with the *Primaplana*.[38] Since Münster had already contributed its contingent to the *Deutsche Allianz*, it was not obliged to contribute any more troops to the Westphalian Circle. However, Galen provided an additional 200 infantrymen for the Westphalian *Kreisregiment Uffeln* and also took over the quota of recruits for some of the

---

38 Tessin, 'Beiträge zur Formationsgeschichte des Münsterischen Militärs', p.89. In May 166, it was ordered that the Nitzau battalion joined the troops of the Electorate of Mainz under *Generalwachtmeister* Leyen, and that the Toller battalion formed a regiment together with the battalion of Trier. In the meantime, Hermann Post had already returned home to take command of the electoral Lower Rhine Circle contingent.

THE PRINCE-BISHOPRIC OF MÜNSTER

states in the circle in return for money.[39] In May 1664 an infantry regiment of 16 companies was raised, from which a field battalion of five companies with 651 men was formed. In the same year the battalion and other companies of foot and horse, totalling 1,000 infantrymen and 200 horsemen, participated under Major General Pleuren at the siege of Erfurt, which had rebelled to the Prince-Bishop Elector of Mainz.

Despite the costs involved in maintaining a permanent armed force, Christoph Bernhard's military policy did not take a pause. The treaty Galen concluded with Charles II of England on 13 June 1665 provided for the raising of an army of 20,000 infantry and 10,000 cavalry, to be employed in the joint war against the Dutch Republic. On 16 February 1665 all companies of horse were called to report their strength, and then merged among the existing cavalry regiments.[40] According to the sources, the infantry totalled 8,000 men not including the *Rheingraf* regiment, which was recruited later and never completed, and the three *eskadronen* (battalions) of captains Leuren, Kalckum and Lohe, which were probably *Landvolk*-militia. Once again, the number of companies forming the regiments shows the usual variety.[41] The infantry consisted of two regiments of 12 companies but with 1,500 and 700 men respectively; a further 10 regiments of eight companies with 100 men each, a regiment of six companies with 750 men, a battalion of five companies with 635 men, 12 battalions of four companies with 500 men for a total of 6,000 men, and two battalions of two companies with 250 men for a total of 500 men; in total, on paper, 166 companies with 18,075 foot.[42] The actual strength was far less, but sources differ considerably on this matter.[43] In June 1665 the cavalry numbered about 7,200 horsemen and 400–500 dragoons, while the infantry could field approximately between 5,000 and 6,000 men, with several regiments and companies still in formation.[44] Another source dated April–May 1666, resulting from a Dutch intelligence

---

39   See Mugnai, *Wars and Soldiers*, vol. 2, p.287.

40   Tessin, 'Beiträge zur Formationsgeschichte des Münsterischen Militärs', pp.92–93: 'On 16 February, the companies of the five squadron commanders Speckmann, Eisengert, Drewitz, Bützow and Haugwitz were probably still being completed. The recruitments of Colonel Clemens – 400 horsemen – and Piron – 4 companies – apparently did not materialise.'

41   The fluctuations in strength of the *Gorgas* cavalry regiment (MüC-4) appears to be one of the most complicated cases to solve. The colonel had left the army of Braunschweig-Lüneburg-Celle and in early 1665 was recruiting in Hamburg 10 companies for Münster totalling 750 men. Tessin (*ibid.*, p.90) adds: 'an account dated 16 August 1665 states that the regiment fielded 12 companies and comprised 900 horsemen. In February 1666 it was reduced to 8 companies, and on 17 August it still appeared in service, but with 1,200 men.' The *Hollandse Mercurius* of 1666 contributes to increase the complexity: according to the newspaper, in April–May 1666, the regiment *Gorgas* had 11 companies with 825 men.

42   Tessin, 'Beiträge zur Formationsgeschichte des Münsterischen Militärs', p.92.

43   Tessin, 'Beiträge zur Formationsgeschichte des Münsterischen Militärs', p.90. According to the author, the main source of information is the Alpen's *Decadis de Vita et Rebus Gestis Christophori Bernardi*, a list regarding the distribution of bread and beer in the encampment of Ochtrup, and a recently discovered list preserved in the Royal Archives in Stockholm.

44   Tessin, 'Beiträge zur Formationsgeschichte des Münsterischen Militärs', p.90. 'The Swedish list, which takes into account the losses suffered at Winschoten and the garrisons remaining in the bishopric, gives a total of 9,408 men. Ochtrup's list states 8,857 men. Both lists, however, do not include the regiments Nath, Carp and Cleuter that would have participated in the campaign in the Netherlands.' Georges Bernard Depping, in *Geschichte des Krieges der Münsterer und Cölner*

investigation, reports that Münster's field army now comprised 18,128 infantrymen divided into 188 companies, 7,400 horsemen in 89 companies, and 810 dragoons in 14 companies.[45] The Dutch agents also intercepted a letter written by one of Galen's generals, who had boasted that the Prince-Bishop would soon have 25,000 men under arms.[46] Although the numbers were still less than what had been agreed with Charles II, Galen had managed to increase the army considerably. The recruitment was not limited to the territory of Münster, but also extended to Paderborn, Lippe, the Electorate of Cologne, Mecklenburg and other German states and free cities. Overall, between 1665 and 1666, 19 infantry, 14 cavalry and one dragoon regiments were raised, and further units joined the army as free companies, battalions or squadrons. This force also included two short-lived Household regiments, one of infantry and another of cavalry.[47] Although the Dutch estimate may not be entirely accurate, in the spring of 1666 the Prince-Bishop could field at least 24,000 professional soldiers. This figure also appears considerable if compared to other armies in Germany; in fact, during the same period Brandenburg had 7,000–8,000 men in all. However, numbers do not always mean military effectiveness. Several reports suggest that discipline was low and training left much to be desired. A letter of the Dutch commander of Wesel, dated August 1665, informed The Hague that:

> His Princely Grace of Münster takes great pleasure in having the cavalry exercised, but they amuse themselves the most when sometimes man and horse fall ... They shoot at the targets there so violently that the farmers are as frightened as ducks.[48]

In what was to become a feature of such arrangements, England failed to pay its subsidies in full and even made one instalment in the form of a shipload of lead. Galen extorted additional 'contributions' from the Dutch provinces of Groningen and Overijssel, but now he was clearly unable to continue the war against the opposition of his own cathedral chapter and the appearance of the Dutch troops with their French allies. Though England fought on until July 1667, Münster signed a peace at Cleves on 18 April 1666, agreeing to reduce the army to 3,000 garrison troops.[49]

---

    im Bundnisse mit Frankreich gegen Holland in den Jahren 1672, 1673 und 1674 (Münster, 1840), calculates that cavalry and infantry did not exceed 11,000 men.

45 *Hollandse Mercurius*, 1666. Thanks to Edwin Groot for this information.

46 Nimwegen, *The Dutch Army*, p.416. Since early 1665, Münster's war preparation did not go unnoticed in the Dutch Republic. An anonymous correspondent sent a warning to The Hague: 'There in Münster, in towns and villages throughout the land, hard work is being carried out and all manner of things useful to war ... In confusion, wherever I have been, from Coesfeld to Münster and from there to Telgre and Warendorf, and thus back to Dülmen again in whatever villages and towns that I passed through I found that people were busily smithying, making wheels, attaching iron reinforcements to wagons and gun carriages.'

47 Tessin, 'Beiträge zur Formationsgeschichte des Münsterischen Militärs', p.90. According to some sources cited by the author, in the spring of 1665 the cavalry *Leibregiment* had 720 horsemen divided into eight companies.

48 Nimwegen. *The Dutch Army*, p.417.

49 Wilson, *German Armies*, p.34.

THE PRINCE-BISHOPRIC OF MÜNSTER

Satirical print, probably from 1665, depicting the alliance between England and Münster. Prince-Bishop Christoph Bernhard von Galen is riding a nun; on the left he keeps dogs on a leash, while on the right, he is in the company of pigs. The English are depicted as the dogs.

The failure did not discourage Galen; on the contrary, German involvement in international conflict continued, and Münster itself was one of the signatories to a string of treaties negotiated by French diplomats in 1667 to isolate the Spanish Low Countries as the intended target of Louis XIV's first major war. Like those signed with Pfalz-Neuburg, Mainz, Cologne and Brandenburg, Münster's new treaty was essentially defensive, binding it only to hold troops in readiness to prevent possible Austrian assistance to Spain.[50] Nevertheless, Galen tried to obtain as much financial gain as possible from the reduction of his army, which was in open violation of the policy of the Rhenish League, as the Prince-Bishop ceded a large number of his former troops to Spain. In 1666 the army of the Spanish Low Countries transferred the rank and file of eight regiments of foot and horse which Galen had been obliged to disband after the Peace of Kleve.[51] The contingent was supposed to include a further cavalry regiment, but the agreement was cancelled because the horsemen found their passage barred by the French, and more critically the Spaniards had paid the soldiers' engagement but not the price requested by the Prince-Bishop.[52]

---

50 Wilson, *German Armies*, p.34.
51 Spanish military preparations included troops hired from Braunschweig-Lüneburg-Celle in 1667; meanwhile Hanover and Osnabrück together provided 4,614 men to reinforce the Dutch as they joined Sweden and England in applying diplomatic pressure on France to abandon the campaign in Flanders in 1668.
52 Tessin, 'Beiträge zur Formationsgeschichte des Münsterischen Militärs', p.91.

Although in 1665 Münster had created a large army in a very short time, this did not mean that the recruitment campaign did not face problems. Resources remained limited, and a clear sign of these difficulties had already emerged before the beginning of the military campaign. In August, while the Prince-Bishop was gathering his force, a report from the border informed the States General about Münster's financial shortage:

> The difficult time [for the Prince-Bishop] is starting to approach: the soldiers want to be paid and still no wages have been distributed … so the men are already starting to desert. If Their High Mightinesses were to start recruiting now then I have no doubt that we shall be riding horses that someone else had saddled.[53]

More troubles derived from some princes and military entrepreneurs who failed to fulfil their promises, and forced the Prince-Bishop to rectify the contracts concluded with them. In the spring of 1665 the *Rheingraf* Johann Ludwig von Salm had agreed with Galen to recruit three infantry regiments and a cavalry troop, but in November Salm requested a change in the agreement to enlist only 2,000 infantrymen. Despite the arrangement, even this number was not completed. The affair also turned out to be a mistake from an economic point of view, because in April 1666 the rank and file mutinied when they learned that they had been ceded to Spain. The soldiers who had not deserted were transferred to Lowen and distributed to the companies of the garrison.[54]

Not much time passed before the basis for a new field army was conceived. On 4 May 1667 the Prince-Bishop signed with France the secret treaty of St Germain: in return for subsidies, Münster committed to maintain 2,500 foot soldiers and 400 horsemen in peacetime, but in the event of war they were to increase to 8,000 foot, 1,700 horse and 400 dragoons.[55] France's support restored Galen's proverbial daring in external policy. In January 1671, following a dispute with the Duke of Braunschweig-Lüneburg-Celle over the borders around Corvey, Galen ordered the army increased again. For this he issued a large number of *Werbpatenten* (enlistment patents) to colonel-proprietors and entrepreneurs for the recruitment of soldiers in Hamburg, Bremen, Frankfurt am Mein, and Aachen. They included some crowned heads of the *Reich*, such as Count August of Lippe. Galen also intended to enlist six Lorraine cavalry regiments into his service, however, armed confrontation was avoided thanks to the mediation of the Prince-Bishop Elector of Cologne.

A new season of war had only been postponed. This time Galen's target was the hated Dutch Republic, which was close to certain destruction thanks to the invasion that Louis XIV was preparing. The new agreement concluded with France at Coesfeld on 3 April 1672 provided for 16,000 infantry, 2,600 cavalry, 400 dragoons and field artillery. Just days before, the French plenipotentiary Verjus had disposed the payment to the Prince-Bishop of

---

53 Nimwegen, *The Dutch Army*, p.422.
54 Tessin, 'Beiträge zur Formationsgeschichte des Münsterischen Militärs', p.92.
55 Depping, *Geschichte des Krieges der Münsterer und Cölner*, p.38.

THE PRINCE-BISHOPRIC OF MÜNSTER

100,000 *Reichsthaler*, requested as an advance on grants and any future subsidies, and with the request to transfer 2,000 infantry and 1,500 cavalry to French service.[56] In the same month, Galen pledged to provide a contingent of 4,000 infantrymen and 1,800 cavalry for a federal army to be formed by his allies of the Rhenish League, but the project did not succeed.[57]

It is difficult to establish the actual number of soldiers that the Prince-Bishop gathered for his second war against the Dutch Republic. Contemporary sources report that in April 1672 a total of 42,072 men on foot, and 17,928 on horseback, supported by 55 guns and 60 mortars, were gathered between Coesfeld and Meppen.[58] However, this figure is considered unlikely by most authoritative scholars.[59] According to them, in the spring of 1672 the infantry numbered 6,500 men in all. As for the cavalry, the total figure was 6,139 men.[60] Another estimate of the actual number of soldiers deployed in 1672 suggests a total of 20,196 men. This figure does not take into account artillery personnel, household units, and the approximately 4,000 men divided into 50 companies of the *Landesausschuss* (territorial militia). This figure is far from the most exaggerated reconstructions, but always a respectable armed force compared to other contemporary German armies.[61]

In 1672 the massive recruitment campaign led to the creation of at least 24 new infantry regiments, followed by a further 14 the following year. When the number of recruits was not sufficient, there was always some German prince who dismissed a part of his troops. In February 1672 Christoph Bernhard recruited half of the Duke of Mecklenburg's soldiers to complete his regiments,[62] and one year later he turned to the local *Wartschützen* (reservists) and the *Ausschuss* (militia) to replace the loss suffered on campaign.[63] The cavalry increase was no less impressive, with 16 regiments raised in 1672 and another in 1673. In the same period two regiments of dragoons were also formed. Once again, a variety of problems affected the recruitment of these units. On 1 February 1672 the *Rheingraf* Ludwig zu Salm again concluded a

---

56 Depping, *Geschichte des Krieges der Münsterer und Cölner*, p 42.

57 Tessin, 'Beiträge zur Formationsgeschichte des Münsterischen Militärs', p.91.

58 Depping, *Geschichte des Krieges der Münsterer und Cölner*, p.43. The author states this force was divided into 25 regiments and 20 battalions of infantry, and 19 regiments and nine autonomous squadrons of cavalry.

59 Tessin, 'Beiträge zur Formationsgeschichte des Münsterischen Militärs', p.95. Alpen lists most of the officers who served in 1672–74. From this uncertain information, in 1782 Ferdinand Fahle, a quartermaster of the Münster infantry Regiment *Stael*, reconstructed for 1672 an *Ordre de Bataille* comprising 17 infantry regiments, nine cavalry squadrons and two dragoon regiments. These figures contrast with the primary source, since according to Alpen, the infantry deployed 27 regiments and 40 battalions or 'half-regiments'.

60 Tessin, 'Beiträge zur Formationsgeschichte des Münsterischen Militärs', p.95. 'If the cavalry regiments Caldenbach, and Wolframsdorff and the Wolframsdorff *Dragoner* are counted as 4 companies each, the total strength would result in 94 companies. The capitulation of the *Rheingraf* regiment, for instance, resulted in only 55 cavalrymen per company, and with the *Primaplana*, the strength was 65 men with 80 horses. This figure also coincides with the only existing muster list of the *Reuss* cavalry regiment, in which only the *Leibkompanie* numbered 82 'heads', while the other seven companies had between 23 and 62 men. The total of 92 companies of 65 men each would bring the cavalry to a field force of 6,130 men.'

61 Depping, *Geschichte des Krieges der Münsterer und Cölner*, p.132.

62 Depping, *Geschichte des Krieges der Münsterer und Cölner*, p.130.

63 Zeigert, 'Die Artillerietruppe des Fürstbistums Münster 1655–1802', p.28.

new capitulation with the Prince-Bishop, in which he promised to recruit two infantry regiments with 16 companies of 75 men each, for 2,400 men in all. By the summer, however, just 700 and 200 men had been under arms, who were therefore joined into a single regiment. By August all the companies were garrisoned in Münster. On 27 February 1673, after the escape of the *Rheingraf*, only the *Leibkompanie* and five other companies quartered in Coesfeld declared their loyalty to the Prince-Bishop.[64]

The mighty army Galen had raised was, however, a colossus with feet of clay. After the dazzling successes in the first phase of the 1672 campaign, Münster's troops found themselves short of supplies due to concomitant factors, the first and foremost being the insufficient number of wagons hired from private civilian suppliers, which was inadequate to support the army on campaign. Among the other various problems that occurred, was that the width of the axles of the Münster wagons became a serious problem on Dutch roads, and caused the collapse of the supply system of the field army. Furthermore, since the officers could bring on campaign an indeterminate number of wagons, this resulted in a train of huge dimensions and an actual nightmare for Münster's army.[65]

The disastrous outcome of the campaigns in the Netherlands and Germany marks the turning point in Galen's military fortunes. The surrender of Bonn on 12 November 1673 forced the Prince-Bishop Elector of Cologne to agree a peace with the Allies, leaving Münster exposed to an invasion of the powerful Triple Alliance. Following the treaty signed at Cologne on 22 April 1674, which ended the war between Münster and the Dutch Republic, Christoph Bernhard broke the alliance with Louis XIV and committed to support the Emperor in the *Reichskrieg*. Galen promised to join the Allies with 8,000–9,000 men, but in early May a mass mutiny occurred. Most of the soldiers fled to the United Provinces or to Bremen, and only a small part could be joined to the Imperial army under *Feldmarschall* Jean-Louis Raduit de Souches; in late May the field army still numbered 4,629 horsemen and 930 dragoons,[66] and possibly 8,000–9,000 infantrymen. Though the mutiny caused the reduction of half of the regular force and the disbanding of many units, six regiments of cavalry and two of dragoon participated in the Alsace campaign of 1674–75 under Major General Hermann Lothar von Post, and after his death, under *Generalwachtmeister* Gustav Wilhem von Wedel by December 1674.[67] As far as the infantry was concerned, a portion of the dismissed soldiers entered the

---

64   Tessin, 'Beiträge zur Formationsgeschichte des Münsterischen Militärs', p.95. In December 1672, both the *Rheingraf* and the Count of Reuss abandoned the alliance with the Prince-Bishop and passed to the Emperor's side. The *Rheingraf zu Fuss* is last mentioned in March 1673 with four companies quartered in Menschede.

65   The same problem was encountered in 1666 by the French corps sent to support the Dutch Republic in the war against England and Münster.

66   Depping, *Geschichte des Krieges der Münsterer und Cölner*, pp.346–347. The author gives the number of soldiers for each regiment, but the total is wrong and therefore the sum of the individual units has been reported.

67   Tessin, 'Beiträge zur Formationsgeschichte des Münsterischen Militärs', p.99. Cavalry regiments *Nagel, Hautin, Macdonnel, Post, Westerholt, Offen*, and dragoon regiments *Nagel* and *Leibregiment*. Regiments *Hautin, Post, Offen* and *Westerholt* are mentioned for the last time in Alsace in autumn 1674.

THE PRINCE-BISHOPRIC OF MÜNSTER

Imperial service between May and July of 1674. In early summer the Prince-Bishop also sent a company of 150 men to Cologne as a contingent for the Westphalian Circle.[68]

In March 1675 Münster agreed to provide the Emperor with 9,000 auxiliary troops – 2,400 horsemen, 600 dragoons and 6,000 infantrymen – for the summer campaign. They were to swear an oath to Galen and be deployed only in the area between Trier, Koblenz, Höxter, Roermonde and Wenloo. However, the Emperor hesitated to ratify the contact since the Austrian treasury had no resources. Instead, on 12 October a treaty was concluded with Spain and the Dutch Republic for 1,000 horsemen, 2,500 infantrymen and 500 dragoons. The Prince-Bishop managed to increase his army, and it is estimated that in the winter of 1675–76 he still had 20,000 professional soldiers.[69] In September 1676, 3,000 soldiers were sent to guard the posts on the Meuse River. In the same month another 8,000 men marched into Bremen territory to face the Swedes. In addition, the newly raised infantry regiments *Lohaus* (MüI-71), with four companies, and *Janson* (MüI-71), joined the allied corps in Bremen but soon both were disbanded and distributed to other regiments.[70]

Other engagements came from neighbouring states of Germany. In the late summer of 1676, Major General Franz von Grandvillers entered East Frisia with a cavalry regiment and 1,000 infantrymen, to support Princess Christine Charlotte in the dispute with the estates of her state. Six other regiments were to follow him, for which not only rations but also engagement were required. However, with the contract of 18 September the Princess took 800 foot and 200 horse from Münster into permanent service.[71] The year after, Colonel Pölling and Major Reinhartz were with their soldiers in East Frisia, the latter quartered in Leer. After Pölling had been defeated by the citizens of Emden, and had himself become a prisoner, Colonel Kalckum arrived in East Frisia in October 1677 with nine infantry companies totalling about 1,000 men to support the Princess. Weeks later another 15 companies followed him.[72]

On 23 April 1677 a new contract was signed between Galen and the Spanish governor of the Low Countries. The *Vertrag* committed the Prince-Bishop to provide 2,000 infantry, 2,000 cavalry and 500 dragoons, to be employed in Flanders. The agreement was modified the following week by

---

68   Tessin, 'Beiträge zur Formationsgeschichte des Münsterischen Militärs', p.99. 'According to Alpen, the infantry regiments *Wedel, Mias, Schwartz, Rollingen* and *Pulling* entered the service of the Emperor. The regiment *Schwartz* may have been formed with the companies of the disbanded *Leibregiment*. Kotzfleisch, instead only mentions the four foot regiments *Wedel, Mias, Erden* and *Lymburg-Styrum*, of which the last two are otherwise never mentioned. Unfortunately, not even the Austrian *Kriegsarchiv* has such information about these troops, and then the matter remains unresolved.'

69   Tessin, 'Beiträge zur Formationsgeschichte des Münsterischen Militärs', p.100.

70   Tessin, 'Beiträge zur Formationsgeschichte des Münsterischen Militärs', p.100. 'Colonel Clauberg was to command a battalion of 350 foot formed with some companies from Wedel's corps, from the Sauerland to Pomerania to join the Brandenburg army against the Swedes. However, since in 1677 Clauburg was still the Lieutenant Colonel in the *Nitzow* regiment (MüI-28), this order was probably not carried out.'

71   Tessin, 'Beiträge zur Formationsgeschichte des Münsterischen Militärs', p.100.

72   Tessin, 'Beiträge zur Formationsgeschichte des Münsterischen Militärs', p.101.

249

raising the number of infantrymen to 3,000.[73] Further adjustments increased the contingent, since in August the muster registered 5,572 infantry, 2,364 cavalry and 574 dragoons.[74]

In the same period, the Prince-Bishop concluded an agreement with the King of Denmark to provide a corps of 4,200 men. The contingent was formed from troops previously quartered in East Frisia, including 600 men already in the service of Princess Christine Charlotte.[75] The corps also included 60 artillerymen. In June, under the orders of General Grandvillers, the soldiers joined the Danish army in Scania which was preparing to besiege Malmö. Six infantry battalions and three cavalry squadrons participated at the Battle of Landskrona on 16 July 1677; the cavalry regiment also participated in the cavalry ride to Christianstadt. The following year, the contingent of Münster participated in the unsuccessful invasion of Rügen, where it was taken prisoner by the Swedes on 9 January 1678. To replace this contingent, Galen sent to Denmark a new corps of 6,092 men under General Wedel by means of the new contract of 3 April 1678. In July, the new contingent was taken over in Ottensten by the Danish commissioners. This included 1,780 horsemen and 469 dragoons, which together with 3,720 infantry totalled 5,969 men.[76]

The trade of soldiers did not stop even when the already formed units were no longer available. In the winter of 1677–78, three new cavalry regiments with six companies each were to be recruited for Spain in the Rhineland and Liège through colonels appointed by Galen. However, only a small part of this recruitment took place. Lion, one of the newly appointed colonels, was assassinated in Aachen in January 1678, and the licence was transferred to Colonel Tserclas von Tilly and Lieutenant Colonel Manderscheid. The latter managed to gather five companies. However, the recruitment campaign must have encountered several problems, considering that until January 1678 Colonel Floris (MüC-37) had only recruited 200 men in the Rhineland. These horsemen were probably later divided among the other regiments when this unit was disbanded in the spring of 1678. Even worse was the result of Colonel Georg von der Nath, who recruited only 20 men because Liège suspended the patent. The corps in the Spanish Low Countries had suffered severely from bad treatment, and the cavalry so much that, in Wedel's opinion, some regiments needed to be recruited again.[77] In the summer of 1678, the cavalry regiments *Bönninghausen* (MüC-18), *Mortaigne* (MüC-35, former *Leibregiment*), which had returned from

---

73 Tessin, 'Beiträge zur Formationsgeschichte des Münsterischen Militärs', p.101.
74 Tessin, 'Beiträge zur Formationsgeschichte des Münsterischen Militärs', p.101.
75 Tessin, 'Beiträge zur Formationsgeschichte des Münsterischen Militärs', p.102. On 20 May 1679, the infantry regiments *Schwartz* (MüI-64), *Frankenstein* (MüI-74), and *Gogreve* (MüI-28) returned to Münster with 624, 430 and 591 men respectively. They had lost 332, 108 and 179 men. With them also returned the dragoons, in unspecified numbers.
76 Tessin, 'Beiträge zur Formationsgeschichte des Münsterischen Militärs', p.102.
77 Tessin, 'Beiträge zur Formationsgeschichte des Münsterischen Militärs', p.102. Regiment *Mandelslohe* (MüC-36) was then disbanded in January 1678. Instead, using rank and file who escaped capture at Rügen, nine companies were raised. Together with two companies transferred from existing units, the new cavalry regiments *Bassem* (MüC-39) and *Rabe* (MüC-40) were formed. Furthermore, by dividing the *Wedel* (MüC-26) regiment, consisting of 12 companies, another cavalry regiment – *Wendt* (MüC-41) – was raised, and with recruits and

THE PRINCE-BISHOPRIC OF MÜNSTER

Denmark, and *Tserclas* (MüC-36), together with the infantry regiments *Eltz* (MüI-52), *Jung Elverfeldt* (MüI-67), *Otthons* (MüI-53), *Körberin* (MüI-75) and *Kalckum* (MüI-37) joined the allied army on the Moselle. This corps was later joined by the *Brun* battalion. In September between Maas and Rhein there were 1,193 cavalry divided into three regiments with 17 companies of unequal strength, 104 partly dismounted dragoons (regiment *Rose*, MüD-37), and 3,093 infantry divided into six regiments and one battalion, with 56 companies in all.

In the winter of 1677–78, the first rational army reform took place, whereby an attempt was made to bring more order to the composition of the regiments and companies. All cavalry regiments were to be increased to 12 companies, and the *Wedel* regiment (MüC-26) was even to deploy 18 companies, but the goal was not achieved.

The Twilight of an Armed State

On 16 September 1678, Christoph Bernhard died. As far as many subjects and neighbours were concerned, the Prince-Bishop's death ended 'a dangerous reign of terror',[78] and decisively changed the military policy of Münster. After the failure of the assignments in the Westphalian Circle to quarter 25,000 foot and horse, the newly elected Prince-Bishop Ferdinand von Fürstenberg, after examining the army's financial burden, decided upon a drastic reduction in military strength; during the winter 1678–79, most of the regiments were disbanded. The Prince-Bishop retained the *Garde zu Pferde* with 88 horse under Colonel Shade, 3,532 infantry, 525 cavalry, and 225 dragoons.[79] It was still a respectable peace establishment which, however, did not allow the continuation of an aggressive foreign policy, at least as it had been until then. Even under the next ruler, Maximilian Heinrich von Wittelsbach, already Prince-Bishop Elector of Cologne, the 'Military' of Münster occupied a secondary position. More or less unexpectedly, the army returned to play a role during the Ottoman offensive of 1683. Maximilian Heinrich adhered to the German princes' initiative to support the Emperor, and in the summer of 1683 gathered a *Hilfskorps* of 6,639 men. The contingent comprised troops of Cologne and Paderborn. Münster contributed with 1,475 infantrymen of the regiment *Schwartz* (MüI-64), and 465 dragoons of the regiment *Hoetensleben* (MüD-2).[80] Before the end of the year, Maximilian Heinrich ordered the raising of three further infantry battalions in Münster, but the project failed due to a shortage of funds. The corps arrived in Austria a few weeks after the

---

some privates from the *Hoetensleben Dragoner* (MüD-2), the squadron – later regiment – *Rose* (MüD-5) entered the Spanish service.

78 Joachim Whaley, *Germany and the Holy Roman Empire*, p.38.

79 Tessin, 'Beiträge zur Formationsgeschichte des Münsterischen Militärs', pp.103–104. There is no certain information concerning the artillery, however, according to Zeigert, 'Die Artillerietruppe des Fürstbistums Münster 1655–1802', p.27, in 1680, there are still registered in the garrisons 936 artillerymen and 744 men of the auxiliary companies serving within the artillery corps.

80 Tessin, 'Beiträge zur Formationsgeschichte des Münsterischen Militärs', p.104.

251

Battle of Vienna and later took part in the campaigns in Hungary until 1689, but it left little information about an active role on the field.

Print dating to the 1670s, depicting the Prince-Bishop Bernhard von Galen and his troops. (Author's Collection) On the left, the *Leibgarde* of the Prince-Bishop is dressed like the French *Mousquetaires* of the *Maison du Roi*, but with a St Andrew cross on the tabard. Thanks to a report about a friendly fire skirmish between Dutch troops, some details of the uniform of the Münster *Leibgarde* are known. It happened that in summer 1673, the Prince Johan Maurits' Frisian Life Guard Company of Horse was targeted by some Dutch horsemen because they had mistaken them for the Prince-Bishop's Guards, who also had red coat with blue facings. (Thanks to Edwin Groot for this notice)

The Prince-Bishop Goes to War

After the submission of Münster in 1660, Bernhard von Galen did not interrupt his aggressive policy and in 1663 came into conflict with neighbouring East Friesland. The matter of dispute was the contested sovereignty over the territories beyond the River Ems, and a debt that Prince Georg Christian had not yet paid. In December, 800–900 infantrymen left Münster and marched into East Friesland.[81] The Prince-Bishop could formally justify his action, since Emperor Leopold I had authorised him to collect the money by armed force, if necessary. The East Friesland militiamen who manned the fort surrendered after the first cannon shot on 18 December, and soon the Prince-Bishop's troops began to collect money and billets from the inhabitants of the region. In The Hague this act sounded like an open challenge, because after seizing the redoubts of Dijlerschans, Galen's troops controlled the navigation on the

---

81 See Mugnai, *Wars and Soldiers*, vol. 1, pp.103–105.

THE PRINCE-BISHOPRIC OF MÜNSTER

River Ems and posed a direct threat to the Dutch territories of Westervwolde on the eastern border of the provinces of Drenthe and Groningen, as well as the Dutch garrisons in Leerort and Emden. The conquest of the Dijlerschans redoubts caused great clamour in the neighbouring provinces of Friesland and Groningen, which asked for a resolute reaction. The Dutch Republic considered it unlikely that Galen would receive assistance from Vienna and the German princes, because currently they had to face the Ottomans in Hungary. The scenario was then auspicious for undertaking a medium-sized expedition with a limited military force. As a result, on 26 December the States General of The United Provinces of the Netherlands voted to raise a field army to expel the Münster troops from East Friesland;[82] on 30 December the Dutch began to gather troops while waiting for the season to allow their use on the field. The Dutch Council of State estimated that 5,000 men would be enough to expel the Münster troops from the Dijlerschans, and on 6 May

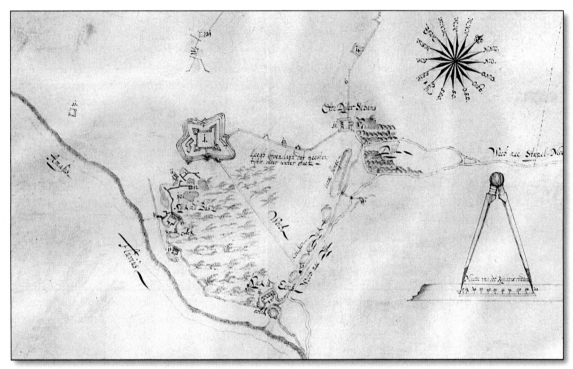

The Dijlerschans area in the 'Account of the siege of Dijler entrenchment. Received on 20 May, expired on 6 June 1664'. (Collection of the Groninger Archieven) About 400 Münster infantry with artillery manned the redoubts, which began an artillery duel which lasted three days. On 28 May two of von Galen's deputies were received in the Dutch encampment, claiming they had been sent by the Prince-Bishop to find a friendly settlement. The Dutch commander, Willem Frederik of Nassau-Dietz agreed to a three-day truce, but the negotiations led to nothing. The Dutch ended the ceasefire and the artillery fire recommenced on 1 June. After three days, the fortifications had been transformed into a ruin and then the defenders offered to surrender. Willem Frederik permitted the garrison to withdraw to Meppen and the evacuation took place two days later. The garrison numbered more than 300 men, including 80 sick and wounded, but the casualties of the Münster soldiers remain unknown, as well as the losses on the Dutch side.

---

82 Nimwegen, *The Dutch Army*, p.411. As a justification for this military operation, the Republic would first lend 135,000 rix-dollars to Prince Georg Christian, so that he could repay the first instalment of his debt.

the Dutch corps marched through Bentheim to the River Ems, and after a week of delay due to supply problems, arrived before the Dijlerschans on 20 May. On 25 May, without offering a surrender, the Dutch battery opened fire, and the Münster troops surrendered on 4 June. The invasion had ended in defeat for the Prince-Bishop, and this exacerbated his resentment against the Dutch Republic.

Münster in the Anglo-Dutch War (1665–66)

In the wake of the English naval victory at Lowestoft on 13 June 1665, Bernhard von Galen felt the time was propitious to launch his own assault on the Dutch Republic. On the same day, Charles II of England and the Prince-Bishop had signed an alliance with which the King promised to pay the first rate of the subsidy as soon as the Münster troops had captured a harbour in the estuary of the River Ems. Münster's plan aimed to seize control of Greersiel in East Friesland and to join the English landing force between Emden and Delfzijl; or alternatively to invade Overijssel with a strong corps and then cross the River Ijssel, in order to establish winter quarters in the region of Weluwe, hoping to take some fortified town to secure its position. The troops at the Republic's disposal were numerically far inferior to their enemy's, however, the Dutch senior commanders did not envisage that the Prince-Bishop could lay siege to one of the towns along the River Ijssel. They had always assumed that Galen would vent his rage against the Republic by launching predatory raids into the Achterhoek and Twente, Drenthe and Groningen. While they would have to thwart the enemy's marauding raids as best they could, The Hague had to wait until the army was complete, the French auxiliary corps had arrived, and the fleet had returned to port. These forces, with the allies from Lüneburg and Osnabrück, would then counter the enemy offensive and recapture the lost territories.

At the end of the summer, Münster's imminent offensive towards the River Ijssel became evident; on 20 September the Prince-Bishop demanded the immediate restitution of Borculo. He did not await a response to the ultimatum, and the following day about 20,000 men under the Scottish soldier-of-fortune and *Generalwachtmeister* John George Gorgas marched into Twente.[83] At this date, the Dutch field commander-in-chief Johan Maurits of Nassau-Siegen reportedly dispersed along the frontier about 15,000 infantry and 1,600 cavalry, but these figures were on paper, since the musters reported that the actual force was only 12,800 effectives, and just 1,250 foot with 1,500 horse could be assembled to form a field corps.[84] Gorgas had divided the army into two columns to deceive the enemy. The main corps entered enemy territory from Gronau, while 5,000 foot and 2,000 horse headed towards the villages of Walchum, Dersum and Heede and crossed the moor to Sellingen after making a wide arc. On 25 September 1665, Münster troops appeared before

---

83   Verspohl, *Das Heerwesen die Münsterischen Fürstbischofs Christoph Bernard von Galen*, p.135.
84   Nimwegen, *The Dutch Army*, p.410.

THE PRINCE-BISHOPRIC OF MÜNSTER

Borculo; the Dutch garrison surrendered after only one day and claimed the loss of 100 dead and wounded due to the heavy bombardment of enemy siege artillery, whose size was impressive.[85] Following the Continental practice, Gorgas was careful not to bypass any fortified stronghold. After Borculo, the Achterhoek towns of Lochem, Lichtenworde, Doetinchem, Keppel and Ulft also surrendered, and in Twente the towns of Oldenzaal, Enschede, Almelo, Ootmarsum Winschoten and Dieppenheim were also lost. The road for the complete conquest of Overijssell was open. The Münster offensive had achieved unexpected results which dismayed the States General: the only success achieved by the Dutch was managing to protect the towns along the River Ijssel. General Gorgas had wanted to take Doesburg or Arnhem by surprise, but Johan Maurits prevented this with his small force. A formal siege was equally impossible, because the heavy rain had left the roads in such a miserable state that the Münster troops had been forced to leave behind their siege artillery.[86] By October Galen's troops suffered greatly from the persistent rainy weather: the roads were impassable, the ground had turned into a swamp and the cold season was approaching. Maintaining the position became impossible.[87]

A war council was convened with the presence of the Prince-Bishop. It was decided to move the offensive northwards, and above all to take Burtange before the upcoming winter. If this fortress fell, the provinces of Friesland and Groningen were available as coveted quartering areas. Based on this consideration, the army was divided again: General d'Ossery, another Scotsman, marched in the direction of the Frisian provinces, while Gorgas entered the province of Groningen, where he entrenched the troops between Winschoten, Westerwolde and Wedde and awaited further orders from the Prince-Bishop. D'Ossery moved via Ootmarsum through the Bentheim county to the

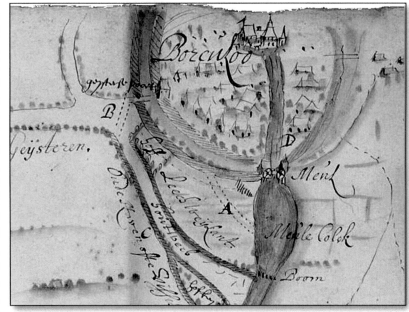

The town of Borculo from a Dutch map of 1642. (Collection of the Gelderarchief) The possession of the town was long disputed by Christoph Bernhard von Galen and in 1665 was used as *casus belli* with the Dutch Republic.

---

85 Verspohl, *Das Heerwesen die Münsterischen Fürstbischofs Christoph Bernard von Galen*, p.138.
86 Verspohl, *Das Heerwesen die Münsterischen Fürstbischofs Christoph Bernard von Galen*, p.139.
87 Various authors, 'Die Geschichte des Emslandes im Rahmen der Allgemeinen Deutschen Geschichte: 2. Der erste Holländische Krieg 1665–1666' in *Emlandsbuch 1928 – Ein Heimatbuch für die Kreise Weppen, Aschendorf, Kümmling* (Osnabrück, 1928), p.6.

Ems where he established the headquarters. The instructions received were to unite with Gorgas, who was still in front of the Bourtange fortress.[88] Here the operations were looking bad for Münster's troops: incessant rains had flooded the area around Bourtange, making a regular siege impossible. Attempts to gain a bridgehead on the northern side had also failed. Gorgas had tried to cross the swamp to reach Jipsinghuizen, where he hoped to hold that position with the troops that were still marching to join his corps; however, when the Dutch discovered the plan they immediately met the enemy, and after a hard fight rejected them back over the dyke they had started to build between Dersum and Sellingen.[89] On 12 October the rain lessened, allowing some 8,000 men to resume their advance towards the north, heading for the Dutch post of Rouveen. The small garrison took to its heels almost immediately. Now Hasselt and Zwartsluis could be invested. Gorgas hoped that the assault on Rouveen was only intended as a feint to draw the Dutch field corps away from Dieren. For this he had left 3,800 men behind in the Achterhoek under d'Ossery, so that he would be able to assemble the main army along the Ijssel, but Johan Maurits had envisaged the enemy plan and resolutely maintained the position. The conquest of Rouveen was the turning point of the campaign. Instead of laying siege to Hasselt, or heading towards the Ijssel line, the Münster army marched onward into the province of Groningen.

The move was obligatory, since the logistical system was collapsing. Food shortages and bad weather were causing illness and desertion. When 1,000 horses had become unserviceable for lack of fodder, General d'Ossery had to leave the Achterhoek to join Gorgas, but from the information he received, every direction appeared uncertain. East Friesland was well manned by Dutch

The fort of Bourtange in 1657, after Matthäus Merian the Younger. (Author's Collection) Located in the North-East of The United Provinces, Bourtange guarded the only road through the swamps into Germany.

---

88   Verspohl, *Das Heerwesen die Münsterischen Fürstbischofs Christoph Bernard von Galen*, p.140.

89   Various authors, 'Die Geschichte des Emslandes', p.8. Local chronicles report that the attack took the guards by surprise as they sat trembling beside the fire. A brave Dutch lieutenant with 100 soldiers went as far as the Moor dam, setting fire with tar to the bridge connecting the two banks and thus 'did the country a great service'. The chronicles also report that the victory was celebrated by the Dutch with floods of beer that put the troops out of action for days afterwards.

garrisons and the roads blocked, forcing d'Ossery into a difficult and tiring march to the north, and taking the quarter between Wedde and the fortified Winschoten. From here, he could move to protect the march of Gorgas in case the Dutch had left Dieren unprotected, but the road to this fortress was hindered by the enemy presence at Ter Apel, and by the rain that had started again incessantly and copiously. Soon the terrain turned in a swamp; the wagons sank in the mud, and supplies were getting scarcer by the day. At the end of October, escorted by his horse Life Guard, Galen took quarters near the village of Heede in order to have a direct knowledge of development of the campaign. The situation seemed without remedy, but Galen was not a man to be put down easily. He ordered the construction of a bridge across the marsh: *Inter Heedam pagum Emslandiae et Apeliam er adversa ripa.*[90] The 'bridge', in fact a pontoon, had to cover about 1.5 German miles (2.4km). With the utmost urgency, soldiers and peasants from the villages on the left bank of the Ems worked on the project. D'Ossery on the north side, and Gorgas on the south had to contribute to the work; in the meantime, supplies were delivered by horses and mules only. Fascines of brushwood, bushes and cane were brought in. With the enemy unable to prevent it, houses in Dutch territory were demolished and timber, beams, planks, staves, and all available wood was removed.[91] Huge masses of earth and sand were poured into the marsh. Branches and whole trees were thrown over it, while beams and poles were driven into the ground on either side of the pontoon. The farmers from the nearby villages of Walchum and Dersum had to deliver their house doors because these were to be used as the upper layer of the artificial road over the swamp.

Meanwhile, the strategic situation was becoming critical for Münster's army. On 4 November, reports indicated that the French auxiliary corps was marching across Dutch territory, heading to the River Ems, and troops from Brunswick-Lüneburg and Osnabrück were gathering near to Münster's border. For their part the Dutch also reacted, and with their artillery targeted the pontoon and the nearby worksites. During one of these bombardments a shell passed through the high ground behind which the Prince-Bishop was dining and grazed him, knocking the dish out of his hand.[92] However, despite all the difficulties the huge pontoon, soon named *Bischoffsdamm*, was completed so that the marsh became passable for men and horses; by mid-November, to everyone's amazement, the troops were able to escape across the moorland into safe territory. The infantry marched in front, followed by the baggage together with 1,000 Frisian oxen as spoils of war; the cavalry closed the column in the rearguard. D'Ossery, with about 2,000 men, manned Winschoten, while the rest of the exhausted troops took winter quarters in Meppen alongside the general staff, leaving some detachments to guard the outposts and garrison the conquered cities in enemy territory. This decision was not a wise one, as it left d'Ossery and his men in a trap.

---

90   Alpen, *Decadis de Vita et Rebus Gestis Christophori Bernardi*, vol. I, p.266.
91   Various authors, 'Die Geschichte des Emslandes', p.9.
92   Various authors, 'Die Geschichte des Emslandes', p.9.

Dutch broadsheet dated 1666 containing a satirical sonnet about the army of the Prince-Bishop of Münster. (Author's Collection) Note the infantry with musketeers and pikemen in decidedly unfashionable clothing, but probably alluding to the poor appearance of the enemy troops on campaign.

The departure of the Münster army gave the Republic some breathing space to prepare the next campaign. The arrival of the French corps near Maastricht on 10 November came as a boost. Johan Maurits sent the cavalry to approach Winschoten, blocking the enemy inside; as soon as the 6,000 Frenchmen had joined the Dutch troops along the Ijssel, Maurits hoped to launch a counter-offensive with the aim of dislodging the enemy from Twente and the Achterhoek. Then, in conjunction with the German troops from Brunswick and Osnabrück, he wanted to move the war into the Prince-Bishopric of Münster itself. Until then, he sought to inflict as much damage as possible on the enemy troops with small-scale operations.[93] Unfortunately for him, supply problems and other drawbacks delayed the plan,[94] but The Hague refused to endorse suspending the struggle against Münster. The Dutch fleet had returned to port and supply had been gathered for the winter campaign, and the Grand-Pensionary Johan De Witt also insisted that the counter-offensive should be executed. The plan was to recapture Lochem and seize Bocholt in enemy territory; on 7 December the Dutch–French headed to Lochem, which surrendered after a four-day siege, but the operation to seize Bocholt had to be abandoned, because the wet ground reduced the speed of the artillery train, as experienced by the enemy months before. Bocholt would therefore have to be taken by surprise, but the approaching Dutch–French troops were discovered and the 800-man garrison could face the threat with readiness.[95] Between December and January the Dutch command submitted a plan to assault the Münster fortresses on the River Ems with the German auxiliaries from Brunswick and Osnabrück, alongside the Dutch corps under Johan Maurits. In the meantime, the Allies achieved a success with the surrender of the starving garrison of Winschoten, which agreed to suspend resistance in exchange for free evacuation, but many soldiers deserted and entered the Dutch army.

---

93 Nimwegen, *The Dutch Army*, p.422.
94 See also Mugnai, *Wars and Soldiers*, vol. I, pp.105–111.
95 Verspohl, *Das Heerwesen die Münsterischen Fürstbischofs Christoph Bernard von Galen*, p.144.

THE PRINCE-BISHOPRIC OF MÜNSTER

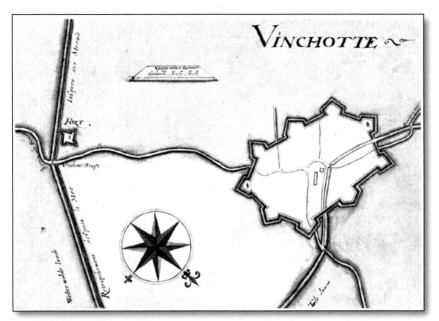

The fort of Winschoten on a Dutch map of the late seventeenth century. After the shelling of the Dutch entrenchments, part of the Münster troops established its headquarters in the fort of Winschoten. The command was entrusted to the Count of Ossery. From here he could control the whole of the Oldambt and the Westerwolde, but when Maurice of Nassau marched with his troops to the River Ems, the Prince-Bishop's troops had already suffered greatly from the climate, poor supply and disease. By mid-November 1665, with the exception of Winschoten, the region was nominally in the hands of the Dutch. The unsuccessful outcome of the campaign and the threatening presence of the coalition forces on the borders of his state convinced the Prince-Bishop to end the war and to sign the Peace of Cleves in April 1666.

In February the States General signed an alliance with Brandenburg, but the Prince-Elector Friedrich Wilhelm would first try to persuade Galen to agree a diplomatic solution; only if he declined would 7,000 Brandenburg troops immediately be made available to the Republic.[96] The Prince-Bishop's acceptance of the Great Elector's mediation meant that there was no need for the Brandenburg troops to take action. The situation was becoming unfavourable for the Prince-Bishop because the aid promised by England was not arriving to the agreed extent, and on 18 April 1666 Münster and the Dutch Republic concluded the Peace of Cleves. Bernhard von Galen renounced the 'territorial right' to Borculo, even though the seigniory formally remained a fief of Münster.

---

96 Nimwegen, *The Dutch Army*, p.424.

WARS AND SOLDIERS IN THE EARLY REIGN OF LOUIS XIV – VOLUME 7 PART 1

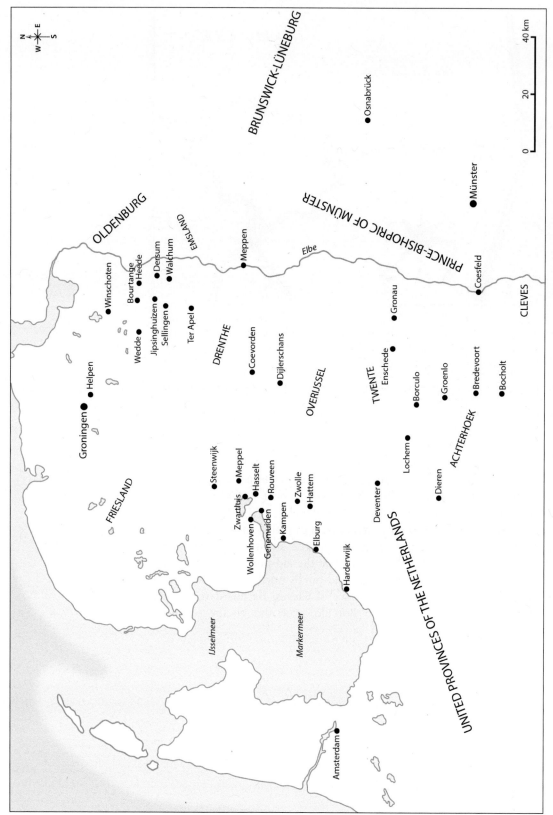

Theatre of the Operations in Overijssel, Friesland, Drenthe and Groningen (1665–66 and 1672–73)

The Münster's Franco-Dutch War, or 'the War on Both Sides' (1672–1678)

The war of 1665–66 had ended with nothing for the Prince-Bishop, but the dispute with the Dutch Republic remained open, waiting for a new opportunity to claim the balance. On 18 May 1672, the day after the beginning of the French invasion of the Republic, the Prince-Bishop published an edict which was read in all churches and posted in all cities, denouncing – in 27 chapters – the hostile actions of the Dutch. Chapter 5 stated that agents provocateurs sent by the Republic had been discovered in the bishopric, 'trying to bribe soldiers and officers with large sums of money'. The document added that the same provocateurs had tried to set fire to magazines and arsenals and raise a rebellion in the towns and fortresses, and that both would pass into the hands of the States General, while 'the troops, released from their oath of loyalty to the Prince-Bishop, would be merged into the army of the United Provinces'.[97] The Prince-Bishop also accused the Dutch of an attempt on his life, since 'the vice of murder, abhorred even by the Turks and barbarians' had induced them to try to kill him in the monastery of Kreuzherren.[98] Months earlier, tension between Galen and The Hague had arisen following disputes between their respective peasants over the use of grasslands on the frontier between Meppen and Westerwolde, but now the dispute had increased to an unbearable extent.[99]

As serious as Galen's charges were, the Prince-Bishop had already exploited French subsidies to raise the field army that on 28 May marched into Dutch territory alongside the troops of Electoral Cologne. About 20,000 Münster soldiers and 10,000 of Cologne under the new field commander, *Generalleutnant* Charles de Siffredy de Mornas, entered the province of Overijssel unopposed. With them, *Maréchal* François Henri de Montmorency-Bouteville, better known as Duke of Piney-Luxembourg, was added as an adviser by Louis XIV, and the cavalry vanguard advanced in the Twente region to cover the march of the main army. After the lesson learned in 1665, the campaign had begun in the dry season so the Prince-Bishop's siege artillery could deploy all its power. In a few days Borculo, Almelo, Enschede, and Ootmarsum opened their gates after a very little resistance.[100] On 9 June Groenlo also surrendered, and a few days later a small detachment seized the forts of Bredevoort. While the main army was marching to Deventer, two corps were detached to seize the Dutch forts in the Veluwe, and those along the River Ijssel. The first task was entrusted to general Christoph Bernhard

---

97 Various authors, 'Die Geschichte des Emslandes', p.13.

98 True or false, the accusation against the Dutch Republic was another attempt to eliminate the Prince-Bishop, since in February 1673 Imperial agents unsuccessfully tried to assassinate him. See Wilson, *German Armies*, p.46.

99 'Der Zweite Holländische Krieg. 1672–1674', p.13. The Dutch soldiers had threatened the peasants of Münster that if they found them on those grasslands again they would capture them, and even threaten them with death. The soldiers had also burnt a bridge over the swamp that the Prince-Bishop had built two years earlier.

100 Depping, *Geschichte des Krieges der Münsterer und Cölner*, p.76.

von Nagel and the second to general Hautin, who in rapid succession seized Hattem, Elburg, Harderwijk and other minor places; meanwhile, Deventer surrendered on 21 June. The siege artillery of Münster played a major role again, since the bombardment had such a paralysing effect on the citizens that they forced the garrison to deliver the city.[101] Days later Lochem and Kampen also came under the control of the Münster and Cologne army. The campaign continued with the conquest of Zwolle, Hasselt, Wollenhoven, Steenwijk, Meppel, Genemuiden, and Zwartsluis, and Rouveen surrendered without resistance between 22 and 24 June.[102]

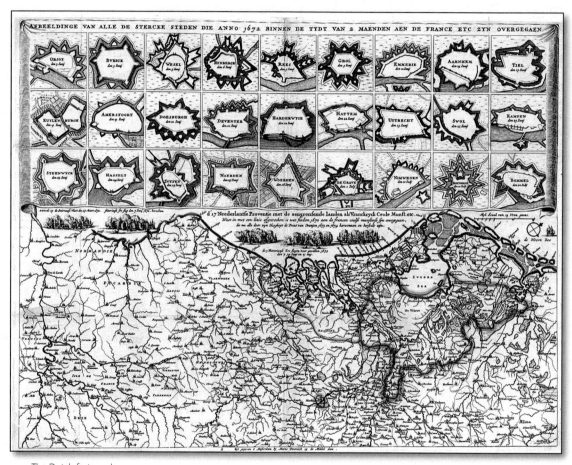

The Dutch forts and towns lost in 1672 in a contemporary print by Marcus Willemsz Doornick. (Rijksmuseum Amsterdam) The list is not complete, since much of the forts taken by Münster and Cologne have been omitted, and only Deventer, Hasselt, Harderwijk, Kampen, Stenwick and Hattem are mentioned as major conquests.

What appeared to be a triumphal march was overshadowed by the disagreements between Bernhard von Galen and his adviser Luxembourg. Already during the siege of Deventer, the intransigent temperament of the Prince-Bishop had caused such a serious quarrel with the General and the Prince-Bishop Elector of Cologne, that it was only thanks to the efforts of the minister of Cologne, Wilhelm Egon von Fürftenberg, that the campaign could continue. The divisions with Luxembourg concerned the division of

---

101 Various authors, 'Die Geschichte des Emslandes', p.14.
102 Depping, *Geschichte des Krieges der Münsterer und Cölner*, p.77.

conquered territories. In the end, an agreement was reached assigning all the lands between the Rhine, the Meuse and the Ijffel to France; Cologne received Rheinberg and Deventer; while to Christoph Bernhard went Groenlo, Breedevoort, Borculo and all present and future acquisitions in the provinces of Overijssel, Friesland and Groningen. Zwolle was to be ruled jointly by Münster and Cologne.[103]

In the meantime, another operation took place north of the Emsland, entrusted to the Münster militia under the orders of Chief War Commissioner Johann Heinrich von Martels. The chronicles of the Franco-Dutch War avoid this secondary campaign, which was nevertheless of some importance for the Dutch Republic, as it succeeded in retaining the fortress of Bourtange. Despite Martels occupying the Dijler's trenches and conquering the field fortifications that guarded access from the Dutch Republic into East Friesland, Bourtange was besieged in vain by his militiamen supported by the peasants of the Emsland. Due to lack of artillery, Martels only managed to block Bourtange on the north-western side.[104]

By late June, Luxembourg had been replaced by the more compliant Marquise of Renel, but differences also emerged in the conduct of the campaign. Cologne's Prince-Bishop Elector Maximilian Heinrich aimed to consolidate the conquests around Deventer and Zwolle, while Bernhard von Galen insisted on a further advance into Friesland and Groningen. The easy and unexpected conquests had outdated the original plans, and now the continuation of the campaign showed up the Allies' conflicting strategies. Moreover, the need to garrison the conquered fortresses and towns had reduced the army by half.

Galen managed to persuade his reluctant ally to continue in the direction of the sea, to meet the English fleet and conquer the entire province of Groningen. However, a prerequisite for an attack on the capital was the conquest of the fortress of Coevorden in Drenthe. The operation on the field did not encounter enemy opposition, since in Utrecht and Holland the situation was even worse. On 4 July the Prince-Bishop's soldiers opened the trenches before Coevorden, and two days later, 20 mortars shelled the fortifications with a tempest of fire.[105] The devastating bombardment employed incendiary bombs, grenades and the infamous projectiles that threw fire and lead, and spread a disgusting smell.[106] On 7 July the artillery opened a breach in the curtain and two days later one of the gates was destroyed. Soon the Münster and Cologne infantrymen stormed the outer edge of the bastion, which came under their control on 10 July; the day after the garrison of Coevorden surrendered. On 19 July a war council was convened to discuss the next operation. The Allies agreed to continue the offensive towards the sea, and on 21 July entered the province of Groningen. Here, Bernhard von Galen ordered contributions to be extorted from the countryside as compensation for the war expenses sustained until then.

---

103 Kohl, *Christoph Bernhard von Galen*, p.403.
104 Various authors, 'Die Geschichte des Emslandes', p.14.
105 Depping, *Geschichte des Krieges der Münsterer und Cölner*, p.79.
106 Various authors, 'Die Geschichte des Emslandes', p.14.

Days before, the Münster cavalry under general Nagel had approached the city with 3,000–4,000 horsemen for a reconnaissance and engaged a small corps of enemy cavalry near the village of Helpen.[107] On 24 July, the field army arrived before Groningen. As usual, the information varies regarding the number of troops. According to the Dutch commander's esteem, they consisted of 13,000–14,000 men in all;[108] instead, the German sources state that the two bishops still had 24,000 men.[109]

The besieging army laid its camp between the Schuitendiep and Hoornsche; the troops of Cologne on the left side and those of Münster on the right. The city of Groningen had a simple curtain with 17 bastions and a wide and deep ditch filled with water. There were no noteworthy external works, but the fortifications appeared to be in good condition because they had received continuous improvements and maintenance. Inside Groningen, 3,000 regular troops and 2,200 militiamen formed the garrison; a large quantity of weapons and ammunition was stored in the city's arsenal.[110] The attempt to surround the city failed due to lack of troops, so the Allies

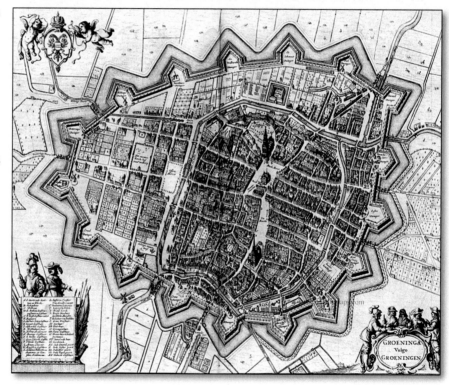

Groningen, from Johannes Janssonius' *Theatrum Urbium Celebriorum Totius Belgii sive Germaniae Inferioris* (Amsterdam, 1657). On 11 July 1672, the strong fortress of Coevorden surrendered after a six days siege. Suddenly, the campaign encountered its first serious obstacle on 18 July, before Groningen, where the military fortunes of Cologne and Münster turned into a painful retreat.

107 Depping, *Geschichte des Krieges der Münsterer und Cölner*, p.79.
108 W. J. Koop, *Krijgs- en Geschiedkundige Beschouwingen over Willem den Derde* (The Hague, 1895), vol. I, p.113.
109 Depping, *Geschichte des Krieges der Münsterer und Cölner*, p.107.
110 W. J. Koop, *Krijgs- en Geschiedkundige Beschouwingen over Willem den Derde*, p.113. The strength of the Groningen garrison is not clear. Estimates range from 1,200 to 2,000 regular forces. Renel reports that after the arrival of 19 new companies from Holland, in Groningen 3,000 regular troops were available. These were 23 or 24 companies of infantry, four companies of cavalry and three companies of dragoons. To them can be added the militia with 18 companies, plus four new companies of citizens and a company of 150 male students. Knoop estimates the total

THE PRINCE-BISHOPRIC OF MÜNSTER

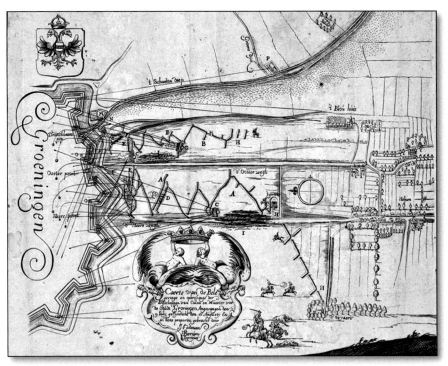

A map of the southern walls of Groningen, made after the siege of 1672, showing the Münster and Cologne trenches and approaches. After the siege and the heavy bombardment of the city, the Prince-Bishop received the nickname *Bommen Berend* (Bombing Bernard). A holiday with this name is still celebrated in the city of Groningen on 28 August to commemorate the breaking of the siege.

A print by Jan Luyken depicting Catholic friars serving as artillerymen during the Siege of Groningen (Author's archive). Differences in the religious faith were turned to matters of propaganda during the Franco-Dutch War; the enemies of the Republic all belonging to the Catholic Church.

number of defenders at 4,000–5000. The stores were well filled and the supply lines were open (thanks to Edwin Groot for this notice).

concentrated the siege on the southern side. The approach trenches were dug before the bastions of Drenkelaars, Oosterport and Heereport, and advanced towards the curtain between the first and second bastions and that between the second and third. This was a forced choice, as the defenders had flooded

In the City Hall of Groningen are two paintings that depict the siege of 1672. The first, entitled *Beleg van Groningen in 1672*, was painted in 1686 by Folkert Bock (1632–1696). The work was commissioned by the city council to capture the already fading memory of that episode for posterity. The details of the city and the landscape are accurately reproduced and it is highly likely that for the preparation of the painting, Bock consulted eyewitnesses to depict the besieging army. Although the Münster soldiers appear conventionally dressed, some details seem quite accurate. The waist scarves of the officers, and some non-commissioned officers, are red, as indeed were the ones that identified the Prince-Bishop's soldiers in the previous decade. In the foreground a commander on horseback is shown talking to some officers, and in the lower left some women are taking care of the wounded. Infantry also appear, wearing brown or grey coats. According to Theodor Werspohl, in 'Das Heerwesen des Münsterschen Fürstbischofs Christoph Bernhard von Galen 1650–1678', brown coats were also worn by the Münster *Ausschuss* (militia).
The second oil painting preserved in Groningen is probably a preliminary study for the previous painting. Here, further interesting details concerning the uniforms of the Münster soldiers are reproduced with some accuracy. Three cavalry are playing dice on a kettledrum; the one depicted from behind with wide cross belts is wearing a dark blue coat with red cuffs, to his right another cavalryman is dressed in brown with a pale ochre hat, while on the left, there is, perhaps, a dragoon dressed in yellow with a red cloth cap trimmed in brown fur. On the opposite side of the painting, other cavalrymen are wearing grey or brown coats of various shades with red cuffs.

THE PRINCE-BISHOPRIC OF MÜNSTER

the surrounding countryside. A second attempt to surround the city on the other side failed. On 25 July, eight companies of foot and 2,000 horse moved against the enemy outpost on the sconce at Aduarderzijl, but failed as the defenders were reinforced by a company of dragoons and 1,000 armed peasants.

On 26 July, the War Council unanimously agreed to force the city to surrender by employing siege artillery. The bombardment began violently. In 14 days, 9,000 cannon shots were fired against the curtain and 5,000 bombs were dropped into the city, including 300lb mortar projectiles. The streets were in ruins and in flames, yet there was no thought of surrender in the unfortunate city. The skilled Karl von Raubenhaupt held the command in Groningen and managed to resist until 16 August, when supplies and reinforcements arrived. The French–English fleet had failed to intercept the Dutch men-of-war under Admiral de Ruyter, who had successfully escorted the merchants to relieve the besieged garrison.

Recognising the impossibility of blocking the route between Groningen and the Dutch fleet, the bombardment resumed the following day, but with less intensity due to the dwindling stock of ammunition. In addition, the food supply became insufficient, and the surrounding marshes made the air unhealthy and a typhus epidemic spread among the besieging troops. On 28 August, the Allies lifted the siege. The artillery was recovered at Coevorden, while the troops began a painful march through the swamps. The columns headed to the Emsland, since the news coming from Germany reported that the Emperor was gathering troops to support the Dutch Republic.

On 11 September the field army took quarters between Meppen and Enschede; the muster registered just 4,400 infantry and cavalry of Münster and 6,300 for Cologne.[111] For the first time since the war began, Galen took note of the cost paid by his army. The figures were dramatic. Between June and August the campaigns had claimed 4,536 dead through disease and a further 1,426 wounded or sick; a further 606 soldiers had been captured and at least 5,000 had deserted.[112] Desertion had increased because already in late July wages had not been issued. Winter quarters brought further negative consequences: the soldiers billeted in the Emsland caused trouble and spread terror among the inhabitants, and according to the contemporary chroniclers, the worst years of the Thirty Years' War seemed to have returned.[113] Discipline had become precarious due to the delay in paying wages, and when the senior officers issued punishments, desertions increased accordingly. The presence of mercenaries from all over Germany aggravated the situation, as soldiers and officers had no connection to the local population, and only a small number were natives of the country. In their writings, the commentators blamed the captains who neglected their soldiers and only cared about procuring plenty of food and beer for themselves.[114] Even the distribution of

---

111 Depping, *Geschichte des Krieges der Münsterer und Cölner*, p.118. Münster troops still numbered 2,500 infantrymen, 1,800 cavalrymen and 100 dragoons.

112 Depping, *Geschichte des Krieges der Münsterer und Cölner*, p.118.

113 Various authors, 'Die Geschichte des Emslandes', p.15.

114 Various authors, 'Die Geschichte des Emslandes', p.15.

bread was irregular. The misery of the soldiers and the promiscuity in their quarters caused the spread of disease, and soon a 'red plague' propagated in Meppen. The contemporary chronicles give a dramatic account of the situation in the winter 1672–73:

> In November 1672 there were [in Meppen] 200 houses, but a month later only 90 were still inhabited and offered shelter to citizens and soldiers. The ferocity of the mercenaries reached intolerable levels. Soldiers of the Wedel [infantry] regiment demolished the abandoned houses, destroyed gardens and mistreated citizens if what they demanded was not delivered immediately. It was not uncommon for individual houses to be occupied by 20–25 soldiers, who demanded their whole livelihood; otherwise there were only threats and beatings. The peaceful citizen was thrown out of his house and the foreign mercenary took over his poor home.

The situation was equally dramatic in the countryside:

> Cows were stolen and horses died under the strain of transport for the army. Young men had disappeared or were serving in the train or at the front. In a short time, the town of Meppen turned into a desert in which hordes of mercenaries wandered. The border villages on the left bank of the Ems were the hardest hit, as they were burdened by both Münster and Dutch soldiers, who, according to the law of war, constantly made predatory incursions into the countryside.[115]

In February 1673, Galen met the War Council to examine the strategic situation. The Prince-Bishop and his generals assumed that the strong French presence in Gelderland, Friesland and Utrecht should have forced the Dutch to divert their attention from Overijssel. Taking advantage of this, the Prince-Bishop planned a new offensive on Drenthe. In December the Dutch had recaptured Coevorden by a surprise action and therefore the possibility of seizing the fortress again was discussed, and the Prince-Bishop's architect and chief military engineer, Petrus Pictorius, was summoned. He presented a plan to exploit the Vechte River that flows near Coevorden to flood the city and force it to surrender. To achieve this goal it was necessary to build several dams to divert the course of the river and its tributaries: a job for at least 1,000 pioneers. If water had saved the Republic in 1672, it would now bring down Coevorden.[116]

Between April and May, peasants were enlisted in Münster, Bentheim and in the province of Overijssel.[117] At the end of May, 6,000 infantrymen and horsemen arrived in front of Coevorden together with the peasants, who immediately started work under the direction of Pictorius. The besiegers also dug six entrenchments and prepared batteries for 60 cannons, to be defended by embankments and fences. The rainy summer made the peasants' work

---

115 Various authors, 'Die Geschichte des Emslandes', p.15.
116 Depping, *Geschichte des Krieges der Münsterer und Cölner*, p.121.
117 The enlistment was considered as legitimate, since on 5 July 1672, delegates of the Overijssel accepted to submit the province to Münster, declaring dissolved the bond with the Dutch Republic.

THE PRINCE-BISHOPRIC OF MÜNSTER

easier and soon the water began to overflow into Coevorden. In mid-August a sortie by the defenders was repulsed. At the end of the month General Rabenhaupt gathered a corps of 4,000 soldiers and militiamen in Groningen and headed for Coevorden. There was no way to reverse the situation, but in September the intensity of the rains increased, and on 1 October a violent downpour damaged the dams, which suddenly collapsed under the pressure of the water. This caused a wave that swept over the besiegers' positions. General Wedel and 100 peasants tried to plug the breach, but in vain. In the flood 1,400 pioneers and soldiers drowned, including an infantry colonel.[118] With difficulty, the expeditionary corps saved its artillery and marched southwards through the Overijssel.

In November 1673, the conquest of Bonn and the surrender of the Prince-Bishop-Elector of Cologne left Christoph Bernhard von Galen alone against Imperialists and Dutch-Spaniards. However, in February 1674 the Prince-Bishop once again tried to save the situation by invading the provinces of Drenthe and Groningen. Taking advantage of the cold March, which froze the swamps, about 5,000 Münster troops advanced as far as Winschoten, which they plundered before returning to Emsland with a rich booty and many hostages. But now the Dutch had enough troops to face their enemies in the Overijssel: Rabenhaupt engaged the Münster cavalry near Northorn and Neuenhaus in the county of Bentheim, prevailing in both the encounters, but later had to retreat to Coevorden. This was the last action of the war on this front. On Easter Day, 22 April 1674, Galen signed the Peace of Cologne. The Prince-Bishop returned all conquests achieved in 1672 and 1673, and the only modest success achieved was the renunciation of the Republic to maintain the fortifications of Dieren on the border with Münster.[119]

The Dutch retook Coevorden on 30 December 1672. In a detail from the painting by Pieter Wouwerman in the Rijksmuseum, Amsterdam, musketeers of the besieged garrison are fighting on the bastion. They are dressed with grey coats and pale coloured broad-brimmed hats.

The Peace of Cologne also meant that Galen had to provide troops for the *Reichskrieg* against Louis XIV. After a negotiation with Vienna, the Prince-Bishop agreed to gather a contingent of 5,000 infantry, 4,000 cavalry and 1,000 dragoons for the campaign in Alsace under *Feldmarschall* Bournonville. On 29 December 1674 the cavalry formed the wing that covered the march of the main army to Mulhouse. Early in the morning, the horsemen of Münster were routed by the surprise assault of the French and lost several standards.[120] Horsemen, infantrymen and artillerymen with six cannons, under Major Renkemeyer, also participated at the unfortunate battle of Türkheim on 5 January 1675, the outcome of which forced the Imperialists to evacuate Alsace. Soon, the Allies considered the soldiers of Münster as the *Schmerzenskind* (pain child) of the army. In 1674 the infantry registered a high rate of desertion, so much so that it was necessary to send most of them

---

118 Various authors, 'Die Geschichte des Emslandes', p.17.
119 Kohl, *Christoph Bernhard von Galen*, p.427.
120 Verspohl, *Das Heerwesen die Münsterischen Fürstbischofs Christoph Bernard von Galen*, p.166.

269

to Hanau as a garrison; [121] regarding their poor performance on campaign there is the authoritative statement of the Margrave Hermann of Baden, who describes them as 'ruined and discontented troops'.[122] The comments of other eyewitnesses are even worse. After the Battle of Mulhouse, Imperial Major General Schultz wrote that 'they deserve to be hanged for the most part'; while Brandenburg's General Goltz declared that they were 'just an embarrassment that prevents sleep'. Pointless were the objections of their commanders, who tried to defend the reputation of their men by claiming that in the unfortunate conditions they were in, it was not possible to achieve more. In substance, the Prince-Bishop's contribution to the coalition was regarded with much doubt by all the allies.[123] In January 1675, the contingent left the field army and marched back home.

The following spring, Münster troops joined the Spaniards and Germans in the campaign against the French in the Electoral Rhine. This time the quality of the troops must have been better, at least because complaints are not recorded. On 11 August the infantry formed the corps under Imperial General Grana del Carretto which faced the French assault against the hill nearby the Konzer Brücke, allowing the final victory for the allied side.[124] By 1676, Münster contributed to the war effort against Louis XIV by hiring troops to the Allies: from 1676 to 1678 between 4,000 and 8,300 soldiers of Münster served in Flanders with the Spanish army of the Low Countries,[125] and in 1678 Münster troops participated at the last campaign of the Franco-Dutch War, which ended on 14 August 1678 with the bloody and unnecessary Battle of Saint-Denis.

Against Sweden (1675–76)

In July 1675 some 8,000 Münster soldiers under Lieutenant General Wedel had joined the Imperial corps in the territory of Bremen after the diet had declared the *Reichsexecution* against Sweden. Notwithstanding his 70th birthday, the Prince-Bishop accompanied his troops on campaign, because he wanted to assume command of the whole allied force in Bremen-Verden. On 16 September he crossed the border alongside his troops and entered enemy territory heading to the Weser. The Münster troops marched from

---

121 Gustav von Kotzfleisch, 'Der Oberelsässische Winterfeldzug und das Treffen von Türkheim', *Beitrage zur Landes- und Volkskunde von Elsass-Lothringen* – H. 29 (Strasbourg, 1904), p.18.
122 Kotzfleisch, 'Der Oberelsässische Winterfeldzug und das Treffen von Türkheim', p.19.
123 Kotzfleisch, 'Der Oberelsässische Winterfeldzug und das Treffen von Türkheim', p.19.
124 Arthur Janke, *Die Belagerungen der Stadt Trier in den Jahren 1673 bis 1675 und die Schlacht an der Conzer Brücke am 11. August 1675* (Trier. 1890), pp.103–105. According to some sources, two infantry battalions of Münster participated at the victorious battle of Konzer Brücke on 11 August 1675. These were two battalions from regiments *Grandvilliers* (MüI-31) and *Keyl* (MüI-55). Otto Elster, in *Geschichte der Stehenden Truppen im Herzogtum Braunschweig-Wolfenbüttel, 1600–1806*, vol. I (Leipzig, 1899–1901), p.463, states that a third battalion from regiment *Kalckum* (MüI-53) also participated to the battle. Janke, instead, places it in the garrison of Trier.
125 Tessin, 'Beiträge zur Formationsgeschichte des Münsterischen Militärs', pp.100–101.

THE PRINCE-BISHOPRIC OF MÜNSTER

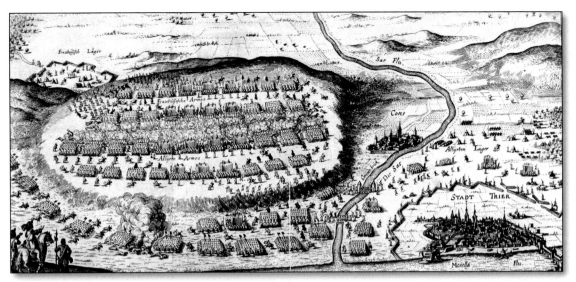

The Battle of Konzer Brücke in a print of 1675, engraver unknown. (Author's Collection)

The Battle of Saint-Denis on a contemporary Dutch print. (Rijksmuseum Amsterdam).

neutral Bremen to the fortress of Langwedel on the Weser, capturing it between 27 and 28 September, and with this conquest, the way into the region of Verden was open. The fortress of Verden upon Aller itself fell into allied hands on 29 September, and Münster troops quickly occupied the town and established their quarters. After Verden the town of Rotenburg was conquered, falling after some resistance. The Münster contingent included the renowned siege artillery, which the *Kanonenbischof* and General Wedel had exploited since the initial phase of the campaign. On 3 October the Münster artillerymen managed to open a large breach in the wall of the Swedish fort of Otterberg, which surrendered on conditions the same day. On 10 October the Allies besieged Buxtehude; this fortress quartered 400 regular soldiers and was plentiful in ammunition and provision. By 11 October a total of 100 mortar bombs and 60 artillery shells were fired into the town from howitzers and mortars, causing much damage, and the day after, the Swedish commander opened negotiations and left the town on 16 October. The garrison was permitted to withdraw to Stade taking its belongings and weapons. Bremerwörde suffered the same fate on 28 October, where the surrender was favoured by the German mercenaries in the Swedish garrison, who had learned of the pronouncement of the Imperial Ban on Sweden, and refused to render military service. The Swedish commander had no choice but to surrender the fort. The Swedish garrison was given free passage with all the possessions and weapons, while most of the German mercenaries switched to the Imperial side.[126] The campaign looked promising for the Allies, who had one last obstacle to seize for expelling the Swedes from the region between the Elbe and the Weser.

Christoph Bernhard von Galen in 1674, in a portrait by Wolfgang Heimbach. (Groningen City Museum) In 1675, Galen marched with his troops on a campaign against the Swedes in Verden-Bremen. Accounts report that he wore a shirt of mail under his ecclesiastical robes.

---

126 Various authors, '6. Die Teilnahme Christoph Bernhards von Galen an dem Gegen die Franzosen 1674 und gegen die Schweden 1675 Erklärten Reichskriege', in *Emlandsbuch 1928 – Ein Heimatbuch für die Kreise Weppen, Aschendorf, Kümmling* (Osnabrück: 1928), p.18.

THE PRINCE-BISHOPRIC OF MÜNSTER

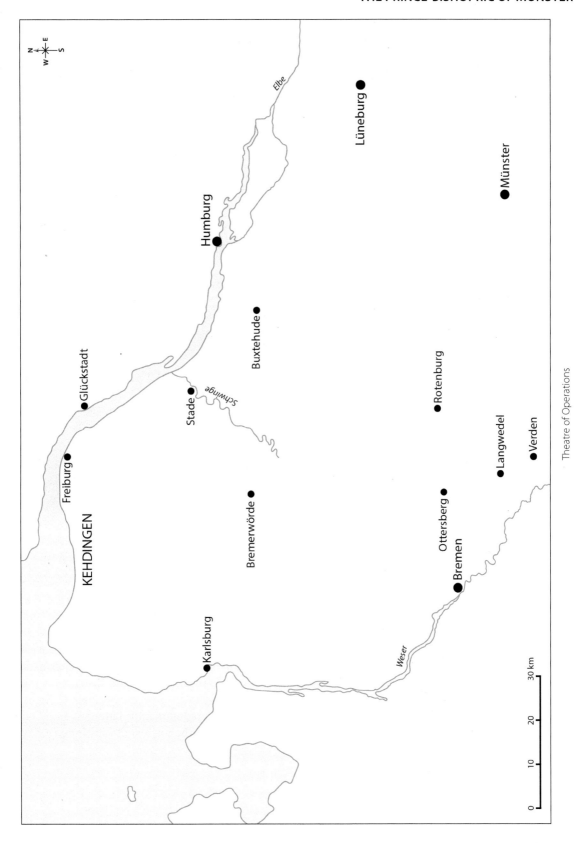

273

Iron *Viertel-Kartaune* dating to 1659 with the Coat of Arms of Christoph Bernhard von Galen, in the collection of Standort Museum of Münster. (Author's photograph)

Bernhard von Galen established his headquarters in Rotenburg. Here, a secret treaty was signed on 14 October, wherein the Prince-Bishop and Welfes Dukes of Brunswick agreed to provide mutual support to one another in the next campaign. Furthermore, a provisional division of the conquests was negotiated that excluded Denmark and Brandenburg. In the aftermath of the campaign there was considerable disagreement and distrust, as the Protestant federated princes did not want to give the Roman Catholic Prince-Bishop too much influence in a predominantly Lutheran Imperial circle.[127] By late October the Allies besieged the fortress of Karlsburg (today

---

127 Kohl, *Christoph Bernhard von Galen*, p.454.

THE PRINCE-BISHOPRIC OF MÜNSTER

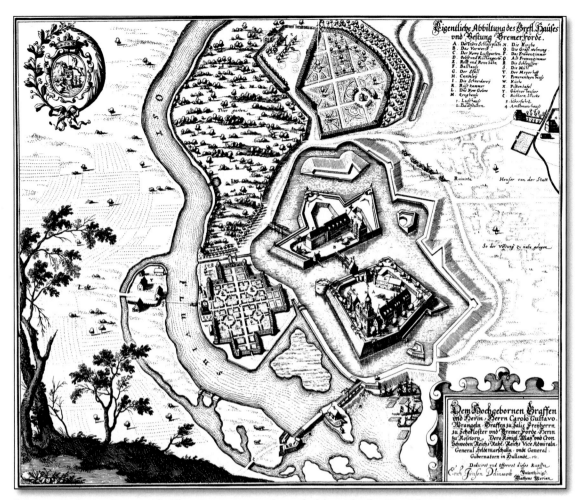

The fortification of Bremerwörde, a print dating to 1653 by Matthäus Merian the Younger. (Author's collection).

Wesermünde, in Germany). The siege was conducted alongside the Danish and Brunswick-Lüneburg contingents.[128]

On 4 November the Allies advanced on Stade, the last Swedish fortress in Bremen-Verden. With them, Brandenburg troops also joined the siege. Field Marshal Henrik Horn held the defence of the city with 5,600 regular soldiers and militiamen. The curtain and bastions of Stade were strong and well designed, and here the siege artillery of Galen did not achieved appreciable results. Repeated attacks on the fortress occurred on 6 and 7 November, but these were unsuccessful, and the Allies could not agree on continuing the siege of the town because of the approaching winter. On 9 November, the besieging army withdrew into winter quarters.[129] The hitherto captured forts remained under allied occupation, in order to maintain the blockade of Stade. The Swedes took advantage of the pause and repeatedly carried out raids, sending out foraging parties in the enemy's rear. In early January the Swedes

---

128 Various authors, '6. Die Teilnahme Christoph Bernhards von Galen an dem gegen die Franzosen 1674,' p.18.
129 Various authors, '6. Die Teilnahme Christoph Bernhards von Galen an dem gegen die Franzosen 1674,' p.18.

engaged the Danish and Münster troops guarding the posts on the River Elbe between Kehdingen and Freiburg. Five hundred Münster infantrymen under Lieutenant Colonel Lamsdorff held the position, but the Swedes managed to outflank the Danes and assaulted them from behind. After routing the Danes, the Swedes assaulted the Münster troops again, who sustained heavy losses, and then abandoned the position and fled. Pursued by Swedish cavalry, 260 were captured.[130] Days later, the Allies achieved a success at Karlsburg, which had been blocked since the end of October. Lack of ammunition and food resulted in the surrender of the fortress on 22 January.

However, because the Prince-Bishop and the Dukes of Brunswick had agreed in advance to exclude Denmark and Brandenburg from the future division of Bremen-Verden, there were serious arguments amongst the Allies, which affected and endangered the continuation of the war. Galen demanded the former Prince-Bishopric of Verden with some districts including Bremervörde and Ottersberg. The rest was to be annexed by Lüneburg Hanover. Denmark and Brandenburg, on the other hand, argued for an equal distribution of the conquests. Denmark demanded Karlsburg

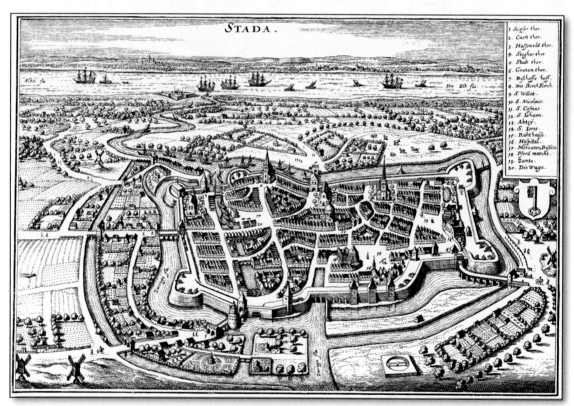

Stade in 1640, engraving by Matthäus Merian the Elder. (Author's collection)

130 *Theatrum Europaeum*, vol. XI (Frankfurt am Main, 1682), p.864. Among the prisoners there were 15 mercenaries who had originally joined up for Swedish service, but had changed sides after the fall of Bremervörde. One was quartered in Stade as a deterrent, five were hanged and nine were branded.

and Stade, and thus the control of the Weser and Elbe estuaries, in order to be able to exchange them later in return for the employment of auxiliary troops from Münster and Lüneburg for the campaigns in Pomerania. The dispute involving conflicting territorial claims escalated to such an extent that it threatened to come to open war between the Allies, and the States General of the Dutch Republic endeavoured to mediate between the parties, so as not to jeopardise the war against France.[131] An agreement was finally reached, but the parties remained in mutual distrust. Brandenburg's envoy to the Dutch Republic wanted to reach a provisional breakdown, and on 28 March he gave his approval to the treaty because he saw no other way to achieve an end to the dispute. Although the Prince-Elector of Brandenburg did not ratify the decision of his envoy, he dropped his objections to the deployment of Lüneburg auxiliaries to Bremen-Verden in the light of the favourable progress being made in the war against Sweden in Pomerania. Nevertheless, Friedrich Wilhelm secured Denmark's support in a secret agreement in early 1677, that Brandenburg should get 'at least one-fifth of territory to be divided in Bremen-Verden'.[132]

The ongoing dispute over the distribution of Bremen-Verden delayed the onset of the siege of Stade until March 1676. The Allies, now reinforced by 2,000 Brandenburg troops, planned the siege of the fortress with 16,000 infantry and 4,000 cavalry. Once conquered, Stade was to be manned by troops from Denmark, Brandenburg, Brunswick-Lüneburg, and Münster. On 19 March 1676, 1,000 Münster and Lüneburg soldiers undertook an unsuccessful surprise action; in early April the besiegers implemented measures to blockade the town. As a consequence, there were almost daily skirmishes and Swedish raids with varying degrees of success; at the same time, the besiegers began to build earthworks and embankments for the artillery. Stade had access to the sea by virtue of its location at the mouth of the Schwinge River, a tributary of the Elbe, and part of the Swedish fortifications included a fieldwork which guarded the mouth of the Schwinge in Stadersand. Under its protection, several Swedish ships were able to reach the town, providing much-needed supplies in the course of the siege. So to prevent access to Stade from the sea, and thus tighten the stranglehold of the siege, the Allies decided to seize the Schwinge fieldwork. To this end, they called for artillery from Glückstadt and also brought in two 18-gun Lüneburg sailing ships into the mouth of the Schwinge. All Swedish attempts to disrupt the preparations were repulsed, and the Allies drew closer and closer to the hill and established a battery which opened a continual fire on the Swedish position. On 23 April the Swedes carried out a new raid with 300 horsemen, but were again driven back after initial success, with a loss of 46 men, according

---

131 Kohl, *Christoph Bernhard von Galen*, p.497. William III of Orange proposed that all fortresses in Bremen-Verden should be slighted, to negotiate the final apportionment of territory at the peace congress in Nijmegen and to transfer provisional administration of both duchies to Lüneburg-Celle and Münster. Brandenburg and Denmark were expressly entitled to retain their rights to territorial interests in Bremen-Verden if, contrary to expectations, they did not achieve 'compensation' in Swedish Pomerania and Scania.

132 Friedrich Förster, *Friedrich Wilhelm, der Grosse Kurfürst, und Seine Zeit* (Berlin, 1885), p.185.

to contemporary sources.[133] On 4 July the Allies completed their earthworks and shelled the Schwinge position so heavily that the 100 infantrymen of the garrison capitulated. With the loss of the Schwinge fieldwork, the resupply of Stade from the sea was no longer possible, and when three Swedish warships held up by unfavourable winds, and six other transport ships loaded with supplies, reached the mouth of the Schwinge River, they were shelled by allied batteries stationed on the banks of the estuary. The Swedish fleet had to withdraw from Stade, and after a few raids into the area around the Elbe, it left. Cut off from all resupply, conditions of life in the fortress of Stade deteriorated considerably. An epidemic of shigellosis reduced the strength of the garrison to around 3,000 soldiers, and morale amongst the besieged fell. Twice there were mutinies amongst the Swedish soldiers which required repressive measures to put down; the desertion of the German mercenaries now increased to such an extent that active defence with patrols and sentinels was no longer possible. In June, the trenches on the allied side were so far advanced that they reached the town ditches. However, the town was not shelled, because the besiegers intended to starve its citizens and not storm it, in order to protect their own forces. Countermeasures by the Swedish garrison consisted of flooding the surrounding area by opening the locks on the river, but the besiegers succeeded in draining the water through two channels to the Elbe. As the supply situation in the town became ever more critical, the citizens and the governor-general, Horn, were forced to negotiate with the besiegers.

The negotiations began on 23 July. However, they were delayed at the behest of the population who, despite the tougher conditions, preferred to be garrisoned by Protestant Lüneburg troops rather than Catholic Münster soldiers. As a result of the surrender negotiations, the town was to be occupied by nine companies of Brunswick-Lüneburg, and the German mercenaries had to terminate their Swedish service. In the early morning of 13 August 1676, Swedish general Horn, with 10 cannon and 800 Swedish soldiers, left Stade. Following the conquest of Stade, 3,000 Lüneburg soldiers were sent to Swedish Pomerania to support the Brandenburg army. At the end of September, Münster troops and the rest of the Lüneburg troops marched to Wetzlar on the River Lahn. During the occupation of Bremen-Verden, Galen tried to revitalise Catholicism in the area he controlled, and Catholic services were reintroduced in many places, but with minimal success.

---

133 *Theatrum Europaeum*, p.865.

THE PRINCE-BISHOPRIC OF MÜNSTER

Leibfahne belonging to one of the infantry regiments hired to Denmark in 1677. Preserved in the collection of the Armémuseum in Stockholm.

Colour Plate Commentaries

Private musketeer and *Lieutenant* of the Brandenburg regiment *Kurfürstin* Dorothea von Schleswig-Holstein, in a late nineteenth century illustration. (Author's Collection). Apart from the inaccuracy and approximation of clothing and equipment, some items, such as the cover of the musketeer's ammunition pouch and the officer's gorget are confirmed from contemporary sources.

Plate A – Electorate of Brandenburg, infantry 1660s–1670s.

1 – *Schwerin zu Fuss*, Musketeer 1657–60
2 – Unknown unit, Pikeman, early 1660s

The clothing and equipment of the Brandenburg infantry in the late 1650s was essentially copied from the Swedish army. This musketeer wears the classic broad-brimmed hat and the *Leibrock*, and carries a musket with a rest, this latter was replaced by the swinesfeather on campaign. He wears a bandolier with 20 'bottles' as established in the infantry Ordinance issued in 1655. A pikeman was expected to wear a helmet and back and breast. Both also carried a sword as a sidearm. Contemporary sources state that in 1656 the Brandenburg infantry was all dressed in blue cloth. The red cravat was issued in 1657, after the reversal of the alliance.

3 – *Markische Leibgarde*, Ensign 1664.

The company of the *Markische Garde* was the oldest Life Guard of foot, and formed the permanent garrison of Berlin. Like Richard Knötel, Carl Röchling also perfectly

COLOUR PLATE COMMENTARIES

captures the style of uniforms in the early age of the Great Elector. The coat, in the typical cut of the 1660s, is still without pockets, but has slits on each side for more comfort. Note the 'puritan-style' broad-brimmed hat, a feature which possibly derives from Dutch influence.

Plate B – Electorate of Brandenburg, Infantry 1680s.

1 – Bolsey Marine Regiment, Marine 1676–80

Although none of the authors who have dealt with the Great Elector's army report on the participation of the Marine battalion in the landing of Rügen in 1678, some evidence seems to suggest otherwise. One of the Oranienburg's tapestries shows this action in great detail. On the right side of the tapestry some fusiliers on board a vessel are depicted wearing a dark blue coat, with equipment and weapons typical of the infantry. The hypothesis that these soldiers are actually marines is reinforced by the fact that the infantry depicted on the same tapestry are equipped with bandoleer and baldric carried over the shoulder, as usual for the infantry in the 1670s. Other clues suggest that these soldiers are actually marines. Since they are the only infantrymen who are aboard a ship, while all the others are either on boats or on the beach. Moreover, the uniform is very similar to the one of the Dutch marines. When Friedrich Wilhelm of Brandenburg decided to raise a battalion for the service with the fleet, he obtained permission from the States General to enlist officers and NCOs experienced in this kind of warfare in the Dutch Republic. The battalion was recruited, equipped and trained

Brandenburg infantry of the late 1670s-early 1680s. Richard Knötel, *Die Grosse Uniformenkunde*, plate XIII.9 (Rathenow, 1903), after the tapestry of the conquest of Stralsund.

Leibstandarte, Brandenburg cavalry regiment *Treffenfeld* (BrC-33), preserved in the Deutschen Historischen Museum, Berlin (Author's photograph). White silk field with silver and golden embroidery and silver fringe. Approximate size: 65cm x 65cm.

Company standard, Brandenburg cavalry regiment *Treffenfeld* (BrC-33) preserved in the Deutschen Historischen Museum, Berlin (Author's photograph). Dark green field with gold embroidery and silver fringe. The museum has, in its collection, a further five standards in the same colours, each with a different inscription:

VOR GOTT,
DIR MEINEM
HERRN
ALLEZEIT
WILLIG ZU
STERBEN
BIN ICH BEREIT

DEIN WERK
ALLEIN
SEI GOTTES
EHR!
AUF DEM ES WAG
DICH REDLICH
WEHR
GOTT IST DER WAHRE KRIEGESMANN
DER DEINE FEINDE SCHLAGEN KANN

WER GOTT VERTRAUT,
DER WIRD BESCHÜTZT,
WIE SEHR DES FEINDES DONNER BLITZT,
WER SICH GETROST AUF GOTT VERLÄSST
DER STEHT VOR FEINDES WAFFEN FEST

MIT GOTT UND GLÜCK DRAN
MIT FREUDEN DAVON
FRISCH UND UNVERZAGT
WER WEISS WER DEN ANDERN JAGT
GOTT ALLEIN DIE EHRE

VERTRAUE GOTT, DICH TAPFER WEHR
DARIN BESTEHT DEIN RUHM UND EHR
DENN WER'S AUF GOTT HERZHAFTIG
WAGT, WIRD NIMMER AUS DEM FELD
GEJAGT

in the Netherlands, and entrusted to Colonel Simon Van Bolsey, a veteran of the States' Army.

2 – Regiment *Spaen zu Fuss*, Musketeer 1685

Richard Knötel derived the information concerning the first uniforms of the Electoral army not only from the sources that still exist today, but also from original documents and items no longer preserved, deteriorated or destroyed during the Second World War. This musketeer comes from an illustration for a German Army post card of the early 1900s, where the artist depicted the new equipment of the infantry introduced after 1681, with sword waist belt and ammunition bag in Dutch-Swedish style. The issuing of new uniforms was seldom completed rapidly, since soldiers were expected first to wear out their old uniforms and equipment. As a result, several styles of uniforms might have appeared simultaneously within the same units. In the 1680s, the prevalent colour for the Brandenburg infantry was dark blue, but some regiments continued to wear coats of a different colour, notably red and grey. In 1686, there were at least three infantry regiments wearing red coats, and another had coats of grey cloth.

3 – Regiment *Dönhoff zu Fuss*, *Hauptmann*, 1678–80

This figure is a reconstruction from Richard Knötel's works illustrating the uniforms of the Brandenburg army in the late 1670s, with the colours also taken from the tapestries in the Oranienburg Palace Museum. As before, officers provided their own uniforms, but in the 1680s the tendency to wear a coat of the same colour seems to be a well established convention in the Brandenburg army, at least at the company level. This was possibly already a convention in previous years, as is suggested by some infantry officers depicted on the tapestries. In action, a company officer would be armed with a pistol carried under the waist scarf. The sword and the partisan completed his armament, and the latter usually identified the rank as was common in the German armies of this age. Gorget also became another typical distinctive of rank for the Brandenburg infantry officers since the late 1670s.

COLOUR PLATE COMMENTARIES

Plate C – Electorate of Brandenburg, Cavalry 1670s

1 – Cavalry Regiment *Markgraf Ludwig von Brandenburg*, *Pauker* Kettledrummer 1678

This figure comes from the tapestry illustrating the landing of Rügen in 1678, where trumpeters and a kettledrummer wearing blue coat with golden laces are depicted in the foreground. The dark blue coat is made with cloth of high quality, since the regiment's facings are in less expensive medium blue. Alongside the colours, the kettledrums represented the most important symbol of the regiment and their loss was considered a disgraceful event. Since the kettledrummer held a prominent role in the regiment, he generally ranked as NCO.

2 – Cavalry Regiment *Markgraf Ludwig von Brandenburg*, Trooper 1678

Like most other Brandenburg horsemen depicted in the tapestries of the Oranienburg Palace series, this trooper wears the classic buff coat and high boots. He is armed with a heavy cavalry 'Walloon' sword and with a carbine and might also carry a pair of pistols at the saddle

Dragoon company guidon, Brandenburg regiment *Derfflinger* (BrD-1), 1673-79. In the collection of Deutschen Historischen Museum, Berlin (Author's photograph). Azure field with silver inscription on an, originally white, scroll, figures in natural colours, silver fringe. Approximate size 65cm x 95cm.

Company colour (left) and Life Colour (right), marine battalion Simon van Bolsey (BrI-54), 1675. Both colours were captured by the Swedes at Carlsborg. Company Colour: Black field, red and white Electoral cap, red fruits, silver figures and inscription.
Life Colour, as above, but white field, green laurels with gold fruits and branch, green leaves with gold fruits, and gold inscripion and electoral sceptre. 203 cm flying x 205 cm on the staff.

283

WARS AND SOLDIERS IN THE EARLY REIGN OF LOUIS XIV – VOLUME 7 PART 1

Leibfahne, Brandenburg regiment Anhalt-Dessau zu Fuss (Brl-39), 1683. Red eagle with gold beak and claws on white field, yellow flames on the corners. The same regiment had its company colours in yellow with the same figures.

bow. According to some contemporary sources, the saddle cover carried the Colonel Proprietor's monogram embroidered in white or yellow, but possibly these were not used in action, as is confirmed in the tapestries illustrating the war episodes of 1675–78.

a-b-c: liveries, 1660–1690

The chequered lace (a) belonged to the earlier livery of the household troops, and it was replaced in the 1670s by the white-black-red lace (c), at least according to the tapestry of the Oranienburg series. The red and white lace (b) is associated with the livery of the Prince Elector's wife, Dorothea of Schleswig-Holstein.

Plate D – Electorate of Brandenburg, Cavalry and Dragoons, 1670s–1680s.

1 – Cavalry Field Officer, 1678

Company's colours of two unknown Brandenburg infantry regiments. Left: green laurel with red fruit, golden monogram and electoral sceptre on scarlet red field. The cap is usually of red trimmed of ermine white fur. Right: carmine red field with silver embroidered figures and inscriptions. Infantry colours during the reign of the Great Elector essentially belong to two styles. The first, coinciding with the initial phase of his rule, is characterised by flags with a single-coloured field and the monogram as the main element, often within a laurel. From the 1670s the Brandenburg red eagle becomes more common, accompanied by laurels and flames disposed in various ways.

Even in austere Brandenburg, officers had their clothing tailored privately, but ultimately the rules established by the Colonel Proprietor had to be adhered to. For this reason, at least by the 1680s onwards, it seems that junior officers and NCOs were required to wear coats in a predetermined colour, which was normally the distinctive colour of the unit. This rule was less severe with regard to senior officers, who

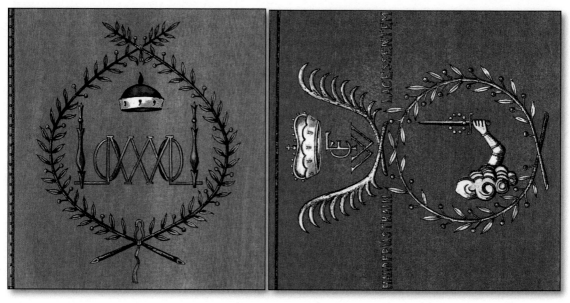

COLOUR PLATE COMMENTARIES

could retain a wider autonomy in matter of their military clothing. According to the items preserved in German museums, 'lobster' helmet and back and breast plates continued to be worn on campaign until the early eighteenth century.

2 – *Leibdragoner* Regiment, Dragoon 1686

The sources relating the uniforms of Brandenburg dragoons generally state that their clothing was the same as that issued to the infantrymen, except for the boots, which although visually similar were usually lighter compared to those of the cavalry. Dark blue coats laced and lined in yellow seem to be issued in the 1670s, but the first iconographic source is dated to 1686 and shows the regiment in the aftermath of the campaigns in Hungary, and the coat seems to be completely dark blue. He is armed with a sword shorter than the one used against western European enemies, and a flintlock musket with bandolier. A pair of pistols in holsters completed the weaponry of this dragoon.

3 – *Du Hamel zu Pferde*, Trooper 1688

According to Gerhard Pelet-Narbonne, the Brandenburg cavalry abandoned the buff coat by the mid to late 1680s, replacing them with the *Rock* of grey-white cloth faced and lined with a distinctive colour. The carbine bandolier also served as a distinctive item, being manufactured in one or more colours.

Colour of the *Markische Landmiliz*, 1675. Red eagle with golden rostrum and claws; green laurel with red fruits, black inscriptions on white field.

Standards of the *Dienstpflichtigen* (mounted militia) of Ducal Prussia, 1675-79. Red field with *destroschiere* in natural colours and gold inscriptions and fringe.

WARS AND SOLDIERS IN THE EARLY REIGN OF LOUIS XIV – VOLUME 7 PART 1

Plate E – Electorate of Brandenburg, *Trabantengarde* **1675–78**

In an alternative to the parade dress, the *Trabanten* wore an 'ordinary uniform' consisting of a dark blue coat with black facings. Other finest details, like plumed broad-brimmed hat, silver lace and buttons qualified the status of this Life Guard when escorting the Prince Elector on campaign.

Plate F – Electorate of Bavaria, 1660s–1670s.

1 – Infantry Regiment *Puech* (BvI-6), Musketeer 1661-64

This figure is based on the drawing depicting a Bavarian musketeer dating to the early 1660s described by Karl Staudinger in his *Geschichte des Kurbayerischen Heeres Insbesondere unter Kurfürst Ferdinand Maria, 1651–1679* (Munich: 1901). He wears an early version of the *Leibrock*, which was substantially the German version of the Dutch and French coat. As for the colour, the grey was the most widespread, but already in 1669 blue became just as usual for the Bavarian infantry.

2 – Cavalry Officer, 1670–75

Back and breast plate of blackened metal with gold fittings, over a buff coat appears in a painting depicting the young Max Emanuel in the 1670s. This is the conventional clothing of the German cavalry officers of this age, but the brocade velvet sleeves with fully decorated cuffs of the buff coat are typical of Italy and Southern Europe. This is relatively unsurprising considering the influence of Italians at the Bavarian court during the rule of Prince Elector Ferdinand Maria.

Coat pattern for Bavarian cavalry kettledrummer, late seventeenthth century. After Anton Hoffmann, *Das Heer des Blauen Königs. Die Soldaten des Kurfürsten Max II. Emmanuel von Bayern. 1682-1726* (Munich, 1909).

3 – Infantry Regiment *Wagenseil* (BvI-8), Musketeer 1679

The Bavarian infantry had a more 'uniform' appearance than many other contemporary German infantry, since medium blue or grey coats had been standard since the late 1660s. By the 1670s, the uniform consisted of a black, broad-brimmed hat edged in white 'tape', a black cravat, knee-length *justaucorps*, knee breeches and stockings. The coat was collarless and worn unbuttoned at the neck. Different regiments used a

286

COLOUR PLATE COMMENTARIES

number of different-coloured coat linings which showed as facings on the turned back cuffs. Since there were more regiments than available lining colours, regiments were further differentiated by breeches and stockings in either red, the lining colour, or other contrasting shades. In 1676, bandoliers with white and blue fringe were also issued to the infantry as distinctive marks. Hats often carried ribbons in the regimental facing colour.

Plate G – Electorate of Bavaria, 1683-85.

1 – Dragoon Regiment *Schier* (BvD-3), Dragoon 1684

Before the 1680s, there is little information about the uniforms of the Bavarian dragoons, but probably they wore grey or medium blue coats. By 1683, the newly formed squadrons received their own uniform which gave the name to the unit: *Blau Dragoner* and *Rote Dragoner*. In 1684, two regiments were raised and both were dressed in medium blue with scarlet or carmine red facings. The pattern of the uniform was the same issued to the infantry, except for the high, above the knee, boots.

2 – Unknown regiment of Cuirassiers, Trumpeter 1683

This trumpeter wears a coat with false sleeves, while the actual sleeves, of contrasting colour, and cuffs are a part of the coat. This can be deduced from the painting of the Battle of the Kahlenberg in the collection of the Heeresgeschichtliches Museum in Vienna.

3 – *Leibregiment zu Fuss* (BvI-17), Grenadier 1685

Grenadiers were introduced in the Bavarian infantry in 1682. They received a flintlock musket with bayonet, a grenade bag with case for the match, and a sword belt with ammunition pouch. However, they continued to wear the broad-brimmed hat until the bearskin cap was finally introduced.

Plate H – Electorate of Saxony, 1660s–1670s.

1 – Pikeman, unknown infantry unit, 1660

This figure comes from the *Kurtze Iedoch Deutliche Beschreibung Des Pique-Spielens* by Johann Georg Pascha, printed in 1660, illustrating the drill for pikemen. As was happening more or less simultaneously throughout Western Europe, armour had fallen into disuse in Saxony and pikemen were dressed in the same way as musketeers.

2 – Musketeer, 1666

Like the previous figure, this also comes from an illustration of Johann Georg Pascha, and according to these sources, Saxon infantrymen were dressed and armed in the Continental pattern. Armed with a musket without rest

WARS AND SOLDIERS IN THE EARLY REIGN OF LOUIS XIV – VOLUME 7 PART 1

Saxon *Leib-Trabantengarde zu Ross*, trooper 1685. Author's Reconstruction after *Uniformes de l'Electorat de Saxe, 1685-1772*. (Bibliothèque Nationale de France, Paris). Black headgear edged of yellow with red and white plumes; white cravat; scarlet red coat with golden laces and buttonholes, white cuffs, shoulder lanyards and lining, breastplate of natural metal; natural leather breeches; golden buttons, carbine blt of red velvet with golden edgings and fittings.

and with a sword as sidearm, he relies on a conventional bandolier with wooden bottles and a powder flask.

3 – *Leibregiment zu Pferde* (SaC-2), 1676–78

A Life Guard or elite cavalryman was expected to wear clothing made with cloth of good quality and colours qualifying his status. In the Electorate of Saxony, all regiments named as *Garde* or *Leib* had a red coat with white or blue facing colour, as is shown here.

Plate I – Electorate of Saxony, 1680-86.

1 – Cuirassier, Trooper 1680

The standard dress of the Saxon cuirassiers was a buff coat worn under a metal back and breast, usually painted black. In the 1680s, the cuirassiers still wore lobster-tail helmets like the one shown. Contemporary sources, like the painting of the battle of the Kahlenberg preserved in the Heeresgeschichtliches Museum of Vienna, shows Saxon cuirassiers wearing buff coats without turned back cuffs. Possibly the colour of the saddle covers and other items like the waist scarf and plumes were used to distinguish the regiments.

2 – Artilleryman, 1683

The same source provides this figure, which was also depicted by Knötel for the work of Martin Lezius *Die Entwicklung des Deutschen Heeres von Seinen Frühesten Anfängen bis Unsere Tage in Uniformtafeln* (Berlin: 1936). The Saxon artillery played an important role during the battle of the Kahlenberg, and rightly the anonymous artist places this constable at the forefront. According to the painting, the carriage is in very dark natural wood, and only the metal parts are painted in black.

3 – Musketeer, 1686

The standard dress of the Saxon infantry was the usual black hat with white edging to the brim; a light grey coat with pockets in the skirts, and cuffs in a regimental colour, breeches in natural leather or regimental colour, stockings and black shoes. It should be noted, however, that the two Leibregiments

COLOUR PLATE COMMENTARIES

had red coats with blue or white cuffs and linings. As concerns weaponry and equipment, in 1683 the Saxon infantry had already received ammunition pouches of Swedish (and Brandenburg) model to replace the bandolier with wooden bottles. However, these items were issued beginning with the *Leibregiments* and some units possibly retained the old equipment for many years.

Plate J – Prince-Bishopric of Münster Infantry, 1670s.

1 – *Feldwebel,* 1672

As with the officers, the senior NCOs could also provide their own clothing. A good number of testaments of sergeants who left the most valuable parts of their clothing as a legacy to their families, and sometimes to their colleagues, have survived. Very often these were weapons and metal protection that had the highest value, however the coat, especially if decorated with lace, could become an item to be preserved to perhaps sell. This sergeant appears on the only reasonably reliable source concerning the uniforms of the Prince-Bishop's army in the 1670s – the paintings preserved in the city hall of Groningen. This NCO wears a fine tailored coat with double laced cuffs and a hat with plumes: two marks very common in the German armies of this period. The painting shows two more figures who are apparently NCOs, one in red and the other in grey.

2 – Musketeer, 1672

Like most armies of this age, coarse, less expensive clothes were used for manufacturing the uniforms issued to the most numerous component of the army, namely the infantry. Grey was the most widespread colour, but brown was also widely used in the Spanish Low Countries and in the Rhineland-Westphalia. Infantrymen wearing brown coats are depicted in the paintings preserved in Groningen. Unfortunately, not many other details are discernible in the painting; however, thanks to the presence of advisers and consultants sent to Münster by Louis XIV, certain features of clothing and equipment could be of French pattern.

3 – Senior Officer, 1670

This senior officer wears a very fashioned *justaucorps* of Dutch or French pattern. In all of the period iconography, the coats, *justaucorps*, are usually just above the knee until the second half of the 1660s, and then increased in length in the next year. In the late 1660s and early 1670s cuffs were higher up the arm and smaller, while in the next decade they become bigger and turned back some inches above the wrist to expose the shirt and eventually the waistcoat sleeves. Laces and ribbons continue to decorate the clothing of high-class men, but in some cases these latter are also typical of the dress for rank and file in the mid to late 1660s.

Plate K – Prince-Bishopric of Münster, Cavalry 1673–73.

1 – *Leibgarde zu Ross*, Trooper 1673

Reports of a friendly fire incident in 1673 confirm that the Life Guard of Prince-Bishop Christoph Bernhard von Galen was dressed in red. The mistake was due to the fact that the Life Guard company of Prince Maurits of Nassau was mistaken for the Münster cavalry because the Prince-Bishop's *Leibgarde* was dressed in the same colours, and as with their Dutch counterpart, they also rode grey horses.

2 – Unknown cavalry unit, Trooper 1672

Due to their almost general absence, the sources relating to military clothing in the 1660s-1670s must be interpreted by turning to analogies. According to the painting preserved in Groningen, the Münster cavalry was dressed similar to the French, with cloth *justaucorps* and a broad-brimmed hat. Apart from the horsemen dressed in blue with red facings, there is a little information of grey as the most common colour, since the painting shows just a few cavalrymen and then only in background. Probably, there were few differences among the clothing of the companies, since regiments were quite frequently raised and then disbanded within a few months. It is likely that they were distinguished by the use of additional ribbons and strips of 'lace' in facing colour.

3 – Dragoon Regiment *Wolframsdorf*, Dragoon 1672

Before the outbreak of the Franco-Dutch War, Münster dragoons were enlisted in Germany but trained following the French drill. This may be the reason why the style of the uniform derives from that of the French dragoons, at least for the headgear. The only iconographic source for a Münster dragoon, in fact, shows the 'slouch hat' trimmed with fur. As with every mounted infantryman, he is armed with a musket, in this case a wheelock musket of French manufacture, and a cavalry 'Walloon' sword.

Plate L – Brandenburg Infantry Colours.

1 – *Leibfahne* regiment *Garde zu Fuss* (BrI-9), 1678

Reconstruction after the tapestry *Die Eroberung von Stralsund* (Oranienburg Palast Museum).

2 – *Kompagniefahne*, possibly regiment *Belling zu Fuss* (BrI-1), 1684 (Zeughaus – Deutsches Historisches Museum, Berlin)
3 – *Kompagniefahne* regiment *Derfflinger zu Fuss* (BrI-51), 1674
4 – *Kompagniefahne* regiment *Dönhoff zu Fuss* (BrI-43), 1680s

COLOUR PLATE COMMENTARIES

5 – *Leibfahne* and *Kompagniefahne* Regiment *Zieten zu Fuss* (BrI-62), 1680s. The company's colour carries the coat of arms of the city of Minden, where the regiment had its quarter since the 1670s.

Reconstructions after Ewald Fiebig's *Unsterbliche Treue. Das Heldenlied der Fahnen und Standarten des Deutschen Heeres* (Berlin: 1936). Fiebig also refers to the hues of further infantry colours of the late seventeenth century. Regiment *Goltz* (BrI-7) had lemon yellow companies' colours in 1678; regiment *Hallart* (BrI-56) blue with gold and red flames in 1679; *Alt-Holstein* (BrI-14) green in 1678; *Görtzke (*BrI-60) green and white in 1678 and *Dohna* (BrI-2) azure-blue in 1675.

Plate M – Brandenburg Cavalry and Dragoon Colours

1 – Standard of the *Trabantengarde* (brc-i), 1670s (Reconstruction after a tapestry preserved in the Charlottenburg Palast)
2 – *Leibstandarte* regiment *Croy zu Pferde* (BrC-39), 1674–79
3 – *Compagnie Standarte* regiment *Spaen zu Pferde* (BrC-28), 1680s
4 – *Compagnie Standarte* regiment *Briquemault zu Pferde* (BrC-43), before 1700
5 – *Compagnie Standarte* regiment *Markgraf Ludwig zu Pferde* (BrC-31), 1682–87

Reconstructions after Ewald Fiebig's *Unsterbliche Treue. Das Heldenlied der Fahnen und Standarten des Deutschen Heeres* (Berlin, 1936). The same author notes that in 1688, the company standard of the *Anhalt-Dessau* cavalry regiment (BrC-27) had a blue field with the monogram 'A' inside a golden oval under the Elector cap. The Brandenburg colours, were similar to the Swedish ones in symbols and style, at least until the 1660s. The use of palm fronds and the monogram remained typical of the ensigns during the reign of the Grand Elector.

6 – Life Colour, *Leibdragoner* regiment (BrD-15) 1678–88. (Author's reconstruction after Fiebig and Knötel)

Plate N – Bavarian Infantry and Cavalry Colours

1, 2 and 3 – Infantry Company Colours, 1688-90

The Colours display the traditional blue and white lozenge pattern that became the standard infantry colour in the next century. After Anton Hoffman, *Das Heer des Blauen Königs. Die Soldaten des Kurfürsten Max II. Emmanuel von Bayern. 1682–1726* (Munich: 1909).

4 – Company's standard, cavalry regiment *Höning* (BvC-3), 1663–64.

The only seventeenth century cavalry standard to survive until today is the one from the cavalry regiment which fought in the Hungarian campaigns against the Ottomans. The cross has lost part of the golden textile, but the standard is still in good condition (Bavarian Army Museum, Ingolstadt).

5 - *Leibstandarte* **for cavalry, 1670s** after Staudinger *Geschichte des Kurbayerischen Heeres*, vol. I.

Plate O – Saxon Infantry, Cavalry and Dragoon Colours

1 – Standard of the *Leibtrabanten Garde zu Ross*, 1676–77.

Reconstruction after Oskar Schuster and Friedrich August Francke, *Die Geschichte der Sächsische Armee von der Errichtung bis in die neueste Zeit: Unter Benutzung handschriftlicher und urkundlicher Quellen*, vol. I (Leipzig, 1885).

2 – Company's Ensigns of the *2. Leibgarde zu Fuss* (SaI-2), 1683.
3 – Company Ensign, *Sachsen-Weissenfels zu Fuss* (SaI-4)

Reconstruction after the painting *Belagerung und Entsatz der Stadt Wien im September 1683* (Heeresgeschichtliches Museum, Vienna). The regiment *Sachsen-Weissenfels* is represented carrying a similar ensign in pink and another with red and yellow bands.

4 – Company's Ensign of an unknown infantry regiment, 1680–94.
5 – Company's standard of an unknown dragoon regiment, late seventeenth century.

(Armémuseum Stockholm). These latter ensigns were captured by the Swedes during the Second Northern War (1700–1721), but the style is typical of an earlier period and they were probably made between 1680 and 1694.

Plate P – Münster Infantry Colours

1 – Infantry *Leibfahne*, Unknown Regiment, 1677–78.
2 and 3 – Infantry Company Colours, Unknown Regiment, 1677–78.
4 - Coat of Arms of Münster

(Olof Holmann's album of flags, Armémuseum Stockholm) The only known Münster infantry colours are preserved in the Military Museum of Stockholm. These, as well as the other 4,519 colours, standards, drum and trumpet banners, were depicted in the 1740s by Olof Hoffmann, in order to preserve the images of the trophies captured by the Swedish army since the sixteenth century. These three colours were captured after the battle of Warskow, on the Island of Rügen, on 8 January 1678.

Currency in Seventeenth-Century Germany

The most recognised currency was the *Rhenish Gulden* (Rhenish florins) or *Thaler*, which was often abbreviated to 'flr' in documents, having its origins in the Florin. There were 60 *Kreuzers* in a *Gulden*.

Appendix I

Regiments, Battalions, Squadrons and Companies, 1657–1690

APPENDIX I

Kur-Brandenburg (Electorate of Brandenburg)

Infantry Companies

Id.	Year:	Colonel Proprietor – Denomination:	Campaigns – Engagements:	History:	Uniforms:
bri-i	1615	Märkische Garde		disbanded in 1701, and merged with the *Garde zu Fuss* (BrI-9)	(1664)[1] Private, Officer and NCO: black headgear; white cravat, dark blue coat with red cuffs and lining; dark blue breeches: red stockings: tin buttons.
bri-ii	1640	Preussische Garde		disbanded in 1672, and merged with the regiment *Kurprinz* (BrI-11)	

Infantry Regiments

Id.	Year:	Colonel Proprietor – Denomination:	Campaigns – Engagements:	History:	Uniforms:
BrI-1	1629	(1657) Pierre de la Cave; 1679 Johann Heinrich von Truchsess-Waldburg; 1684 Belling; 1689 Brandt	Bonn (1689)	*Östpreussen Inf. Regt. Nr.3* in 1808	(1690)[2] Private: black headgear with white edging black cravat; dark blue coat with carmine cuffs and lining; natural leather breeches; red stockings; brass buttons.
BrI-2	1631	(1656) Christian Albrecht zu Dohna; 1677 Johann Albrecht von Barfus	Türkheim (1675); Stettin (1677); Rügen, Stralsund (1678); Buda (1686)	disbanded in 1807 as *Kalckreuth Infanterie*	(1650s)[3] Private: dark blue coat with deep yellow facing. (1680)[4] Private: black headgear; dark blue coat with scarlet red cuffs and lining; natural leather breeches; red stockings; brass buttons. (1686)[5] Private: black headgear; red coat with blue facings, red stockings Officer: black headgear; dark blue coat with red facings, dark blue stockings. NCO: black headgear; dark blue coat with red facings; red stockings. *Spielleute:* Private: black headgear; red coat with blue facings; red stockings

295

BrI-3	1644	(1650) Otto Christoph von Sparr; 1660 Gröben	Warsaw (1656); Fredriksodde, Funen, Stettin (1659)	disbanded in 1661	
BrI-4	1646	(1656) Kannenberg; 1673 Eller; 1680 Gerhard Bernhard von Pöllnitz; 1684 Briquemault	Stade (1677)	disbanded in 1807 as *Schenk Infanterie*	
BrI-5	1651	Sparr; 1668 Otto von Schwerin; 1678 Heinrich von Schlabrendorff	Stade (1677)	disbanded in 1715 as *Schöneneck zu Fuss*	
BrI-6	1655	Wolrad von Waldeck; 1657 Belcum	Poland (1656–57)	*Wibranzen* regiment; disbanded in 1660	
BrI-7	1655	(1657) Johann Rüdiger von der Goltz	Warsaw (1656); Fredriksodde, Funen, Stettin (1659); Türkheim, Wolgast (1675); Stade (1676); Stettin, (1677); Rügen, Stralsund (1678)	disbanded in 1679	
BrI-8	1655	Wladislaw von Sparr		ceded to Austria in 1661	(1664)[6] Private: black headgear, dark grey coat and breeches, dark red stockings. Officer: red coat.
BrI-9	1655	*Churfürstliche Leibgarde* (La Cave; 1661 Pöllnitz); 1679, *Garde zu Fuss* (Wrangel; 1684 Schöning; 1691 Flemming)	Warsaw (1656); Fredriksodde, Funen, Stettin (1659); Türkheim; Wohlgast (1675); Stade (1676); Stettin, (1677); Rügen, Stralsund (1678); Buda (1686)	*Fusilergarde* in 1703	(1675)[7] Private: black headgear; dark blue coat with white cuffs and lining; grey-white stockings; tin buttons. (1678)[8] Private: black headgear; white cravat; dark blue coat and lining, white cuffs; natural leather breeches; grey-white stockings; brass buttons. Officer: black headgear, white coat and cuffs. (1685)[9] Private: dark blue coat with white facings.

					Officer: black headgear with white plumes; dark blue coat laced of gold and silver. (1686)[10] Private: black headgear; dark blue coat with white facings; white stockings. NCO: black headgear; dark blue coat with white facings; dark blue stockings. Officer: black headgear; dark blue coat and facings. *Spielleute*: black headgear; dark blue coat and facings; red stockings.
BrI-10	1655	Joachim Ernst von Görtzke	Poland (1656–57); Fredriksodde, Funen, Stettin (1659)	disbanded in 1661	
BrI-11	1655	Eulenberg; 1667 Boguslav Radziwill; 1670 *Kurprinz*; 1674 Schöning	Poland (1656–57); Türkheim (1675); Stade (1676); Stettin, (1677); Rügen, Stralsund (1678)	*Wibranzen* regiment until 1660; disbanded in 1684	(1675)[11] Private: dark blue coat with white facings
BrI-12	1655	Dobeneck		disbanded in 1660	
BrI-13	1655	Klinspoor		*Wibranzen* regiment; disbanded in 1660	
BrI-14	1655	Georg Friedrich von Waldeck; 1658 Georg von Ritterforth; 1659 Barfus; 1659 Holstein; 1677 Alt-Holstein;	Warsaw (1656); Fredriksodde, Funen, Stettin (1659); Niytra, Szent-Benedek, Léva (1664); Türkheim (1675); Stettin, (1677); Rügen, Stralsund (1678)	*Wibranzen* regiment until 1660; disbanded in 1697 as *Jung-Heiden zu Fuss*	
BrI-15	1655	Halle	Poland (1656–57)	disbanded in 1660	
BrI-16	1655	Otto von Schwerin; 1668 Bogislaw von Schwerin	Wolgast, Wismar (1675); Stettin (1677); Rügen, Stralsund (1678)	*Östpreussen Inf. Regt. Nr.1* in 1808	(1660s)[12] Private: straw-yellow headgear; red cravat; dark blue coat with grey-white lining; natural leather breeches; dark grey stockings; tin buttons.

WARS AND SOLDIERS IN THE EARLY REIGN OF LOUIS XIV – VOLUME 7 PART 1

Brl-17	1655	Spaen: 1655 Johann Georg von Syburg	Warsaw (1656); Fredriksodde, Funen, Stettin (1659)	disbanded in 1661	
Brl-18	1655	Kalckstein		ceded to Sweden in 1656	
Brl-19	1655	Cluyt		disbanded in 1656	
Brl-20	1655	Dobeneck		*Wibranzen* regiment; disbanded in 1660	
Brl-21	1655	Christian Albrecht zu Dohna		*Wibranzen* regiment; disbanded in 1656	
Brl-22	1656	Joachim Rüdiger von der Goltz; 1657 Wetzel		disbanded in 1657	
Brl-23	1656	Borwinckel		disbanded in 1657	
Brl-24	1656	Groende		disbanded in 1660	
Brl-25	1656	Hundebeck		disbanded in 1660	
Brl-26	1656	Bodelschwing; 1658 Alexander von Spaen	Fredriksodde, Funen, Stettin (1659); Grave (1674) Maastricht (1676); Saint-Denis (1678)	disbanded in 1697 as *La Cave zu Fuss*	(1685)[13] Private: medium grey coat with green cuffs; leather breeches; red stockings; brass buttons.
Brl-27	1656	Johann von Wittgenstein		disbanded in 1660	
Brl-28	1656	Nettelhorst		disbanded in 1661	
Brl-29	1656	Boroffsky		disbanded in 1657	
Brl-30	1656	Ritterforth		ceded to Sweden in 1656	
Brl-31	1657	Bawyr		disbanded in 1658	
Brl-32	1658	Uffeln		disbanded in 1660	
Brl-33	1658	Lynar		disbanded in 1660	
Brl-34	1658	Burgdorff		disbanded in 1660	
Brl-35	1658	Moll		disbanded in 1660	
Brl-36	1658	Bonin; 1659 Zastrow		disbanded in 1660	

BrI-37	1660	Plattenberg		disbanded in 1660	
BrI-38	1663	Heinrich von Sparr		disbanded in 1664	
BrI-39	1665	Johann von Fargell; 1679 Johann Georg II von Anhalt-Dessau	Wolgast, Wismar (1675); Stettin, (1677); Rügen, Stralsund (1678); Buda (1686)	in Dutch service in 1688; disbanded in 1806 as *Renouard Infanterie*	(1679)[14] Private: dark blue coat with red facings. (1683)[15] Private: black headgear with red tassel and yellow lanyard; white cravat; dark blue coat with red cuffs and lining; natural leather breeches, red stockings; dark blue cloak with red collar and lining; tin buttons. *Spielleute*: red coat with blue false sleeves laced of white. Officer: natural metal gorget with golden fittings. (1686)[16] Private: black headgear; dark blue coat with red facings; dark blue stockings. Officer: black headgear; red coat and facings, white stockings. NCO: black headgear; dark blue coat with red facings; red stockings. Officer: Black headgear; red coat with dark blue facings; red stockings *Spielleute*: black headgears; red coat and facings, dark blue stockings. (1688)[17] Private: black headgear; white cravat; dark blue coat with red cuffs and lining; leather breeches; red stockings; brass buttons.
BrI-40	1665	Kaspar von Syberg		disbanded in 1666	
BrI-41	1666	Schmidt		disbanded in 1666	
BrI-42	1666	Ruel		disbanded in 1666	

BrI-43	1669	Friedrich von Dönhoff	Türkheim, Wolgast, Wismar (1675); Stettin (1677); Kahlenberg, Párkány (1683), Buda (1684); Esztergom (1685); Buda (1686)	*Östpreussen Inf. Regt. Nr.2* in 1808	(1670s)[18] Private: dark blue coat with grey-white cuffs; carmine red stockings; tin buttons. Officer: black headgear; red coat with white cuffs; white breeches and stockings; golden buttons and laces. (1680)[19] Private: black headgear, dark blue coat with white cuffs and lining; white stockings; tin buttons. (1684)[20] Private: dark blue coat with white facings. (1686)[21] Private: black headgear; dark blue coat and carmine red facings; dark blue stockings. NCO: black headgear; carmine red coat with dark blue facings; carmine red stockings. Officer: black headgear; dark blue coat with carmine red facings; carmine red stockings. *Spielleute*: black headgear; dark blue coat and carmine red facings; dark blue stockings.
BrI-44	1669	Node; 1672 Flemming	Türkheim Wolgast, Wismar (1675)	disbanded in 1675	
BrI-45	1672	Görtkze; 1672 Bomsdorf; 1676 Schlieben	Wolgast, Wismar (1675); Stettin (1677)	disbanded in 1679	
BrI-46	1672	Syberg		disbanded in 1673	
BrI-47	1672	Reuss		disbanded in 1673	
BrI-48	1672	Eller		disbanded in 1673	
BrI-49	1672	Berlepach		disbanded in 1673	
BrI-50	1672	Chieze		disbanded in 1673	
BrI-51	1674	Georg von Derfflinger; 1675 Hans Georg von Marwitz	Türkheim, Wolgast, Wismar (1675) 1675); Stettin (1677); Rügen, Stralsund (1678)	disbanded in 1679	

APPENDIX I

BrI-52	1674	Micrander	Grave (1674) Maastricht (1676)	disbanded in 1679	
BrI-53	1674	Carnitz	Wolgast, Wismar (1675)	disbanded in 1677	
BrI-54	1674	Simon van Bolsey	Carlsborg (1675)	Marine battalion; disbanded in 1689	(1675)[22] Private: straw-yellow headgear; white cravat; dark blue coat and breeches; light grey stockings; tin buttons.
BrI-55	1675	Prinz Friedrich von Hohenzollern (*Kurprinz*)	Wismar (1675); Stettin (1677); Rügen, Stralsund (1678); Buda (1686)	*Grenadier Garde* in 1801	(1686)[23] Private: black headgear; dark blue coat with red facings; red stockings. NCO: black headgear; dark blue coat with red facings; dark blue stockings. Officer: black headgear; red coat with dark blue facings; dark blue stockings. *Spielleute*: black headgear; red coat with dark blue facings; dark blue stockings
BrI-56	1675	Helldorf; 1677 Hallart	Wismar (1675)	disbanded in 1679	
BrI-57	1676	Dorothea von Schleswig-Holstein *Kurfürstin* zu Brandenburg; 1689 Markgraf Christian Ludwig von Brandenburg	Stettin (1677)	in Dutch service in 1688; *Infanterie Regiment Nr.7* in 1807	(1681)[24] Private: black headgear with red-white edging; white cravat; scarlet red coat with grey-white cuffs and lining; scarlet red waistcoat; natural leather breeches; scarlet red stockings; tin buttons. *Spielleute*: black headgear with red-white edging; dark blue coat with livery lace of white and red; natural leather breeches; scarlet red stockings; tin buttons. (1683)[25] Private: red coat with white facings. Officer: Captain violet coat; Lieutenant and Ensign: crimson red coat. (1686)[26] Private: black headgear; red coat with green facings; white stockings NCO: black headgear; red coat with white facings; red stockings. Officer: black headgear; red coat with white facings; white stockings.

BrI-58	1677	Jung-Holstein	Saint-Denis (1678)	disbanded in 1679	*Spielleute:* black headgear; green coat with red facings; red stockings. (1690s) [27] Private: dark blue coat with red cuffs.
BrI-59	1677	Candal		disbanded in 1679	
BrI-60	1677	Görtzke; 1680 Derfflinger; 1690 Kurt Hildebrand von der Marwitz	Buda (1686)	*Infanterie Regiment Nr.25* in 1807	(1686)[28] Private: black headgear; red coat with black facings; black stockings. NCO: black headgear; red coat with black facings; red stockings. Officer: black headgear; red coat and facings; dark blue stockings. *Spielleute:* black headgear; red coat and facings; red stockings
BrI-61	1678	Ernst von Croy; 1684 Johann Heinrich von Truchsess-Waldburg		*Infanterie Regiment Nr.26* in 1807	
BrI-62	1678	Hutten; 1679 Zieten; 1688 Günther von Anhalt-Zerbst		*Infanterie Regiment Nr.8* in 1807	
BrI-63	1684	Karl Heinrich zu Dohna	Buda (1684); Esztergom (1685)	disbanded in 1685	(1684)[29] Private: dark blue coat with red facings.
BrI-64	1684	Alexander *Prinz von Kurland*	Buda (1684); Esztergom (1685)	disbanded in 1685	(1684)[30] Private: black headgear; dark blue coat with yellow lining; natural leather breeches; red stockings; tin buttons; dark blue cloak with yellow lining.

BrI-65	1685	*Markgraf Philipp Wilhelm* von Brandenburg-Schwedt	Buda (1686)	*Infanterie Regiment Nr.12* in 1807	(1686)[31] Private: black headgear; dark blue coat with orange facings; dark blue stockings. NCO: black headgear; dark blue coat with orange facings; orange stockings. Officer: black headgear; red coat and facings; dark blue stockings. *Spielleute*: black headgear; dark blue coat with orange cuffs; orange stockings. (1690s)[32] dark blue coat with orange facings.
BrI-66	1685	Holsterin-Beck or *Jung-Holstein*	Bonn (1689)	*Infanterie Regiment Nr.11* in 1807	
BrI-67	1686	Alexander *Prinz von Kurland*; 1686 Ferdinand *Prinz von Kurland*; 1689 Heiden	Buda (1686)	*Infanterie Regiment Nr.10* in 1807	(1686)[33] Private: dark grey headgear with white edging and black ribbon; black cravat; dark blue coat with carmine red cuffs laced of white; natural leather breeches; carmine red stockings; tin buttons NCO: dark grey headgear with white edging; white cravat; carmine red coat with dark blue cuffs double white lace; pale blue stockings, tin buttons (1686)[34] Private: black headgear, dark blue coat with dark red facings; dark blue stockings NCO: black headgear, dark red coat with dark blue facings; dark blue stockings. Officer: black headgear, dark blue coat with dark red facings; dark red stockings. *Spielleute*: black headgear, dark red coat with dark blue facings; dark red stockings. (1687)[35] Private: dark blue coat with red cuffs laced of white.

WARS AND SOLDIERS IN THE EARLY REIGN OF LOUIS XIV – VOLUME 7 PART 1

Id.	Year	Name	History	Uniforms
BrI-68	1686	Varenne	Huguenots, disbanded in 1697	(1690)[36] Private: black headgear; white cravat; dark blue coat with deep yellow cuffs; deep yellow waistcoat; light grey stockings; tin buttons. (1694)[37] Private: dark blue coat with yellow facings. (1698)[38] Private: red cravat; dark blue coat with red cuffs and lining; natural leather breeches; dark blue stockings. Officer and NCO: red coat with dark blue cuffs and facings.
BrI-69	1686	Courneaud	Huguenots, disbanded in 1697	
BrI-70	1688	Briquemault; 1688 Lottum	*Infanterie Regiment Nr.15* in 1807	
BrI-71	1689	Schonberg; 1691 Hutten	disbanded in 1697	
BrI-72	1689	Karl Emilius zu Dohna	*Infanterie Regiment Nr.16* in 1807	
BrI-73	1690	Horn	disbanded in 1697	

Cavalry Companies

Id.	Year:	Colonel Proprietor – Denomination:	Campaigns – Engagements:	History:	Uniforms:
brc-i	1632	*Leibgarde zu Ross*, 1656 *Trabantengarde*	Stettin (1659); Türkheim, Fehrbellin (1675); Stettin, (1677); Rügen, Stralsund (1678)	*Garde du Corps* in 1701	(1670s)[39] Trooper: black headgear; with silver edging; dark blue coat laced of silver, black facings laced of silver; silver buttons.
brc-ii	1672	*Prinz Friedrich Liebgarde*	Türkheim (1675)	disbanded in 1675	

APPENDIX I

Id	Year	Colonel Proprietor – Denomination	Campaigns – Engagements	History	Uniforms
brc-iii	1687	*Grands Mousquetaires*	Bonn (1689)	*Gens d'Armes* in 1710	(1687)[40] Trooper: black headgear with golden edging; white cravat; red coat and cuffs laced of gold, red breeches, golden buttons; azure bandolier piped and edged of gold; red saddle cover with golden trim.
brc-iv	1687	*Grenadiers à cheval*	Bonn (1689)	disbanded in 1698	(1688)[41] Trooper: grenadier cap with white frontal plaque and scarlet bag laced of white; white cravat; dark blue coat with scarlet cuffs and lining laced of yellow; natural leather breeches; brass buttons; dark blue saddle cover with golden trim and embroidered red eagle.

Cavalry Regiments

Id.	Year:	Colonel Proprietor – Denomination:	Campaigns – Engagements:	History:	Uniforms:
BrC-1	1655	Christoph von Kannenberg	Warsaw (1656); Funen, Nyborg (1659)	disbanded in 1660	
BrC-2	1655	Georg Friedrich von Waldeck	Warsaw (1656)	disbanded in 1658	
BrC-3	1655	Spaen; 1656 Johann Georg von Sachsen-Weimar	Warsaw (1656); Stettin (1659)	disbanded in 1660	
BrC-4	1655	Wolf Ernst von Eller; 1658 Anhalt-Dessau	Warsaw (1656); Stettin (1659)	disbanded in 1660	
BrC-5	1655	Dietrich von Lesgewang; 1656 Strein; 1658 Boguslav Radziwill	Upper Hungary and Transylvania: Niytra, Szent-Benedek, Léva (1664)	disbanded in 1664	
BrC-6	1655	Georg Heinrich von Wallenrodt	Poland (1656–57)	disbanded in 1657	
BrC-7	1655	Georg von Schöneich	Warsaw (1656)	disbanded in 1660	
BrC-8	1655	Manteuffel; 1656 Polenz		disbanded in 1660	
BrC-9	1655	Halle	Warsaw (1656)	disbanded in 1659	

Code	Year	Colonel	Campaigns	Fate	Notes
BrC-10	1655	Georg Wallenrodt; 1659 Joachim Rüdiger von der Goltz	Poland (1656–57)	disbanded in 1660.	
BrC-11	1655	Wylich-Lottum; 1656 Brunell; 1656 Nahmer	Warsaw (1656)	disbanded in 1656	
BrC-12	1656	*Leibregiment zu Pferde* (Alexander von Spaen)	Warsaw (1656); Stettin (1659)	disbanded in 1660	
BrC-13	1656	Georg von Derfflinger	Stettin (1659)	disbanded in 1660	
BrC-14	1656	Joseph Katzler	Stettin (1659)	disbanded in 1660	
BrC-15	1656	Hille	Stettin (1659)	disbanded in 1660	
BrC-16	1656	Pfuel	Stettin (1659)	disbanded in 1660	
BrC-17	1656	Johachim Ernst von Görtzke	Stettin (1659)	disbanded in 1660	
BrC-18	1656	Albrecht Christoph von Quast	Funen, Nyborg (1659)	disbanded in 1660	
BrC-19	1656	Zastrow		disbanded in 1660	
BrC-20	1656	Johann von Wittgestein; 1659 Georg Heinrich von Gröben	Funen, Nyborg (1659)	disbanded in 1660	
BrC-21	1656	Schmidt; 1659 Versen		disbanded in 1660	
BrC-22	1656	Marwitz	Stettin (1659)	disbanded in 1660	
BrC-23	1659	Brockdorff		disbanded in 1660	
BrC-24	1659	Basse		disbanded in 1659	
BrC-25	1659	Küssow		disbanded in 1660	
BrC-26	1659	Bonin		disbanded in 1659	
BrC-27	1659	Wallenrodt		disbanded in 1660	
BrC-28	1665	Alexander von Spaen	Saint-Denis (1678); Buda (1686)	disbanded in 1718 as *Hondt Cuirassieren*	(1678)[42] Trooper: black polished lobster helm (and armour ?) (1688)[43] Trooper: grey-white coat with orange facings.

BrC-29	1666	Johann Georg II von Anhalt-Dessau	Türkheim, Wolgast (1675); Rügen, Stralsund, (1678)	*Kürassieren Regiment Nr.1* in 1807	(1688)[44] black headgear with silver edging; white cravat with black band, buff coat with blue cuffs; grey waistcoat (?); natural leather breeches; black waist scarf with orange and silver fringes, blue saddle cover with red-white edge and a silver 'A' and Electoral hat embroidered on the corner; grey cloak with dark blue lining and collar. Officer and NCO; dark blue coat laced of gold and silver. (1690)[45] Trooper: black headgear; black cravat; grey-white coat with indigo blue cuffs and lining; natural leather breeches; tin buttons; grey cloak with indigo blue facings; indigo blue saddle cover with white trim. Officer: white cravat; indigo blue coat with golden-yellow piping and embroideries; indigo blue waistcoat; golden buttons; silver scarf; red saddle cover with golden-yellow trim.
BrC-30	1666	Georg von Derfflinger; 1672 Osten; 1673 Derfflinger	Türkheim, Fehrbellin (1675); Stettin (1677); Rügen, Stralsund, (1678); Buda (1686)	disbanded in 1697 as *Heyne Cuirassieren*	

Code	Year	Name	Battles	Fate	Uniform
BrC-31	1666	Kannenberg; 1673 Görtzke; 1682 *Markgraf Ludwig von Brandenburg*; 1687 Lüttwitz	Türkheim, Fehrbellin (1675); Stettin, (1677); Rügen, Stralsund, (1678)	disbanded in 1697 as *Thyme Cuirassieren*, and merged with *Kurprinz* (BrC-36)	(1680s)[46] Trooper: black headgear with yellow ribbon; black cravat; buff coat with medium blue cuffs; azure blue breeches; tin buttons; medium blue carbine belt edged of white; medium blue saddle cover with white trim. Officer: black headgear with yellow ribbon and white edging; white cravat; straw-yellow coat with medium blue cuffs and lining, silver laces and buttons; white waistcoat; silver scarf.
BrC-32	1666	Pfuel; 1672 *Prinz Friedrich von Hohenzollern*; 1688 *Kronprinz*	Türkheim, Fehrbellin (1675); Stettin (1677); Saint-Denis (1678); Buda (1686)	*Kürassieren Regiment Nr.2* in 1807	
BrC-33	1666	Quast; 1669 Berndt Joachim von Mörner; 1675 Joachim Hennings von Treffenfeld	Türkheim, Nauen, Fehrbellin (1675); Stettin (1677); Rügen, Stralsund, (1678)	disbanded in 1679	(1677)[47] Trooper; black headgear with white edging; red cravat; buff coat with dark green cuffs; natural leather breeches; dark green carbine belt edged of white; tin buttons; dark green saddle cover with white trim.
BrC-34	1666	Eller; 1672 Lütke	Türkheim, Fehrbellin (1675); Saint-Denis (1678)	disbanded in 1679	
BrC-35	1672	*Leibregiment* (1675 Ulrich von Promnitz)	Türkheim; Fehrbellin (1675); Stettin (1677); Rügen, Stralsund, (1678); Buda (1686)	*Kürassieren Regiment Nr.3* in 1807	(1672)[48] Trooper: black polished lobster helm and armour; medium blue cravat; buff coat with red facing; brass buttons; red saddle cover. (1680s)[49] Officer: red coat laced of gold and silver.

APPENDIX I

BrC-36	1672	*Kurprinz*	Türkheim, Fehrbellin (1675); Stettin; (1677); Rügen, Stralsund, (1678)	disbanded in 1679	
BrC-37	1672	Friedrich von Hessen-Homburg; 1675 Sachsen-Gotha; 1676 Hessen-Homburg	Türkheim, Fehrbellin (1675); Stettin (1677); Rügen, Stralsund, (1678)	disbanded in 1679	
BrC-38	1672	Mecklenburg; 1674 Brockdorff; 1676 Du Hamel	Türkheim, Fehrbellin (1675); Stettin (1677)	disbanded in 1679	
BrC-39	1672	Joachim Ernst von Görtzke; 1674 Ernst von Croy	Türkheim; Fehrbellin (1675); Stettin (1677)	disbanded in 1679	
BrC-40	1672	Ulrich von Promnitz		disbanded in 1673	
BrC-41	1675	Eller	Saint-Denis (1678)	disbanded in 1679	
BrC-42	1677	Küssow	Rügen (1677)	disbanded in 1679	
BrC-43	1683	Briquemault, 1693 *Markgraf Philipp Wilhelm von Brandenburg*	Buda (1686)	*Kürassieren Regiment Nr.5* in 1807	(1688)[50] Trooper: grey-white coat. (1690s)[51] Trooper: black headgear with white edging; red cravat; grey-white coat with royal blue cuffs and lining; grey-white waistcoat; natural leather breeches; tin buttons; royal blue carbine belt edged of white; royal blue saddle cover with white trim. Officer: black headgear with white edging; white cravat; carmine red coat with blue cuffs and lining, silver laces and buttonholes; natural leather waistcoat; white breeches; silver buttons and scarf.

309

Dragoon Companies

Id.	Year:	Colonel Proprietor – Denomination:	Campaigns – Engagements:	History:	Uniforms:
BrC-44	1686	Hans Christoph von Straus	Buda (1686)	disbanded in 1686	(1686)[52] Private: black headgear; grey-white coat with azure facings; azure saddle cover. NCO: black headgear; grey-white coat, azure cuffs. Officer: black headgear; dark blue coat and facings. Trumpet: dark blue coat with white facings.
BrC-45	1686	*Prinz Heinrich von Sachsen-Barby*; 1691 Flemming	Buda (1686)	disbanded in 1702 as *Wartensleben Cuirassieren*	(1690s)[53] Trooper: grey-white coat with pink facings.
BrC-46	1688	Du Hamel		Huguenots; Kürassieren Regiment Nr.6 in 1807	(1690s)[54] Trooper: black headgear; white cravat; grey-white coat with dark red cuffs and lining; brass buttons; black carbine belt edged of red and white; dark red saddle cover with white trim.
BrC-47	1689	Lethmate; 1691 Ansbach-Bayreuth		*Kürassieren Regiment Nr.8* in 1807	

Id.	Year:	Colonel Proprietor – Denomination:	Campaigns – Engagements:	History:	Uniforms:
brd-i	1640	*Leibgarde Dragoner*	Warsaw (1656);	*Leibdragoner* Regiment in 1657	

Dragoon Regiments

APPENDIX I

Id.	Year:	Colonel Proprietor – Denomination:	Campaigns – Engagements:	History:	Uniforms:
BrD-1	1655	Georg Friedrich zu Waldeck; 1658 Georg von Derfflinger; 1672 Marwitz; 1673 Derfflinger	Warsaw (1656); Fredriksodde, Funen, Stettin (1659); Mulhouse (1674); Türkheim, Rathenow, Fehrbellin, Wolgast (1675); Stettin (1677); Rügen, Stralsund, (1678); Buda (1686)	disbanded in 1697	(1675)[55] Trooper: black headgear; deep yellow coat with blue cuffs; natural leather breeches; brass buttons; blue saddle cover with white trim.
BrD-2	1655	Elias von Kanitz	Warsaw (1656); Funen, Nyborg (1659)	disbanded in 1660	
BrD-3	1655	Christian Ludwig von Kalckstein	Warsaw (1656)	disbanded in 1656	
BrD-4	1655	Schlieben; 1655 Halle, 1656 Ritterforth	Warsaw (1656)	became infantry regiment in 1656	
BrD-5	1656	Auer	Warsaw (1656)	disbanded in 1660	
BrD-6	1656	Halle; 1657 Otto Christoph von Sparr	Warsaw (1656)	disbanded in 1658	
BrD-7	1657	Leibdragoner	Fredriksodde, Funen, Stettin (1659)	disbanded in 1660	
BrD-8	1656	Boguslav Radziwill	Stettin (1659)	disbanded in 1664	
BrD-9	1665	Kanitz		disbanded in 1666	
BrD-10	1666	Bornsdorff		disbanded in 1666	
BrD-11	1672	Bornsdorff	Wolgast (1675)	disbanded in 1678	
BrD-12	1672	Schlieben; 1676 Görtzke; 1678 Sydow; 1679 Köpping	Podolia (1674); Nauen, Fehrbellin (1675); Stettin (1677); Rügen, Stralsund, (1678)	disbanded in 1679	

BrD-13	1672	Block; 1674 Hohendorf; 1676 Schlieben	Podolia (1674); Stettin (1677)	disbanded in 1679	(1674)[56]: Private: dark blue coat and cloak.
BrD-14	1672	Grumbkow		disbanded in 1673	
BrD-15	1674	*Leibdragoner*; (Grumbkow; 1682 Dietrich zu Dohna; 1688 Schomberg; 1689 Wresch)	Mulhouse (1674): Türkheim, Fehrbellin (1675); Stettin, (1677); Rügen, Stralsund, (1678); Buda (1686)	*Kürassieren Regiment Nr.4* in 1807	(1686)[57] Private: black headgear; dark blue coat and cuffs; dark blue saddle cover. NCO: black headgear; dark blue coat and cuffs. Officer: black headgear; dark blue coat and cuffs Trumpet: dark blue coat with black cuffs. (1690s)[58] Private: black headgear with white edging; black cravat; dark blue coat and cuffs with yellow lining; natural leather breeches; dark blue buttons; dark blue saddle cover.
BrD-16	1674	Bomstorff; 1675 Holstein	Türkheim, Wolgast, Wismar (1675); Stettin (1677)	disbanded in 1679	
BrD-17	1679	Croy; 1684 Perbandt		disbanded in 1694 as *Rauter Dragoner*	
BrD-18	1686	Dohna		disbanded in 1686	
BrD-19	1688	Perbandt, 1689 Sonsfeld		*Kürassieren Regiment Nr.7* in 1807	
BrD-20	1689	Ansbach-Bayreuth		*Dragoner Regiment Nr.1* in 1807	

APPENDIX I

Kur-Bayern (Electorate of Bavaria)

Infantry Battalions

Id.	Year:	Colonel Proprietor – Denomination:	Campaigns – Engagements:	History:	Uniforms:
bvi-i	1672	Jean-Louis de la Perouse	Ovada (1672)	in Savoy-Piedmont service in 1672; becomes regiment Perouse (BvI-12) in 1673	(1673)[59] Private and NCO: medium blue coat with red cuffs and lining.

Infantry Regiments

Id.	Year:	Colonel Proprietor – Denomination:	Campaigns – Engagements:	History:	Uniforms:
BvI-1	1657	Maximilian Willibald von Wolfsegg		disbanded in 1660	
BvI-2	1657	Franz von Fugger-Kirchberg		disbanded in 1660	
BvI-3	1657	Franz von Royer		disbanded in 1660	
BvI-4	1657	Ferdinand von Puech		disbanded in 1660	
BvI-5	1658	Negron or *De Baviere*		ceded to Venice in 1659	
BvI-6	1661	Puech	Szigetvár, Pécs, Kanisza, Szentgotthárd (1664)	with the *Bayerischer Kreis* in 1661; disbanded in 1664	(1664)[60] Private: grey coat.
BvI-7	1669	Bühren	Candia (1669)	in Venetian service; disbanded in 1669	(1669)[61] Private: blue coat.
BvI-8	1672	Prospero d'Arco; 1675 Philipp zu Sulzbach; 1676 Lorenz von Wagenseil		disbanded in 1679	(1679)[62] Private: grey coat with yellow facings.
BvI-9	1672	Johann Berlo de Coquier		disbanded in 1679	
BvI-10	1672	Johann Wilhelm von Culer; 1673 Bibow; 1676 Louis d'Anglure	Deventer, Coevorden, Groningen (1672)	in Electoral Cologne service from 1672 to 1674; disbanded in 1679	(1672)[63] Private: blue coat.

313

WARS AND SOLDIERS IN THE EARLY REIGN OF LOUIS XIV – VOLUME 7 PART 1

BvI-11	1672	Wilhelm Beltin; 1677 David William Graham	Ovada (1672)	in Savoy-Piedmont service in 1672; disbanded in 1679	(1673)[64] Private and NCO: medium blue coat with red cuffs and lining.
BvI-12	1673	Perouse		disbanded in 1673	
BvI-13	1673	Puech		disbanded in 1679	
BvI-14	1673	Anton von Montfort		disbanded in 1679	
BvI-15	1673	Siegfried von Bibow		former Mecklenburg regiment; disbanded in 1674	
BvI-16	1675	Perouse, 1676 Fileno Spolverini		disbanded in 1679	
BvI-17	1682	Berlo; 1683 Mercy; 1684 *Leibregiment*	Kahlenberg, Esztergom (1683); Buda (1684); Esztergom, Érsekújvár, (1685); Buda (1686); Mohács (1687); Belgrade (1688); Mainz (1689)	*Infanterie Regt. Nr.10* in 1778	(1684)[65] Private: black headgear; medium blue coat with white cuffs; medium blue breeches. (1690s)[66] Private: black headgear with white edging; white cravat; medium blue coat with white cuffs; pale blue-white striped stockings; tin buttons.
BvI-18	1682	Puech; 1685 Johann Veit Sartorius von Schwanenfeldt		disbanded in 1688	(1682)[67] Private: green coat with yellow facings. (1684)[68] Private: black headgear; light grey coat with medium blue cuffs; carmine red breeches.
BvI-19	1682	Hannibal von Degenfeld; 1683 Franz Emanuel La Rosee, 1685 Georg von Gallenfels; 1689 Schwanenfeldt	Kahlenberg, Esztergom (1683); Buda (1684); Érsekújvár, (1685); Buda (1686); Mohács (1687); Belgrade (1688); Mainz (1689)	*Infanterie Regt. Nr.2* in 1778	(1684)[69] Private: black headgear; medium blue coat with deep yellow cuffs; medium blue breeches. (1690s)[70] Private: medium blue coat with dark lilac facings.

APPENDIX I

Id.	Year	Colonel Proprietor or Denomination	Campaigns – Engagements	History	Uniforms
BvI-20	1682	Jakob von Preysing; 1685 Alexander Ludwig von Seyboltdorff	Kahlenberg, Esztergom (1683); Buda (1684); Esztergom, Érsekújvár, (1685); Buda (1686); Mohács (1687); Belgrade (1688); Mainz (1689)	disbanded in 1704	(1684)[71] Private: black headgear; medium blue coat with lemon yellow cuffs; natural leather breeches.
BvI-21	1682	Montfort	Buda (1684); Érsekújvár, (1685); Buda (1686); Mohács (1687); Belgrade (1688)	disbanded in 1688	(1684)[72] Private: black headgear; light grey coat with medium blue cuffs; natural leather breeches. (1688)[73] Private: dark grey coat with blue facings.
BvI-22	1682	Adam Heinrich von Steinau	Kahlenberg, Esztergom (1683); Buda (1684); Esztergom, Érsekújvár, Košice (1685); Buda (1686); Mohács (1687); Belgrade (1688); Mainz (1689)	disbanded in 1705	(1684)[74] Private: black headgear; medium blue coat with deep purple cuffs and breeches. (1690s)[75] Private: black headgear with white edging; white cravat; medium blue coat with scarlet cuffs; grey breeches and stockings; brass buttons.
BvI-23	1682	Perouse; 1683 Johann Friedrich von Rummel; 1686 August von Weldenz; 1689 Antonio Zacco	Kahlenberg, Esztergom (1683); Buda (1684); Érsekújvár, (1685); Buda (1686); Mohács (1687); Belgrade (1688); Mainz (1689)	disbanded in 1705	(1684)[76] Private: black headgear; medium blue coat with carmine red cuffs; natural leather breeches.

Cavalry Companies

Id.	Year	Colonel Proprietor or Denomination	Campaigns – Engagements:	History:	Uniforms:
bvc-i	1594	*Leibgarde zu Ross*		disbanded in 1669	

Id.	Year	Colonel Proprietor or Denomination	Campaigns – Engagements:	History:	Uniforms:
bvc-ii	1669	*Leibgarde der Hartschiere*	Buda (1684); Esztergom (1685); Buda (1686); Mohács (1687); Belgrade (1688)	disbanded in 1706	(1680s)[77] campaign dress: Trooper: black polished lobster helm and breast armour; medium blue coat laced of white, black cuffs with white lace and buttonholes; medium blue saddle cover with black–white trim.
bvc-iii	1669	*Korbinergarde or Leichte-Korbinern*		disbanded in 1684	(1670s)[78] Trooper: black polished lobster helm and breast armour, buff coat; medium blue saddle cover (laced of white?). Parade uniform: red coat.

Cavalry Regiments

Id.	Year	Colonel Proprietor or Denomination	Campaigns – Engagements:	History:	Uniforms:
BvC-1	1657	Georg Truckmüller zu Brunn		disbanded in 1660	
BvC-2	1657	Andreas Kolb von Reindorf		disbanded in 1660	
BvC-3	1661	Nikolaus von Höning	Szigetvár, Pécs, Kanisza Szentgotthárd (1664)	with the *Bayerischer Kreis* in 1661; disbanded in 1664	(1664)[79] Trooper: black polished lobster helm and breast armour, buff coat; red saddle cover.
BvC-4	1674	Johann Bärtls		disbanded in 1674	
BvC-5	1674	Höning		disbanded in 1679	
BvC-6	1674	Martin Kleining		disbanded in 1674	
BvC-7	1674	Charles de Harancourt		disbanded in 1679	
BvC-8	1674	Günther Erich Clau; 1675 Bärtls		disbanded in 1679	
BvC-9	1675	Culer; 1676 Daniel McKay; 1677 Louis de Beauvau		disbanded in 1679	(1675–77)[80] Trooper, buff coat; yellow saddle cover
BvC-10	1675	Spinchal		disbanded in 1679	

APPENDIX I

BvC-11	1682	Harancourt; 1683 Johann Baptist d'Arco	Kahlenberg (1683); Buda (1684), Esztergom, Érsekújvár, (1685); Buda (1686); Mohács (1687);	Dragoner Regt. Nr.1 in 1778	(1682)[81] Trooper: light grey coat with blue facings. (1686)[82] Trooper: black polished lobster helm and breast armour; light grey coat with medium blue cuffs; medium blue saddle cover with white trim.
BvC-12	1682	Bärtls; 1683 Münster; 1684 Walser	Kahlenberg (1683); Buda (1684);	Cuirassiers, disbanded in 1685	
BvC-13	1682	Louis de Beauvau; 1685 Franz Ferdinand von Salburg; 1691 Carl Lothar von Weickhel	Buda (1684); Érsekújvár (1685); Buda (1686), Mohács (1687);	Cuirassiers, Dragoner Regt. Nr.2 in 1778	(1682)[83] Trooper: light grey coat with red facings. (1686)[84] Trooper: black polished lobster helm and breast armour; light grey coat with carmine red cuffs; light grey cloak with carmine red facing; medium blue saddle cover with white trim.
BvC-14	1682	Johann Christoph Schüz von Schüzenhofen; 1685 Lamoral de Latour	Kahlenberg (1683); Buda (1684); Esztergom, Érsekújvár, (1685); Buda (1686); Mohács (1687);	Cuirassiers, disbanded in 1757 as Frohberg Cuirassiers	(1686)[85] Trooper: black polished lobster helm and breast armour; light grey coat with deep yellow cuffs; light grey cloak with deep yellow facing; medium blue saddle cover with white trim.
BvC-15	1683	Harancourt, 1684 Latour	Kahlenberg (1683); Buda (1684)	Cuirassiers, disbanded in 1685	
BvC-16	1683	Johann Matthias von Löbell	Buda (1684)	Cuirassiers, disbanded in 1685	
BvC-17	1685	Bielke	Buda (1686); Mohács (1687);	Cuirassiers, disbanded in 1688	(1686)[86] Trooper: black polished lobster helm and breast armour; light grey coat; medium blue saddle cover with white trim.
BvC-18	1689	Leibregiment		Cuirassiers, ceded to Spain in 1690	

Dragoon Companies and Squadrons

Id.	Year	Denomination	Campaigns – Engagements:	History:	Uniforms:
bvd-i	1672	Philippe de Martin		In Electoral Cologne service from 1672 to 1674; disbanded in 1675	
bvd-ii	1672	Nicola Dubelier		In Electoral Cologne service from 1672 to 1674; disbanded in 1675	
bvd-iii	1683	*Blau Dragoner* (squadron)	Kahlenberg (1683)	disbanded in 1684	(1683)[87] Private: blue coat.
bvd-iv	1683	*Rote Dragoner* (squadron)	Kahlenberg (1683)	disbanded in 1684	(1683)[88] Private: red coat.
bvd-v	1684	*Leibdragoner* (squadron)	Érsekújvár (1685)	disbanded in 1686	

Dragoon Regiment

Id.	Year	Colonel Proprietor or Denomination	Campaigns – Engagements:	History:	Uniforms:
BvD-1	1676	Bärtls; 1675 Leoprechting		disbanded in 1679	
BvD-2	1684	1684 Friedrich August von Sachsen-Eisenach; 1685 Philipp d'Arco	Buda (1684); Esztergom Érsekújvár (1685); Buda (1686); Mohács (1687);	disbanded in 1704	(1683)[89] Private: light grey or black headgear; medium blue coat with scarlet red cuffs; medium blue saddle cover with white trim. Drummer: scarlet red coat with medium blue cuffs. (1684)[90] Private: black headgear; medium blue coat with scarlet red cuffs; medium blue saddle cover and pistol holsters with white trim and embroideries.

BvD-3	1684	Schier	Érsekújvár (1685); Buda (1686); Mohács (1687);	disbanded in 1704	(1683)[91] Private: black headgear; medium blue coat with carmine red cuffs; medium blue cloak; medium blue saddle cover with white trim.
BvD-4	1685	Bielke		disbanded in 1685	

Hussars

Id.	Year	Colonel Proprietor or Denomination	Campaigns – Engagements:	History:	Uniforms:
BvH-1	1688	Johann Baptist Lidl von Borbula	Belgrade (1688)	disbanded in 1689	(1688)[92] Trooper: brown fur cap with red bag; medium blue *Attila* and trousers with white lanyards and laces; brown fur pelisse; medium blue saddle cover.

Kur-Sachsen (Electorate of Saxony)

Infantry Companies and Battalions

Id.	Year:	Colonel Proprietor – Denomination:	Campaigns – Engagements:	History:	Uniforms:
sai-i	1656	Schweizer Leibkompagnie der Musketiere		disbanded in 1669	
sai-ii	1666	Hochteutsche Leibgarde		disbanded in 1681	

Infantry Regiments

Id.	Year:	Colonel Proprietor – Denomination:	Campaigns – Engagements:	History:	Uniforms:
SaI-1	1663	*Leibregiment* (Brandt; 1676 Johann Kuffer; 1682 Joachim Rüdiger von der Goltz; 1683 Heinrich IV von Reuss)	Léva (1664); Kahlenberg (1683)	*Kurfürst Infanterie* in 1764	(1683)[93] Private: red scarlet coat with azure cuffs and lining.

SaI-2	1675	2. *Leibregiment*; (Rudolph von Schönfeld; 1686 Erskin, 1687 Lüttig)	Kahlenberg (1683); in Venetian service from 1685 to 1687: Calamata (1685); Navarino, Modone, Nauplia (1686)	disbanded in 1702 as *Steinau zu Fuss*	(1686)[94] Private: black headgear; white cravat; red scarlet coat with grey-white cuffs and lining, natural leather breeches; scarlet red stockings; brass buttons. (1685)[95] NCO: black headgear; white cravat; red scarlet coat with white cuffs, lining and stockings; natural leather breeches; brass buttons.
SaI-3	1675	Hannibal von Degenfeld		disbanded in 1676	
SaI-4	1680	Herzog Christian von Sachsen-Weissenfels; 1689 Prinz Christian August of Sachsen-Weimar	Kahlenberg (1683); Buda (1686); Mainz (1689)	*Kurprinz zu Fuss* in 1700	(1685)[96] Private: black headgear edged of yellow with azure and yellow plumes; white cravat; light grey coat with deep yellow cuffs, lining and stockings; natural leather breeches; brass buttons.
SaI-5	1682	Löben; Trauttmannsdorff; Haubitz; 1687 Promnitz	Buda (1686)	disbanded in 1697 as *Schachmann zu Fuss*	
SaI-6	1682	Kuffer; 1689 Ütterodt	Buda (1686)	*Königin zu Fuss* in 1699	(1685)[97] Private: black headgear edged of yellow with azure and yellow plumes; white cravat; light grey coat with dark green cuffs, lining and stockings; natural leather breeches; brass buttons. (1689)[98] NCO: black headgear; black cravat; light grey coat with red cuffs, lining and stockings; natural leather breeches; tin buttons.

APPENDIX I

Id.	Year:	Colonel Proprietor – Denomination:	Campaigns – Engagements:	History:	Uniforms:
Sal-7	1683	Heino Heinrich von Flemming	Kahlenberg (1683)	disbanded in 1694 as *Reuss zu Fuss*	(1685)[99] Private: black headgear edged of yellow with white and yellow plumes; white cravat; light grey coat with pink cuffs, lining and stockings; natural leather breeches; brass buttons.
Sal-8	1683	Löben; 1688 Sinzendorff	Kahlenberg (1683)	disbanded in 1702 as *Steinau zu Fuss*	(1685)[100] Private: black headgear edged of yellow with azure and yellow plumes; white cravat; light grey coat with azure cuffs, lining and stockings; natural leather breeches; brass buttons.
Sal-9	1685	Bernhard von Troppau	in Venetian service from 1685 to 1687: Calamata (1685); Navarino, Modone, Nauplia (1686)	disbanded in 1687	(1686)[101] Private: grey coat.
Sal-10	1685	*Kleist*	in Venetian service from 1685 to 1687: Calamata (1685); Navarino, Modone, Nauplia (1686)	disbanded in 1686	(1686)[102] Private: grey coat.
Sal-11	1688	*Kurprinz* (Cuno Christoph von Birckholz)	Belgrade (1688)	disbanded in 1692	

Cavalry

Id.	Year:	Colonel Proprietor – Denomination:	Campaigns – Engagements:	History:	Uniforms:
sac-i	1656	*Kroatische Leibgarde*		disbanded in 1680	
sac-ii	1656	*Leib-Eskadron*		*Leibregiment* in 1668	
sac-iii	1656	*Deutsche Leibgarde zu Ross*		disbanded in 1657	

sac-iv	1657	*Leib-Trabantengarde zu Ross*; 1686 *Garde-trabanten zu Ross*	Kahlenberg (1683)	disbanded in 1689	(1685)[103] Trooper: black headgear edged of yellow with red and white plumes; white cravat; scarlet red coat with golden laces and buttonholes, white cuffs, shoulder lanyards and lining, breastplate of natural metal; natural leather breeches; golden buttons.
sac-v	1671	Mousquetaires		disbanded in 1680	

Id.	Year:	Colonel Proprietor – Denomination:	Campaigns – Engagements:	History:	Uniforms:
SaC-1	1664	Wolframsdorf		disbanded in 1665	
SaC-2	1668	*Leibregiment* (Kanne; 1676 Dernath)	Sinsheim (1674); Salzbach, Altenheim (1675); Philippsburg (1676); Gengenbach (1677); Kahlenberg (1683)	disbanded in 1689	(1678)[104] Trooper: scarlet red coat with azure cuffs and lining. (1685)[105] Trooper: black headgear edged of yellow; white cravat; scarlet red coat with golden laces and buttonholes, scarlet cuffs and lining, natural leather breeches; azure bandolier with golden edgings; golden buttons.
SaC-3	1673	*Kurprinz*, Neitschütz; 1689 *Leibregiment*	Sinsheim (1674); Salzbach, Altenheim (1675); Philippsburg (1676); Gengenbach (1677); Kahlenberg (1683)	disbanded in 1717	(1682)[106] Trooper: and black polished metal breast armour and lobster helm; buff coat. (1690) Private: black headgear edged of white; black cravat; scarlet red coat with yellow cuffs and lining; natural leather breeches; tin buttons.[107]

APPENDIX I

Id.	Year:	Colonel Proprietor – Denomination:	Campaigns – Engagements:	History:	Uniforms:
SaC-4	1680	Promnitz; 1682 Plotho; 1689 Haugwiz	Kahlenberg (1683)	*Kurfürst Cuirassieren* in 1764	(1682)[108] Trooper: black polished metal breast armour and lobster helm; buff coat. (1685)[109] Trooper: natural metal lobster helm with yellow-red plumes and breast armour; buff coat with red cuffs and lining; natural leather breeches. (1690) Private: black headgear edged of white; red cravat; scarlet red coat with white cuffs and lining; natural leather breeches; tin buttons.[110]
SaC-5	1682	Goltz; 1683 Trauttmannsdorff; 1686 Bronne;	Kahlenberg (1683)	disbanded in 1697 as *Rosen zu Pferde*	(1682)[111] Trooper: buff coat and black polished metal breast armour and lobster helm. (1690) Private: black headgear edged of white; red cravat; scarlet red coat with straw yellow cuffs and lining; natural leather breeches; tin buttons.[112]
SaC-6	1688	Prinz Friedrich August		disbanded in 1697 as *Kurfürstin zu Pferde*	
SaC-7	1689	Flemming		disbanded in 1704 as *Jordan Cuirassieren*	

Dragoons

Id.	Year:	Colonel Proprietor – Denomination:	Campaigns – Engagements:	History:	Uniforms:
sad-i	1665	*Leibgarde*		disbanded in 1667	
sad-ii	1667	*Leibdragoner* (squadron)	Sinsheim (1674)	disbanded in 1680	

Prince-Bishopric of Münster — Infantry tables continued

Id.	Year:	Colonel Proprietor – Denomination:	Campaigns – Engagements:	History:	Uniforms:
SaD-1	1675	Maltzan		disbanded in 1676	
SaD-2	1682	Reuss; 1688 Minkwitz	Kahlenberg (1683)	disbanded in 1717 as *Leibregiment Dragoner*	
SaD-3	1689	Riedesel; 1690 Trützscher		disbanded in 1703 as *Kurprinz Dragoner*	(1690) Private: red coat with blue facing; tin buttons.[113]

Prince-Bishopric of Münster

Infantry Companies or Battalions

Id.	Year:	Denomination:	Campaigns – Engagements:	History:	Uniforms:
müi-i	1664	*Leibgarde zu Fuss* (Heiducks)		disbanded in 1674?	(1668)[114] Private: Hungarian style brown cap and coat.
müi-ii	1679	*Garde zu Fuss*		disbanded in 1688	
müi-iii	1679	Geismar (battalion)		disbanded in 1684	

Infantry Regiments

Id.	Year:	Colonel Proprietor – Denomination:	Campaigns – Engagements:	History:	Uniforms:
MüI-1	1660	Dietrich Philipp von Wylich		disbanded in 1660	
MüI-2	1660	Rudolf Heinrich von Plettenberg		disbanded in 1660	
MüI-3	1660	Johann Waldbott von Bassenheim	Münster (1660–61)	disbanded in 1662	
MüI-4	1660	Nikolaus von Elverfeldt	Münster (1660–61)	disbanded in 1663	
MüI-5	1661	*Münster*	Hungary and Transylvania (1661–62)	ceded to Austria in 1661	

MüI-6		Spielberg	Hungary and Transylvania (1661–62)	from Pfalz-Neuburg, ceded to Austria in 1661.	
MüI-7	1663	Hermann Lothar von Post	Hungary and Transylvania (1663–64)	disbanded in 1664	
MüI-8	1665	Oswald von Pleuren		disbanded in 1666	
MüI-9	1665	John George Gorgas	Borculo, Rouveen, Bourtange (1665); Winschoten (1665–66)	disbanded in 1666	
MüI-10	1665	Denis de l'Espines Saint-Antoine	Borculo, Rouveen, Bourtange (1665)	ceded to Spain in 1666	
MüI-11	1665	Schermberg	Borculo, Bourtange (1665)	ceded to Spain in 1666	
MüI-12	1665	Oldenhaupt	Borculo, Bourtange (1665)	disbanded in 1666	
MüI-13	1665	Waldbott	Borculo, Rouveen (1665); Winschoten (1665–66)	ceded to Kur-Pfalz in 1666	
MüI-14	1665	Lothar von Toller	Borculo, Rouveen, Bourtange (1665); Winschoten (1665–66)	disbanded in 1666	
MüI-15	1665	Ernst von Ilten	Borculo, Rouveen (1665)	disbanded in 1666	
MüI-16	1665	Elverfeldt	Borculo, Rouveen (1665)	disbanded in 1666	
MüI-17	1665	*Rheingraf* (Johann Ludwig zu Salm)		Walloon, ceded to Spain in 1666	
MüI-18	1665	Gerhard von der Nath		disbanded in 1666	
MüI-19	1665	Carp		Walloon, disbanded in 1666	
MüI-20	1665	Leonard de Cleuter		Walloon, disbanded in 1666	
MüI-21	1665	*Leibregiment*	Borculo (1665)	disbanded in 1665	
MüI-22	1665	Johann Casimir Moll	Winschoten (1665–66)	disbanded in 1666	
MüI-23	1665	Grunacker	Lochem (1665); Winschoten (1665–66)	disbanded in 1665	
MüI-24	1665	Schultze		disbanded in 1666	
MüI-25	1665	Georg Krohne	Bocholt (1665); Groningen (1672)	disbanded in 1672	

Code	Year	Commander	Towns (campaigns)	Service / disbandment	Uniform
MüI-26	1666	Brembt		disbanded in 1666	
MüI-27	1672	Johann Georg Daurer	Groenlo, Deventer, Kampen, Zwolle, Coevorden, (1672); Verden, Karlsburg (1675); Stade (1676);	in Spanish service from 1677 to 1678; disbanded in 1679	
MüI-28	1672	Philipp Nitzow; 1678 Adam Jobst von Gaugreben (or Gogreve)	Deventer (1672), Groningen (1672) Langakershanz (1673); Demmin (1676); Landskrona (1677); Warskow, (1678)	in Danish service from 1677 to 1678; disbanded in 1679	
MüI-29	1672	Gustav Wilhelm von Wedel	Zwolle, Groningen (1672); Coevorden (1673); Mulhouse (1674); Türkheim, Verden, Karlsburg (1675); Stade (1676)	in Spanish service from 1677 to 1678; in Danish service from in 1678; ceded to Denmark in 1679	
MüI-30	1672	Mias; 1676 Esche	Groenlo, Groningen (1672); Mulhouse (1674); Türkheim, Verden, Karlsburg (1675); Stade (1676);	in Spanish service from 1677 to 1678; in Danish service in 1678; ceded to Denmark in 1679	
MüI-31	1672	Franz Gomar von Grandvilliers; 1678 George de Mortaigne	Deventer (1672), Conzer Brücke (1675); Landskrona (1677); Warkow (1678)	in Danish service from 1677 to 1678; disbanded in 1678	(1673)[115] Private: grey coat with red facings.
MüI-32	1672	Alt-Reuss	Deventer (1672), Groningen (1672)	disbanded in 1673	
MüI-33	1672	Jung-Reuss	Deventer (1672), Groningen (1672)	disbanded in 1673	
MüI-34	1672	Bernhard von Sehlinger	Groningen (1672)	disbanded in 1673	
MüI-35	1672	Rheingraf	Groningen (1672)	disbanded in 1673	
MüI-36	1672	Saint-Paul	Bentheim (1673)	disbanded in 1673	
MüI-37	1672	Berlepsch	Groningen (1672) Bentheim (1673)	disbanded in 1673	
MüI-38	1672	Pillach	Groningen (1672)	disbanded in 1673	

APPENDIX I

MüI-39	1672	Toller	Deventer (1672), Groningen (1672)	disbanded in 1673
MüI-40	1672	Thilo Heinrich Nymphius	Deventer (1672)	disbanded in 1673
MüI-41	1672	Grubbe		disbanded in 1673
MüI-42	1672	Burggraf	Groningen (1672)	disbanded in 1672
MüI-43	1672	Franz Rovelli	Groningen (1672)	disbanded in 1672
MüI-44	1672	Twickel		disbanded in 1672
MüI-45	1672	Croy		disbanded in 1672
MüI-46	1672	Märnich		disbanded in 1672
MüI-47	1672	Hautmarez		from Liège, disbanded in 1672
MüI-48	1672	Tilmann		disbanded in 1672
MüI-49	1672	Schneider		disbanded in 1672
MüI-50	1672	Plettenberg		disbanded in 1672
MüI-51	1673	Braun	Landskrona (1677); Warskow (1678)	in Danish service from 1677 to 1678; disbanded in 1678
MüI-52	1673	Einschaten; 1677 Eltz		in Spanish service from 1677 to 1678; disbanded in 1679
MüI-53	1673	Johan Bernhard Kalckum	Trier (1675); East Frisia (1677–78)	in Spanish service in 1678; disbanded in 1679
MüI-53	1673	Otthons; 1678 Bletzowski		in Spanish service from 1677 to 1678; disbanded in 1678
MüI-54	1673	Friedrich Moritz von Bentheim-Tecklenburg	Landskrona (1677); Warskow (1678)	in Danish service from 1677 to 1678; disbanded in 1678
MüI-55	1673	Keyl	Conzer Brücke (1675)	disbanded in 1677
MüI-56	1673	Oger de Pölling	Mulhouse (1674); Türkheim (1675); East Friesia (1677)	disbanded in 1677
MüI-57	1673	Schilder (*Garde zu Fuss*)		disbanded in 1673

Mül-58	1673	Johann Georg Körberin (or Corberin)		disbanded in 1673
Mül-59	1673	Klepping		disbanded in 1673
Mül-60	1673	Rheinhard		disbanded in 1673
Mül-61	1673	Messignies (or Vitry)		disbanded in 1673
Mül-62	1673	Reemen		disbanded in 1673
Mül-63	1673	Leemput		disbanded in 1673
Mül-64	1674	Anton Günter Schwartz	Mulhouse (1674); Türkheim (1675); Stade (1676)	in Spanish service from 1677 to 1678; in Danish service from 1678 to 1679; disbanded in 1801 as *Droste Infanterie*
Mül-65	1674	Rollingen	Mulhouse (1674); Türkheim (1675)	in Spanish service from 1677 to 1678; disbanded in 1678
Mül-66	1674	Erden (or Lymburg-Styrum?)		disbanded in 1674
Mül-67	1676	Jung Elverfeld		in Spanish service from 1677 to 1678; disbanded in 1679
Mül-68	1676	Reinhardts		disbanded in 1679
Mül-69	1676	Vischer		disbanded in 1679
Mül-70	1676	Brancador		disbanded in 1676
Mül-71	1676	Lohaus		disbanded in 1676
Mül-72	1676	Janson		disbanded in 1676
Mül-73	1676	Clauberg		disbanded in 1676
Mül-74	1677	Frankenstein		in Danish service from 1678 to 1679; disbanded in 1679
Mül-75	1677	Körberin (or Corberin)		in Spanish service from 1677 to 1679; disbanded in 1679
Mül-76	1677	Wantzheimb		disbanded in 1677
Mül-77	1685	Elverfeld		ceded to Prussia in 1803

MüI-78	1685	Corfey		disbanded in 1767 as *Wenge Infanterie*	
MüI-79	1685	Landesberg		disbanded in 1767 as *Bönninghausen Infanterie*	
MüI-80	1685	Gogreve		in Danish service from 1678 to 1679; disbanded in 1767 as *Seyboltsdorf Infanterie*	

Cavalry Companies or Squadrons

Id.	Year:	Colonel Proprietor – Denomination:	Campaigns – Engagements:	History:	Uniforms:
müc-i	1651	*Leibgarde zu Ross* or *Trabanten*		disbanded in 1689	(1672)[116] Trooper: red coat with dark blue facings, red cassock with silver St. Andrew cross.

Cavalry Regiments

Id.	Year:	Colonel Proprietor – Denomination:	Campaigns – Engagements:	History:	Uniforms:
MüC-1	1654	Johannes de Reumont	Münster (1660–61)	disbanded in 1662	
MüC-2	1657	Dietrich Hermann von Nagel		disbanded in 1657	
MüC-3	1661	Hermann Lothar von Post		ceded to Austria in 1662	(1662)[117] Trooper: buff coat and black polished metal breast armour.
MüC-4	1665	Gorgas	Borculo, Rouveen, Bourtange (1665); Winschoten (1665–66)	disbanded in 1666	
MüC-5	1665	Ägidius Christoph von Lützow		ceded to Sweden in 1666	
MüC-6	1665	Brabeck		ceded to Kur-Pfalz in 1666	
MüC-7	1665	Korff		disbanded in 1666	

ID	Year	Name	Campaigns	Fate
MüC-8	1665	*Leibregiment*; Massiette		ceded to Spain in 1666
MüC-9	1665	Georg Christian von Hessen-Homburg		disbanded in 1666
MüC-10	1665	Efferen		ceded to Spain in 1666
MüC-11	1665	Buttlar		disbanded in 1666
MüC-12	1665	Post		ceded to Spain in 1666
MüC-13	1665	Barthels		ceded to Kur-Pfalz in 1666
MüC-14	1665	d'Ossery	Winschoten (1665–66)	ceded to Spain in 1666
MüC-15	1665	Herbaix		Walloon, ceded to Spain in 1666
MüC-16	1665	Meinerzhagen		disbanded in 1666
MüC-17	1666	Waldenburg		disbanded in 1666
MüC-18	1668	Nagel; 1674 Bönninghausen; 1688 Christoph Bernhard von Nagel	Groenlo, Deventer, Twente, Coevorden (1672); Veldhausen, Muhlouse (1674); Türkheim (1675); Saint-Denis (1678)	in Spanish service from 1677 to 1678; ceded to Prussia in 1803
MüC-19	1672	Hautin	Groenlo (1672); Muhlouse (1674)	disbanded in 1674
MüC-20	1672	Courcelles		ceded to the Electorate of Cologne in 1672
MüC-21	1672	Wasternhagen		disbanded in 1672
MüC-22	1672	Heinrich IV von Reuss	Zwolle (1672)	disbanded in 1673
MüC-23	1672	Meinerzhagen		disbanded in 1673
MüC-24	1672	*Rheingraf*		disbanded in 1673
MüC-25	1672	Massenbach		disbanded in 1674
MüC-26	1672	Alexander Macdonnel; 1676 Wedel	Veldhausen, Muhlouse (1674); Türkheim (1675)	in Spanish service from 1677 to 1678; in Danish service in 1678; ceded to Denmark in 1679

ID	Year	Commander	Locations	Notes
MüC-27	1672	Friedrich Moritz von Bentheim-Tecklenburg		disbanded in 1672
MüC-28	1672	Post; 1674 Grandvilliers	Zwolle (1672); Veldhausen, Muhlouse (1674); Türkheim (1675); East Frisia (1676); Landskrona (1677); Warskow (1678)	in Danish service from 1677 to 1678; disbanded in 1678
MüC-29	1672	Westerholt	Twente (1672); Muhlouse (1674)	disbanded in 1674
MüC-30	1672	Andreas Probst; 1673 Offen; 1677 Mandelslohe	Zwolle (1672); Muhlouse (1674); Türkheim (1675);	in Spanish service from 1677 to 1678; disbanded in 1678
MüC-31	1672	Lennarts	Zwolle, Twente (1672)	disbanded in 1674
MüC-32	1672	Caldenbach		disbanded in 1672
MüC-33	1672	Wolframsdorff		disbanded in 1674
MüC-34	1672	Claude La Roche		disbanded in 1673
MüC-35	1673	*Leibregiment zu Pferde*; 1677 Mortaigne	Veldhausen (1674); Saint-Denis (1678)	in Spanish service from 1677 to 1678; disbanded in 1679
MüC-36	1677	Lion; 1678 Tserclaes de Tilly		in Spanish service in 1678; disbanded in 1679
MüC-37	1677	Floris		in Spanish service in 1678; disbanded in 1678
MüC-38	1677	Georg von der Nath		in Spanish service in 1678; disbanded in 1678
MüC-39	1678	Bassem		in Danish service in 1678; ceded to Denmark in 1679
MüC-40	1678	Rabe		in Danish service in 1678; ceded to Denmark in 1679
MüC-41	1678	Wendt		ceded to Denmark in 1679

Dragoon Squadrons

Id.	Year:	Colonel Proprietor – Denomination:	Campaigns – Engagements:	History:	Uniforms:
müd-i	1661	*Leibdragoner*		*Leibdragoner Regiment* in 1674	

Dragoon Regiments

Id.	Year:	Colonel Proprietor – Denomination:	Campaigns – Engagements:	History:	Uniforms:
MüD-1	1665	Heinrich Reinhard von Wolframsdorff		ceded to Kur-Pfalz in 1666	
MüD-2	1672	Wolframsdorff; 1674 Nagel; 1674 Wedel; 1676 Hoetensleben	Groningen (1672); Muhlouse (1673); Türkheim (1674)	in Spanish service from 1677 to 1678; in Danish service from 1678 to 1679; disbanded in 1767 as *Droste Cuirassieren*	(1672)[118] Private: fur cap with red bag; white cravat; yellow coat; cuffs and lining; brass buttons.
MüD-3	1672	Heinrich Ubach; 1677 Schönemacher	Landskrona (1677)	disbanded in 1678	
MüD-4	1674	*Leibdragoner*	Muhlouse (1674); Türkheim (1675)	disbanded in 1678	
MüD-5	1678	Rose		in Spanish service in 1678; disbanded in 1679	

Artillery

Id.	Year:	Colonel Proprietor – Denomination:	Campaigns – Engagements:	History:	Uniforms:
MüA-1	1673	Braun		disbanded in 1678	

APPENDIX I

Endnotes

1   Carl Röchling, *Fürstliche Leibcompagnie im Jahre 1664* (Wehrgeschichtlichen Museum Rastatt).

2   Karl Redlin, 'L'Armée Brandebourgeoise' in *Le Bivouac*, no.13 Septembre 1984.

3   Fedor von Köppen, *Preussens Heer in Bild und Wort, 1619–1889* (Glogau, 1900).

4   Redlin, 'L'Armée Brandebourgeoise' in *Le Bivouac*, no.13 Septembre 1984.

5   Hessische Staatsarchiv, Marburg, WHK 6/19: *Plan vom Feldlager der Armee des Kurfürsten von Brandenburg* (1686).

6   Reconstruction after the fresco of the battle of Szentgotthárd preserved in the Castle of Lysá, Czech Republic.

7   Redlin, 'L'Armée Brandebourgeoise' in *Le Bivouac*, no.13 Septembre 1984.

8   Reconstruction after the tapestry *Die Eroberung von Stralsund*, Oraniengburg Palace Museum.

9   Jany, *Geschichte der Königlich Preußischen Armee bis zum Jahre 1807*, Vol. I (Berlin, 1928), p.342.

10 Hessische Staatsarchiv, Marburg, WHK 6/19: *Plan vom Feldlager der Armee des Kurfürsten von Brandenburg* (1686).

11 Jany, *Geschichte der Königlich Preußischen Armee*, p.342.

12 Redlin, 'L'Armée Brandebourgeoise' in *Le Bivouac*, no.13 Septembre 1984.

13 *Ibid.*

14 Jany, *Geschichte der Königlich Preußischen Armee*, p.342.

15 *Ibid.*, p.345.

16 Hessische Staatsarchiv, Marburg, WHK 6/19: *Plan vom Feldlager der Armee des Kurfürsten von Brandenburg* (1686).

17 Belaubre, *Les Triomphes du Louis XIV*, p.7.

18 Redlin, 'L'Armée Brandebourgeoise' in *Le Bivouac*, no.13 Septembre 1984.

19 Martin Lezius, *Die Entwicklung des Deutschen Heeres von Seinen Frühesten Anfängen bis Unsere Tage in Uniformtafeln* (Berlin, 1936), plate 1.

20 Jany, *Geschichte der Königlich Preußischen Armee*, p.342.

21 Hessische Staatsarchiv, Marburg, WHK 6/19: *Plan vom Feldlager der Armee des Kurfürsten von Brandenburg* (1686).

22 Reconstruction after the tapestry *Die Landung auf Rügen*, Oraniengburg Palace Museum.

23 Hessische Staatsarchiv, Marburg, WHK 6/19: *Plan vom Feldlager der Armee des Kurfürsten von Brandenburg* (1686).

24 Jany, *Geschichte der Königlich Preußischen Armee*, p.345.

25 *Ibid.*, 342.

26 Hessische Staatsarchiv, Marburg, WHK 6/19: *Plan vom Feldlager der Armee des Kurfürsten von Brandenburg* (1686).

27 Redlin, 'L'Armée Brandebourgeoise' in *Le Bivouac*, no.13 Septembre 1984.

28 Hessische Staatsarchiv, Marburg, WHK 6/19: *Plan vom Feldlager der Armee des Kurfürsten von Brandenburg* (1686).

29 Jany, *Geschichte der Königlich Preußischen Armee*, p.342.

30 *Ibid.*, p.345.

31 Hessische Staatsarchiv, Marburg, WHK 6/19: *Plan vom Feldlager der Armee des Kurfürsten von Brandenburg* (1686).

32 Karl Redlin, 'L'Armée Brandebourgeoise' in *Le Bivouac*, no.13 Septembre 1984.

33 Knötel, *Die Grosse Uniformenkunde*, Regiment Kurland 1686.

34 Hessische Staatsarchiv, Marburg, WHK 6/19: *Plan vom Feldlager der Armee des Kurfürsten von Brandenburg* (1686).

35 Jany, *Geschichte der Königlich Preußischen Armee*, p.342.

36 Belaubre, *Les Triomphes du Louis XIV*, p.64.

37 Jany, *Geschichte der Königlich Preußischen Armee*, p.342.

38 Redlin, 'L'Armée Brandebourgeoise' in *Le Bivouac*, no.13 Septembre 1984.

39 *Ibid.*

40 Fedor von Köppen, *Preussens Heer in Bild und Wort, 1619–1889* (Glogau, 1900)., p.7, and Karl Redlin, 'L'Armée Brandebourgeoise' in *Le Bivouac*, n. 13 – September 1984.

41 Redlin, 'L'Armée Brandebourgeoise' in *Le Bivouac*, no.13 Septembre 1984.

42 Romeyn de Hooghe's print, *Slag bi St. Denis, 1678*.

43 Belaubre, *Les Triomphes du Louis XIV*, p.129 and Ewald Fiebig, *Unsterbliche Treue. Das Heldenlied der Fahnen und Standarten des Deutschen Heeres* (Berlin, 1936), p.18.

44 Pelet-Narbonne, *Geschichte der Brandenburg-Preußischen Reiterei*, p.19, and Jany, *Geschichte der Königlich Preußischen Armee*, p.349.

45 Belaubre, *Les Triomphes du Louis XIV*, p.76.

46 Redlin, 'L'Armée Brandebourgeoise' in *Le Bivouac*, no.13 Septembre 1984.

47 Reconstruction after the colours preserved in the Deutschen Historischen Museum, Berlin.

48 Redlin, 'L'Armée Brandebourgeoise' in *Le Bivouac*, no.13 Septembre 1984.

49 Jany, *Geschichte der Königlich Preußischen Armee*, p.349.

50 Belaubre, *Les Triomphes du Louis XIV*, p.129.

51 Knötel, *Die Grosse Uniformenkunde*.

52 Hessische Staatsarchiv, Marburg, WHK 6/19: *Plan vom Feldlager der Armee des Kurfürsten von Brandenburg* (1686).

53 Reconstruction after Fiebig, *Unsterbliche Treue*, p.19.

54 Belaubre, *Les Triomphes du Louis XIV*, p.13.

55 Knötel, *Die Grosse Uniformenkunde*.

56 Jany, *Geschichte der Königlich Preußischen Armee*, p.349.

57 Hessische Staatsarchiv, Marburg, WHK 6/19: *Plan vom Feldlager der Armee des Kurfürsten von Brandenburg* (1686).

APPENDIX I

58   Knötel, *Die Grosse Uniformenkunde.*

59   Archivio di Stato di Torino (ASTo), *Sezioni Riunite, Patenti Controllo Finanze*, m. 84 (1672).

60   ASV (Archivio Segreto Vaticano), Segreteria di Stato 1026, *Avvisi, Avvisi di Germania*, 23 Aprile 1663.

61   Karl Staudinger, *Geschichte des Kurbayerischen Heeres Insbesondere unter Kurfürst Ferdinand Maria, 1651–1679* (Münich, 1901), p.353.

62   Staudinger, *Geschichte des Kurbayerischen Heeres*, vol. I, p.354.

63   *Ibid.*, p.353.

64   Archivio di Stato di Torino (ASTo), *Sezioni Riunite, Patenti Controllo Finanze*, m. 84 (1672).

65   Anton Hoffmann, *Das Heer des Blauen Königs – Die Soldaten des Kurfürsten Max II. Emanuel von Bayern 1682 – 1726* (Münich, 1909), plate 52.

66   Jean Belaubre, *Les Triomphes du Louis XIV* (Paris: self-publishing, 1971), p.62.

67   Friedrich Münich, *Geschichte der Entwicklung der Bayerischen Armee seit zwei Jahrhunderten* (Münich, 1864), p.41.

68   Hoffmann, Das Heer des Blauen Königs, plate 52.

69   *Ibid.*

70   Münich, *Geschichte der Entwicklung der Bayerischen Armee*, p.41.

71   Hoffmann, *Das Heer des Blauen Königs*, plate 52.

72   *Ibid.*

73   Münich, *Geschichte der Entwicklung der Bayerischen Armee*, p.41.

74   Hoffmann, *Das Heer des Blauen Königs*, plate 52.

75   Belaubre, *Les Triomphes du Louis XIV*, p.63.

76   Hoffmann, *Das Heer des Blauen Königs*, plate 52.

77   Staudinger, *Geschichte des Kurbayerischen Heeres*, vol. II, p.15.

78   Staudinger, *Geschichte des Kurbayerischen Heeres*, vol. I, p.357.

79   *Ibid.*

80   *Ibid.*, p.353.

81   Münich, *Geschichte der Entwicklung der Bayerischen Armee*, p.41.

82   Hoffmann, *Das Heer des Blauen Königs*, plate 53.

83   Münich, *Geschichte der Entwicklung der Bayerischen Armee*, p.41.

84   Hoffmann, *Das Heer des Blauen Königs*, plate 53.

85   *Ibid.*

86   *Ibid.*

87   Staudinger, *Geschichte des Kurbayerischen Heeres*, vol. II, p.43.

88   *Ibid.*

89   Hoffmann, *Das Heer des Blauen Königs*, plate 53.

90   *Ibid.*, plate 53.

91   *Ibid.*, plate 53.

92   *Ibid.*, plate 53.

93   Oskar Schuster and Friedrich August Francke, *Die Geschichte der Sächsische Armee von der Errichtung bis in die neueste Zeit: Unter Benutzung handschriftlicher und urkundlicher Quellen*, vol. I (Leipzig, 1885), p.112.

94 Schuster – Francke, *Die Geschichte der Sächsische Armee*, p, 110 and *Manfroni Manuscript*, plate 239; Rossi-Cassigoli Collection 199 – Biblioteca Nazionale Centrale, Florence.

95 *Uniformes de l'Electorat de Saxe, 1685–1772* (Bibliothèque Nationale de France, Paris), plate 1.

96 *Ibid.*, plate 3.

97 *Ibid.*, plate 6.

98 *Ibid.*, plate 1.

99 *Ibid.*, plate 4.

100 *Ibid.*, plate 5.

101 Schuster and Francke, *Die Geschichte der Sächsische Armee*, p, 110.

102 *Ibid.*

103 *Uniformes de l'Electorat de Saxe, 1685–1772* (Bibliothèque Nationale de France, Paris), plate 8.

104 Schuster and Francke, *Die Geschichte der Sächsische Armee*, p, 113.

105 *Uniformes de l'Electorat de Saxe, 1685–1772* (Bibliothèque Nationale de France, Paris), plate 7.

106 Friedrich, *Die Uniformen der Kurfürstlich Sächsischen Armee, 1683–1763*, p.58.

107 Dan Schorr, *The Saxon Army 1700-1716* (selfpublishing, 2008), author's reconstruction.

108 *Ibid.*

109 *Uniformes de l'Electorat de Saxe, 1685–1772* (Bibliothèque Nationale de France, Paris), plate 9.

110 Dan Schorr, *The Saxon Army 1700-1716* (selfpublishing, 2008), author's reconstruction.

111 Friedrich, *Die Uniformen der kurfürstlich Sächsischen Armee, 1683–1763*, p.58.

112 Dan Schorr, *The Saxon Army 1700-1716* (selfpublishing, 2008), author's reconstruction.

113 Dan Schorr, *The Saxon Army 1700-1716* (selfpublishing, 2008), author's reconstruction.

114 Theodor Verspohl, 'Das Heerwesen des Münsterschen Fürstbischofs Christoph Bernhard von Galen 1650–1678', in *Beiträge für die Geschichte Niedersachsens und Westfalens*. 18. Heft, Universität Münster (1909).

115 *Ibid.*

116 Reconstruction after Gualdo Priorato, *Relatione delle Corti e Stati* (Leyden, 1668).

117 Reconstruction after Fritz Lallemand, *Die k.k. Österreichische Armee im Laufe zweyer Jahrhunderte* (Vienna, 1840).

118 Reconstruction after Folkert Bock's painting *Beleg van Groningen in 1672* (City Hall of Groningen).

Appendix II

Army Lists and Orders of Battle

Brandenburg

Garrisons, April 1655

	Strength	Quarters
Infantry		
Leibgarde, Märkische Kompagnie (bri-i)	1 comp.	Kleve-Mark
Sparr (BrI-3)	9 comp.	Colberg, Minden and Lippstadt
Goltz (BrI-7)	8 comp.	Brandenburg
Wolrad von Waldeck (BrI-6)	12 comp.	Brandenburg
Spaen (BrI-17)	11 comp.	Ravensberg
Cavalry		
Leibgarde zu Ross (brc-i)	69 men	Berlin
Kannenberg (BrC-1)	10 comp.	Brandenburg
Georg Friedrich zu Waldeck (BrC-2)	12 comp.	Kleve-Mark
Spaen (BrC-3)	6 comp.	Ravensberg
Eller (Brc-4)	6 comp.	Preussen
Lottum (BrC-11)	2 comp	Preussen
Dragoons		
Georg Friedrich zu Waldeck (BrD-1)	1 comp.	Kleve-Mark
Kanitz (BrD-2)	1 comp.	Brandenburg
Artillery		
34 cannons and 3 howitzers		

Source: Curt Jany, *Geschichte der Königlich Preußischen Armee bis zum Jahre 1807*, vol. I (Berlin, 1928), pp.116–117.

The *Defensionwerk* in Prussia (Militia in Ducal Prussia), 1655

District:	Infantry	Cavalry	Dragoons
Samland	7 companies Ragnit 1 Insterburg 3 Schaaken 1 Tilsit 1 Memel 1	5 companies Schaaken 1 Fischausen 1 Tapiau 1 Neuhäuser 1 Insterburg 1	
Ratingen	4 companies Brandenburg 1 Angerburg 1 Oletzko 1 Rhein 1	5 companies Brandenburg1 Rastenburg 1 Balga 1 Angerburg 1 Eylau 1	4 companies Oletzko 1 Johannisburg 1 Lötzen 1 Rhein 1
Oberland	2 companies: Holland 1 Neidenburg 1	6 companies: Ortelsburg 1 Osterode 1 Mark 1 Holland 1 Reidenburg 1 Marienwerder 1	
Total	3,592 *Musketiere*	1,788.5 *Reiter*	389.5 *Dragoner*

Source: Curt Jany, *Geschichte der Königlich Preußischen Armee*, p.112.

Brandenburg Army; Campaign of Poland, 1656

Infantry

#	Regiment or Battalion:	Officers	Men
BrI-9	*Churfürstliche Leibgarde*	6	279
BrI-3	*Sparr*	12	1,200
BrI-6	*Wolrad von Waldeck*	12	1,200
BrI-7	*Goltz*	8	800
BrI-10	*Götkze*	10	1,000
BrI-11	*Eulenburg*	10	1,000
BrI-14	*Georg Friedrich von Waldeck*	6	600
BrI-15	*Halle*	4	400
BrI-17	*Syburg*	12	1,200

APPENDIX II

Cavalry

#	Regiment or Squadron/Company:	Officers	Men
BrC-12	*Churfürstliche Leibregiment*	7	700
BrC-1	*Kannenberg*	10	1,000
BrC-2	*Georg Friedrich von Waldeck*	12	1,200
BrC-3	*Sachsen-Weimar*	6	600
BrC-4	*Eller*	6	600
BrC-5	*Lesgewang*	2	200
BrC-6	*Heinrich Wallenrodt*	4	400
BrC-7	*Schöneich*	8	400
BrC-9	*Halle*	3	300
BrC-10	*Georg Wallenrodt*	8	800
BrC-11	*Brunell*	3	300
-	*Schmidt* (squadron)	2	200
-	*Putlitz* (free company)	1	100
-	*Massenbach* (free company)	1	100

Dragoons

#	Regiment or Squadron/Company:	Officers	Men
BrD-i	*Leibgarde Dragoner*	1	200
BrD-1	*Georg Friedrich von Waldeck*	5	555
BrD-2	*Kanitz*	4	400
BrD-3	*Kalckstein*	5	500
BrD-6	*Halle*	3	300
BrD-5	*Auer*	3	300
BrD-4	*Ritterforth*	8	800
-	*Kannenberg* (free company)	1	100
-	*Heinrich Wallenrodt* (free company)	1	100

Artillery:

30 Cannons and 5 howitzers

Source: Curt Jany, *Geschichte der Königlich Preußischen Armee*, pp.121–122.

Brandenburg Order of Battle at Warsaw, 28–30 July 1656

Infantry

Churfürstliche Leibgarde zu Fuss (BrI-9) 2 comp.
Sparr (BrI-3) 11 comp.
Goltz (BrI-7) 8 comp.
Waldeck (BrI-6) 12 comp.
Syburg (BrI-17) 11 comp.

Cavalry

Leibregiment zu Ross (BrC-12) 3 sqn
Waldeck (BrC-2) 6 sqn
Kannenberg (BrC-1) 3 sqn
Eller (BrC-4) 2 sqn
Schönheich (BrC-7) 2 sqn
Lesgewang (BrC-5) 1 sqn
Brünell (BrC-11) 1 sqn
Weimar (BrC-3) 2 sqn

Dragoons

Waldeck (BrD-1) 4 sqn
Kanitz (BrD-2) 3 sqn
Kalckstein (BrD-3) 3 sqn
Artillery: 30 cannons and 5 howitzer.

Source: (Various authors), *Stammliste der Königlich Preußischen Armee Seit dem 16ten Jahrhundert bis 1840* (Berlin, 1840), p.5.

Troops in Brandenburg and Pomerania, October 1657

Infantry

#	Unit	Strength
BrI-i/ii	*Garde zu Fuss*	2 comp.
BrI-3	*Sparr*	12 comp.
BrI-6	*Wolrad von Waldeck*	8 comp.
BrI-7	*Goltz*	8 comp.
BrI-10	*Götkze*	8 comp.
BrI-17	*Syburg*	9 comp.

Total: 47 companies

APPENDIX II

Cavalry

#	Unit	Strength
BrC-i	*Churfürstliche Trabanten*	1 comp.
BrC-12	*Churfürstliche Leibregiment*	10 comp.
BrC-13	*Derfflinger*	8 comp.
BrC-1	*Kannenberg*	9 comp.
BrC-17	*Görzke*	4 comp.
BrC-18	*Quast*	4 comp.
BrC-16	*Pfuel*	4 comp.
BrC-4	*Eller*	6 comp.
BrC-3	*Sachsen-Weimar*	8 comp.
BrC-20	*Wittgenstein*	5 comp.
BrC-9	*Halle*	4 comp.
BrC-14	*Katzler*	4 comp.
BrC-19	*Zastrow*	8 comp.
BrC-21	*Schmidt*	3 comp.
BrC-22	*Marwitz*	5 comp.

Total: 83 companies

Dragoons

#	Unit	Strength
BrD-7	*Leibdragoner*	5 comp.
BrD-6	*Sparr*	5 comp.
BrD-9	*Kanitz*	4 comp.

Total: 14 companies

Source: Curt Jany, *Geschichte der königlich preußischen Armee*, p.138.

Winter Quarters in 1658

Province/Towns	Infantry	Cavalry	Dragoons
Brandenburg	54 comp.	53 comp.	10 comp.
Prussia	47 comp.	17 comp.	9 comp.
Pomerania	8 comp.	41 comp.	5 comp.
Halberstadt	2 comp.	5 comp.	-

Source: Adolph von Crouzas, *Die Organisationen des Brandenburgischen und Preußischen Heeres von 1640, Sowie Neuzeitig Diejenigen des Norddeutschen Bundes und Deutschen Reichsheeres*, vol. I (Berlin, 1873), p.10.

341

Brandenburg Standing Army, July 1672

Infantry

#	Unit:	Strength	
		Garrison	**Field**
BrI-9	*Garde zu Fuss*	639	1,016
BrI-11	*Kurprinz*	?	?
BrI-2	*Dohna*	?	166
BrI-4	*Kannenberg*	600	-
BrI-14	*Holstein*	600	-
BrI-7	*Goltz*	-	1,008
BrI-26	*Spaen*	-	1,008
BrI-48	*Eller*	402	-
BrI-45	*Görtkze*	200	1,008
BrI-46	*Syberg*	-	1,008
BrI-44	*Plettenberg (Flemming)*	600	-
BrI-39	*Fargel*	756	-
BrI-49	*Berlepach*	504	-
BrI-47	*Reuss*	504	-
BrI-50	*Chieze*	604	-
BrI-5	*Schwerin*	?	?
-	Freicompagnie Peitz	200	-

Cavalry

#	Unit:	Strength:	
		Garrison	**Field**
BrC-i	Trabanten	200	-
BrC-35	*Leibregiment*	522	-
BrC-36	*Kurprinz*	522	-
BrC-37	*Hessen-Homburg*	262	-
BrC-32	*Prinz Friedrich*	101	-
BrC-34	Eller	101	-
BrC-31	*Kannenberg*	101	-
BrC-28	*Spaen*	101	-
BrC-29	*Anhalt*	101	-
BrC-30	*Derfflinger*	101	-
BrC-38	Mecklenburg	101	-
BrC-39	*Görtkze*	101	-
BrC-40	*Promnitz*	101	-

Dragoons

#	Unit	Strength	
		Garrison	Field
BrD-1	Derfflinger	388	-
BrD-11	Bomsdorff	388	-

Georg Adalbert von Mülverstedt, *Die brandenburgische Kriegsmacht unter dem Großen Kurfürsten* (Magdeburg, 1888), pp.788–789.

Brandenburg Corps in Alsace, 1674

Infantry

#	Unit	Strength	
BrI-9	*Garde zu Fuss*	8 comp.	1,000
BrI-11	*Kurprinz*	8 comp.	1,000
BrI-51	*Derfflinger*	8 comp.	1,000
BrI-2	*Dohna*	8 comp.	1,000
BrI-7	*Goltz*	8 comp.	1,000
BrI-45	*Görtzke*	8 comp.	1,000
BrI-14	*Holstein*	5 comp.	625
BrI-39	*Fargell*	5 comp.	625
BrI-43	*Döhnoff*	4 comp.	560
BrI-44	*Flemming*	4 comp.	500

Cavalry

#	Unit:	Strength	
BrC-i	Trabanten	1 comp.	150
BrC-ii	Prinz Friedrich Leibgarde	1 comp.	100
BrC-35	Leibregiment	6 comp.	516
BrC-36	Kurprinz	6 comp.	600
BrC-32	Prinz Friedrich	6 comp.	600
BrC-30	Derfflinger	6 comp.	516
BrC-29	Anhalt	6 comp.	516
BrC-31	Görtzke	6 comp.	600
BrC-33	Mörner	6 comp.	600
BrC-34	Lütke	6 comp.	516
BrC-37	Hessen-Homburg	4 comp.	400
BrC-38	Brockdorff	3 comp.	270
BrC-39	Croy	2 comp.	200

Dragoons

#	Unit:	Strength	
BrD-15	Leibdragoner	1 comp.	100
BrD-1	Derfflinger	6 comp.	616
BrD-16	Bomstorff	6 comp.	616

Artillery

40 cannons, 2 mortars (1,000 artillerymen, assistants and drivers)

Source: Curt Jany, *Geschichte der Königlich Preußischen Armee*, pp.225-226

Brandenburg Order of Battle at Fehrbellin, 18 June 1675

Right Wing Cavalry (Friedrich of Hessen-Homburg)
Leibregiment (BrC-45)
Hessen-Homburg (BrC-37) 3 sqn
Mörner (BrC-33) 3 sqn
Görtzke (BrC-31) 3 sqn
Prinz Friedrich (BrC-32) 2 sqn
Brockdorff (BrC-38) 1 sqn; *Kurprinz* (BrC-36) 3 sqn
Lütke (BrC-34) 2 sqn.

Left Wing Cavalry and Dragoons (Georg von Derfflinger)
Trabanten (brc-i) 1 sqn
Anhalt (BrC-29) 3 sqn
Derfflinger (BrC-30) 3 sqn
Schlieben (BrD-12) 1 sqn
Derfflinger (BrD-1) 1 sqn
Leibdragoner (BrD-15) 1 sqn
Croy (BrC-39) 1 sqn
Frankenberg (Pfalz-Neuburg) 2 sqn.

1,350 mounted infantry from various infantry regiments.

Artillery: 9 light guns (3 lb), 2 field guns (12 lb) 2 howitzers

Source: Ernst Friedrich Christian Müsebeck, *Die Feldzüge des Grossen Kurfürsten in Pommern 1675–1677* (Marburg, 1897), p.66.

APPENDIX II

Brandenburg Order of Battle at Stettin (July 1677)

Infantry

Kurfürstin (BrI-57)
Kurprinz (BrI-55)
Görtkze (BrI-60)
Dohna (BrI-2)
Holstein (BrI-14)
Goltz (BrI-7)
Fargell (BrI-39)
Schwerin (BrI-16)
Donhoff (BrI-43)
Schöning (BrI-11)
Montgomery Grenadier Company

Cavalry

Trabanten (BrC-i)
Leibregiment (BrC-35); *Kurprinz* (BrC-36); Anhalt (BrC-29); *Derfflinger* (BrC-30); *Hessen-Homburg* (BrC-37); *Görtzke* (BrC-39); *Prinz Friedrich* (BrC-35); *Croy* (BrC-39); *Treffenfels* (BrC-33); *Hamel* (BrC-38); *Freycompagnie Kussow*

Dragoons

Leibregiment (BrD-15); Derfflinger (BrD-1); Görtzke (BrD-12); Schlieben (BrD-13); Holstein (BrD-16); *Freycompagnie Schwerin*.

Source: Curt Jany, *Geschichte der königlich preußischen Armee*, p.255.

345

The Brandenburg *Militäretat*, February 1679

Infantry

#	Unit	Strength
BrI-2	*Barfus*	1,374
BrI-7	*Goltz*	1,174
BrI-9	*Leibregiment*	1,395
BrI-11	*Schöning*	1,374
BrI-14	*Alt-Holstein*	1,174
BrI-26	*Spaen*	1,158
BrI-43	*Döhnoff*	1,158
BrI-39	*Fargell*	1,158
BrI-45	*Schlieben*	1,158
BrI-51	*Marwitz*	1,151
BrI-52	*Micrander*	1,158
BrI-55	*Prinz Friedrich*	1,379
BrI-56	*Hallart*	1,158
BrI-57	*Kurfürstin*	1.379
BrI-58	*Jung-Holstein*	1,174
BrI-59	*Candal*	290
BrI-60	*Görtkze*	1,379
BrI-61	*Croy*	586
(BrI-62)	*Bataillon Eckebrecht* (later *Zieten zu Fuss*)	256
BrI-1	Truchsess	?
BrI-4	*Eller*	?
BrI-5	*Schlabendorff*	?
BrI-16	*Schwerin*	?
BrI-54	*Bolsey* (marine battalion)	?

Cavalry

#	Unit	Strength
BrC-i	*Trabanten*	340
BrC-35	*Leibregiment*	698
BrC-28	*Spaen*	638
Brc-41	*Eller*	548
BrC-34	*Lütke*	614
BrC-33	*Treffenfeld*	698
BrC-29	*Anhalt-Dessau*	698

APPENDIX II

BrC-30	*Derfflinger*	698
BrC-31	*Görtzke*	698
BrC-36	*Kurprinz*	698
BrC-37	*Hessen-Homburg*	698
BrC-38	*du Hamel*	698
BrC-39	*Croy*	698
BrC-42	*Kussow*	474
-	*Brand* (free company)	166

Dragoons

#	Unit	Strength
BrD-15	Leibdragoner	710
BrD-1	Derfflinger	710
BrD-12	Sydow	710
BrD-16	Holstein	478
BrD-17	Croy	178

Mülverstedt, *Die Brandenburgische Kriegsmacht unter dem Großen Kurfürsten*, pp.20-30.

Brandenburg Army Peace Strength, January 1680 – April 1681

Infantry

#	Unit	Strength		Quarters
BrI-9	*Garde zu Fuss*	10 comp.	1,500	Berlin
BrI-57	*Kurfürstin*	8 comp.	1,200	Prussia
BrI-55	*Prinz Friedrich*	8 comp.	1,200	Prussia
BrI-60	*Derfflinger*	8 comp.	1,200	Altmark
BrI-39	*Anhalt-Dessau*	9 comp.	1,350	Halberstadt and Regenstein
BrI-11	*Schöning*	8 comp.	1,200	Magdeburg
BrI-2	*Barfus*	8 comp.	1,200	Prussia
BrI-26	*Spaen*	13 comp.	1,625	Kleve
BrI-62	*Zieten*	8 comp.	1,000	Minden
BrI-4	*Pöllnitz*	5 comp.	575	Lippstadt and Sparenberg
BrI-43	*Dönhoff*	4 comp.	500	Prussia
BrI-61	*Croy*	2 comp.	300	Prussia

347

BrI-14	*Holstein*	4 comp.	800	Colberg
BrI-54	*Bolsey* (Marine battalion)	4 comp.	?	Emden
BrI-1	*Truchsess*	6 comp.	900	Kustrin and Driesen
BrI-4	*Pöllnitz*	4 comp.	600	Pillau
BrI-5	Schlabrendorff	2 comp.	300	Spandau
-	Free companies	2 comp.	300	Peitz
-	Free companies	2 comp.	300	Memel
-	Free company	1 comp.	150	Oberberg and Löchnitz
-	Free company	1 comp.	150	Frankfurt
-	Free company	1 comp.	150	Friedrichsburg

Cavalry

#	Unit	Strength		Quarters
BrC-i	*Trabanten*	2 comp.	150	Mittelmark
BrC-35	*Leibregiment*	6 comp.	384	Mittelmark
BrC-32	*Prinz Friedrich*	6 comp.	384	Neumark
BrC-29	*Anhalt-Dessau*	6 comp.	384	Prussia
BrC-30	*Derfflinger*	6 comp.	384	Pomerania
BrC-31	*Görtzke*	6 comp.	384	Prussia
BrC-28	*Spaen*	3 comp.	192	Prussia
-	Free companies	3 comp.	192	Kleve
-	Free companies	3 comp.	192	Mark

Dragoons

#	Unit	Strength		Quarters
BrD-15	*Leibregiment*	8 comp.	512	Brandenburg
BrD-1	*Derfflinger*	8 comp.	512	Prussia
BrD-17	Croy	2 comp.	128	Prussia

Artillery

Officers:	Feurwerker	Petardier	Korporal	Büchsenmeister	Quarters
8	19	2	14	169	Brandenburg
4	2	-	4	60	Prussia
3	4	-	3	44	Magdeburg
1	3	-	2	30	Colberg
3	2	-	2	39	Minden
2	3	-	2	32	Kleve

Source: Curt Jany, *Geschichte der Königlich Preußischen Armee*, pp.275-277. Stammlisten

APPENDIX II

The Artillery Corps in 1681

2 *Oberst-Lieutenante*	7 *Zeugschmiede* with
3 *Oberhauptleute*	7 *Gesellen*
6 *Hauptleute*	7 *Stellmacher* with
6 *Lieutenante*	4 *Gesellen*
11 *Zeugwärter*	1 *Wagenbauer*
1 *Secretair*	1 *Windenmacher*
1 *Feuerwerkmeister*	1 *Laffetenmacher*
4 *Stückjunker*	1 *Zimmermann*
6 *Zeugschreiber*	2 *Büchsenmacher* with
32 *Feuerwerker*	1 *Gesellen*
1 *Zeugmeister*	5 *Artillerie-Knechte*
2 *Petardierer*	1 *Profoss*
1 *Gefreiten-Corporal*	1 *Steckenknecht*
25 *Corporale*	Total: 514 men
374 *Constabler* and *Büchsenmeister*	

Source Louis von Malinowsky – Robert von Bonin, *Geschichte der Brandenburgisch-Preussischen Artillerie* (Berlin, 1842), vol. I, p.27.

Brandenburg Campaign in Hungary, 1686

Infantry

#	Unit	Strength		
BrI-9	*Garde zu Fuss*	8 comp.	2 bat.	1,000
BrI-55	*Prinz Friedrich*	4 comp.	1 bat.	500
BrI-65	*Markgraf Philipp*	4 comp.	1 bat.	500
BrI-60	*Derfflinger*	4 comp.	1 bat.	500
BrI-39	*Anhalt-Dessau*	4 comp.	1 bat.	500
BrI-2	*Barfus*	4 comp.	1 bat.	500
BrI-43	*Dönhoff*	4 comp.	1 bat.	500
BrI-67	*Kurland*	4 comp.	1 bat.	500
BrI-57	*Kurfürstin*	4 comp.	1 bat.	?

349

WARS AND SOLDIERS IN THE EARLY REIGN OF LOUIS XIV – VOLUME 7 PART 1

Cavalry

#	Unit	Strength		
BrC-35	*Leibregiment*	6 comp.	3 sqn	600
BrC-32	*Prinz Friedrich*	6 comp.	3 sqn	600
BrC-44	*Straus*	?	?	?

Dragoons

#	Unit	Strength		
BrD-15	*Leibregiment*	4 comp.	2 sqn	390
BrD-1	*Derfflinger*	4 comp.	2 sqn	390

Source: Curt Jany, *Geschichte der Königlich Preußischen Armee*, p.289.

Brandenburg Regiments and Garrisons, spring 1688.

Infantry

#	Unit:	*Primaplana*:	*Gemeine*:	Quarter:
BrI-9	Garde zu Fuss	24	3,000	Berlin and Magdeburg
BrI-57	*Kurfürstin*	8	1,200	Magdeburg
BrI-55	*Prinz Friedrich*	8	1,000	Altmark, Prignitz, Rathenow
BrI-65	*Markgraf Philipp*	8	1,000	Neumark
BrI-39	*Anhalt-Dessau*	8	1,000	Wesel
BrI-60	*Derfflinger*	8	1,000	Altmark
BrI-14	*Alt-Holstein*	8	1,000	Wesel and Rees
BrI-66	*Jung-Holstein*	8	1,000	Emmerich and Wesel
BrI-26	*Spaen*	8	1,200	Wesel and Kleve
BrI-43	*Dönhoff*	8	1,000	Prussia
BrI-2	Barfus	8	1,000	Pomerania
BrI-62	*Zieten*	8	1,200	Minden
BrI-67	*Kurland*	8	1,000	Prussia
BrI-61	*Truchsess-Waldburg*	3	375	Prussia
BrI-70	*Lottum*	5	750	Lippstadt and Sparenberg
BrI-68	*Varenne*	16	620	Goest, Stift, Essen, Werden, Bielefeld, Herford
BrI-69	*Courneaud*	4	140	Brandenburg
BrI-54	*Bolsey* (marine)	3	375	Emden
BrI-1	*Belling*	6	900	Kustrin and Driesen

350

APPENDIX II

BrI-4	*Briquemault*	6	750	Pillau
BrI-5	Schlabrendorff	4	600	Colberg
-	Free companies	2	300	Spandau
-	Free companies	2	300	Peiz
-	Free companies	2	250	Memel
-	Free company	1	150	Oberberg
-	Free company	1	150	Frankfurt
-	Free company	1	150	Magdeburg
-	Free company	1	125	Friedrichsburg

Cavalry

#	Unit:	*Primaplana*	*Gemeine*	Quarters
BrC-i	*Trabanten**	2	347	Berlin and Potsdam
BrC-iii	*Grands Mousquetaires*	2	130	Prenzlau and Fürstenwalde
BrC-iv	*Grenadiers*	1	30	Beeskow and Storkow
BrC-35	*Leibregiment*	6	300	Altmark
BrC-32	*Kurprinz*	6	300	Neumark
BrC-29	*Anhalt-Dessau*	5	300	Prussia
BrC-30	*Derfflinger*	6	300	Pomerania
BrC-28	*Spaen*	6	300	Kleve
BrC-31	*Lüttwiz*	6	300	Prussia
BrC-43	*Briquemault*	10	400	Minden, Ravensberg, Kleve
BrC-45	*Prinz Heinrich*	6	300	Prussia

* Included 47 *Alte-Trabanten* (veterans) quartered in Friedrichswerder.

Dragoons

#	Unit	*Primaplana*	*Gemeine*	Quarters
BrD-15	*Leibregiment*	8	512	Brandenburg
BrD-1	*Derfflinger*	8	512	Prussia
BrD-19	*Perbandt*	2	128	Prussia

Source: Curt Jany, *Geschichte der königlich preußischen Armee*, pp.300–302; Mülverstedt, *Die brandenburgische Kriegsmacht unter dem Großen Kurfürsten*, pp.502–546.

351

Brandenburg Auxiliary Corps In the Netherlands (October 1688)

Infantry

#	Unit	Primaplana	Gemeine
BrI-57	*Kurfürstin*	4	480
BrI-55	*Kurprinz*	6	720
BrI-65	*Markgraf Philipp*	6	720
BrI-60	*Derfflinger*	6	720
BrI-39	*Anhalt-Dessau*	4	480
BrI-14	*Alt-Holstein*	4	480
BrI-66	*Jung-Holstein*	4	480
BrI-26	*Spaen*	4	480
BrI-62	*Zieten*	6	720
Total		44	5,280

Cavalry

#	Unit:	Primaplana	Gemeine
BrC-28	*Spaen*	6	300
BrC-43	*Briquemault*	6	300
Total		12	600

Curt Jany, *Geschichte der Königlich Preußischen Armee*, p.361.

APPENDIX II

Bavaria

Professional Troops under Prince-Elector Ferdinand Maria (Late Spring 1657)

Infantry:

#	Regiments or Companies	Strength	
BvI-1	*Wolfsegg*	5 comp.	1,000
BvI-2	*Fugger*	5 comp.	1,000
BvI-3	*Royer*	5 comp.	1,000
BvI-4	*Puech*	5 comp.	1,000
-	Freikompagnue Culer	1 comp.	200
-	Freikompagnie Leoprechting	1 comp.	200
Total (on paper)		22	4,400
Final Total			4,384

Cavalry (Life Guards and *Arquebusieren*):

#	Regiments or Companies	Strength	
BvC-i	*Leibgarde zu Pferd*	1 comp.	100
BvC-1	*Truckmüller*	3 comp.	300
BvC-2	*Kolb*	3 comp.	300
-	Freikompagnie Giel	1 comp.	100
-	Freikompagnie Bärtls	1 comp.	100
-	Freikompagnie Mittelsohn	1 comp.	100
-	Freikompagnie Franz	1 comp.	100
-	Freikompagnie Höning	1 comp.	100
-	Freikompagnie Lamingen	1 comp.	100
-	Freikompagnie Hoffstätten	1 comp.	100
-	Freikompagnie Lichtenau	1 comp.	100

Dragoons

-	Freikompagnie Bärtls	1 comp.	100
Total Cavalry and Dragoons (on paper)		16	1,600
Final Total			1,547

Source: Karl Staudinger, *Geschichte des kurbayerischen Heeres insbesondere unter Kurfürst Ferdinand Maria, 1651–1679* (Münich, 1901), vol. I, pp.171–174.

353

Garrisons (June-August 1660)

In Bavaria	Infantry	Cavalry
Münich	2 comp.	1 comp.
Ingolstadt	1 comp.	1 comp.
Landshut	1 comp.	1 comp.
Straubing	1 comp.	1 comp.
Keltheim	1 comp.	-
Burghausen	1 comp.	-
Donauwörth	1 comp.	-
Abensberg	1 comp.	-
Ried	1 comp.	-
Branau	1 comp.	-
Ötting	1 comp.	-
Traunstein	1 comp.	-
Aichach	1 comp.	-
Cham	-	1 comp.
Lindau	-	1 comp.
Schärding	-	1 comp.
Eggenfelden	-	1 comp.
Wasserburg	-	1 comp.
?	-	2 comp.

In the High-Palatinate	Infantry	Cavalry
Amberg	4 comp.	2 comp.
Neumarkt	1 comp.	-
Rothenberg	1 comp.	-

Source: Staudinger, *Geschichte des Kurbayerischen Heeres Insbesondere unter Kurfürst Ferdinand Maria*, vol. I, pp.180–181.

Bavarian Army Strength (early 1675)

Infantry: 11,400 men in 9 regiments/battalions*, 2 free companies and 1 garrison company (57 companies)
Cavalry: 4,000 men in 5 regiments (40 companies)
Dragoons: 500 men in 4 companies

Total on paper: 15,900 men

In Bavaria 2,120 infantry. In the High-Palatinate 852 infantry.

APPENDIX II

Field army: 8,428 infantry; 4,000 cavalry and 500 dragoons.

Actual total: 12,928 men

* The number included two *Offenen* (open) field battalions.

Source: Staudinger, *Geschichte des kurbayerischen Heeres insbesondere unter Kurfürst Ferdinand Maria*, vol. I, p.252.

Bavarian Artillery Classification, 1660

	Calibre:	*Constablers*	*Servants*	Draw Horses
Doppelte Kartaune	96 lb	6	24	40
Ganze Kartaune	48 lb	4	20	32
Dreiviertel Kartaune	36 lb	3	15	26
Halbe Kartaune	24 lb	2	10	20
Viertel-Kartaune	12 lb	2	8	16
Ganze Feldschlange	18 lb	3	10	20
Halbe Feldschange	9 lb	2	6	10
Falkone	6 lb	2	4	8
Regimentstück	3 lb	1	3	4
Falkonett	1 lb	1	1	2
Serpentine	½ lb	1	1	2

Source: Staudinger, *Geschichte des Kurbayerischen Heeres Insbesondere Unter Kurfürst Ferdinand Maria*, vol. I, p.283.

Bavarian Standing Army, 1673

In Dietfurt (Upper Palatinate)
27 infantry companies:	5,400 men
16 cavalry companies:	1,600 men
3 dragoon companies:	200 men
Total	7,200 men

In Bavaria
15 infantry companies:	3,000 men
7 cavalry companies:	700 men
1 dragoon company:	125 men
Total:	3,825 men

7 Infantry regiments and 3 Cavalry regiments.

Source: Friedrich Münich, *Geschichte des Königlich-Bayerischen I. Chevaulegers-Regiments Kaiser Alexander von Rußland. 1: Die Stämme des Regiments (1645–1682) : Gleichzeitig ein Beitrag zur Ältesten Bayerischen Heeres-Geschichte von 1611–1682* (Münich, 1862), p.48.

Bavarian Standing Army, 1679

Infantry companies
General-Feldzeugmeister	Berlo
Feldmarschall-Lieutenant	Puech
Generalwachtmeister	Montfort
Obrist	Culer
	Perouse
	Lünth,
	Behm
	Wollendorf
Obristwachtmeister	Mercy
	Opfler
	Braunschmidt
	Aufsess
	Compagni
Hauptmann	Pienzenau
	Geissler
	Vögel
	Della Rosa
	Notthasst
	Lichtenau
	Zwitterda
	Croisil
	Manteuffel

Cavalry Companies:
*Generalleutnant*Haracourt	
Generalwachtmeister	Höning
	Spinckal
Obrist	Bärtls
	Kleining
	Beauvau
Obrist Lieutenant	Schüs
	Lützelburg
Obristwachtmeister	Berlo
	Pendler

Dragoon Companies:
Obristlieutenant	Leoprechting
Obristwachtmeister	Schäffer
Hauptmann	Aufsess

Source: Staudinger, *Geschichte des kurbayerischen Heeres Insbesondere Unter Kurfürst Ferdinand Maria* (Münich, 1901), vol. I, p.274.

APPENDIX II

Bavarian Order of Battle at Kahlenberg (12 September 1683)

Centre: *Reichs-Generalfeldmarschall* Prince Friedrich zu Waldeck
Bavarian Infantry: *Generalfeldmarschall-Lieutenant* Hannibal von Degenfeld
Mercy (BvI-19), Degenfeld (BvI-19), Perouse (BvI-23), Steinau (BvI-22),
Preysing (BvI-20),
Total: 8 battalions
Beck (Imperialists) 1 bat., Steindorf (Salzburg), 1 bat., Rummel (Bavarian
Circle) 2 bat., Rodern (Pfalz-Neuburg) 2 bat.
Artillery: 12 guns and 26 regimental guns.

Cavalry reserve under Caprara and Dünnewald
Cuirassiers: Arco (BvC-11), Beauvau (BvC-13), Bärtls (BvC-12), Schüz
(BvC-14), Harancourt (BvC-15),
Total: 10 squadrons
Dragoons: *Blau Dragoner* (BvD-iv), *Rote Dragoner* (bvd-v),
Total: 2 squadrons

Source: George Nafziger, *Relief of Vienna, l3 (sic) September l683* (US Army
Combined Arms Research Digital Library, 2016)

Bavarian Order of Battle at Mohács (12 August 1687)

Left Wing: Prince-Elector Max Emanuel,
Feldzeugmeister Giovanni Carlo Sereni, *Feldmarschall-Lieutenant* Adam
Heinrich von Steinau
First line: *Latour Cuirassieren* (BvC-14) 3 sqn., *Bielke Cuirassieren* (BvC-17
) 3 sqn.
Seibolsdorff zu Fuss (BvI-20) 2 bat., *Steinau zu Fuss* (BvI-22) 2 bat.,
Leibregiment (BvI-17), 2 bat.
Second line: *Salburg Cuirassieren* (BvC-13) 3 sqn., *Arco Cuirassieren* (BvC-
11), 3 sqn., *Schier Dragoner* (BvD-3) 3 sqn., *Arco Dragoner* (BvD-4), 3 sqn.
Veldenz zu Fuss (BvI-23) 2 bat., *Gallenfels zu Fuss* (BvI-19) 2 bat.

Source: Karl Staudinger, *Geschichte des Kurbayerischen Heeres Insbesondere
Unter Kurfürst Max II Emanuel, 1680–1736* (Münich, 1901), vol. II, p.255.

357

Winter Quarters in Hungary (October 1687)

Infantry:	Leibregiment (BvI-17) (with the Grenadier company):	604 men
	Steinau (BvI-22)	492 men
	Seybolstorff (BvI-20)	549 men
	Gallenfels (BvI-19)	521 men
	Weldenz (BvI-23)	500 men
Cavalry:	Arco (BvC-11)	487 men
	Latour (BvC-14)	510 men
	Salburg (BvC-13)	518 men
Dragoons:	Arco (BvD-2)	427 men
	Schier (BvD-3)	474 men

Source: Staudinger, *Geschichte des Kurbayerischen Heeres Insbesondere Unter Kurfürst Max II Emanuel* (Münich, 1901), vol. II, p.257.

APPENDIX II

Saxony

Standing Army in 1666 (October-November)

Infantry

Hochdeutsche Trabanten (*Hauptmann* Pfugl)	56 men
Schweizer Trabanten (*Obrist* de Magny)	132 men
Schweizer Leibkompagnie der Musketiere (*Hauptmann* Escher)	200 men
Deutsche Leibgarde (*Hauptmann* Instedt)	204 men
Unterguardia in Dresden (*Obristwachtmeister* Göss)	501 men
3 Freikompagnien Leibregiment (*Obrist* Kuffer)	600 men
Garrison of Wittenberg	200 men
Garrison of Pleissenburg	100 men
Garrison of Königstein	40 men
Garrison of Sonnestein	30 men
Garrison of Stolpen	30 men
Artillerymen in Dresden and in the garrisons	150 men
6 companies of *Defensionsfändel* (militia)	6,000 men

Cavalry

Deutsche Leibgarde zu Ross (*Obrist* Reitschütz)	256 men
Leibgarde Kroaten (*Rittmeister* Perainsty)	132 men
Leibgarde Dragoner (*Obrist* Reitschütz)	120 men
Leib-Eskadron (*Obrist* Kanne), 2 companies	205 men
Eskadron Obrist Wolffersdorff. 3 companies	202 men

Source: Oskar Schuster – Friedrich August Francke, *Die Geschichte der Sächsische Armee von der Errichtung bis in die neueste Zeit: Unter Benutzung handschriftlicher und urkundlicher Quellen* (Leipzig, 1885), Vol. I, p.86.

The Standing Army after the Reduction of 1680

Hochdeutsche Leibgarde zu Fuss,	4 companies:	325 men
Trabanten Leibgarde zu Fuss	1 company:	65 men

Garrison of Dresden (new and old city),	4 companies:	807 men
Garrison of Wittenberg	1 company:	213 men
Garrison of Pleissenburg	1 company:	153 men
Garrison of Königstein	1 company:	87 men
Garrison of Sonnenstein, Stolpen and Senftenberg	1 company:	90 men

Kurprinzliche Garde zu Ross | 1 company: | 105 men
Leibkompanie zu Ross | 1 company: | 105 men
Kompagnie zu Ross Herzog Moritz, | 1 company: | 105 men
Leibdragoner | 1 company: | 76 men

1. Leibregiment zu Fuss (SaI-1) | 5 companies: | ?
2. Leibregiment zu Fuss (SaI-2) | 4 companies: | ?
Prinz Christian zu Fuss (SaI-4), | 6 companies: | ?
Freifändel Waldau | 4 companies: | ?
Leibfändel Sebottendorff | 1 company: | ?

Source: Schuster – Francke, *Die Geschichte der Sächsische Armee*, p.88.

'The State of the Standing Army in 1682' (late September)

Generalfeldmarschall: Joachim Rüdiger von der Golz, *Feldmarschall-Lieutenant* Heino Heinrich von Flemming. *Generalwachtmeister*: Christian zu Sachsen-Weimar; Heinrich VI von Reuß; Trauttmannsdorff.

Infantry

#	Regiment or Company	Companies	Men
-	Leibgarde-Trabanten	1	65
SaI-1	*Leibregiment zu Fuss*	8	1,182
SaI-2	*Goltz*	8	1,182
SaI-4	*Herzog Christian*	8	1,182
SaI-5	*Löben*	8	1,182
SaI-6	*Kuffer*	8	1,182

Total: 5,975

Cavalry

#	Regiment or Company	Companies	Men
SaC-iii	*Leibgarde-Trabanten zu Roß*	1	172
SaC-2	*Kurfürstliches Leibregiment*	6	609
SaC-3	*Löben (Kurprinz)*	6	609
SaC-4	*Promnitz*	6	609
SaC-5	*Goltz*	6	609

Total: 2,608

APPENDIX II

Dragoons

#	Regiment	Companies	Men
SaD-2	Reuss	6	614

Artillery: 1 *Oberzeugmeister*; 1 *Obristlieutenant*; 1 *Stückhauptmann*; 1 *Zeugleutnant*; 1 *Oberfeuerwerker*; 16 *Feuerwerker*, 32 *Büchsenmeister* and *Konstabler*; assistants, and drivers.
Total: 142 men with 24 cannons and 64 wagons.

Source: Schuster – Francke, *Die Geschichte der Sächsische Armee*, p.99.

Münster

The Standing Army, June 1665

Infantry

#	Regiments	Strength (a)		Strength (b)	
		companies	men	companies	men
MüI-8	Pleuren	8	950	8	580
MüI-9	Gorgas	12	-	8	400
MüI-10	Saint-Antoine	8	600	8	400
MüI-11	Schermberg	8	891	6	320
MüI-12	Oldenhaupt	8	-	8	700
MüI-13	Waldbott	8	800	8	700
MüI-14	Toller	6	660	6	500
MüI-15	Ilten	8	-	8	430
MüI-16	Elverfeldt	8?	860	8	430
MüI-17	Rheingraf	-	-	?	?
MüI-18	Gerhard von der Nath	8?	?	-	-
MüI-19	Carp	8?	?	-	-
MüI-20	Cleuter	8?	?	-	-
MüI-21	Leibregiment	-	-	12	700

Eskadronen (battalions) and *Freikompanien*: Brembt; Nitzau; Cadet; Pilack; Funke; Westerholt; Honervijk; Kirlitz; Plettenberg; Crimbell; Klepping; Windtgens; Wintzheim; Rosenbach; Fischer; Pleuren; Lohe (61 companies).

Cavalry

#	Regiments:	Strength (a)		Strength (b)	
		companies	men	companies	men
MüC-4	Gorgas	12	?	8	690
MüC-5	Lützow	10	?	8	736
MüC-6	Brabeck	9*	600	6	460
MüC-7	*Korff* (a) *Pleuren* (b)	7	600	8	800
MüC-8	Leibregiment	6	375	8	720
MüC-9	*Landgraf* (Hessen-Homburg)	6	?	8	630
MüC-10	Efferen	6	300	8	450

APPENDIX II

MüC-11	Buttlar	6	?	6	370
MüC-12	Post	5	400	8	470
MüC-13	*Deiters* (a) *Barthels* (b)	5	600	6	380
MüC-14	d'Ossery	4	?	8	800
MüC-15	Herbaix	4	450	8	700

* included a dragoon company.

18 *Freikompanien*: Waldenburg; Meinerzhagen; Speckmann, Gosäus, Pleuren; Brembt; Monnich; Lohaus; Walrave; Houmann; Romer; Berkenbush; Hesse; Deiters; Kissel; Mensing; Unna; Knyphausen; Schiffart.

Dragoons

#	Regiments	Strength (a)		Strength (b)	
		companies	men	companies:	men
MüD-1	Wolframsdorff	6	450	6	520

Source: Georg Tessin, 'Beiträge zur Formationsgeschichte des Münsterischen Militärs', *in Westfälische Forschungen. Mitteilungen des Provinzialinstituts für Westfälische Landes- und Volksforschung des Landschaftsverband Westfalen-Lippe*, vol. 32 (Münster: Aschendorffsche Verlagsbuchhandlung, 1982), pp.90-93.

(a) Theodor Verspohl, 'Das Heerwesen des Münsterschen Fürstbischofs Christoph Bernhard von Galen 1650–1678', in *Beiträge für die Geschichte Niedersachsens und Westfalens*. 18. Heft, Universität Münster (1909).

(b) Riksarkivet Stockholm, Krigshist. Handl. XIII (without date), in '1657'.

Münster Campaign against the Dutch Republic, April-May 1666

Infantry

#	Regiments	Strength	
		companies	men
MüI-8	*Pleuren*	18	1,298
MüI-9	*Gorgas*	12	1,250
MüI-13	*Aelbooft* (*Waldbott?*)	12	1,200
MüI-10	*Walpes* (*l'Espines?*)	12	1,200
MüI-16	*Eberfels*	12	1,081
MüI-14	*Zoller*	12	1,036

?	Saintoran	12	800
MüI-11	*Scharrenbergh*	13	937
MüI-15	*Ilten*	12	900
?	Lieut. Beremb.	8	800
-	Lt. Pillarckx	4	465
-	Nitzauer	4	480
-	Furcks	4	465
-	Oversten Lt. Rosenbach	4	481
-	Lt. Drussen	4	479
-	Vestervels	4	400
-	Wachtmeister Ketzliz	4	460
-	Wachtm. Hohnerpleck	4	432
-	Wachtm. Bupauer	5	516
-	Wachtm. Weshouder	4	514
-	Wachtm. Plettenberg	4	516
-	Wachtm. Leon	4	511
-	Wachtm. Klepping	4	456
-	Wachtm. Wingers	4	506
-	Wachtm. Fabr	4	428
-	Wachtm. Engerbell	4	481
Total		188	18,092

Cavalry

#	Regiments	Strength	
		companies	men
MüC-8	*Liif-Regiment*	8	575
MüC-9	*Landgraf*	7	525
MüC-4	*Gener. Wachtm. Gorgas*	11	825
MüC-14	*Wachtm. Deofferi*	4	300
MüC-15	*Oversten Herbos*	4	300
MüC-12	Post	5	375
MüC-10	*Erfferen*	6	450
?	Loef	7	525
MüC-11	*Borthel*	8	600
?	Lutzouw	10	570
MüC-6	*Brabeck*	8	600
-	Lut. Meinershagen	4	300
-	Lt. Hondt	4	300

APPENDIX II

-	Lt. Josias	6	450
-	Wachtm. Sprincken	4	300
-	Noch 3. Compagnie	3	225
Total:		99	7,220

Dragoons:

#	Regiments:	Strength	
		companies:	men:
MüD-1	*Oversten Wolframsdorff*	8	400
-	Oversten Deossery	2	140
-	Oversten Scharrenberg	1	60
-	Oversten Brabach	1	100
-	Noch 2. Compagnien	2	117
Total		14	817

General Total: 26,129 men.

Source: *Hollandse Mercurius*, April-May 1666: *Lyste van de Armee die den Bisschop van Münster dit Iaer in't Velt fonde brengen*

The Field Army in 1672 (May-June).

Infantry:

#	Regiments:	Strength	
		companies:	men:
MüI-25	Krohne	12?	957
MüI-31	Grandvilliers	12	2 bat.
MüI-29	Wedel	12?	900
MüI-30	Mias	12?	800
MüI-41	Burggraf	12?	2 bat.
MüI-34	Rheingraf	?	900
MüI-35	Saint-Paul	6?	300
MüI-36	*Berlepsch**	6?	300
MüI-32	Alt-Reuss	6	300
MüI-33	Jung-Reuss	?	?
MüI-34	Schlinger	6	800
MüI-43	Rovelli	6?	250
MüI-39	Toller	6	?

365

MüI-44	Twickel	6	?
MüI-27	Daurer**	6	?
MüI-28	Nitzow	12	?
MüI-40	Nymphius	6	226
MüI-45	Croy	6?	230
MüI-41	*Grubbe***	?	?
MüI-46	Mernich	4	?
MüI-47	Hautmarez	6?	
MüI-48	Tilman	?	300
MüI-49	Schneider	?	300

* In the spring 1673, the regiment was quartered in Bentheim with 1,200 men.
** In the spring 1673, the regiment deployed a field strength of 800 men.
*** 1,500 men in November 1672.

Cavalry

#	Regiments	Strength	
		companies	men
MüC-18	Nagel	8	649
MüC-19	Hautin	7	457
MüC-22	Reuss	3	280
MüC-25	Massenbach	8	553
MüC-26	Macdonnell	6	398
MüC-28	Post	7	572
MüC-29	Westerholt	7	515
MüC-30	*Offen* (*Probst*)	8	604
MüC-31	Lennarts	2	143
MüC-33	Wolframsdorff	5	271
MüC-20	*Courcelles**	?	?
MüC-21	Wasternhagen	?	?
MüC-23	Meinerzhagen	?	?
MüC-32	Caldenbach	?	?
MüC-27	Bentheim	?	?
MüC-34	La Roche	?	?

* Ceded to the Electorate of Cologne in June 1672.

APPENDIX II

Dragoons

#	Regiments:	Strength	
		companies	men
MüD-2	Wolframsdorff	6	385
MüD-3	Ubach	2	150
MüD-4	Leibregiment	6	437

Three *Frei-Kompanien* with a further 155 dragoons.

Overall: 10,647 infantry; 4,819 cavalry; 972 dragoons (artillery?)

Source: Tessin, 'Beiträge zur Formationsgeschichte des Münsterischen Militärs', pp.96-97.

Siege of Groningen, Münster Order of Battle (August 1672)

Infantry

(From the regiments) (MüI-25) *Krohne* 200 men; (MüI-29) *Wedel* 420 men; (MüI-30) *Mias* 400 men; (MüI-42) *Burggraf* 204 men; (MüI-35) *Rheingraf* 545 men; (MüI-37) *Berlepsch* 247 men; (MüI-32) *Alt-Reuss* 294 men; (MüI-33) *Jung-Reuss* 156 men; (MüI-34) *Sehlinger* 270 men; (MüI-43) *Rovelli* 402 men; (MüI-38) *Pilack* 407 men; (MüI-39) *Toller* 477 men; (MüI-28) *Nitzau* 88 men; (MüI-50) *Plettenberg* 122 men.
Freikompanien: *Leemputt* 122 men; *Hartig* 106 men; *Heusch* 65 men; *Puling* 54 men.

Cavalry: ?

Dragoons: (MüD-2) *Wolframsdorff* ?

Source: Gräflich von Galensches Archiv zu Assen, Landessachen II, nr. 557, cited by Georg Tessin in 'Beiträge zur Formationsgeschichte des Münsterischen Militärs', p.96.

Field Army's Cavalry and Dragoons (May 1674).

Cavalry

#	Regiments	Strength	
		Companies:	Men:
MüC-18	Nagel	8	652
MüC-35	Leibregiment	6	500
MüC-19	Hautin	6	481
MüC-25	Massenbach	5	448
MüC-26	Macdonnell	6	398
MüC-28	Post	8	610
MüC-29	Westerholt	6	487
MüC-30	Offen	8	630
MüC-31	Lennarts	6	417
Total:		59	4,623

Dragoons;

#	Regiments	Strength	
		Companies	Men
MüD-2	*Nagel*	4	400
MüD-3	*Ubach*	3	180
MüD-4	*Leibregiment*	2	200
-	Freykompagnien	3	150
Total		12	930

Source: Georges Bernard Depping, *Geschichte des Krieges der Münsterer und Cölner im Bundnisse mit Frankreich gegen Holland in den Jahren 1672, 1673 und 1674 (Münster, 1840)*, pp.346–347.

APPENDIX II

Generallieutenant Wedells' Corps, Winter Quarters in the Rhineland (Autumn 1676)

Infantry

(MüI-29) *Wedel*   14 companies
(MüI-30) *Esch*   10 companies
(MüI-27) *Dauer*   10 companies
(MüI-52) *Eenschaet*   4 companies
(MüI-54): *Ottons*:   ?

Cavalry

(MüC-26) *Wedel* 10 companies
(MüC-30) *Mandelslohe*   9 companies
(MüC-35) *Leibregiment*   8 companies

Dragoons

(MüD-2) *Hoetensleben*:   4 companies

Source: Tessin, 'Beiträge zur Formationsgeschichte des Münsterischen Militärs', p.99.

First Münster Corps hired to Denmark (26 April 1677)

Infantry

#	Regiments	Strength	
		Companies	Men
MüI-31	*Grandvillers*	10	1,000
MüI-28	*Nitzau*	10	1,000
MüI-54	*Tecklenburg*	10	1,000
MüI-51	*Braun*	5	500
Total		35	3,500

Cavalry

#	Regiments	Strength	
		Companies	Men
MüC-28	*Grandvillers*	4	332

369

Dragoons:

2 companies from the regiment *Schönemacher* (MüD-3), 200 men

Source: Tessin, 'Beiträge zur Formationsgeschichte des Münsterischen Militärs', pp.101-102.

Münster Corps hired to Spain (August 1677)

Infantry

#	Regiments:	Strength	
		Companies	Men
MüI-29	Wedel	12	969
MüI-30	*Esch*	9	678
MüI-27	*Dauer*	9	614
MüI-64	*Schwartz*	9	605
MüI-67	*Elverfeldt*	9	725
MüI-52	Eltz	7	371
MüI-53	*Ottons**	5	953
MüI-65	*Rollingen*	5	657
Total		65	5,572

* Merged with regiment *Keyl* (MüI-54)

Cavalry

#	Regiments	Strength	
		Companies	Men
MüC-18	*Bönninghausen*	10	574
MüC-26	*Wedel*	12	761
MüC-30	*Mandelslohe*	6	471
MüC-35	*Mortaigne*	6	558
Total		34	2,364

Dragoons

#	Regiments	Strength	
		Companies	Men
MüD-2	*Hoetensleben*	10	574

Source: Tessin, 'Beiträge zur Formationsgeschichte des Münsterischen Militärs', p.101.

APPENDIX II

Second Münster Corps hired to Denmark (3 April 1678)

Infantry

#	Regiments	Strength	
		Companies	Men
MüI-29	*Wedel*	13	956
MüI-30	*Esch*	10	730
MüI-64	*Schwartz*	10	726
MüI-74	*Frankenstein*	10	538
MüI-28	*Gogreve*	8	770
Total		51	3,720

Cavalry

#	Regiments	Strength	
		Companies	Men
MüC-26	*Wedel*	12	892
MüC-39	*Bassum*	6	457
MüC-40	*Rabe*	6	431
Total		24	1,780

Dragoons

#	Regiments	Strength	
		Companies	Men
MüD-2	*Hoetensleben*	6	469

Source: Tessin, 'Beiträge zur Formationsgeschichte des Münsterischen Militärs', pp.102-103.

The Army of Münster under Prince-Bishop Ferdinand von Fürstenberg (March-April 1679)

Infantry

#	Units	Strength		Quarters
		Companies	Men	
MüI-ii	Garde zu Fuss	1	132	Neuhaus
MüI-67	Elverfeldt	8	800	Münster
MüI-64	*Schwartz*	10	800	Coesfeld
MüI-27	*Dauer*	5	500	Warendorf
MüI-28	*Gogreve*	3	300	Vechta
MüI-iii	Geismar	5	500	Meppen
-	Freikompanie Seyboltsdorff	1	100	Rheine
-	Freikompanie Fischer	1	100	Bevergern
-	Freikompanie Schilder	1	100	Burgsteinfurt
-	Freikompanie Walrave	1	100	Bentheim
-	Freikompanie Stingel	1	100	Rheda

Cavalry and Dragoons:

#	Units	Strength	
		Companies	Men
MüC-i	Garde zu Pferd	1	88
MüC-18	Bönninghausen	7	525
MüD-2	Hoetensleben	3	225

Source: Tessin, 'Beiträge zur Formationsgeschichte des Münsterischen Militärs', p.104.

About the author

Bruno Mugnai was born in Florence in 1962 and still lives there with his partner Silvia. Active for years as a historical researcher and illustrator, he is the author of several titles published by, among other, the Historical Office of the Italian Army and Helion& Co. His books focus on the historical periods and geographical areas of his interest – the ancient Italian states, central and Eastern Europe in the sixteenth, seventeenth, and eighteenth centuries, and South America after the conquest. He is a member of 'La Sabretache', the Society for Military History Studies, and of the Italian Society of Military History. As an illustrator, he collaborates with important Italian and foreign specialists, and with the Stibbert Museum of Florence. Bruno is a Rugby Football Union enthusiast, who still believes in an Italian Grand Slam in the Six Nations Tournament.

Other titles in the Century of the Soldier series

No 24 *The Last Army: The Battle of Stow-on-the-Wold and the End of the Civil War in the Welsh Marches, 1646*

No 25 *The Battle of the White Mountain 1620 and the Bohemian Revolt, 1618–22*

No 26 *The Swedish Army in the Great Northern War 1700–21: Organisation, Equipment, Campaigns and Uniforms*

No 27 *St. Ruth's Fatal Gamble: The Battle of Aughrim 1691 and the Fall Of Jacobite Ireland*

No 28 *Muscovy's Soldiers: The Emergence of the Russian Army 1462–1689*

No 29 *Home and Away: The British Experience of War 1618–1721*

No 30 *From Solebay to the Texel: The Third Anglo-Dutch War, 1672–1674*

No 31 *The Battle of Killiecrankie: The First Jacobite Campaign, 1689–1691*

No 32 *The Most Heavy Stroke: The Battle of Roundway Down 1643*

No 33 *The Cretan War (1645–1671): The Venetian-Ottoman Struggle in the Mediterranean*

No 34 *Peter the Great's Revenge: The Russian Siege of Narva in 1704*

No 35 *The Battle Of Glenshiel: The Jacobite Rising in 1719*

No 36 *Armies And Enemies Of Louis XIV: Volume 1 - Western Europe 1688–1714: France, Britain, Holland*

No 37 *William III's Italian Ally: Piedmont and the War of the League of Augsburg 1683–1697*

No 38 *Wars and Soldiers in the Early Reign of Louis XIV: Volume 1 - The Army of the United Provinces of the Netherlands, 1660–1687*

No 39 *In The Emperor's Service: Wallenstein's Army, 1625–1634*

No 40 *Charles XI's War: The Scanian War Between Sweden and Denmark, 1675–1679*

No 41 *The Armies and Wars of The Sun King 1643–1715: Volume 1: The Guard of Louis XIV*

No 42 *The Armies Of Philip IV Of Spain 1621–1665: The Fight For European Supremacy*

No 43 *Marlborough's Other Army: The British Army and the Campaigns of the First Peninsular War, 1702–1712*

No 44 *The Last Spanish Armada: Britain And The War Of The Quadruple Alliance, 1718–1720*

No 45 *Essential Agony: The Battle of Dunbar 1650*

No 46 *The Campaigns of Sir William Waller*

No 47 *Wars and Soldiers in the Early Reign of Louis XIV: Volume 2 - The Imperial Army, 1660–1689*

No 48 *The Saxon Mars and His Force: The Saxon Army During The Reign Of John George III 1680–1691*

No 49 *The King's Irish: The Royalist Anglo-Irish Foot of the English Civil War*

No 50 *The Armies and Wars of the Sun King 1643–1715: Volume 2: The Infantry of Louis XIV*

No 51 *More Like Lions Than Men: Sir William Brereton and the Cheshire Army of Parliament, 1642–46*

No 52 *I Am Minded to Rise: The Clothing, Weapons and Accoutrements of the Jacobites from 1689 to 1719*

No 53 *The Perfection of Military Discipline: The Plug Bayonet and the English Army 1660–1705*

No 54 *The Lion From the North: The Swedish Army During the Thirty Years War: Volume 1, 1618–1632*

No 55 *Wars and Soldiers in the Early Reign of Louis XIV: Volume 3 - The Armies of the Ottoman Empire 1645–1718*

No 56 *St. Ruth's Fatal Gamble: The Battle of Aughrim 1691 and the Fall Of Jacobite Ireland*

No 57 *Fighting for Liberty: Argyll & Monmouth's Military Campaigns against the Government of King James, 1685*

No 58 *The Armies and Wars of the Sun King 1643–1715: Volume 3: The Cavalry of Louis XIV*

No 59 *The Lion From the North: The Swedish Army During the Thirty Years War: Volume 2, 1632–1648*

No 60 *By Defeating My Enemies: Charles XII of Sweden and the Great Northern War 1682–1721*

No 61 *Despite Destruction, Misery and Privations..: The Polish Army in Prussia during the war against Sweden 1626–1629*

No 62 *The Armies of Sir Ralph Hopton: The Royalist Armies of the West 1642–46*

No 63 *Italy, Piedmont, and the War of the Spanish Succession 1701–1712*

No 64 *'Cannon played from the great fort': Sieges in the Severn Valley during the English Civil War 1642–1646*

No 65 *Carl Gustav Armfelt and the Struggle for Finland During the Great Northern War*

No 66 *In the Midst of the Kingdom: The Royalist War Effort in the North Midlands 1642–1646*

No 67 *The Anglo-Spanish War 1655–1660: Volume 1: The War in the West Indies*

No 68 *For a Parliament Freely Chosen: The Rebellion of Sir George Booth, 1659*

No 69 *The Bavarian Army During the Thirty Years War 1618–1648: The Backbone of the Catholic League (revised second edition)*

No 70 *The Armies and Wars of the Sun King 1643–1715: Volume 4: The War of the Spanish Succession, Artillery, Engineers and Militias*

No 71 *No Armour But Courage: Colonel Sir George Lisle, 1615–1648 (Paperback reprint)*

No 72 *The New Knights: The Development of Cavalry in Western Europe, 1562–1700*

No 73 *Cavalier Capital: Oxford in the English Civil War 1642–1646 (Paperback reprint)*

No 74 *The Anglo-Spanish War 1655–1660: Volume 2: War in Jamaica*

No 75 *The Perfect Militia: The Stuart Trained Bands of England and Wales 1603–1642*

No 76 *Wars and Soldiers in the Early Reign of Louis XIV: Volume 4 - The Armies of Spain 1659–1688*

No 77 *The Battle of Nördlingen 1634: The Bloody Fight Between Tercios and Brigades*

No 78 *Wars and Soldiers in the Early Reign of Louis XIV: Volume 5 - The Portuguese Army 1659–1690*

No 79 *We Came, We Saw, God Conquered: The Polish-Lithuanian Commonwealth's military effort in the relief of Vienna, 1683*

No 80 *Charles X's Wars: Volume 1 - Armies of the Swedish Deluge, 1655–1660*

No 81 *Cromwell's Buffoon: The Life and Career of the Regicide, Thomas Pride (Paperback reprint)*

No 82 *The Colonial Ironsides: English Expeditions under the Commonwealth and Protectorate, 1650–1660*

No 83 *The English Garrison of Tangier: Charles II's Colonial Venture in the Mediterranean, 1661–1684*

No 84 *The Second Battle of Preston, 1715: The Last Battle on English Soil*

No 85 *To Settle the Crown: Waging Civil War in Shropshire, 1642–1648 (Paperback reprint)*

No 86 *A Very Gallant Gentleman: Colonel Francis Thornhagh (1617–1648) and the Nottinghamshire Horse*

No 87 *Charles X's Wars: Volume 2 - The Wars in the East, 1655–1657*

No 88 *The Shōgun's Soldiers: The Daily Life of Samurai and Soldiers in Edo Period Japan, 1603–1721 Volume 1*

No 89 *Campaigns of the Eastern Association: The Rise of Oliver Cromwell, 1642–1645*

No 90 *The Army of Occupation in Ireland 1603–42: Defending the Protestant Hegemony*

No 91 *The Armies and Wars of the Sun King 1643–1715: Volume 5: Buccaneers and Soldiers in the Americas*

No 92 *New Worlds, Old Wars: The Anglo-American Indian Wars 1607–1678*

No 93 *Against the Deluge: Polish and Lithuanian Armies During the War Against Sweden 1655–1660*

No 94 *The Battle of Rocroi: The Battle, the Myth and the Success of Propaganda*

No 95 *The Shōgun's Soldiers: The Daily Life of Samurai and Soldiers in Edo Period Japan, 1603–1721 Volume 2*

No 96 *Science of Arms: the Art of War in the Century of the Soldier 1672–1699: Volume 1: Preparation for War and the Infantry*

No 97 *Charles X's Wars: Volume 3 - The Danish Wars 1657–1660*

No 98 *Wars and Soldiers in the Early Reign of Louis XIV: Volume 6 - Armies of the Italian States 1660–1690 Part 1*

No 99 *Dragoons and Dragoon Operations in the British Civil Wars, 1638–1653*

No 100 *Wars and Soldiers in the Early Reign of Louis XIV: Volume 6 - Armies of the Italian States 1660–1690 Part 2*

No 101 *1648 and All That: The Scottish Invasions of England, 1648 and 1651: Proceedings of the 2022 Helion and Company 'Century of the Soldier' Conference*

No 102 *John Hampden and the Battle of Chalgrove: The Political and Military Life of Hampden and his Legacy*

No 103 *The City Horse: London's militia cavalry during the English Civil War, 1642–1660*

No 104 *The Battle of Lützen 1632: A Reassessment*

No 105 *Monmouth's First Rebellion: The Later Covenanter Risings, 1660–1685*

No 106 *Raw Generals and Green Soldiers: Catholic Armies in Ireland 1641–1643*

Polish, Lithuanian and Cossack armies versus the might of the Ottoman Empire

No 108 *Soldiers and Civilians, Transport and Provisions: Early Modern Military Logistics and Supply Systems During the British Civil Wars, 1638-1653*

No 109 *Batter their walls, gates and Forts: The Proceedings of the 2022 English Civil War Fortress Symposium*

No 110 *The Town Well Fortified: The Fortresses of the Civil Wars in Britain, 1639-1660*

No 111 *Crucible of the Jacobite '15: The Battle of Sheriffmuir 1715*

No 112 *Charles XII's Karoliners Volume 2 - The Swedish Cavalry of the Great Northern War 1700-1721*

No 113 *Wars and Soldiers in the Early Reign of Louis XIV: Volume 7 - Armies of the German States 1655–1690 Part 1*

SERIES SPECIALS:

No 1 *Charles XII's Karoliners: Volume 1: The Swedish Infantry & Artillery of the Great Northern War 1700–1721*

For the complete range of Century of the Soldier titles please go to
www.helion.co.uk/series/century-of-the-soldier-1618-1721.php